M000208642

Stone by Stone

Reflections on the Psychology of C.G. Jung

Stone by Stone

Reflections on the Psychology of C.G. Jung

Edited by Andreas Schweizer and Regine Schweizer-Vüllers

DAIMON
VERLAG

Cover image: *Speculum humanae salvationis* (15th cent.), Ms. Latin 512, fol. 34
© Bibiothèque Nationale de France, Paris

ISBN 978-3-85630-765-3

Copyright © 2017 Daimon Verlag, Einsiedeln, and the individual authors

Contents

Jonah emerging from the whale. Beside it the masons with the *lapis angularis* (cornerstone) as an image of the "treasure hard to attain."

Foreword

"Stone by Stone" – in view of its hundredth anniversary of the Psychology Club Zurich (1916-2016) the board decided to publish a collected volume of various articles. The title "Stone by Stone" and its accompanying frontispiece from the *Speculum humanae salvationis,* however, require an explanation. What is it that needs to be built? And what do the individual building stones represent?

Today, Jungian psychology has spread throughout the entire world. It speaks to an ever-increasing number of people in various countries and in different continents. People of different religions, cultures and worldviews are drawn to it. Ever more and new institutional training centres are being founded and this will continue in the future. However, this development began around hundred years ago through the efforts of a small group of students, friends and colleagues of C.G. Jung who, after a few tentative attempts, met on the 26th of February, 1916 to found the Psychology Club of Zurich.[1] There were 40 members listed at the time. Emma Jung was elected as the Club's first president.

The first few years of the Club's existence were anything but peaceful. The so-called "Club problem" had to be repeatedly discussed, which means, for instance, that its members showed little engagement, it lacked funds, and personal differences erupted. The members of the board frequently changed. Even C.G. Jung, upon whose initiative the Psychology Club had originally been called into existence, withdrew from the Club, along with Emma Jung, Toni Wolff and a small group of members for one and a half years. It was only in the mid-1920's, particularly after Toni Wolff became President of the Club in 1928, that quieter and decidedly productive years ensued for the Club. This period saw regular lectures held by its members, talks were given by well-known personalities, for example Richard Wilhelm

---

1   For the following see: Friedel Elisabeth Muser, *Zur Geschichte des Psychologischen Clubs von den Anfängen bis 1928.* Sonderdruck aus dem Jahresbericht des Psychologischen Clubs, Zürich 1984 [History of the Psychology Club from its beginning till 1928. Special print from the annual report of the Psychology Club, Zurich 1984], without page numbering.

or Heinrich Zimmer, and C.G. Jung held lectures in which he introduced his new writings one by one for his listeners. Jung placed great importance upon presenting and discussing his research work within the framework of a small group. From its inception and into the early 1930's, the Psychology Club of Zurich provided him with such a suitable circle, while later the Eranos conferences in Ascona became the appropriate forum. Thus, in a certain sense, one can say that the Psychology Club was the place from which Jungian psychology sprang, or to be more exact, it was the place from which Jungian psychology made its way out into the world.

But what does the title of our publication mean and what is the meaning of the building in the frontispiece? With hammer and trowel in hand, two masons are preparing the capstone of a building. This stone has the word "lapis" above it. It is rectangular or square. It is clearly a special stone. The building, too – as can be seen by its church-like windows – is a spiritual structure, and not a worldly building. And above the image is the well-known verse from the Synoptic Gospels, "Lapidem quem reprobaverunt edificantes hic factus est in caput anguli," "The stone that the builders rejected has become the cornerstone."[2] This stone represents Christ – the risen Christ. According to the illuminated manuscript *Speculum humanae salvationis* of the late Middle Ages, it is connected to the Prophet Jonah who, on the left half of the image is emerging with folded hands from the throat of the whale.[3] He is thanking God for his rescue from his underworld journey. C.G. Jung, who integrated this image into his paper *Psychology and Alchemy*, wrote beneath it, "Jonah emerging from the belly of the whale. The goal of the night sea journey is equivalent to the *lapis angularis* or cornerstone."[4] In this manner, Jung compares the capstone of the building that the two masons are working on with the philosopher's stone.

The philosopher's stone, the *lapis*, was infinitely precious to the alchemists. It healed illness, brought about miracles, endowed long life, but it was so mysterious and so puzzling that they ascribed to it an endless number of names and qualities, and could only describe it through paradoxes. No alchemist, as Jung emphasized, was ever able to produce nor to find the stone in his retort. And yet it remained the goal that the alchemists

2 Mt. 21:42; Mk. 12:10; Lk. 20:17. Biblical references are from *The New Oxford Annotated Bible*, edited by Michael D. Coogan (Oxford: Oxford University, 2010).
3 See picture, p. 6: Jonah emerging from the whale. Beside it the masons with the *lapis angularis* (cornerstone) as an image of the "treasure hard to attain."
4 Carl Gustav Jung, *Psychology and Alchemy*, vol. 12 of *The Collected Works of C.G. Jung*, translated by R.F.C. Hull (Princeton: Princeton University Press, 1968), figure 172.

pursued for centuries. The *lapis* is a living stone. It is a stone "with a spirit." Simultaneously, it is small and inconspicuous, thrown out into the streets, and trodden upon in the dunghill. "Help me, so that I can help you," it cries out to the adept.[5] In psychological terms, it is an image of the Self, for the complete, or whole man within us; in other words, for that never-to-be-quite-realized mysterious inner quality that embraces all parts of one's personality, even the meagre, inconspicuous or despised aspects of oneself. C.G. Jung speaks of the "insignificant assortment of man 'as he is'," that is essential for self-realization or individuation.[6] And it is precisely what we despise – or even despise most – about ourselves, this "stumbling block," as Jung formulates it, that paradoxically should become the cornerstone, that is, the intrinsic foundation of a unified personality.[7] This would be, then, the end of the night sea journey that Jonah had to bear and the prize or attainment of the "treasure hard to attain."[8] Marie-Louise von Franz describes just such an experience in the following way: "The experience of the Self brings a feeling of standing on solid ground inside oneself, on a patch of inner eternity which even physical death cannot touch."[9] Thus, a kind of inner assuredness, together with a feeling of being alive or being enlivened, is part of the alchemical stone. The "stone is water of a living fountain," one alchemist says.[10] Simultaneously, the stone is the firestone that, without ever becoming exhausted, generates fire or sparks of fire – emotions, feelings or also love.[11]

At different points in several of his works, C.G. Jung points to the parallel between the alchemical *lapis* and the Christian Redeemer. But he also repeatedly underscores their differences. The alchemical stone represents man's entire nature, not only his spiritual soul aspects. It is "God's mystery in matter,"[12] as Marie-Louise von Franz writes, a spirit in matter or – as it is

---

5 Joachim Telle (ed.) *Rosarium philosophorum. Ein alchemisches Florilegium des Spätmittelalters* [Rosarium philosophorum. An alchemical Florilegium of the late Middle Ages], facsimile reproduction of the first edition Frankfurt 1550, vol. 1 (Weinheim: Verlagsgesellschaft Weinheim, 1992), p. 39.
6 C.G. Jung, *Psychology and Alchemy*, vol. 12, § 105.
7 Ibid., § 247.
8 Ibid., § 155.
9 Marie-Louise von Franz, *C.G. Jung. His Myth in Our Time*, translated by William H. Kennedy (Toronto: Inner City Books, 1998), p. 74.
10 C.G. Jung, *Psychology and Alchemy*, vol. 12, § 336, footnote 7.
11 Ibid., § 451.
12 M.-L. von Franz, *C.G. Jung. His Myth in Our Time*, p. 220.

sometimes said – "hidden in the human body."[13] In his work, the alchemist does not so much seek to achieve his own personal redemption in the manner of a Christian believer, but rather his aim is to redeem and transform those qualities that at first were considered unsightly and were rejected, but which finally attain the highest possible value, for they are the *lapis*, or the divine spirit in nature.

It is of great significance, however, that the alchemical opus and the production or attainment of the *lapis* rest upon the efforts of the individual, or of individual people. And just as Jonah had to endure both involuntarily and unwillingly his night sea journey in the belly of the whale, so, too, did C.G. Jung have to face the "Spirit of the Depth" in the years of his confrontation with the unconscious during which he felt completely alone and without any sure ground under his feet. "Others have been shattered by them," he writes in *Memories, Dreams, Reflections*. "But there was a demonic strength in me, and from the beginning there was no doubt in my mind that I must find the meaning of what I was experiencing in these fantasies. When I endured these assaults of the unconscious I had an answering conviction that I was obeying a higher will, and that feeling continued to uphold me until I had mastered the task."[14] One's individuation process and its concomitant encounter with the unknown within oneself – one's night sea journey and one's descent into one's own inner depths – are the tasks of the individual. Attainment of the *lapis* – one's experience of the Self – however, mysteriously appears to connect us with other people and with the world around us.

> Pursuit who never grows weary of labor,
> who slowly forms but never destroys
> and – to the building of eternities
> but grain on grain of sand does lay,
> yet minutes, days and years effaces
> from the great debt of ages.[15]

13 Ibid.
14 Aniela Jaffé (ed.), *Memories, Dreams, Reflections by C.G. Jung*, (London: Fontana Press, 1995), p. 201.
15 Friedrich Schiller, *Werke* [Works], vol. 1, (Munich/Zurich: Droemersche Verlagsanstalt, 1962), p. 70. This prose translation corresponds as best as possible with the German poetic text.

These final lines of Friedrich Schiller's poem *The Ideals* speaks of "the building of eternities" slowly, one grain of sand at a time, but each grain causing it to continually grow through the collaboration of patient, creative, human effort. Schiller's "pursuit" does not refer to some simple activity or some frenzied bustle. Rather, it is referring to what the alchemists tried to achieve with the *lapis*, and to what we refer to as becoming conscious of one's inner soul kernel, or individuation. It is, indeed, a matter of building. And just as each individual is able over time to build an inner house, an inner fortress, an inner solid realm of the spirit, perhaps it is also possible that over the course of centuries, far-reaching constructive changes in the collective unconscious connected to the efforts of individual people striving to become more conscious and more whole, may occur. This would be the "building of eternities." Being a part of this effort, and thereby being connected to the infinite within ourselves, endows us with meaning, and can liberate us from feeling separate and isolated. "Meaninglessness inhibits fullness of life and is therefore equivalent to illness. Meaning makes a great many things endurable – perhaps everything," Jung writes in *Memories*.[16]

In 1949, four years after the end of the Second World War, Max Zeller, a doctor and analyst from Berlin, visited Europe many years after his emigration to Los Angeles.[17] He came to Zurich to see Jung and, he could meet again the circle of Jungian friends and colleagues, but the entire time, as he himself wrote, he was preoccupied with *one* question: "What am I doing as an analyst? With the overwhelming problems in the world, to see twenty or twenty-five patients, that's nothing. What are we doing, all of us?"[18] The night before he was to leave to return to the States he had a dream about which he himself said, "There was the answer to my question what we, as analysts are doing."[19]

---

16 A. Jaffé (ed.), *Memories, Dreams, Reflections by C.G. Jung*, p. 373.
17 According to his daughter, Jacqueline Levin-Zeller, immediately after the "Kristall-nacht," Max Zeller was brought to the Concentration camp of Sachsenhausen. Six weeks later he was released thanks to the help of his wife, Lore Zeller. He emigrated with his family firstly to London, in order to emigrate to Los Angeles later. There he founded, together with James Kirsch and others, the C.G. Jung Institute of Los Angeles. (I am grateful to Jacqueline Levin-Zeller, who gave me this information.)
18 Max Zeller, „The Task of the Analyst", in: Max Zeller, *The Dream. The Vision of the Night*, edited by Janet Dallet (Los Angeles: Analytical Psychology Club and C.G. Jung Institute of Los Angeles, 1975), p. 1.
19 Ibid., p. 2.

A temple of vast dimensions was in the process of being built. As far as I could see – ahead, behind, right and left – there were incredible numbers of people building on gigantic pillars. I, too, was building on a pillar. The whole building process was in its very first beginnings, but the foundation was already there, the rest of the building was starting to go up, and I and many others were working on it.

After Max Zeller told him the dream on the morning of his departure, C.G. Jung said at that time, „Ja, you know, that is the temple we all build on. We don't know the people because, believe me, they build in India and China and in Russia and all over the world. That is the new religion. You know how long it will take until it is built?" And when Max Zeller asked, "How should I know? Do you know?" Jung said, "About six hundred years." "Where do you know this from?" Jung, "From dreams. From other people's dreams and from my own."[20] Max Zeller ended his little, but thereby even more meaningful, report by saying, "That is what happens in our work... We see it every day... Each person works on his own pillar, until one day the temple will be built."[21]

It is to this greater building that the editors feel committed. And it is in this sense that the various contributions in this publication on the hundredth anniversary of the Psychology Club Zurich are to be understood. Most are based upon lectures that have been held at the Club over the last years. They are creative contributions from individuals who feel that they are a part of something bigger. Together, they cover a wide spectrum of Jungian psychology. Almost all areas of Analytical Psychology are represented.

The first two papers concern the Psychology Club itself. In his article "I Ching – The Book of the Play of Opposites," Andreas Schweizer begins with the often underestimated difficulties that we in the West have in truly understanding "the wisdom of the Orient." C.G. Jung often warned against a too-hasty adaptation to the East. Which is why the author's point of departure is the Taoist background of the *Book of Changes*. His focus is upon the inner structure of the I Ching, as well as some of the individual Chinese written characters of the hexagrams, in order to shed light upon his own question to the I Ching, namely, how the Psychology Club should proceed with its centenarian heritage and how to pass it onto future generations? The second contribution is also about the Psychology Club. In what was

20 Ibid.
21 Ibid., p. 5.

one of her last public appearances, Marie-Louise von Franz speaks in a very touching manner about her personal relationship to the Club, particularly in her younger years. She describes how she, as an introverted person, experienced the Club's community and what was important to her at that time. At the end of her talk, she answers questions from her listeners.

The article that follows leads the reader into the world of fairy tales. Marie-Louise von Franz's unpublished (until now) interpretation of the Grimm fairy tale "The Goose Girl" opens with the fact that in this fairy tale two distant kingdoms co-exist. What does this mean in psychological terms? The problem of the shadow – particularly the shadow of the feminine – is discussed at length. Marie-Louise von Franz emphasizes several times that "The Goose Girl" is a special tale. Here, the old king does not mean, as he does in most other tales, an old and therefore in-need-of-renewal viewpoint. Rather, he stands for wisdom and careful insight. It is the old king who is responsible for the princess being where she should be at the end of the tale. Within the realm of feminine psychology, he is the equivalent of a sovereign spiritual-religious animus.

The following two articles are concerned first with the world of alchemy, and next with mysticism or, more precisely, with Jewish mysticism of the Kabbalah. The contribution by Regine Schweizer-Vüllers, "He struck the rock and the waters did flow," looks at the alchemical background of Marie-Louise von Franz and Barbara Hannah's gravestone. Initially looking at what is represented on the stone itself – the circle or also the mandala – the model of which can be found in an alchemical text, she goes on to discuss the inscription and its interpretation according to Marie-Louise von Franz herself in her work *Aurora Consurgens*. "I came across this impressive doctrine" – the title of Toni Woolfson's essay had its origins in a letter from C.G. Jung. In a refreshingly lively, but also profound, manner, the author sheds light upon the Jewish Kabbalah as a whole, and in particular the relationship between C.G. Jung and Gershom Scholem.

C.G. Jung and the world of Christianity, especially the world of Protestantism is the theme of the next three papers. In January 1952 the "Psychologische Gesellschaft Basel" invited C.G. Jung to talk on his recently published book *Aion – Researches into the Phenomenology of the Self.* C.G. Jung answered questions from his listeners. They were on the function of the unconscious, particularly its compensatory function; on alchemy and its relationship to Christianity; on the meaning of the feminine; on the problem of evil; and on the Jewish, as well as Christian, concept of

God and the transformation of the God image. Murray Stein's article on "Jungian Psychology and the Spirit of Protestantism" looks at the special meaning that Protestantism, or more specifically Swiss Protestantism, had for Jung. This spiritual-religious and cultural background had, according to the author, a bigger impact on both Jung and his psychology than we had previously thought. This is particularly the case with the emphasis upon the individual and the responsibility that each individual carries. At the end of his paper, Murray Stein shows the effect Jung had upon his listeners through two situations, both of which took place in 1937 – one in Germany, the other in New York.

Marianne Jehle-Wildberger's contribution, "Stations of a Difficult Friendship – Carl Gustav Jung and Adolf Keller," is based upon the talk she gave at the vernissage that was held at the Psychology Club for the book she edited on the exchange of letters between C.G. Jung and Adolf Keller. Jung and the theologian Adolf Keller knew each other for over fifty years. Especially in the early years of Analytical Psychology, Adolf Keller and his wife, Tina Keller-Jenny, were close friends of C.G. Jung and Emma Jung. Later, their paths separated. Marianne Jehle-Wildberger describes this "difficult friendship" – as she calls it – in a knowledgeable and empathetic manner, elucidating in the process certain unknown aspects of both personalities.

"Aloneness as Calling," the paper by Hermann Strobel is a legacy. Hermann Strobel passed away in 2006. The thoughts he presents here may comprise his last creative work. As the author himself says, they "revolve" around the theme of being alone, whereby his thoughts, ponderings and insights seem to spiral ever deeper. It is like diving into one's own depths. For Herman Strobel "aloneness" means, at bottom, "all-one-ness," that is, the encounter with the Self. At various points in his paper he touches upon times of dictatorship, National Socialism in Germany and the Second World War. This time left its traces upon the Psychology Club also, even though the Club had the good fortune of being based in Zurich in a comparatively peaceful country. Herman Strobel's paper shows how people at that time confronted such terrifying darkness without being broken, Deo concedente, with God's grace.

Claudine Koch-Morgenegg describes her work with a 90-year-old woman. "The great Mystery – Individuation in Old Age" is the title of her article. It is, indeed, a process of individuation – of "becoming one's Self" – that is revealed in this article. Dreams accompany and trigger this spiritual process from the outset. In addition one is struck by the personality of the analysand herself and the deeply human connection between her and her analyst. It would appear that individuation – in this world, at least – never comes to an end and is always also the destiny of the respective individual. To be able to communicate "the great mystery" to another human being and thereby become conscious of it oneself was the path of healing, or of becoming whole, for this woman.

Rudolf Högger's contribution is also about a decisive moment in an individual's life. The author had the opportunity to be a part of the initiation ceremony of a seven-year-old Hindu boy in Nepal, and he was struck by a central symbol of this ceremony – the so-called "Treasure Vase." His paper follows the trail of this archaic god-image, especially within the religious context of the Indian sub-continent, but also in the dreams of modern man. Fundamentally it is the great goddess in all her richness – the great feminine – that finds expression in this symbol of the "treasure vase."

The editors would like to thank the authors for their contributions. We would also like to give our special thanks to those who helped in the background – to the members of the editing commission, to Ursula Stüssi-Scholian for her work on the transcriptions, to the translators of the English edition – especially Alison Kappes-Bates, Brigitte Jacobs-Fröhlich and Joan Smith, to Judith Dowling for her assistance in correcting the English texts – and to the staff at Daimon publishing house. Without the financial support of the "Psychology Club Zurich," the "Foundation of the Psychology Club," the "Linda Fierz Fund," and the "Foundation for the Promotion of Jungian Psychology," this publication would not have been possible.

Regine Schweizer-Vüllers
Zollikon, October 2016

Andreas Schweizer

I Ching (*Yì jīng*) – The Book of the Play of Opposites

1. Preliminaries

The difficulties in approaching the I Ching, this basic work of Eastern wisdom, can scarcely be overestimated. We have imposed our Western values on the East, and with our materialism and rationalism, nearly, if not totally, destroyed a culture thousands of years old and "perhaps destined to disappear forever."[1] I therefore consider it our duty to approach the I Ching with the greatest respect, in order not to destroy once again with Western prejudices that precious inheritance of the Chinese spirit, through which, as Jung once said, the sickness of Western culture could perhaps be healed. Yet also, the majority of modern Chinese, Taiwanese, Koreans and Japanese, in particular the younger generation, hardly have any understanding of the "wisdom of the East" any longer. In contrast, as shown by the numerous new translations of the I Ching, the *Dao de jing* and of Zhuangzi,[2] the Chinese classics have such a strong appeal, that it is no exaggeration to speak of a veritable renaissance of Taoism. An open question, however,

---

1   C.G. Jung, "Richard Wilhelm: In Memoriam," in: *The Spirit in Man, Art, and Literature*, vol. 15 of *The Collected Works of C.G. Jung.* Translated by R.F.C. Hull. (Princeton: Princeton University Press, 1966), § 74.

2   Given the confusing usage of Chinese expressions and names I decided to generally use the today's common Pinyin transcription. Only for the *Book of Changes* I keep the more familiar *I Ching* instead of the actually correct transcription of the Chinese term *Yì jīng*.

remains, whether this renaissance can even remotely take up the treasures of the astounding primordial wisdom of ancient China.

C.G. Jung, in a letter to an anonymous recipient who planned an institute to spread the wisdom of the I Ching in the Western world, answered, "If I understand anything of the *I Ching*, then I should say it is *the* book that teaches you your own way and the all-importance of it." But he utterly warns him against such plans because "an institute that hands out the wisdom is the quintessence of horror to me." In the Western world the wisdom of the East, Jung continues, is hardly understood at all and he adds, "You don't know what a hell of trouble I have to instill the smallest drop of wisdom into the vein of the 'Technicalized Savage' called European."[3] Considering these difficulties we must meet the I Ching with greatest caution and respect, so not to destroy once again the precious and most valuable heritage of the Chinese spirit, through which the illness of Western culture might be healed.

The problem already begins with the name. Richard Wilhelm called the *Book of Changes* the *I Ging*. I have often asked myself why he chose exactly this German expression. In Chinese it is called *Yì jing*, which is why the English *I Ching* would actually fit better. However, this is only partially true. In Chinese, a word may take a completely different meaning, depending upon how it is intoned, that is, upon its particular articulation. The English articulation of *I Ching* descends in pitch, whereas the German articulation of *I Ging* ascends, as in the Chinese. The correct Chinese is *Yì jing*. For Wilhelm, it was evidently more important to preserve the intonation than the actual wording. With this apparently minor example, I want to make two things clear: first, how sensitive Richard Wilhelm's translation is, and second, how difficult it is to find a mutual expression of language. In dialogue with the East, small nuances can give rise to large misunderstandings.

Noting these difficulties, I decided to proceed as follows. First I asked the I Ching itself how I should approach it (section 2). The answer, Hexagram 20, *Contemplation*, was enlightening, but, with the first line stressed, warned me not to ask boyishly, that is, with a too naive mind, because to do that, according to the I Ching, would be humiliating in a superior man. I'll come back to this in a moment. Apparently, when contemplating the I Ching today, we must be careful not to lose sight of the great universal

---

3   C.G. Jung, *Letters*, selected and edited by Gerhard Adler in collaboration with Aniela Jaffé. Translated by R.F.C. Hull (Princeton: Princeton University Press, 1975), Anonymous, 25 October 1935, vol. 1, pp. 201-202.

connections that continually resonate through the *Book of Changes*. Given this warning, based on this questioning of the I Ching, I decided to begin with an introduction to the intellectual and historical background of the *Book of Changes* (section 3). We will therefore approach the I Ching by a circuitous route, which corresponds perfectly to the Eastern circling of thoughts around the center.

In this third section, I want to touch on four themes:

1. The origin and textual history of the I Ching.
2. The structuring of the 64 hexagrams on the background of the Chinese celestial mind of *Hotu* and *Lo-shu*.
3. C.G. Jung's commentary on the I Ching: Taoism and analytical psychology.
4. The basic idea of the I Ching: the *Dao* of the *Yi* (change) or the secret of the transformation of all things, based on several examples.

Finally, in the fourth and last section, I will present a concrete example of how to work with the I Ching; for this I will consult the I Ching about a specific question, namely: What should a community such as the Psychology Club of Zürich, immersed in the spirit of analytical psychology, look like? This question I ask myself as the President of the Psychology Club again and again, a question that has been put more than once during the history of the Club, mainly in the early years.

But before going into the particular sections let me anticipate the following thought:

The encounter between Richard Wilhelm and Carl Gustav Jung

In December 1921 Richard Wilhelm was invited to the Psychology Club Zürich. It was the first time that he had spoken about the I Ching in the Western world. For C.G. Jung and his psychological research, the encounter with Richard Wilhelm and with the spirit of the East was essential and revealing. Only nine years later, on May 10th 1930, Jung gave a very moving talk at the memorial service for Wilhelm. I elaborately quote from this address because it is not well known and now so beautiful. Here Jung said about his relationship with Wilhelm:

I stand indeed as a stranger outside that vast realm of knowledge and experience in which Wilhelm worked as a master of his profession. He as a sinologist and I as a doctor would probably never have come into contact had we remained specialists. But we met in a field of humanity which begins beyond the academic boundary posts. There lay our point of contact; there the spark leapt across and kindled a light that was to become for me one of the most significant events of my life.[4]

And referring to Richard Wilhelm's translation he added:

To me the greatest of his achievements is his translation of, and commentary on, the I Ching... This book embodies, as perhaps no other, the living spirit of Chinese civilization, for the best minds of China have collaborated on it and contributed to it for thousands of years...
Anyone who, like myself, has had the rare good fortune to experience in association with Wilhelm the divinatory power of the I Ching cannot remain ignorant of the fact that we have here an Archimedean point from which our Western attitude of mind could be lifted off its foundations.[5]

These words mirror the deep gratitude for Wilhelm's work through which "he has inoculated us with the living germ of the Chinese spirit, capable of working a fundamental change in our view of the world." It is his merit that we "find ourselves partaking of the spirit of the East to the extent that we succeed in experiencing the living power of the *I Ching*."[6]

The creative spirit then and now

But how can we, in our time, even remotely live up to the creative spirit that is so livelily radiated by the I Ching and its wisdom? Or to put the question in psychological terms: How can western people connect with the *objective spirit* of the unconscious and how, for instance, by consulting the I Ching, can they integrate this spirit into their way of life? A painting of Peter Birkhäuser (1911-1976), painted during a difficult period of his life, might

4   C.G. Jung, "Richard Wilhelm: In Memoriam," CW 15, § 74.
5   Ibid., CW 15, § 77-78.
6   Ibid., CW 15, § 78.

offer an answer to this question. He called the painting *Sun of the Night*.[7]
(See plate 1, p. 225) It beautifully illustrates why it is so important that the
individual is committed in a very concrete way, in his own house, as it were,
to the spirit of the collective unconscious.

A nocturnal, owl-like creature with uncanny eyes rises from the horizon
like the moon. Its look seems somehow foreboding as if it were in possession
of a remote knowledge which certainly surpasses human consciousness. Its
strangeness and even eeriness make clear that the encounter of the individual with the spirit of the unconscious isn't anything like an easy task. On
the contrary, the human being in his small house seems to be completely
and utterly at the mercy of that supreme and alien power of the "Other."
Compared to the powerful *Sun of the Night* the small house with its warm
human light appears rather unimportant. And now this dwelling place
offers a vessel to the human, that is, a protected place of shelter. The human
being needs such a place, where he or she can get in contact with and listen
to the objective psyche, that is, to the spirit of the unconscious.

This is why C.G. Jung and Marie-Louise von Franz each created such
a place, quite concretely built in stone, a protective place in the midst of
nature sheltering them in their life-long investigation into the unknown
depths of the unconscious: he his *round* tower below at the shore of the
upper lake Zurich in Bollingen and she her *square* tower above on the ridge
of the mountain. To these places protected by Mother Nature they regularly
retreated in order to reconnect with the "cosmic depths of the soul"[8] as Jung
once expressed it.

But let's come back to Peter Birkhäuser's painting. In comparison to the
stunning grandiosity of the cosmic spirit the small house of the artist is but
a hovel. However, despite the poverty of the human hut, its importance
should not be underestimated. In the small house there is a light, a poor
light, truly, but it is a *warm human light*. I get the impression that the divine
spirit is yearning for the earthly light, if not to say, for the warmth of the
human blood; yearning for the little spark of human consciousness. There
is an intimate connection between the two, a mutual flow of energy, as
the power pole at the horizon shows. There is a vibration between the

7 Eva Wertenschlag-Birkhäuser and Kaspar Birkhäuser (eds.), *Der Rote Faden, Malerei
  und Grafik von Peter Birkhäuser* (Einsiedeln: Daimon Verlag, 2013), picture 166, p. 132;
  reproduced with kind permission of the Stiftung Peter und Sibylle Birkhäuser-Oeri.
8 C.G. Jung, *Introduction to Jungian Psychology. Notes of the Seminar on Analytical Psychology given in 1925 by C.G. Jung*, edited by William McGuire, Sonu Shamdasani
  (Princeton: Princeton University Press, 2012), lecture 8, p. 68.

two disparate partners, and it seems that the protective night makes their encounter possible, if at all.

The protective quality of the night is beautifully expressed in the many stars of the nocturnal sky arising high above the rather uncanny looking *Sun of the Night*. This points to a cosmic order existing beyond the ambivalence of human consciousness and the unconscious. Since primordial times human beings oriented themselves towards the stars, always longing for the cosmic heavenly order so formidably presented by the old Chinese sages who created the I Ching. This heavenly order, I feel, is also expressed by Peter Birkhäuser's painting. However vast the creative spirit of the unconscious emerging above the horizon, as represented by the *Sun of the Night* may be, and however small the human light of consciousness, seemingly threatened to be swallowed by the divine spirit seems to be, behind of that is that cosmic order. It is the cosmic depths of the soul, as it were, through which the opposites of human consciousness and the objective psyche, that is, the collective unconscious are reconciled if not to say united.

It is precisely this cosmic spirit or mind as suggested by Peter Birkhäuser's painting which makes the world of the I Ching so precious to me and which I feel in every single hexagram not to speak of the deeply meaningful sequences of the respective hexagrams. From its very beginning in early times in the I Ching the simple reigns. Within this simplicity arises the profoundly impressive cosmic spirit that flowed into Taoism centuries later. This is why Richard Wilhelm's translation of the ancient *Book of Changes* was of such importance for C.G. Jung; it was a tremendous experience for him to hear through this book, in clear language, "things [he] had dimly divined in the confusion of our European unconscious."[9]

I now come back to the first consulting of *the Book of Changes* in which I asked how to approach this cosmic order, that is, the Taoist celestial mind.

2. The First Consultation of the I Ching

So how should I proceed dealing with the I Ching?

The answer to the question posed above reads: no. 20, *Guan, Contemplation* ☶, and changes to no. 42, *Yi, Increase.*

However, before looking at this hexagram some preliminary remarks concerning the translations of the I Ching may be necessary. The various

---

9 C.G. Jung, "Richard Wilhelm: In Memoriam," CW 15, § 96.

translations differ quite a lot from each other. At heart it is the personal decision of each individual who uses the I Ching which translation he or she will chose. For me Richard Wilhelm's translation[10] is still one of the best. Various sinologists, as well as actively practicing Taoists, occasionally reproach him, suggesting that his commentary for this or that passage is made from a one-sided Western perspective. Nevertheless, I deeply agree with C.G. Jung, who, in his moving speech at the memorial service for Richard Wilhelm in Munich (10 May 1930), said of him: Richard Wilhelm was a "master of his profession," a master who knew the secret of the Chinese mind as nearly no other, and who "sacrificed his European prejudices for the sake of this rare pearl."[11]

In my opinion, the best English translation is *The Complete I-Ching* by the Taoist master Alfred Huang.[12] After the communists seized power in China in 1949, they forbade any activity with the I Ching. Huang had the opportunity, or perhaps I should rather say the fate, to find an old master (Master Yin), who, at over eighty, introduced him to the I Ching. Naturally the meetings took place in secret, which did not save Master Huang from being imprisoned by the communists for thirteen long years for his, as they called it, anti-revolutionary activities. During these years he was daily confronted with execution. They starved him almost to death, but eventually set him free after all. He immigrated to the United States, where to his great surprise he encountered a lively interest in the I Ching, not least thanks to Wilhelm's translation.

After his dreams asked him several times to make a translation in English, he finally submitted himself to the will of the unconscious. First he translated the Old Chinese text into modern Chinese, and then this text in turn into English. The Old Chinese text appears to differ in many respects from the text that Wilhelm used. To take only one example, the heading to Hexagram 4 is not *Youthful Folly*, as in Wilhelm, but rather simply *Childhood*. Whereas Wilhelm's commentary speaks of the "helpless folly of youth," in the text of Huang we find no negative aspects whatsoever. By contrast, he says that the Old Chinese compare the nature of childhood with an unpolished jade stone, whose beauty is still hidden. This hexagram is about

10 *The I Ching* or *Book of Changes*, The Richard Wilhelm Translation rendered into English by Cary F. Baynes, 3rd ed. (Princeton: Princeton University Press, 1967).
11 C.G. Jung, "Richard Wilhelm. In Memoriam," CW 15, § 74-75.
12 *The Complete I Ching, The Definitive Translation by the Taoist Master Alfred Huang* (Rochester, Vermont: Inner Traditions, 1998).

discovering the hidden wisdom of childhood and gradually bringing it into the light, just as, during the course of a long life, one would polish a precious stone to the highest brilliance.

I myself use almost exclusively these two translations. Also to be mentioned would be the edition of Ritsema;[13] it attempts to avoid any interpretation and to adhere to the Chinese wording verbatim. However, I have had difficulties finding an entry to it.

Finally, there are still those translations that come from the so-called *Complete Reality School* of Taoism, from which school the *Golden Flower* also derives. One example would be *The Taoist I-Ching* by Liu I-ming, a Taoist and alchemist from the eighteenth century.[14] A recurring Taoist proverb illustrates the basic position of the *Complete Reality School* beautifully:

"Empty the mind, fill the belly,"

"free yourself from your thoughts, fill your belly."[15] With the latter, it is naturally not meant that one should only gorge and booze, quite the opposite. As soon as one looks inward and lets go of the ten thousand worries, one begins to breathe deeply. One fills the belly. Filling the belly is a metaphor for the realization of the Tao of going along with time, as Master Liu I-ming put it in his treatise *Awakening to the Tao*. "Plants and trees," he said, "first flower and then produce fruit, each in its season. This is why they can live a long time."[16] Psychologically this equals the daily turning towards the unconscious. This branch of Taoism aspires to a life wholly related to the unconscious or the Self, or to express myself more carefully, as wholly related as possible. Free yourself from your wishes and prejudices and follow your true nature, or as C.G. Jung once said, listen to the advice of the two million-year-old human in yourself and act accordingly.[17]

---

13 Rudolf Ritsema, *The Classic Chinese Oracle of Change, The First Complete Translation With Concordance* (Shaftesbury: Element, 1995).

14 Liu I-ming, *The Taoist I Ching* (1796). Translated by Thomas Cleary, *The Taoist Classics*, vol. 4 (Boston: Shambhala, 2003).

15 Chang Po-tuan (Zhang Boduan, d. 1082), *Understanding Reality* with a commentary by Liu I-ming, in: *The Taoist Classics*, translated by Thomas Cleary, vol. 2 (Boston: Shambhala, 2003), pp. 73-74. Ibid., *The Inner Teachings of Taoism*. Commentary by Liu I-ming, in: *The Taoist Classics*, vol. 2, p. 252.

16 Liu I-ming, *Awakening to the Tao* (1816). Translated by Thomas Cleary, *The Taoist Classics*, vol. 3 (Boston: Shambhala, 2003), p. 504.

17 *C.G. Jung Speaking. Interview and Encounters*, ed. by William McGuire and R.F.C. Hull (Princeton: Princeton University Press, 1977), pp. 359-362. See also pp. 71-72.

After these introductory remarks concerning the various translations, let us come back to the concrete sample of how to use the I Ching. Before writing about this ancient old book I questioned the I Ching on how I should approach it.

As mentioned above, the answer reads: no. 20, *Guan, Contemplation* ䷓, the image of a tower, and changes to no. 42, *Yi, Increase.*

Master Huang begins his commentary to each of the individual hexagrams with a description of the Old Chinese pictogram. This is often very helpful. In our case, *Guan, Contemplation*, the left half of the character shows a bird with wide-open eyes. Next to it, to the right, the image of a human eye and under this the character for human is found. The hexagram therefore shows a bird and a human, each observing something precisely from its own perspective. My question was: how should I approach the I Ching? Does the picture of a bird and a human give an answer? If so, what?

Apparently the pictogram for *Contemplation* suggests connecting the heavenly or spiritual with the earthly, that is, contemplating both viewpoints together. One could also say, however, that the human must always himself be conscious that he is accurately observed by the other side, the heavenly bird. Another painting of Peter Birkhäuser entitled *The Observer,* shows a bird-like or cat-like creature watching the observer with a dark aura of power shining from his eyes. Marie-Louise von Franz commented on it as follows: "Before we know ourselves we are already 'known'. The self watches us like a superior observer… allowing no self-deception. He is both subhuman and superhuman and sees things far beyond our conscious mind."[18] This describes the psychic reality of the bird in pictogram 20, *Contemplation* very well. Therefore we may say, that the Chinese character for *Guan* alone points to contemplation both from this side and from the other side. In China, the Taoist temple is called *Dao Guan;* that is, the temple is a place where one carefully contemplates the Tao, or the Self and where human consciousness approaches the beyond, the "other," and the alien, integrating it as far as ever possible. In this sense, active imagination – a

18 "The Observer" in: *Light from the Darkness. The Paintings of Peter Birkhäuser,* ed. by Eva Wertenschlag-Birkhäuser and Kaspar Birkhäuser with a commentary by Marie-Louise von Franz (Basel: Birkhäuser Verlag, 1980), p. 64.

method developed by Jung of *consciously* approaching unconscious contents – may be called a *Dao Guan*.

The hexagram thus recommended a meditative stance in contact with the I Ching. This is also expressed in Wilhelm's translation: "The ablution has been made, but not yet the offering [that is, the sacrifice]." In the commentary, it says that through the ablution the deity is invoked. The moment of time between the ablution and the offering of the sacrifice is the most sacred of all, a moment of deepest inner composure.[19]

When we approach the I Ching, a religious attitude is essential. It is as though we were to enter a temple, which requires certain preparations, such as the ablution. This corresponds completely with the original meaning of *religio*: *religere* in the sense of "to contemplate something exactly or carefully," "to stand in awe in front of something," which precisely corresponds to *Dao Guan*. In the commentary of Confucius, we find "contemplation of the divine meaning underlying the workings of the universe" that is, the laws of nature.

The Taoists have always distinguished between two ways of using the I Ching. One can employ it as an *oracle book*, to receive an answer to a specific question; the I Ching can, however, also help one to find one's own center, or as Wilhelm perhaps would have said, to find the inner meaning of a certain situation. Then it becomes a *book of meditation*. A nineteenth-century Taoist, *Lu Tung-pin*, formulated it as follows:

> Although the words [of the I Ching] are very clear, yet they are also very vague. The shallow may take the I Ching to be a book of divination, but the profound consider it the secret of the celestial mechanism.[20]

Accordingly the real meaning of the I Ching for the Taoists of the School of Inner Alchemy[21] did not value so much the questioning of the oracle, but

---

19 R. Wilhelm, *I Ching*, p. 82.
20 Thomas Cleary, *The Taoist Classics*, vol. 4, p. 6.
21 The goal of *Inner Alchemy* or the *Way of the Golden Elixir*, Chinese *neidan*, is to achieve immortality or a state of union with the *dao* through various techniques such as meditation, breathing, and sexual hygiene. *Neidan* is complementary to *waidan*, the *External Alchemy*, which is focused on the compounding of elixirs, and is mainly concerned with the world of deities and demons, and with the performance of ceremonies and other ritual actions addressed to deities. See the respective articles in: *The Routledge Encyclopedia of Taoism*. Ed. by Fabrizio Pregadio (London and New York: Routledge, 2008), vol. II.

rather the reflection upon and the restoration of the original *wholeness* or, as they called it, the original celestial mind. I will come back to this.

In my questioning of the I Ching the first line of Hexagram 20, *Contemplation*, was stressed:

> Six at the beginning means:
> Boylike contemplation
> For an inferior man, no blame,
> For a superior man, humiliation.[22]

This is a clear warning. Apparently I must watch that I don't approach the I Ching too superficially. For this reason, I decided to give a careful introduction to the background and spiritual world of the I Ching, to the best of my ability. "Boylike contemplation" remains too much on the surface. As Wilhelm says in his commentary to this line, it is important to contemplate the deeper connections, and so far as possible, to understand them. I don't want to evade this admittedly difficult work.

In the original version of the foreword to the English edition of Wilhelm's translation, Jung says that two things would make dealing with the I Ching difficult. To begin with, there is the remarkably strange symbolism, which often remains closed to us despite Wilhelm's brilliant commentary. Here, however, a basic knowledge of the psychology of the unconscious with its symbolic language helps us, because here, as there, in the Western tradition as in the world of Chinese thought, it concerns the world of the archetypes. However, the greater difficulty, according to Jung, is the inferior side of the individual personality, the shadow, to which we are often astonishingly blind.[23] Above all, the changing lines refer to these shadow aspects. This is frequently the case when the third or the top line is stressed. He who avoids his own shadow, to him the celestial mind cannot disclose itself. I must certainly make a point of avoiding boylike contemplation! For

---

22 R. Wilhelm, *I Ching*, p. 84.
23 C.G. Jung, Vorwort zum I Ging (1948/1950), in: C.G. Jung, *Zur Psychologie westlicher und östlicher Religion* (Olten/Freiburg i.Br.: Walter Verlag, ²1973), GW 11, § 975. This paragraph is not in the English edition of the *Collected Works*. The English translation of the foreword diverges in many parts from Jung's original version reproduced from the German text. Therefore the paragraphs differ in the two versions. C.G. Jung, Foreword to the "I Ching," in: *Psychology and Religion: West and East*, vol. 11 of *The Collected Works of C.G. Jung*, translated by R.F.C. Hull. (Princeton: Princeton University Press, ⁸1989), § 964-1018.

an "inferior man" this may carry no blame; for a "superior man," however, it is humiliating. In other words, whoever strives for higher, spiritual values in his or her life, or as the Chinese would put it, whoever searches for the *dao*, must investigate the deeper mysteries of the I Ching. In this sense, I will now discuss some aspects of the Chinese history of thoughts.

3. The I Ching in the Light of the Chinese History of Thoughts

3.1. Origin and textual history of the I Ching

There were four wise ones, who gave to the I Ching its current form, the first of whom, the legendary *Emperor Fu Xi*, goes back to mythical times. With this the Taoists want to argue – and they do this quite rightly from a psychological perspective – that the source of the I Ching is of an archetypal nature. Legend has it that Fu Xi introduced the eight trigrams:

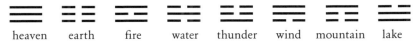

heaven   earth   fire   water   thunder   wind   mountain   lake

King Wen, founder of the Chou Dynasty, who lived around 1000 B.C.E., formed the 64 hexagrams from these eight trigrams. His son, the *Duke of Chou*, added the line texts, and finally, *Confucius* and his students (sixth to fifth century B.C.E.) supplemented the book with their commentaries. However, the I Ching first appeared with these commentaries not before the time of the Han Dynasty, between 206 B.C.E. and 220 C.E. In this exceedingly turbulent time politically, the I Ching achieved the form that it now has retained for a good two thousand years – astoundingly, at exactly the same time as the Bible found its final form.

I don't doubt that the origins of the I Ching go back to the world of the shamans. The idea that a person, as like the shaman, must orient him- or herself between heaven and earth is a basic concept of shamanism, as well as of Taoism and the I Ching. In working with the I Ching, it is important to keep this archaic, universal background in mind. Behind every personal difficulty there is a cosmic dimension, and only if we take this into account, do we not lose ourselves in the egotism of "boylike [or girlish] contemplation." Which brings us to the cosmic dimension of the I Ching.

3.2. Hotu and Lo-shu, the inner and the outer celestial mind. The inner structure of the I Ching

The legend tells us that a horse rose out of a river and revealed to the legendary Emperor Fu Xi the original celestial mind or, as the Taoist also called it, the Older Heavenly Order, *Hotu*. This is contrasted with the worldly, or social order, also called the Younger Heavenly Order, *Lo-shu*, which was engraved on the shell of a turtle that surfaced from the River Lo. Richard Wilhelm refers to both celestial minds as the "Primal Arrangement" and the "Inner-World Arrangement."[24] Behind this is the idea of two separate time systems; *Hotu*, the timeless, otherworldly and cosmos creating time, or eternity, as opposed to, *Lo-shu*, the cyclic, worldly time. The Chinese speak also of the earlier or inner and the later or outer celestial mind.

In her book on divination and synchronicity, Marie-Louise von Franz mentions the French-Jewish mathematician and physicist, Albert Lautmann, who was murdered by the Nazis at the age of thirty-two. He had developed a theory of two qualities of time, which is astoundingly reminiscent of the ancient Chinese idea of the two celestial minds. Lautmann called these qualities *linear time* and *cosmogonic time*. "The latter he conceives of as a field in which he says, 'topological accidents would take place,'" says Marie-Louise von Franz, and she continues, "This field of topological accidents would be another intuitive hypothesis which approaches my idea of the collective unconscious conceived of as a one continuum field ordered by the rhythms of the archetypes."[25] This means that the collective unconscious is not simply a chaotic accumulation of unconscious material; much more, through precise contemplation (*guan*) it is revealed as a hidden enigmatic, eternal or archetypical order.

The idea of a field continuum that is ordered by an archetypal rhythm similar to sacred dance also lies behind the Chinese notion of the original celestial mind, *Hotu*. In this the Chinese see an ideal condition, in which everything is united harmoniously with the Tao. The knowledge of this celestial mind is embedded in everyone, but the older we become, the more distant we are from it, until we, as it is called in the Golden Flower and also in the I Ching, *return* in order to reconnect with the original or the heavenly mind. This is what we do when we attempt to recognize the messages from the unconscious and to follow them; we re-establish, even if only for an

24 Richard Wilhelm, *I Ching*, pp. 266-268.
25 Marie-Louise von Franz, *On Divination and Synchronicity* (Toronto: Inner City Books, 1980), p. 104.

infinitesimal part, what the Chinese call the original cosmic mind or the mind of Tao.

Taoists are practitioners and, as such, less interested in theory. Consequently, the idea of the two celestial minds has for them quite practical outcomes. To understand these, they say, means to understand when it is time to act and when it is time *not* to act and rather to wait. "Before the appropriate time has arrived," or as we would say, before the creative spirit of the collective unconscious stirs, "there is preservation of tranquility and silence." Once the time [to act] has arrived, however, then one must take care that the fullness doesn't overflow,[26] that is, now one must act, or as the I Ching says, now is the time arrived to cross the great water. Or as the Taoist text of the Golden Flower from the 12th Century puts it: "If one moves too quickly, as long as the celestial mind is still calm and tranquil, one loses one's true mind, because one is too young. However, if the heavenly mind starts to move and one follows this movement too late, one loses one's true mind, because one is too old."[27] Likewise, the uses of the I Ching are correspondingly different. In times of rest, says Wilhelm, one should meditate on the images of the I Ching. In times of action, however, one consults the oracle to receive appropriate advice.[28]

The separation of the 64 hexagrams of the I Ching into two sections also has to do with the two celestial minds. While the first section with Hexagrams 1-30 deals with the inner celestial mind, the second (31-64) turns to the realization of the celestial mind in the social environment. Correspondingly, the first section begins with the description of heaven and earth, the two basic powers of nature. The second, however, contains a description of human relationship, that is, of Eros as the foundation of the social order: no. 31, *Influence* (wooing) (to take a maiden to wife brings good fortune!) and no. 32, *Duration*, in which a lasting relationship or connection is accorded the highest value. This means no less than that the love relationship is the basis of every social order, also of the state.

Besides *Heaven*: *The Creative*, and *Earth*: *The Receptive*, *yang* and *yin*, there are two further cardinal signs: *water*, which embodies the darkness of the moon, and *fire*, which represents the brightness of the sun. Accordingly,

---

26 Thomas Cleary, *The Taoist Classics*, vol. 4, p. 7.
27 Mokusen Miyuki (ed.), *Die Erfahrung der Goldenen Blüte. Der Basistext taoistischer Meditation aus dem China des 12. Jahrhunderts*, Teil 2: *Die Lehre von der Goldenen Blüte des großen Einen* (Bern/München/Wien: O.W. Barth Verlag, 2000), p. 141 (my translation).
28 Richard Wilhelm, *I Ching*, p. 290.

the trigrams *water* and *fire* stand in their pure forms at the close of the first section: nrs. 29, *Kan* and 30, *Li*. In their mixed form they stand at the close of the second section: water over fire in no. 63 ☷☰, *After Completion*, and fire over water in no. 64 ☰☷, *Before Completion*.

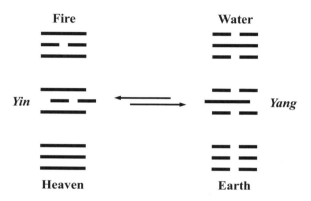

The Taoist and alchemical writings, for which the I Ching served as a basis, are full of speculations about the opposing transformations of these two cardinal signs. If *fire* and *water* interact, and the middle *yang* of *water* interchanges with the middle *yin* of *fire*, the original celestial mind arises: pure *yang* and pure *yin*, heaven and earth. The alchemists call this "filling fire with water" or "the immersing of fire in water."

Regarding the interaction between fire and water, the Taoists have some wonderful speculations and expressions about the creative and enlivening relationship of masculine and feminine where the female was considered to hold the most significant value. I quote from the classical sixth chapter of the *Dao de jing*, most likely the oldest text in which the great and unnamable mystery of the *Dao* is intimately connected with the dark feminine:

> The valley spirit (*gŭshén*) never dies,
> it is called the mysterious female (*xuánpìn*).
> The gate of the mysterious female
> is called the root of heaven and earth.
> Smooth like an ongoing silk thread is his existence.

Utilize it, and his effect is never exhausted.[29]

The same Taoist spirit, open to the female, imbues the eighteenth century text of the *Golden Flower*. Here, in chapter eight, we read: "In the midst of the moon the true *yang* is collected. It is the true light of the sun."[30] The interplay of *yin* and *yang* leads to the birth of the divine child: "The moon gathers up the ten thousand waters. In the midst of this darkness, the Heavenly Heart [or: Spirit] suddenly begins a movement. This is the return of the one Light, the time when the child comes to life."[31] In these texts the golden flower represents the light of the pure *yang* that is received into the stillness of the pure *yin*, in the deepest introspection of meditation.[32]

3.3. C.G. Jung and the I Ching. Taoism and Analytical Psychology

Jung's address at the memorial service of Richard Wilhelm (1930)

C.G. Jung spoke only four times in a definitive way about the I Ching despite the fact that he once called himself a "jealous lover of the I Ching."[33] The first time was in May 1930 at a memorial service in Munich on the occasion of the death of Richard Wilhelm.[34] This talk moves me as has no other text of Jung about the light of the East, which, as he says, is able to give us so much healing in our spiritual need. On this occasion Jung talked

29 My translation. I thank Hsing-Chuen Schmuziger-Chen for her support. A possible interpretation of the chapter can be found in: Andreas Schweizer, Chinas Berge – zwischen Himmel und Erde. Der Geist des Tao und das Fenster in die Ewigkeit, in: Erik Hornung and Andreas Schweizer (Ed.), *Heilige Landschaft*, Eranos 2013 und 2014 (Basel: Schwabe, 2015), pp. 153-190, especially p. 174.

30 Translation by Andreas Schweizer from the revised and completed German edition of the original text of the *Golden Flower*; I couldn't find a translation of this text in English. Wilhelm's translation ends in the midst of chapter 8. The German translation of the completed text can be found in: Richard Wilhelm/C.G. Jung, *Geheimnis der Goldenen Blüte. Das Buch von Bewusstsein und Leben*. Mit ergänzenden Übersetzungen aus dem Chinesischen von Barbara Hendrischke. Neu herausgegeben und mit einem Nachwort versehen von Ulf Diederichs (München: Eugen Diederichs, ⁷1996), p. 129.

31 *The Secret of the Golden Flower. A Chinese Book of Life*. Translated and explained by Richard Wilhelm with a European Commentary by C.G. Jung, translated [from German] into English by Cary F. Baynes (London: Kegan Paul, Trench, Trubner & Co, 1931) p. 61.

32 See Mokusen Miyuki, *Die Erfahrung der Goldenen Blüte*, p. 12. It seems that the original English version of Miyuki's thesis at the C.G. Jung Institute entitled *The Secret of the Golden Flower* has not been published in English.

33 C.G. Jung, *Letters*, Vol. 1, 25.10.1935, p. 201.

34 C.G. Jung, "Richard Wilhelm: In Memoriam," CW 15, § 74-96.

with greatest respect of Wilhelm whose mind "created a bridge between East and West and gave to the Occident the precious heritage of a culture thousands of years old, a culture perhaps destined to disappear forever."[35] In the spiritual exchange with Wilhelm, Jung experienced the divinatory power of the I Ching – a rare good fortune, as he called it – and he knew that through the I Ching Wilhelm "has inoculated us with the living germ of the Chinese spirit, capable of working a fundamental change in our view of the world."[36] However, he was painfully aware, that "the light of this wisdom shines only in the dark, not in the brightly lit theater of European consciousness and will." This is an allusion to the thousands of years old, bloody and cruel Chinese history, which caused so much suffering to the people of China. The wisdom of the I Ching issued from "the nameless poverty and hopeless filth and vices of the Chinese masses."[37] From the background of this darkness and suffering has emerged the light of the East.

Foreword to the English edition of the I Ching (1948)

Not until eighteen years later (1948) did Jung speak again about the I Ching. At that time he was asked to write a foreword to the English edition of Wilhelm's translation. Again he hesitated, and finally asked the I Ching itself what it had to say. The answer was totally positive, Hexagram 50, *The Caldron*; this is a hexagram that emphasizes very strongly the religious dimension of the I Ching. As so often is the case, Jung's interpretation of this hexagram comes as a surprise. He regarded the text "as though the *I Ching* itself were the speaking person. Thus it describes itself as a caldron…"[38] The caldron serves in the offering of sacrifice to God, whose revelation appears to prophets and holy men. Accordingly, the I Ching says, "The will of god, as revealed through them, should be accepted in humility." This brings enlightenment, or as Master Huang suggests with his title of hexagram 50: *Establishing the New*, it symbolizes a new era. "Nine in the second place" says:

> There is food in the *ting* (caldron).
> My comrades are envious,
> But they cannot harm me.

35 Ibid., CW 15, § 74.
36 Ibid., CW 15, § 78.
37 Ibid., CW 15, § 88.
38 C.G. Jung, "Foreword to the I Ching," CW 11, § 977.

Good fortune.[39]

Jung follows from this that the I Ching contains "spiritual nourishment," which the envious try to rob. But their enmity is in vain, for no one can take away its richness of meaning and its positive achievements.[40] However, "Nine in the third place" carries a warning:

> The handle of the *ting* (caldron) is altered.
> One is impeded in his way of life.

This suggests – and here I follow the commentary of Master Huang – that a new era has started and thus it is time to change, time to establish the new. And Jung, referring to his question continues, "We are no longer supported by the wise counsel and deep insight of the oracle; therefore we no longer find our way through the mazes of fate and the obscurities of our own natures… the *I Ching* is complaining, as it were, that its excellent qualities go unrecognized and hence lie fallow."[41] However, the top line speaks of the jade rings of the sacrificial vessel and of great good fortune, and thus Jung's commentary ends quite optimistically "with the pleasant conclusion that the *I Ching* approves of the new [English] edition."[42]

The I Ching in the light of the phenomenon of synchronicity (1952)

In 1952, soon to be eighty years old, Jung wrote about the I Ching and Taoism for the first time in a *scholarly* work in the essay *Synchronicity: An Acausal Connecting Principle.*[43] To my knowledge, Jung refers to the synchronistic principle for the first time in the memorial for Richard Wilhelm, already mentioned. There he speaks of a certain Englishman who had expressed surprise "that so highly intelligent a people as the Chinese had produced no science." This must be an optical illusion, replied Jung, since they definitely had developed a science. The "standard text book of this science was the I Ching."[44] Its principle, however, as so much else in China, was altogether

39 R. Wilhelm, *I Ching*, p. 195.
40 C.G. Jung, "Foreword to the I Ching," CW 11, § 980.
41 Ibid., § 981.
42 Ibid., § 993.
43 C.G. Jung, "Synchronicity: An Acausal Connecting Principle," in: *The Structure and Dynamics of the Psyche*, vol. 8 of *The Collected Works of C.G. Jung*. Edited and translated by Gerhard Adler and R.F.C. Hull (Princeton: Princeton University Press, 1970), § 816-997.
44 C.G. Jung, "Richard Wilhelm: In Memoriam," CW 15, § 80-81.

different from the principle of our Western science. Anticipating his later research into synchronicity, Jung, as already mentioned, stated that we are touching here, "an Archimedean point from which our Western attitude of mind could be lifted off its foundations."[45]

And indeed, not only the I Ching, but Jung, too, lifted the Western attitude of mind off its foundations, not least because of his deep interaction with the light of the East. Characteristic for the I Ching and the Chinese way of thought are its intuitive methods "which start with the psychic factor and take the existence of synchronicity as self-evident," that is, its "intuitive technique for *grasping the total situation*."[46] Behind the I Ching stands the structure of the original celestial mind or, as the Chinese also called it, the Older Heavenly Order, Ho-tu, which due to its transcendental character can only be grasped intuitively. In its orientation toward wholeness, precisely the celestial mind, Chinese science is completely bound to the acausal orderedness of the synchronistic principle. Isolated phenomena and individuals are always seen as a part of the whole. Due to this closeness between Chinese thought and the synchronistic principle, Jung, in his work on synchronicity, quotes Zhuangzi (Chuang-tzu) (fourth century BCE) from his book, *Das Wahre Buch vom südlichen Blütenland* (*The True Book from the Southern Flower Land*), translated by Richard Wilhelm: "The state in which ego and non-ego are no longer opposed is called the pivot of Tao."[47] What this actually means and which consequences this has becomes clear a few chapters later:

> Forget the time! Forget opinions!
> Leap into the boundless! Dwell in the boundless![48]

In the text from the Southern Flower Land follows the famous story of Zhuangzi, who dreamt that he was a butterfly, free and happy, knowing nothing about Zhuangzi. Then suddenly he woke up and was once again Zhuangzi. Now, he didn't know whether Zhuangzi had dreamt that he was a butterfly, or whether the butterfly had dreamt that he was Zhuangzi. It is

45 Ibid., § 78.
46 C.G. Jung, "Synchronicity: An Acausal Connecting Principle," CW 8, § 863.
47 Dschuang Dsï (Zhuangzi), *Das Wahre Buch vom südlichen Blütenland*, Aus dem Chinesischen übertragen und erläutert von Richard Wilhelm (Zürich: Ex Libris, 1972), Buch II, Kap. 3, p. 43. See: C.G. Jung, "Synchronicity: An Acausal Connecting Principle," CW 8, § 923.
48 My translation from Richard Wilhelm's German text, Zhuangzi, Book II, Chapter 10, p. 51.

exactly like this, says the story, with the transformation of things.[49] And so it is with the I Ching, I might add. What is it really about? Is it about the individual asker of the I Ching or about the hidden reality of the original celestial mind, about an individual person or about the infinity of the spiritual world? These questions, however, stem from a Western mind; for the Chinese synchronistic way of thought the two sides are but one, even if this oneness can only be comprehended as a paradox.

Jung, in his treatise on synchronicity suggests that there exists "in the unconscious something like an a priori knowledge or an 'immediacy' of events which lacks any causal basis."[50] A little later he speaks of "absolute knowledge" and compares it with Agrippa's late medieval notion of an all-pervasive *spiritus mundi.*[51] The divinatory technique of the I Ching, the origin of which goes back to the early millennium B.C.E., rests on "the *simultaneous occurrence* of a psychic state [of whoever consults the oracle] with a physical process [techniques like throwing the coins]," which might be called the *equivalence of meaning.*[52] This underlying meaning of everything that exists in the world is what the Chinese called the Tao. Therefore Richard Wilhelm suggested translating "the Tao that cannot be spoken and whose name cannot be named," as "meaning." It is this *a priori* meaning that Jung called the "psychoid factor;"[53] this factor is inherent in any synchronistic principle with its quality of meaning. Thus Jung's concept of synchronistic principle as compensatory to the principle of causality echoes the age-old Chinese wisdom of Tao.

Referring to the dark mystery of the eternal feminine, the already mentioned sixth chapter of the *Dao de jing* beautifully describes the mystery of Tao or Meaning which also lies at the bottom of the I Ching, I quote the first two lines again:

> The valley spirit (*gŭshén*) never dies,
> it is called the mysterious female (*xuánpìn*).

"The valley spirit never dies…" What could this mean? First we must forget our preconceived notions of valley. Valley does not refer to the constricting

49 Richard Wilhelm, Zhuangzi, Book II, Chapter 11, p. 52.
50 C.G. Jung, "Synchronicity: An Acausal Connecting Principle," CW 8, § 856.
51 Ibid., CW 8, § 931; Agrippa von Nettesheim (1486-1535).
52 Ibid., CW 8, § 865 (emphasis mine).
53 Ibid., CW 8, § 962.

day-to-day realities, nor is it meant as opposed to the vastness of heaven.
Valley rather denotes the empty and open space between the rock walls.
The primordial spirit pervades this space of emptiness just as an echo
resonates throughout a mountain valley. The valley receives the sound
without holding it back, unintentionally, like a mirror that reflects the
image without any effort. This image illustrates a central truth of the Taoist
core; it gives witness to the strong Chinese intuition of the reality of the
collective unconscious. If humans succeed to go along the path of utter
simplicity and ease, to become empty, quiet and intent, and thus to reach
tranquility of mind, then they are like the valley between the mountains.
For sure, the valley spirit, that is, the primordial spirit of Tao or, to put it
in psychological terms, the creative power of the unconscious, will move in
spontaneous reply. It is precisely this spirit of Tao which pervades the *Book
of Changes*. Receive it and your life will be filled with Meaning.

Memories, Dreams, Reflections (1961)

The fourth and last time Jung discussed the I Ching was in his recollec-
tions of Richard Wilhelm and the I Ching in *Memories, Dreams, Reflections*
(appendix iv).[54] Jung recounts how around 1920 he began experimenting
with the I Ching, discovering more and more amazing coincidences. He
was preoccupied with mainly one question: "Are the *I Ching's* answers
meaningful or not?" And if they are, "how does the connection between
the psychic and the physical sequence of events come about?"[55] Not much
later when he met Richard Wilhelm and his "wealth of knowledge of the
Chinese mentality," "some of the most difficult problems that the European unconscious has posed on [him]" had been clarified.[56] In his encounter
with Wilhelm Jung found answers to his most besetting questions about the
synchronicities and meaningful connections that he discovered in his own
research. This caused a deep, however, short friendship between the two in
the spirit of the I Ching, which ended with Wilhelm's death in March 1930.

3.4. The Tao of the Yì or the secret of the transformation of all things

The idea of the transformation of all things (yì) runs throughout the entire
I Ching, but above all is expressed in two aspects: firstly, in the sequential

---

54 Aniela Jaffé (ed.), *Memories, Dreams, Reflections by C.G. Jung*, translated from the
    German by Richard and Clara Winston (London: Fontana Press, 1995) pp. 407-410.
55 Ibid., p. 407.
56 Ibid., p. 408.

order of the hexagrams, which is why it is helpful to look each time at the preceding and following hexagrams; and secondly, in the sequence of the individual lines, which is why all of the lines should be looked at each time, and not just the one which has been stressed. I want to give an example of each aspect.

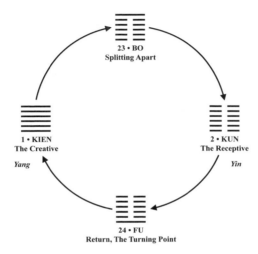

The succession of the hexagrams

In the eighth chapter of the *Golden Flower* the shift from darkness to the new light, as we have seen already, is described as *return* or *reversal*:

> In the midst of this darkness, the Heavenly Heart [or: Spirit] suddenly begins a movement. This is the return of the one Light, the time when the child comes to life.[57]

Or in Mokusen Miyuki's version:

> In the midst of this profound depth and darkness, suddenly the heavenly spirit begins to move. This moment is meant when it is said, "that a *yang* joins *fu* [referring to the single *yang* line entering at the bottom of Hexagram 24, *Return*]." This is the hour of return.[58]

---

57 R. Wilhelm, *Golden Flower*, p. 61.
58 M. Miyuki, *Die Erfahrung der Goldenen Blüte*, p. 140 (my translation).

In order to better understand this, we must look at the preceding hexagram, no. 23, *Splitting Apart*, or as Huang translates, *Falling Away*. Hexagram 23, *Splitting Apart*, consists of five *yin* lines and at the top a *yang* line. When this *yang* line falls away, there remain only the *yin* lines, which correspond to Hexagram 2. The masculine falls, as the text of the *Golden Flower* expresses, into the profound depth and darkness of the pure *yin*; it is, so to speak, devoured by the feminine. Now *yang*, or the creative is invisible, but it doesn't vanish completely; it broods, so to speak, in the shelter of the darkness of the feminine; it waits for the hour of the return, Hexagram 24.

The return or turning back within the course of the year corresponds to the time of the winter solstice, through which the entire creation will appear in a new light. Now a new and creative time dawns. As already explained, the wise of China emphasize again and again that everything depends on knowing the difference between when it is necessary to wait and be still, and when the time for action has arrived. The commentaries on these two Hexagrams could not illustrate this difference more: "It does not further one to go anywhere," it says in Hexagram 23. One should therefore wait in all quiet until the hour of the return appears. Don't force anything! And suddenly, in the following hexagram, everything comes to life anew: "Friends come without blame. To and fro goes the way," etc. He who now does *not* act, the top line of Hexagram 24 warns, misses the return. Then misfortune threatens. Therefore, "If a man misses the right time for return, he meets with misfortune." And why? Because one has not taken to heart the universal connection, the celestial mind.

The succession of the individual lines

To close this chapter, we will cast a glance at the significance of the individual lines. Each line has its own quality of transformation and so contributes decisively to an understanding of the respective hexagram. I will use as an example the individual lines in Hexagram 2, *Kun, The Receptive*, the earth, or the feminine *yin*. As Hexagram 1, heaven, describes the quality of strength and solidity, so Hexagram 2, earth, features movement and flexibility. The individual lines then describe the use and the misuse of the *yang* and *yin* qualities. We will therefore take a closer look at these lines. They give us valuable information about the most important characteristics of the feminine *yin*.

Six at the beginning means:

When there is hoarfrost underfoot,
Solid ice is not far off.[59]

When the first frost comes, winter is approaching and with it the time of darkness and death. If our spirit is sufficiently agile and open, reflecting and being aware of the flexibility of the feminine *yin*, it is prepared. It does not defend itself against the encroaching darkness. And why? Because it knows about the return and turning point, which, sooner or later, with certainty will follow. Therefore with this changing line, the hexagram changes into no. 24, *Return*.

Six in the second place means:
Straight, square, great. Without purpose,
Yet nothing remains unfurthered.

Straightforwardness and sincerity are virtues of the wise, who follow the laws of earth, of the feminine *yin*. The square is the basic form of the temple. So this is about simple devotion to the laws of the creative and of nature. "The essence of the receptive is to offer the right vessel, the appropriate form, to everything that heaven initiates, that heaven 'begets' and 'bears'."[60] This devotion is based on the secret of the receptive. In the center of one's own being lays great strength. Therefore with this changing line, the hexagram changes into no. 7, *The Army*. And why? Because the army is the inner strength of a people or the power of the creative, as Marie-Louise von Franz once interpreted this hexagram.[61]

Six in the third place means: …
Seek not works but bring to completion.

"Seek not works but bring to completion," this means: "Conceal your strengths!" The wise one acts within the secrecy of the *yin*. His wisdom resembles a slowly developing embryo. He seeks no profit for himself, and nevertheless, he completes. He waits patiently for his time. Then he

59 R. Wilhelm, *I Ching*, p. 13.
60 *I Ging, Das Buch der Wandlungen*, neu übersetzt und kommentiert von Georg Zimmermann (Düsseldorf: Patmos Verlag, 2007), p. 56 (my translation).
61 Marie-Louise von Franz, "Nike and the Waters of the Styx," in: *Archetypal Dimensions of the Psyche* (London: Shambhala, 1999), pp. 278-279.

acts, without any consideration of individual interests. Therefore with this changing line, the hexagram changes into no. 15, *Modesty*.

> Six in the fourth place means:
> A tied-up sack. No blame, no praise.

This line recommends the strongest reserve and the strictest reticence. The time is dangerous. Caution is indicated. There is no praise, because one cannot act creatively. Now is the time to wait, until the thunder finally breaks out of the earth. Therefore with this changing line, the hexagram changes into no. 16, *Enthusiasm*: "Thunder over the earth!" "Thunder comes resounding out of the earth: the image of Enthusiasm," an image of spring.

> Six in the fifth place means:
> A yellow lower garment brings supreme good fortune.

Yellow is the colour of the center and of the earth; reliable and genuine. The undergarment is simple, without any decoration. This speaks of the utmost discretion and modesty. "Humility is of an inner beauty,"[62] as the interpretation runs. The hexagram changes into no. 8, *Holding Together*. Holding together is only possible, it says in Hexagram 8, when a center point is there. This center point is created within the stillness of the feminine. That is the great power of the stillness and simplicity of the feminine, the receptive.

> Six at the top means:
> Dragons fight in the meadow.
> Their blood is black and yellow.

Here the dark and shadowy element should yield to the light. When it wills to assert itself and to dominate, instead of serving, it incurs the wrath of the strong. In this way, both sides come to harm, both bleed, the heaven (blue-black) and the earth (yellow). That leads to a merciless battle of the genders and of their opposites. Thus one loses one's center. Therefore with this changing line, the hexagram changes into no. 23, *Splitting Apart*.

This sequence demonstrates the inexhaustible network of relationships, in which we are enmeshed each time we consult the I Ching. Using a

---

62 Master Huang, *I Ching*, p. 46.

concept from mathematics, Marie-Louise von Franz called it the field continuum of the collective unconscious. The Taoists call it the original celestial mind or the older heavenly order. When we follow this, then the I Ching promises us great good fortune. When, however, we want to dominate, then misfortune looms. Perhaps we would do better to follow the maxim of the Old Chinese: "Forget your thoughts, fill your belly."

* * *

So much for the Taoist background of the I Ching and the original celestial mind in ancient China. This, however, brings up the question of how we can approach this thousand of years old wisdom in our time. Let us first cast another glance at C.G. Jung's foreword to the English edition of Wilhelm's *I Ching*. At first he hesitated to write it. Behind this hesitation was most likely the basic question, whether the *I Ching* and its use were, after all, practicable in the Western world. Jung then asked the I Ching itself whether spreading its wisdom in the Western world could turn out to be meaningful, and the answer, as we have seen, was absolutely positive. However, in conclusion one thing is clear: only the individual, practicable and thoughtful usage of the I Ching can prove its value. In this sense, and to conclude, a concrete example of a consultation of the I Ching will follow here.

It is some years ago that I asked the I Ching concerning the Psychology Club. I then was deeply preoccupied with the question of how a *community* in the spirit of *Analytical Psychology*, as the Psychology Club certainly represents, should look like. What do we have to draw our attention to in order to bestow a living creative spirit on this community? As we know from the Club archives, this question also concerned the members of previous times, and they too consulted the I Ching.

4. The Second Consultation of the I Ching – an Example

In January 2013, during the time of the total renovation of the Club house at Gemeindestraße 27 in Zürich, the question was posed:

In which way do we have to be mindful at the Psychology Club in order to pass on the precious, nearly hundred years old tradition to, and transform it for, future generations?

The answer was significant and encouraging too:

> 14, *Dà yŏu, Possession in Great Measure*, or as Master Huang translates it, *Great Harvest*. With the Nine in the first and second place it changes to 56, *Lü, The Wanderer*.

Sequence of the hexagrams

Let's first have a look at the sequence of the hexagrams, which is quite revealing regarding the question we asked. The proceeding Hexagram 13, *Pi, Fellowship with Men*, offers some sort of a basis for the resulting hexagram. The *Book of Changes* seems to be of the opinion that fellowship with humans leads to Hexagram 14, *Great Harvest*. However, "True fellowship among men must be based upon a concern that is universal. It is not the private interests of the individual that create lasting fellowship among men, but rather the goals of humanity,"[63] as King Wen beautifully commented on *The Judgment*. In that way even difficult tasks, such as crossing the great water, can be accomplished. The focus of each group member on a cosmic participation or, in psychological terms, on the collective unconscious and its archetypal structure is crucial. Regardless of individual differences the members of the Psychology Club must remain focused on the transpersonal and uniting aspect.

Master Huang translated Hexagram 13 as *Seeking Harmony*.[64] This mirrors the ancient Chinese belief that people cannot live in harmony unless the individual members meet in a spirit of equality, thus obtaining harmony by "seeking common ground on major issues while reserving differences on minor ones."[65] A similar idea can be found in Paul's letter to the Corinthians. Paul used the image of the body and its many members:

> For in the one Spirit we were all baptized into one body – Jews or Greeks, slaves or free – we were all made to drink of one Spirit…
> But as it is, God arranged the members in the body, each one of them, as he chose. If all were a single member, where would the body be? …
> The eye cannot say to the hand, "I have no need of you," nor again the head to the feet, "I have no need of you." On the contrary, the members

63 R. Wilhelm, *I Ching*, p. 56.
64 Master Huang, *I Ching*, p. 134.
65 Ibid., p. 135.

of the body that seem to be weaker are indispensable… If one member suffers, all suffer together with it; if one member is honoured, all rejoice together with it. (1 Corinthians 12, 12-26)

The sequence of the hexagrams 13 and 14 therefore suggests exploring and fostering analytical psychology in a way that creates a spirit of a community in which the objective psyche and the unconscious is vividly and mandatorily present.

That this only can be reached through greatest modesty and humbleness is stressed by the first line of Hexagram 14 (Nine at the beginning) and its commentary as well as by the following Hexagram 15, *Modesty*. The first line of Hexagram 14 states that many difficulties are still to be overcome. If, however, one remains conscious of these difficulties one keeps inwardly free of possible arrogance and wastefulness.[66] Only in a spirit of modesty can the work be successful. Therefore, the Judgment in Hexagram 15 says: "Modesty creates success."[67] The deep conviction that success can only be reached through modesty belongs to the core of Taoist thought. This ancient wisdom, however, is valuable for analytical psychology too. The danger in this psychology is precisely that inflation in which the individual, or a group of psychologists as a whole, identify themselves with the self or with various archetypal images, with the result that they overestimate themselves beyond all measure. The Delphic "Know thyself," therefore, more than anything else, means, "Be aware of your own shadow!"

Hexagram 14, Dà yǒu (大有)

Let's come back to hexagram 14. Master Huang's description of the Chinese pictogram for *Dà yǒu* is very helpful. He translates it, as already mentioned, as *Great Harvest*. On top we see a "person standing upright with arms and legs wide open," the pictogram for *dà*, "great." In Chinese tradition three things are great: Heaven, Earth, and the human being standing and mediating between the two.[68] The upper part of the second ideograph beneath shows "a hand with three fingers open

66 R. Wilhelm, *I Ching*, p. 61.
67 Ibid., p. 63.
68 Master Huang, *I Ching*, p, 143.

as in the act of grasping [or harvesting] something. Underneath the hand is the ideograph of a moon."[69] For the ancient Chinese the moon with its ever-changing nature and particularly the lunar eclipse, when the world fell into darkness, suggested the transitory nature of possession. At this place *yŏu* does not indicate "to possess" or "to have," as in modern Chinese, but, following the old meaning of *yŏu*, it points to the "harvest" or to "harvesting." Thus this pictogram does not suggest any individual possession. On the contrary, *dà yŏu* includes the transience of every possession, since every storage of the harvest, however big as it may be, will sooner or later decline. It taught people that it was not right to appropriate others' possessions. In that sense harvest as a gift of heaven and earth is not a "possession."

The gifts of nature belong to humanity. This is how the Chinese read the order of the two trigrams, *Fire* above, *Heaven* below, ☲☰. The sun shines in the sky giving light and heat for myriad beings on earth. If all people participate in the abundant gifts of nature, freedom reigns the world. Yet the sun has another, ethical meaning too. In Wilhelm's commentary on *The Image* we read:

> The sun in heaven above, shedding light over everything on earth, is the image of possession on a grand scale. But a possession of this sort must be administered properly. The sun brings both evil and good into the light of day.[70]

From this Confucius concluded, that *Great Harvest* requires an ethical obligation. I follow Master Huang's translation:

> The superior person represses evil and promotes good,
> Carrying out the glorious virtue of Heaven.[71]

Indeed, the Psychology Club Zürich as one of the oldest places of origin of analytical psychology may have a certain leading position and "ethical obligation" as suggested by the I Ching. This, however, requires its members to stay modest und strong within. But what could the "evil" be that must be repressed? Following the spirit of the I Ching, I believe, it would be any form of egotism, which certainly would destroy the original heavenly mind

---

69 Ibid.
70 R. Wilhelm, *I Ching*, p. 60.
71 Master Huang, *I Ching*, p. 144.

by not being in tune anymore with the creative forces of the collective unconscious, that is, with the will of God. Regarding the Club as a community it would, for instance, be the temptation to turn it into an institution that uses its authority for its own purpose or that even intends to "spread its wisdom!"[72]

The single lines

Let's now have a look at each line and their meaning. The first two lines have been discussed already. They contain a warning against arrogance and wastefulness. In Master Huang's translation they read:

> Initial Nine
> No pride, no harm.
> Of course no fault.
> Being aware of hardship:
> No fault.

"No pride, no harm." Whoever takes the plunge to approach the new and to build it up, remaining modest all the same, makes no fault. Yet it is essential to always be aware of hardship.

> Second Nine.
> A big wagon for loading.
> There is somewhere to go.
> No fault.

The second line is a *yang* element in the middle of the lower trigram. One at this place, due to its central and humble position, is strong and able and would not be self-opinionated. This line responds to the six at the fifth place; she is the only *yin*-line, and all the strong lines are in harmony with her. She occupies the place of honour. Therefore the commentary says, "One in a leading role [*yin*-line in the fifth place] should be humble and sincere, gentle and magnanimous [*yang*-line in the second place], willing to seek harmony with people, then blessing will descend to him from *Heaven*."[73] Strength (*Heaven*) and clarity (*Fire*) are united. *Big Harvest* is

---

72 I remind the reader of Jung's letter from October 25, 1935, mentioned above, in which he expressed his horror about "an institute that hands out the wisdom."
73 Master Huang, *I Ching*, p. 145.

fated. The big wagon carrying a heavy load means that there are able helpers at hand who offer their strong support. However, it also refers to movability, that is, flexibility, which enables one to reach faraway goals. Referring to the initial question of how to pass over the living heritage to future generations the I Ching suggests that this task can only be fulfilled successfully with the help of individuals who strongly support the community: "One can load great responsibility upon such persons, and this is necessary in important undertakings."[74]

Yet, the "big wagon," refers to a specific historical constellation. After his military victory over a rebellious foreign clan King Wen received a great award from the Tyrant of Shang. The gifts he received would have filled a whole wagon. Thus he remained conscious of the hardship to come and maintained his humble attitude; he did not forget that the aim he wanted to achieve would still cause hardship and pain. And, even more important, he knew that real blessing came from Heaven.[75]

As we have seen, it is always worthwhile to have a closer look at all lines, even if they are not moving lines.

> Nine in the third place means:
> A prince offers it [great possession or great harvest]
> to the Son of Heaven.
> A petty man cannot do this.[76]

Whatever success one achieves and however great the possession, it is not private property. A petty man is harmed by great possessions, because instead of sacrificing them and sharing them with others, he would keep them for himself. In respect to our questioning of the I Ching about the future of the Psychology Club, the *Book of Changes* clearly recommends a spirit of openness towards the world, not by listening or following the spirit of this time, but by being devoted to the creative gift of heaven, for "the movement of heaven is full of power."[77]

The *fourth line* is a warning to remain free of envy, neither looking to the right nor to the left, trying to imitate them, and to shun the temptation to vie with others. This does not mean to exclude one's own strength, only

---

74 R. Wilhelm, *I Ching*, p. 61.
75 Master Huang, *I Ching*, p. 146.
76 R. Wilhelm, *I Ching*, p. 61.
77 *The Image* in: Hexagram 1, *The Creative*. Richard Wilhelm, *I Ching*, p. 6.

that one should not be proud of it. The *fifth line* has been mentioned above. They all are crowned by the Nine at the top:

> From heaven comes blessing.
> Good fortune.
> Nothing that does not further.

I particularly like Wilhelm's commentary: "In the fullness of possession and at the height of power, one remains modest and gives honor to the sage who stands outside the affairs of the world. By this means one puts oneself under the beneficent influence descending from heaven, and all goes well." For thousands of years the shaman and the sage standing apart from the world of myriad beings have been *the* ideal of the Taoists. Countless Taoists sought retirement from the world by going into the mountains in order to cultivate tranquility, be it as hermits or as members of a monastic community. Others, however, were not striving for outer solitude, but rather were of the opinion that "the true lead [the true spirit] must be sought out in the midst of the social world."[78] Thus, they practiced concealment within the world, as Wu Cailuan, a female Chinese alchemist, put it, "My body lives in the city, my essence dwells in the mountains."[79]

The Changing Hexagram: 56 Lü, The Wanderer, Traveling

In closing, some reflections on the changing Hexagram 56, *The Wanderer*, are necessary. The changing hexagram points to the potentialities inherent in the resulting hexagram, that is, to the potentials of future development. Applied to the specific consultation, *The Wanderer* might offer an answer to the question of how the Psychology Club can develop in order to preserve and transform the wealth of the "great harvest" of analytical psychology for future generations, a question which today is of particular interest given that we celebrate the hundredth anniversary in 2016.

Richard Wilhelm's lecture given at the Psychology Club in December 1921 has already been mentioned. *Der I Ging, Chinas mantische Weisheit, The I Ching, China's mantic wisdom*, was its title. At the end of this event, Richard Wilhelm was asked to throw an I Ching for the Club, which he did. The outcome was *The Wanderer*, however, obviously with the *Top Nine*. This line must have caused a great shock as it reads like this:

---

78 Chang Po-tuan *Understanding Reality*, in: *The Taoist Classics*, vol. 2, p. 73.
79 Poem by Wu Cailuan, in: *The Taoist Classics*, vol. 3, p. 446.

The bird's nest burns up.
The wanderer laughs at first,
Then laments and weeps.
Through carelessness he loses his cow.
Misfortune.

The minutes of this evening, written by Club member Ida Bianci and preserved in the archives state: "The I Ching suggested a lack of harmony between different factions of the Club members. We attempt to burn the nest (collectivity, tradition), before we actually can be independent."[80] It is possible that C.G. Jung, too, in his foreword to Richard Wilhelm's *I Ching*, referred to this 1921 questioning of the I Ching. Jung asked Wilhelm to throw a hexagram about the Psychology Club and wrote, "The diagnosis, he gave, was astoundingly correct and so was the prognosis too, describing an event that happened only later and which I did not foresee."[81] It refers to conflicts among Club members in the following years. Due to this C.G. Jung as well as Emma Jung resigned from the Club temporarily.[82]

However, apart from the sixth line, Hexagram 56, *The Wanderer*, is quite an auspicious answer with a promising future. Master Huang translated it as *Traveling* and commented on it, "Traveling suggests that after the declining of *Abundance* [Hexagram 55], one should move forward, exploring the new world and starting a new cycle. Staying at the old place and moving with the old pace is only to stagnate."[83] If abundance becomes poor, the time of traveling must start; thus is the law of the eternal cycle of life following the wisdom of the *Book of Changes*. The play of the opposites never ceases. Whoever remains open to the continual change of life, accepting one's own transformation, can develop. Such openness keeps one alive; it is the key

---

80 Notes of Ida Bianci, Club Archive (15.12.1921). Years later, in the annual general meeting of May 8, 1937 the I Ching was consulted once again. This time the result was Hexagram 7, *The Army*. In his commentary, Jung emphasized the big difference between this result and the previous I Ching, No. 56, *The Wanderer*, and particularly mentioned that the image of the burnt nest in the top line is unpropitious; it shows a state of disorder that must be changed. *The Army*, however, suggests an ordered hierarchy that must *not* be changed (Minutes of the general meeting of May 8, 1937 in the archives of the Psychology Club, *Protokolle*, 5th vol. pp. 87-89).
81 C.G. Jung, Vorwort zum I Ging, GW 11, § 968. This passage is not in the English edition. Translation by Andreas Schweizer.
82 See Marie-Louise von Franz in her talk about the Psychology Club, p. 51ff below.
83 Master Huang, *I Ching*, p. 441.

to success. As Master Huang in his commentary states, all the yielding *yin*-lines "bring good fortune because they are docile and tend to be central and harmonious with others. On the other hand, all the solid lines are not that auspicious because they tend to be willful and opinionated and difficult for others to deal with."[84] Many groups, including political and governmental groups, would most probably function better, if along with firmness and strength, they would respect this most advantageous yielding and docile attitude. "The firmness of *yang* and yielding of *yin* is the wellspring of essence and life," said the Chinese eighteenth century alchemist Liu I-ming.[85]

Wilhelm's comment on this Hexagram points to a slightly different aspect. "Strange lands and separation are the wanderer's lot."[86] Everything personal must be sacrificed. Behind this view of the wanderer stands the figure of the shaman, who sacrifices himself, in order to commune with the spirits of the other world during his journey to the beyond. Richard Wilhelm's son, Helmut Wilhelm, in a lecture about *The Wanderer* given at the Club on September 26, 1965, referred to this idea. According to him the original meaning of this hexagram was the journey of the shaman. The wanderer, therefore, is an image of the individuation process.[87] The journeys of the shaman to the beyond, of which there are many examples in Chinese literature, mirror deep yearning for immortality. The feeling of being a stranger in this world and the yearning for immortality are two aspects of human life that can be found throughout the entire I Ching as well as throughout the ages of Chinese history, and they occur in ever-new transformations. Hexagram 56, *The Wanderer*, places the emphasis on a new start, leaving behind the old and establishing the new. The above mentioned Liu I-ming, alchemist and annotator of the I Ching from the 18th century, described this journey as follows,

Practitioners of Tao should first see through worldly things, looking upon all conditions, all existents, as passing by, not injuring the real by delighting in the false, not disturbing the inward because of the outward... One can thereby transcend the world while in the world.[88]

---

84 Ibid., p. 443.
85 *Understanding Reality*, in: *The Taoist Classics*, vol. 2, p. 52.
86 R. Wilhelm, *I Ching*, pp. 216-217.
87 See Marie-Louise von Franz in a talk about the Psychology Club, see p. 59.
88 Liu I-ming, *The Taoist I Ching*, in: *The Taoist Classics*, vol. 4, p. 207.

He/she who succeeds on this way understands stillness and preserves insight. Then he/she remains true to the Way. This is a way into the future.

To abide in the way, being committed to the unending stream of life, this is the hopeful expectation regarding the future of the Psychology Club that arises from our consultation of the I Ching. May it bestow good fortune! *Deo concedente.*[89]

89 I express my gratitude to Joan Smith and Judith Dowling for their help with the translation into English.

Marie-Louise von Franz

Conversation on the Psychology Club Zurich,

Club Life and her Relationship to the Club

Preliminary remarks of the editors

The following contribution goes back to a recorded talk that Marie-Louise von Franz gave on the Psychology Club Zurich. We found the tape cassette at the Club some years ago and decided to transcribe its contents. Unfortunately we could not find any detailed information about the event nor about its exact date. Considering the obvious difficulties Marie-Louise von Franz had to enunciate, due to her Parkinson's disease, the discussion must have taken place in the mid-nineties (Marie-Louise von Franz died in 1998). Whenever possible the editors followed the literal recording. Changes were made only when it was necessary, in order to clarify the meaning of what she expressed.

Following a few introductory and truly personal statements of Marie-Louise von Franz regarding her relationship to the Psychology Club, she answers questions from the audience. These questions have not been recorded. The editors attempted to reconstruct the questions based upon Marie-Louise von Franz's responses, in order to capture the lively, conversational spirit of the discussion.[1]

*

Marie-Louie von Franz on her Experience as a Club Member

Marie-Louise von Franz: After I had met Jung, he invited me to attend the series of public lectures that took place approximately every two weeks at the Psychology Club. And he arranged for me to always be given a free entry ticket – it cost three francs at the time. So, for eight years, I simply

---

1 We are grateful to the "Foundation for Jungian Psychology, Küsnacht" for their permission to publish the talk.

listened to all the scientific lectures without participating in the Club's social life. I was twenty at the time and extremely shy, and I had a negative mother complex. With its infinite number of grey-haired old ladies, the Club seemed to me to be a frightful gathering. What meant most to me was being able to hear Jung speak. He participated in the discussion after each lecture, and he almost always gave a short introduction in which he drew connections between the speaker's academic background and Jungian psychology. I was impressed by how tactfully and carefully he slowly awoke the interest of those speakers who felt uneasy about Jungian psychology. Unlike the tactless and naïve manner in which Club members spoke of psychology, spooking the speakers in the process, Jung always tried to build a bridge.

Of course, I lacked sufficient education to follow all that was said. But I learnt an enormous amount over those eight years and it motivated me to do my own research. And slowly I began to be less isolated from the others. In this respect, I gratefully recall two Club members – Frau Mathilde Geiser,[2] an extroverted feeling type who accepted me in a friendly mothering fashion; and most importantly Barbara Hannah[3] whom I met by collaborating with her on some translation work, and with whom I enjoyed many hours of drinking tea. She took away my fear of the Psychology Club. A friend of Toni Wolff's, it was through her that I got to hear about the human – the all-too human – side of the group, which I found most amusing and this helped me to slowly overcome my fear of this organisation. As I am an introverted thinking type, I did not get too involved in the social activities of the Club, and remained more on its periphery. A further motherly woman who helped me was the Club's housekeeper, Frau Anni Ammann,[4] who continually offered me her steady and warm-hearted friendship and affection, for which I shall always be extremely grateful.

In my dreams, the Club was where Jungian psychology – which, for me, was an introverted affair – encountered collective and social problems. After eight years, Jung asked me whether I did not want to join the Club,

2 Mathilde Geiser was a Club member from 1921 to 1967.
3 Barbara Hannah was a Club member from 1933 to 1985 and from 1945 to 1952 she was a member of its Board.
4 Anni Ammann was the Psychology Club's housekeeper for more than forty years. Barbara Hannah wrote about her: "She remained well over forty years and was extraordinarily and unusually warmhearted and almost universally beloved. She retired in the spring of 1979, to the lasting regret of the members." See Barbara Hannah, *Jung: His Life and Work* (Boston: Shambhala, 1976), p. 194.

or if I could not join it. I said the latter was the case. He then promised to help me join, to help me become a member of the Psychology Club, but he added, "But we shall wait for a dream." The same night I had the following dream:

> I went to a biological institute where an old wise researcher, who resembled Jung, had set up an experimental laboratory in order to observe how animals of different species get along together. I entered his room. He was sitting at a table and writing down his observations. There were aquariums with fish in them. Cats were sitting in a row on the central heating radiator. Dogs, elephants and cows were moving freely around the room. And the old man was writing down his observations on their behaviour. Then I saw myself. I was a flying fish in an aquarium and, now and again, I would spring out of the aquarium and fly around the room. The old cats tried to bat me down with their claws, but without success.

Jung howled with laughter and said, "So now you are ready to join.[5] You've understood what it's all about. I founded the Club in order to see how introverts work on themselves, and to see how Jungians get on together socially, to observe the group dynamics, and to see the social impact of that. And now that you know what it's all about, you may join."

As time went by, I was able to feel close to many other Club members. And little by little it became a group to which I felt I belonged. With time, I took on the post of being the Club's librarian – which suited me down to the ground. I thoroughly enjoyed looking after this highly cultivated library that, while small, was filled with the most precious books that one cannot get a hold of today. Sadly, it was my experience that members made little use of this library and showed little understanding of it. For me, who had no money to buy books, it was heaven to make myself at home in it, and to even be able to read all the new publications. An unpleasant aspect of the Club was always the huge number of intrigues and power struggles that went on in the background which, I have learnt meanwhile, go on in all groups and seem to be the human – again, all too human – background of all social groups.

So that's what I have to say about that.

5 On the tape one hears that, even after all the intervening years, Marie-Louise von Franz still had to laugh about this dream.

Marie-Louise von Franz answers questions from the audience

Question: On the significance of the inferior function and the role of the persona within the social context of the Club and its members.

Marie-Louise von Franz: You are asking, whether the people…, that Jung said he wanted to see how people without persona interact with their inferior function. This was one of his aims. It really was like that. Unfortunately, this is increasingly less so today, but in those early years of the Club its members really did make an effort to be truly honest with each other. And this, of course, led to the constant struggles and confrontations. But it did clear the air and it was an education for me. For naturally I was not conscious of my lack of feeling connection and had to hear that these elderly ladies thought I was intellectual, arrogant, unrelated etc. On the whole, compared to other social groups, the Club had a lower *niveau* of human contact because of this, but it was, instead, more honest.

Question: How did C.G. Jung interact with the Club members?

Marie-Louise von Franz: Yes – Jung was not conventional. And sometimes, when he consciously – he never did it unconsciously, but consciously – had the feeling that someone needed to be straightened out, he would "give them a roasting." He never did it to me in public, as far as I recall. But occasionally he would coldly ignore me if I were somehow off-key, and of course, I would then go home in tears and ask myself, "What is amiss with me?" So he never dispensed persona friendliness if it was not appropriate.

Question: On C.G. Jung's presence at the Club.

Marie-Louise von Franz: Jung was not always present at the Club. But he almost always came to the lectures. He would only not be present if he were away or ill. Even though he was so overworked and sometimes swore terribly if he had to go to the Club, he was very loyal and always came. When he was absent, I found it boring. But when I look back, I realize it was also meaningful for then more attention was paid to other relationships. Otherwise, everyone was focussed upon him. But [when Jung was absent] we had to be more related to each other and show more interest in each other. And this had a positive effect. This was true for me, too. If Jung were present, I watched and heard only what he did and said. But when he was absent, the others then existed for me, too.

Question: On the so-called "Alleluia game."

Marie-Louise von Franz: No, I never experienced the "Alleluia game."[6] It was played at social events. For the first eight years, I did not attend the social events. When I began to, after eight years – that was around 1942 – the game was no longer being played.

Question: On the experience of the Self at the Club.

Marie-Louise von Franz: This is a question on the social function of the Self. And that is a very rare and mysterious thing. But sometimes the Self does, indeed, manifest in a group, and when it does, everyone is in a kind of supernatural harmony with each other. This is exceptionally rare, something that I experienced only once or twice in all the time I was a member of the Club, and in small groups elsewhere. And it is more impressive than one's own solitary experience of the Self. On the other hand, individuation is one's experience of one's uniqueness and one may not speak about it. Both exist side by side: the mystery that may never be spoken of and being a part of a shared experience of the Self. When I put it like this, it sounds like a paradox. But they do indeed go together and exist side by side very well. The group phenomenon of experiencing the Self has something to do with what I imagine certain religious celebrations amongst primitive peoples elicit, and what is actually sought after and aimed for in the Catholic Mass. It very rarely happens spontaneously. But if you have ever been present at such a "celebration," you remain more warmly connected to the others who were also present. It is the function of generating fellowship.

Question: Do these experiences still happen at the Club today?

Marie-Louise von Franz: I do not know how it is today for my health prevents me from attending any longer. But I always see that my students

6 Barbara Hannah writes about this game, "Jung, moreover, invented a special game for such occasions, called the Alleluia game. In it all the members sat around the room with one member in the center. A knotted cloth (usually a napkin) was thrown from one to the other. It was *de rigueur* to throw it as far across the space in the middle as possible, not just to pass it to your nearest neighbours. The member in the center had to catch it on its way; when he succeeded in doing so, he might sit down, and his place was taken by the member who had thrown the cloth. The game often waxed fast and furious and always efficiently banished stiffness and formality. It had an amazing relating effect bringing the group together in an almost magical way." The name of the game stems from the medieval ball games which took place in the churches at certain times. See Barbara Hannah, *Jung: His Life and Work,* p. 195.

who have been in analysis for a longer period of time participate in some kind of group, be it the Turmgruppe[7], or the Interdisciplinary Talks held by the Stiftung für Jung'sche Psychologie[8], or the Club. I do not exert any influence upon people. But if they come across some kind of group and feel drawn to join in, I encourage them to do so. And when they are disgusted by such "wretched simpletons" and want to leave, I try to explain that it is important and one should remain socially connected. But I do not persuade them to join any particular group. I let them choose.

Question: Why did C.G. Jung temporarily resign from the Club once or twice?

Marie-Louise von Franz: Jung resigned from the Club when a majority wanted to deviate from Jungian psychology. I know of only one instance when a majority of the so-called "Oxford Movement"[9] – a tyrannical, Christian sect who accused Jung himself of being a heathen – joined the Club. He then resigned. Later, they came to him meekly and asked him to return. This "Oxford Movement" disappeared into thin air. It was a momentary collective drunkenness that disappeared without a trace. But whenever the majority at the Club went wrong, Jung did not use power to insist it should be otherwise. He only said, "Good, then I shall no longer be a part of it." I believe this happened twice. The second occasion I can no longer recall.

Question: This question could not be reconstructed (editor's note).

Marie-Louise von Franz: I know nothing about this. He was sometimes disappointed that so few people truly grasped what he was saying. He often mentioned this.

Question: Was it at the Club in particular that C.G. Jung made his observations about psychological types?

Marie-Louise von Franz: No, I do not think so. He did his research on psychological types mostly within his own practice, and with his Freudian colleagues even earlier than that. The Club possibly contributed to this.

---

7   The so-called "Turmgruppe" was founded by Dieter Baumann and José Zavala. It held its meetings in the tower room of the Hotel "Sonne" in Küsnacht.
8   The "Stiftung für Jung'sche Psychologie" [Foundation of Jungian Psychology] was founded in 1974 by Marie-Louise von Franz, René Malamud, Willi Obrist, Alfred Ribi and Paul Walder.
9   The "Oxford Movement" was a Christian revivalist movement of the first half of the 20th century, especially widespread throughout the USA.

But, in my view, he observed wherever he was, not especially at the Club. At the Club he particularly observed how people who had had a Jungian analysis got on together – or did not, which is a very specific situation. Analysis changes one. One has quite different values. And it was to be expected that all the Club members had undergone these changes of one's inner values – the shift of one's values onto one's inner life and the Self. How do people get on (together) then? Do they get on better, or not? If Jungian psychology were to establish itself throughout the world, would it contribute to world peace or not? This is a burning question. What effect does Jungian psychology have socially? And this is what he was trying to observe.

Question: Is a group of people who have been analysed a better group? Are there no longer any difficulties?

Marie-Louise von Franz: Yes, this is still an open-ended question. At all events it is not quickly or noticeably better, but rather there are...[10] Certain difficulties – for example, problems concerning typology – are often resolved and improved with a good sense of humour. And people are more reconciliatory and forgiving of each other. And then there is the animus and anima. Hardly anyone has overcome them. So we cannot say anything about this. Jung said that coming to terms with the anima and animus is a masterpiece. We cannot say that this masterpiece was achieved by a majority of the Club members. So we cannot say what a group of people who have mastered this would be like. We need another five hundred years for this. There are many people who think they have achieved this. But the next time their earth is shaken a little, out comes their old self.

Question: Do women more readily grasp Jungian psychology than men?

Marie-Louise von Franz: I am not sure about this. It is my impression that women have more time. With all the improvements that are now available in the home, married women of today have more time at their disposal. They are a privileged class, whereas men are busier and face greater challenges in our society today, and in our technological world. Men who come to us most often sit there looking pale and exhausted, while the women appear fresh and perky. And because women are more interested in relationship problems, they are more interested in psychology out of their own natural

10 Marie-Louise von Franz's train of thought shifted here and she made a new start to talk about the value of humour.

inclination. Women were certainly the driving force at the Club. Men were the more rare, but very appreciated, birds.

Question: Did the high regard awarded to Emma Jung and Toni Wolff at the Club influence Marie-Louise von Franz's relationship to these two women?

Marie-Louise von Franz: Because everyone knew that Frau Jung[11] was Jung's wife, and that Toni Wolff[12] was his girlfriend, they were treated with great respect, and this really annoyed me as a young person which is why I was always polite but not respectful. As time passed I was able to see that they were held in high esteem not only because of their relationship to Jung, but rather because both women were truly remarkable personalities in their own right, personalities that demanded respect. And, like everyone else, I, too, came to respect both women.

Question: On Barbara Hannah's position within the Club.

Marie-Louise von Franz: Miss Hannah was one of the founding members. In addition, she was very close to Emma Jung and Toni Wolff. She was thus a member of the inner circle and was, for a time, on the Board. I learnt a great deal from her about the Club that I would not have known otherwise for she was quite "outspoken." Together with these two women, and Linda Fierz[13], she played a leading role.

Question: This question was on Marie-Louise von Franz's relationship to the Club in the early years.

Marie-Louise von Franz: I benefited greatly from the lectures. For everything else, I was too introverted. At the age I was at that time, I was not interested in the social functions of people. Now it would interest me. But at that time I was one-sidedly introverted and interested in science.

---

11 At the inaugural general assembly of the Psychology Club on 26th February 1916, Emma Jung was elected to be the first president. She was on the Board from 1917 to 1923 and was President of the Club until 1920.
12 Toni Wolff was a founding member of the Club and was on the Board for many years. From 1928 to 1945 she was the Club President and later from 1949 to 1952 she was the Actuary.
13 Linda Fierz was a member of the Club from 1930 to 1954 and a member of the Board from 1933 to 1945.

Question: On hexagram 56, The Wanderer, that Richard Wilhelm threw at the end of his lecture on 15th December, 1921, at the request of the audience.[14]

Marie-Louise von Franz: Members do not know this. Many years later there was a lecture given by Helmut Wilhelm, his son, on this hexagram. He said that the original meaning of this sign is the journey of the shaman. And the journey of the shaman is an important image of individuation. So this was a very positive I Ching for the Club.[15]

Question: A participant asks whether dreams were discussed openly at the Club?

Marie-Louise von Franz: Dreams were occasionally told, but not very often. They were looked at and discussed within the context of personal disputes. This was the main difference between the Club and other clubs: when members got on each others nerves, one felt committed to meeting up for a cup of tea and clearing the air. And of course, dreams were then discussed. Publicly, we rarely looked at a dream together. There were a few meetings at which dreams that related to Club issues were discussed. But that was seldom. The most important thing was, of course, that we all had dreams about the Club which were then worked on in analysis, or privately with the person concerned. They establish the truth. One cannot discuss it with ten people, but with two people it is possible.

Question: The following question concerns an event with which the Club was preoccupied for years afterwards. Towards the end of the Second World War, some members of the Board proposed making it more difficult for

14 On this I Ching, see Friedel Elisabeth Muser, *Zur Geschichte des Psychologischen Clubs von den Anfängen bis 1928.* Sonderdruck aus dem Jahresbericht des Psychologischen Clubs, Zürich 1984 [History of the Psychology Club from its beginning till 1928. Special print from the annual report of the Psychology Club, Zurich 1984], without page numbering: "At the end, there was a discussion of an event from the year 1921. On 14th of December, 1921, the missionary Richard Wilhelm from Frankfurt am Main gave a lecture. He lectured on "The I Ching. China's Mantic Wisdom." At the end of this lecture he was asked to throw a hexagram for the Club. In the protocol is written, "It was a very negative result – it is number 56 – The Wanderer – that speaks of a bird that burns its nest (number nine in the top position). The I Ching has shown us that there is a lack of cohesion amongst different tendencies within the group. We are trying to burn our nest (the collective/tradition) before we can actually be independent."
15 The lecture by Helmut Wilhelm with the title "'The Wanderer' in the I Ching" took place on 26.9.1964.

foreigners, and thereby also Jewish people, to join the Club. As Marie-Louise von Franz reports here, the proposal was clearly rejected by C.G. Jung and the members.

Marie-Louise von Franz: The document was prepared by the Board and I got to hear of it through an indiscretion on the part of Miss Hannah. But the members only voted on it six weeks later and clearly rejected it. So it was the Board that created the document. I had no part in it. I only heard that it had been discussed. Then, at the meeting, it was rejected. Jung was against it and was fairly certain it would be rejected. Which is why he said to Siegmund Hurwitz[16], "Just wait it out." He was not in a position to say that he knew it would be rejected. So the blame lies with the Board who discussed it and weighed it up.

* * *

The discussion ends here. It is evident on the tape that, because of her illness at that time, Marie-Louise von Franz was having increasing difficulty in speaking. (Editor's note)[17]

16 Siegmund Hurwitz was at that time a statutory guest of the Psychology Club and was concerned by the proposal. He was from 1952 to 1993 a member, for many years on the board, and from 1957 to 1961 President of the Psychology Club.
17 Translated from German by Alison Kappes-Bates, Wädenswil, Switzerland.

Marie-Louise von Franz

The Goose Girl (Grimm's Fairy Tales, nr. 89)

Lecture held at the Psychology Club Zurich
14th November 1970

Preliminary Remarks of the Editors

The following interpretation of the fairy tale "The Goose Girl" is based upon a recording of a lecture that Marie-Louise von Franz held in November 1970 at the Psychology Club, Zurich. Christian Tauber kindly gave it to the Psychology Club for its archives.[1]

To the best of their ability, the editors strove to uphold the lively and engaged manner of delivery of the lecturer. To assist comprehension, small endorsements were made where it was deemed necessary. They are indicated with square brackets []. Those places on the tape where it was impossible to grasp what was being said despite our repeated efforts to do so have been indicated with dots ... The sub-titles and footnotes were added by the editors. We are grateful to the "Stiftung für Jung'sche Psychologie, Küsnacht" [Foundation for Jungian Psychology, Küsnacht] for their permission to publish the lecture for the first time.

*

---

1 A shorter interpretation of this fairy tale including many variations can be found in Marie-Louise von Franz (previously Hedwig von Beit), *Symbolik des Märchens. Versuch einer Deutung* [Symbolism of Fairy Tales. An attempt to interpret them], vol. 1 (Bern/Munich: Francke Verlag, 1971), pp. 778-789. Concerning the authorship of this work see Emmanuel Kennedy's Foreword of the new German edition, the first volume of which came out recently: Marie-Louise von Franz, *Symbolik des Märchens. Versuch einer Deutung*, vol. 1/1 (Küsnacht: Stiftung für Jung'sche Psychologie, 2015). An English translation is in preparation.

Two Kingdoms

The fairy tale begins with a queen who has only one very beautiful daughter.
She lost her spouse long ago. It is she who therefore raises her only daughter
and promises her in marriage to someone *"far beyond the meadow"*[2], meaning
a prince who lives far away in another kingdom.

> *When the time came for her to be married, and she had to depart for the distant
> kingdom, the old queen packed up for her many costly vessels and utensils of
> silver and gold, and trinkets also of gold and silver, and cups and jewels, – her
> entire dowry – for she loved her child with all her heart.*[3]

She also gives her a handmaiden who is to ride with her, along with two
horses. The princess' horse is called Falada and it can speak – a talking
horse. At the hour of her departure, her mother cuts her own finger and
lets three drops of blood fall onto a small white cloth and she gives it to
her daughter saying, *"Dear child, take good care of these. They will be of service
to you on your way"* – so it is a kind of magical protection. They then part
sorrowfully. And the girl and her handmaiden ride off. Let's pause here.

In the kingdom where the princess is headed there also lives an old king.
One only finds this out, however, much later in the story. At first, one has
the impression there is only the young king, her bridegroom. But later an
old king, the young king's father, appears and he has a very important
function … Thus, we have here a strange image. There are two kingdoms.
In the one there is a mother and her daughter, but no husband. And in the
other there is a father and his son, but no mother – no female figure – so it
is clear that the opposites have drifted too far apart and need to be reunited.
This is why, of course, the daughter of the one realm finds her way to the
prince of the other realm and marries him.

You may recall that I described this in an earlier lecture: there should
actually always be only one realm [in a fairy tale] for this would mean that
only one dominant concept of the Self exists to establish a cultural entity.
But if there are several kingdoms – and there are often various kingdoms

2   Literal translation according to the original German text. (Translator's note)
3   Concerning the text see *Grimm's household tales*, translated and edited by Margaret
    Hunt (1884), revised and corrected by D.L. Ashliman (website, © 2000-2002). See
    also: *The Complete Grimm's Fairy Tales*, translated by Margaret Hunt, revised by James
    Stern (New York/Toronto: Pantheon Books, Random House, 1972), nr. 89, pp. 404-
    411.

in a fairy tale, and [various] ways that lead from one kingdom to the other – then it has to do with a certain degree of compartmentalisation[4] of the collective consciousness. In the one kingdom, *one* dominant concept rules, while in the other, a different one rules. And here the decay of the culturally ruling concept is so advanced that while both the masculine and feminine do exist, in the one kingdom everything is purely masculine, while in the other everything is purely feminine.

We need to ask ourselves, of course, what this means in practical terms? What does a culture or ethnic community look like in which there is such a distance between the feminine and the masculine? We can see this in certain periods of Chinese history. In China, the religious ruling concepts include both male and female; consider, for example, the Tao that is made up of both the Yin and the Yang principles. So it is not a purely patriarchal culture. Nevertheless, areas of administration and government were organised in a purely patriarchal way and women held a subordinate position – except in farming communities. In rural operations, or generally in agricultural cultures, women could not be as suppressed as they were in other cultures simply because they were a too important economic factor. And this gave them secret power. If you read Pearl S. Buck's book *The Good Earth*[5] you will see that women at that time were treated as larger workhorses and they were oppressed, but they nevertheless held, as it were, a hidden noble position. So one cannot say that in rural China the feminine element played no role. And yet there was very little genuine relationship between men and women.

In ancient China, the men went into the fields in spring to till the rice fields, and they lived in the fields in order to shoo away the birds, but even more so, to always be close to their seeds, and they lived apart from their women until after the harvest. They returned to their family home and their women only when winter came. This illustrates how little relationship there was between both sides. The women raised the children, and men and women worked together, but, in human terms, they did not speak to each other very often, or take each other seriously. Seen from outside, this would be a culture like the one described above. Of course, it also happens on a psychological level that men live in their own world and while they acknowledge women, they do not want to have anything to do with their

4 The expression means a partially conscious, and partially unconscious co-existence of psychic entities.
5 Pearl S. Buck, *The Good Earth* (New York: Washington Square Press, 2004).

world. And women live in their own world and simply acknowledge the masculine. But there is no interaction or relationship between the two worlds. And seen psychologically, or as an inner problem, this would mean that a rift has sprung up between ideological concepts that are of a purely intellectual nature, bereft of the feminine element, and of those concepts that are connected to one's feeling or feeling relationships in practical life.

And this is probably the state of affairs that this fairy tale is alluding to since this is quite often what happens psychologically. In other words, where morals are concerned, people live a double standard: they have ideals that they cannot live up to, for example, a too spiritual religion which they cannot live up to as it is simply too hard – one would have to be a saint to live up to it. So officially one adheres to a high level of spirituality in one's religion that cannot be reconciled with one's practical life and one's normal human feelings. In such a situation, a community of people defend their behaviour by adopting a double standard where morals are concerned, and in their everyday life, while still upholding the high ideals of the ruling religion, they actually hold different beliefs, or have a different feeling about life, or a different life attitude.

One can see this, for example, amongst the Catholic farmers of Bavaria. Officially, they are Catholic, but they have a pagan ritual that allows them to circumvent the all too high moral demands of the Catholic Church. For example, it is usual there – or at least it was until recently – for a boy to sleep with his girlfriend before getting married in order to see if she were fertile. And most often they got married only after the birth of one or two illegitimate children. Of course the priest did not like it, but it was absolutely official and generally practiced. There is also, for example, a nice folksong that expresses this. A boy goes to his mother and asks, "May I kiss my girlfriend?" And she says, "Oh be careful, that will bring you misfortune." And then he goes to the priest and asks, "May I kiss my girlfriend?" And the priest says, "If you do, you will burn in hell." And the song continues, "And then I went to God Himself and I asked Him, "May I kiss my girlfriend?" "Of course you may," said God and laughed, "It is for you boys that I made the girls."

So you see, this is a sort of feeling religion. It is Eros, or a feminine religion. And this is an official folksong that is sung there. This means that this song would be a part of the ruling feminine ideals. Here one has a completely different approach to life. One respects and accepts all that the Church demands in its patriarchal, spiritual way. That is for Sundays, and for special people who have the moral ability to live such a holy life. But normal people live differently.

In this case we have – if applied to a whole cultural group of people – a kind of split. One thing is officially believed while quite a different thing is lived. And there is no connection between the two things. It is a kind of double standard. And this is always the case if the king and queen are not connected, i.e. when spiritual ideas – the principle of logos – are not in unison with the feeling principle, with how people feel and experience their feelings. Both things are, in their own way, in order. But they are two one-sided things that cannot connect. And thus, natural psychological processes are generated in the unconscious that aim at reuniting these opposites, for it is actually not good for people to live like this. One sees, for example, that in a community like this, the younger people live quite happily with such double standards. But as they get older, they begin to ponder upon such questions and begin to feel guilty about what they did in their youth, even though it was quite normal and so on. So it is a kind of split that causes problems for those who are more developed and more inclined to reflect. Precisely the Christian tradition has always generated splits like this for the feminine element was never sufficiently recognized in the official dogma, which led to double standards being adopted.

I would therefore view this fairy tale as being a compensation for the epoch of Christianity, for I know of no pre-Christian versions that resemble this type of fairy tale, especially with a beginning like this one.

So a dynamic has been introduced. The beautiful daughter of one realm is to go to the distant king of a different realm. This daughter has a … mother who sets her up with all she needs – a talking horse, a blood talisman and all worldly treasures: three good things. Then she gives her a fourth gift to take on her way – her handmaiden. Later, the latter proves to be the murderous enemy of the princess. But she, too, is from the mother. If you were to view this situation from the perspective of an individual's personal problem, it would reflect the problems of a "mother's daughter" – earlier in Rumpelstiltskin, we saw the "father's daughter"[6] type; a "mother's daughter" would mean a daughter who primarily has an intimate, deeply positive relationship to her own mother. On the surface, everything is positive. If a woman has a positive relationship to her own mother, it means that she has a good relationship to her own feminine instinctual side, and

---

6 Marie-Louise von Franz had previously held a lecture on "Rumpelstiltskin" (*Grimm's Fairy Tales*, nr. 55) at the Club.

to her feminine Eros; indeed, to her femininity as a whole. And of course, this seems to be very positive at first glance. But, from this same well-intentioned mother comes the evil handmaiden. And we need to look at what that means. If we now imagine that this queen is a woman, one could say, "Her mother must have very poor instincts to have sought out such an evil servant as her companion." Psychologically speaking, I would say that with her left hand she has ... If she had been really connected to her feelings, she would not have done this. So while she richly endowed her daughter with her right hand, she gave her a clip on the ear with her left hand. This then would be the shadow or dark aspect of such a positive mother complex in a woman, or in a purely feminine constellation.

The Princess and the Handmaiden

So the princess and the handmaiden ride off. And after they had been travelling for an hour, the princess was thirsty and said to her handmaiden,

> *"Dismount, and take my cup which you have brought with you for me, and get me some water from the brook." –* And she replies, – *"If you are thirsty ... get off your horse yourself, and lie down near the water and drink. I won't be your servant." –* And so she gets down, leans over the brook – *and she was not allowed to drink out of the golden cup. Then she said, "Oh, Lord," and the three drops of blood answered, "If this your mother knew, her heart would break in two." But the king's daughter was humble. She said nothing and mounted her horse again.*

And the same thing was repeated. It happened a second time.

> *... and the drops of blood again replied, "If this your mother knew, her heart would break in two." As she was thus drinking, leaning over the stream, the cloth with the three drops of blood fell from of her bosom and floated away with the water, without her taking notice of it, so great were her concerns. However, the chambermaid had seen it, and she rejoiced to think that she now had power over the bride, for by losing the drops of blood, the princess had become weak and powerless.*

And then they swap horses. The handmaiden forces her to swap clothes with her, and she rides on as the princess and forces the real princess to take on the role of maid and, by threatening to murder her, she gets the princess to swear that she will never reveal that she is the real princess. And in these reversed roles, they make their way to the court of the young king.

In nearly all traditions and primitive religions blood is considered to be the soul essence of a being. When, in the Middle Ages, much thought was given in a more differentiated way to the various parts of the soul, the blood soul was considered to be what we would call the soul of affects – the emotional soul. It was also referred to as the "animal soul." This would be, as it were, "the soul of animal stirrings," primarily of emotions and affects. Even today, blood is very often still a symbol of this. This can be taken quite literally, for our circulatory system strongly reacts to affects and emotions. We blush or go pale when we are emotionally hit by something. Our blood vessels react. We go pale with shock. We go red with anger or with embarrassment. In other words, our blood vessels are, so to speak, involved with our emotions. They express them. And as our bloodstream is connected to our heart, the seat of our feelings, blood was quite rightly considered to be the emotional part of the soul. This would mean that as long as the daughter had her mother's drops of blood with her, as a sort of magical protection, she is, so to speak, connected to the mother in a positive way through her instincts and through her animal-soul. In practical terms this means that she still has, as it were, a healthy feminine instinct that protects her from evil.

This means that if she becomes entangled in some dangerous life situation, she would instinctively feel, "Don't put yourself into this situation." This is what we call having a "healthy instinct." It is something that simply protects us from certain dark aspects of life and of oneself through an uncanny feeling, so that we feel, "Something smells fishy, and I need to withdraw," either inwardly or outwardly. And at the very instant that the princess loses the drops of blood, she no longer has this connection and thus lands in the hands of this maid. In Jungian terms, this maid is a shadow figure. This begs the question: is she a shadow figure of the old queen or of the girl herself? I believe "somewhere in between." She is both. She represents something dark, something feminine that apparently was already a part of the old queen for otherwise she would not have chosen this maid and linked her up to her daughter. But, from the psychological standpoint, she is, for this reason, psychologically also a part of the daughter. If you read the other, partially parallel fairy tale by Grimm, "The White Bride and the Black Bride,"[7] you will find a similar story of deception.

It is altogether an enormously widespread motif in fairy tales with heroines that an ambitious, fraudulent devilish woman takes the place of the heroine, edging her way in at the side of her future husband, with the truth coming out only at the very last minute. It is a very widespread motif that must, therefore, point towards a widespread problem of the feminine.

With the term "shadow," we have primarily said nothing more than that we are simply dealing with a dark, negative side of the princess. We need to now be more specific. Allow me to digress. If one looks for the opposite or shadow figure of male heroes, for inferior companions, for shadows, then one notices that in the realm of masculine fairy tales there are many varieties. There is the somewhat inferior servant/companion. … I always call this the likeable nature shadow. This is the somewhat rough, natural, not quite fully moral, but therefore most often more realistic and more humane, person within us – a positive side of oneself that one absolutely needs to integrate. It is our inner Sancho Panza, without whom Don Quixote could never have survived and who is actually the more likeable one of this pair.[8] He thinks of eating and drinking. And he is not what you would call refined. But, in fact, he is the more reliable and the more sensible one of the two.

This is, so to speak, one's nature shadow, an aspect of the shadow that absolutely – and relatively easily – can be integrated by one's ego. But there are more dangerous qualities that form a part of the shadow, for example, a possessive, devilish ambition and a cold intellectualism, or even murderous aspects etc. In this case, the shadow is a much more serious problem for an individual. What is one to do with such a side, and how can one integrate something like that?

If one studies masculine fairy tales – fairy tales in which the main figure is a hero – one finds a wide range of shadow figures: some that are nice, some that are not so nice, some that are like animals, some that are fools, some that are devilish. There is, as it were, a whole drove of them …

If one studies feminine fairytales – fairytales in which the main figure is a heroine – one finds hardly any nature shadow figures. Mind you, there

---

7   *The Complete Grimm's Fairy Tales* (nr. 135), "The White Bride and the Black Bride," pp. 608-612.

8   Miguel de Cervantes Saavedra, *The Ingenious Hidalgo Don Quixote de la Mancha*, translated with an introduction by John Rutherford (London: Penguin Books, 2003).

is one fine feminine nature shadow figure. It is in a Scandinavian fairy tale, "Tatterhood."[9] In it, a queen gives birth to two girls. The one is a beautiful, ideal princess, as in the fairy tale we are discussing. But she has another daughter whom she actually should not have given birth to. She should have eaten only one flower, instead of two, and has therefore broken a taboo, and as a result gives birth to two daughters. The second daughter rides upon a ram with a wooden spoon in her hand and she has a tatterhood on her head. She is a wild figure, but an absolutely positive girl. Women trolls kidnap the beautiful princess and Tatterhood, riding upon her ram, rescues her from the trolls. Later the princess is to marry. And Tatterhood rescues her again, but then says that the younger prince must marry her. So she sets her terms, and it is to marry. And when the two couples are on their way to the church – the older prince with the beautiful daughter and the younger one, gloomy with ugly Tatterhood at his side (he is, of course, not at all pleased that he has to take her as his bride) – Tatterhood asks her younger prince several riddles, and then she is transformed into an even more beautiful princess than the first sister, and a double marriage with both of these figures then ensues.

This is the only feminine European fairy tale that I have found in which such a nature shadow figure appears – a positive shadow. In masculine fairy tales one often comes across a shadow that redeems and, at the end, is completely integrated into collective consciousness. Of course, with her ram and wooden spoon, Tatterhood has some witch-like qualities. There are suggestions of her being a positive "witch" and this would make her a shadow of the feminine. But this fairy tale is a rare exception. I racked my brains about this, asking myself, "Do women have no shadow problem?" To assert this, God forbid, would be far from the truth.

The ordinary, western woman has a shadow problem. Nevertheless, one can say that, for the most part, women from the lower class, out of which fairy tales arise, do indeed have fewer shadow problems than men, for, unlike men, they do not even try to be white in the first place. As a result, they are not so black. In other words, what is light and what is dark is very often not so far apart or as polarised in women. Jung says, for example, women seldom do injury to their affects by repressing them for moral reasons. In other words, women allow themselves to have fits of rage, or to make a scene, or to cry, or to use little tricks, and they do it all without being

9   Ethel Johnston Phelps, (Ed.), *Tatterhood and Other Tales* (Old Westbury/New York: Feminist Press, 1978).

terribly morally bothered by it. They therefore live quite naturally closer to their shadow.

If a woman has completely repressed her shadow or has it strongly under control, one can be fairly sure that it is the work of a morally bound animus. Her feminine side would not do this. But if she is animus possessed, she becomes a moralist, like a man, and thereby divides herself into two and represses her shadow. But if a woman is not completely animus possessed, she most often has enough instinct to not repress her shadow too strongly, but rather to tolerantly let it live. This has a certain charm for men. In this sense, women are instinctively closer to nature. This explains why a nature shadow is more seldom split off. In other words, women generally allow their natural self to live.

For now, I am disregarding the unusual situation of the modern woman who has to work in her profession. But if we consider how, in earlier times, women mainly worked in the family or in nursing and in professions with human contact, where masculine principles were not so important, we see that they were able to live out their natural side. And this was even important. I would say that a mother who does not sometimes have a bad mood and snarls at her children is an unnatural person. It does not hurt the children to grow up in a natural human atmosphere. In my view, if this is missing, life is missing. So it is my belief that this is why feminine fairy tales seldom deal with the problem of a split between the ego and what I choose to call our "nature shadow," that is so often present in masculine fairy tales. I found only this one example – "Tatterhood."

By contrast there is what I call the "devilish shadow." And this appears as frequently in feminine fairy tales as it does in masculine fairy tales and it is absolutely stereotypical. The behaviour of the handmaiden in our tale is simply the quintessence of this shadow. This is always the one who wants to take the jewellery, the clothes, the role of queen. It is utterly boring and stereotypical, one could say. And its motivation is worldliness and ambition. The motif of swapping is important here. The figure of the handmaiden pretends to be the princess. This involves lying and cheating. It is a trick and a fraud. This is the stereotype of the shadow of the feminine. And we need to ask what this looks like in practice.

Psychologically speaking, I believe there is a typical feminine shadow in practical life – and its name is jealousy. Jung once said that jealousy is the blot on feminine nature. And if one were to investigate why women do nasty things, in ninety-nine percent of the cases it would be out of jealousy, specifically out of "wanting what others have," for example, "wanting the other person's partner," or "wanting the other person's relationship." It is a matter of "simply wanting" what the other person has got, without asking, "Would this be right for me?" or "Is this what I really want?" There are women who want everything other women have got, even if they do not really want it, and if they were to get it, they would discard it. But if the others have it, then they must have it, too. This drive is insanely dark. It is, so to speak, *the* dark shadow of the feminine, a kind of greed, a desire to always take away what the other person has got. This has the effect of – and this is where we come to the motif of fraudulence – falsifying one's own personality. The devil or the devilish danger, the dark danger of the feminine, is the danger of being fraudulent towards one's own inner self for one's eye is upon what others have got, and wanting it for oneself. This is the truly great danger.

This figure of the "servant who becomes the master" appears in masculine fairy tales, too.[10] Here it is not as schematic or absolute. In other words, while it is a problem of the masculine, it appears infinitely more often in "feminine fairy tales" and much more stereotypically. So it would appear to be a much bigger problem for women. This may well have to do with the softness of the female being, and how easily it can be influenced: women do not readily know what it is that they really want, what fits for them, and what does not. If they see that their sister has something, suddenly they want the same thing, convinced that it is the right thing for them, too. And this introduces jealousy into the situation and when jealousy walks through the door, it brings all the other devils with it. When I open this door, in walk telling lies and intrigue and all the others. This is what jealousy does. When one sees how a woman gets all worked up … When an analysand leaves her analytical hour feeling fine but returns the following week all askew, you can be fairly certain that she has somehow been stung by jealousy. This sets off her animus and everything is once again in the hands of the devil.

So jealousy is *the* great danger of the feminine. It makes one false. In other words, when jealousy rules, when this aspect of a woman's personality rules, her genuine personality gets pushed into the shadow: it is suppressed, just as the handmaiden suppresses the princess in our story. What is genuine is pushed aside. This is why I believe that the psychological problem with women is very often not so much about being morally good or bad in

10 Marie-Louise von Franz is here referring to fairy tales in which the main figure is
   masculine.

a conventional sense, but rather the problem is much more about knowing who one is and being authentic, to find out who you are and to be authentic in your own eyes. This seems to me to be particularly difficult for women. And it is, actually, their great and very important task. This is why so many fairy tales are about the real bride, the one who clings to her own authenticity which always brings with it great suffering, who is the one who finally becomes queen. So this means that a woman's individuation, her process of becoming conscious or her individuation process, leads her and moves her in the direction of becoming conscious of her own genuine self, and that she must then summon up enough civil courage to stand up for who she is and not to doubt it.

This is, of course, also true for the feminine – for a man's anima. A man's anima also has the tendency of allowing itself to be deluded. Men who consciously believe that A is A, and B is B, and that three is not four – in other words, men who are able to make clear distinctions – are capable of deceiving themselves into believing a feeling matter is wonderful, even when it is not! For example, many men are convinced that a beautiful woman is a good woman. And when they see a beautiful woman they are, not surprisingly, enthusiastic and feel attracted to her. And then this beauty causes a great deal of trouble, playing a game about which any other person would say, "Oh dear! Beautiful on the outside, but rotten on the inside!" But there are always men who, out of desperation, will talk their way around it saying that she must be a nice person really, or is a nice person at bottom. All the havoc she is wreaking is forgiven. It is all an accident. If she lied, then she did not really lie. She meant well. There are other men – and it is a tragic thing – who have had the misfortune of landing a shocking wife, and who, over a period of fifteen or more years of married life, tell themselves that she is actually a nice person. They do this for sentimental reasons, or because they simply want to paint a nice picture of their marriage – they have a nice wife, and nice children. They simply do not want to admit, "Yes, I've made the wrong choice."

In analysis, too, this can be absolutely awful. One recognizes the witch and thus has a sense of the lengths to which the poor man will go, and how he bends over double in order to convince himself that his wife is a nice person. And then she betrays him with another man. And then he feels sorry for her and says that it is because of a psychological problem she has. It is certainly his fault. It is moving to see the effort he makes. I think it is quite tragic. He goes out of his way and lays himself at her feet, and is convinced that it is all his fault that she behaves as she does with him, and all of this because he does not want to wake up to such a repugnant insight. Put simply, this is sentimentality distorting true feeling. It is also a distortion of a genuine reaction. In fact, it is not the man or the woman doing all of this; it is the feminine. The feminine in man and in women is easily distorted – obviously. And this would appear to be the actual and bigger problem. It is also a kind of moral problem, just a bit different to how one normally thinks about it.

If a woman has a positive relationship to her mother – and one can generally also say this about a positive mother complex in a man – and a child has had the good fortune of growing up with a kind mother by whom it feels understood in a positive way, the disadvantage of this is most often that of being too innocent. When I was younger, I used to admire and envy those who had a positive mother for I thought it must have been wonderful. In child therapy books today you can read all about motherly love, and how a child needs the warm love of its mother and all misfortune goes back to a child not feeling "a primal sense of being safe" with its mother, etc. I always find this exaggeratedly one-sided. It is all true, of course. But everything good also has its shadow side, and all that is bad has its positive side. And the shadow side of a positive mother complex is that people grow up in an atmosphere of "*meilleur des mondes possibles*" – as Leibniz[11] would say, and they are therefore too naive and too innocent when it comes to the evil in the world. And this is why these people are often the lambs that become the victims of wolves. They walk dewy-eyed into the darkness of the world, without a trace of distrust. Their origins were too good and too bright. If a series of bitter disappointments does not usher in more realism in people, a positive mother complex is actually also a problem.

This situation can also be seen in this fairy tale. The king's daughter behaves in a dreadfully naive manner. Instead of defending herself, she says, "Oh God! If mother knew about this!" "Mama, if only mama were here!" This is, of course, naive – such an innocent child! One could say it will necessarily attract the other side. It simply has to constellate darkness, either within or on the outside.

That she is so thirsty is also an interesting motif. The source from which one drinks is very often a place where disaster happens – for example, Siegfried who kills the dragon Fafnir. While hunting, he drinks thirstily

11 Gottfried Wilhelm Leibniz (1646-1716).

from a well and just at that moment Hagen thrusts his spear into where
Siegfried is vulnerable.[12] This is generally a mythological motif. When a
hero or heroine bends over a river thirstily, very often the dark side attacks
them from behind. Quenching one's thirst at a river or stream has to do
with one's need for the water of life, or one could say with one's need for
contact with one's soul, or life itself. Flowing water is an image of the river
of life. Indeed, we talk about "the river of life." This is actually the river of
psychic energy. If one's psychic energy stagnates, one has the feeling one is
not really alive. But when one's psychic energy flows, one feels interested,
fascinated, enthusiastic, attracted, enterprising, etc., and this is psychic
energy. When it flows, one feels really alive.

Whether one feels alive or not is a purely subjective feeling. There are
people who feel they are dead, or not really alive, for decades. In other
words, they simply vegetate and exist physically. And conversely there are
people who are very old and while they vegetate physically, psychically they
are very much alive for their psychic life is still flowing. They continue to
pursue their interests, and are able to feel happy etc. They feel they are still
alive. This is the flow of psychic events.

And now the princess and her handmaiden go through a "lean period."
This is not the princess' fault. It is because of the objective situation,
because the kingdom of the men and the kingdom of the women lie so far
apart. Thus there is, as it were, a kind of lean period between them. This
would mean that in this collective situation, the masculine – the spiritual
principle – and the feminine are too far apart, as I tried to describe earlier.
And it is not such an easy matter to bring them together. Between them lies
a hot issue. And this is why the princess feels the need to connect to the
source of life and to drink from it.

Firstly, she orders her maid to bring her water. This means, she wants to
use this dark aspect to get in touch with life. But she says to her, "Fetch it
yourself!" And then the maid forces her to be subservient to her. One has
the feeling that it is somehow in order that she does this. If she had not been
so idiotically naive, she would have been alerted by the maid's response –
"If you want a drink, get it yourself. I won't be your servant." Then, when

---

12 Das Nibelungenlied [The Lay of the Nibelungs], 2 vols., edited and translated by
   Helmut Brackert (Frankfurt a.M.: Fischer TB, 1979), p. 217, verses 980-982; English:
   The Nibelungenlied. The Lay of the Nibelungs, translated with an introduction by Cyril
   Edwards (Oxford: Oxford University Press, 2010).

she drank, she would have been on the alert and said to herself, "I had better keep an eye on her for she does not mean me well."

Instead of which she goes and turns her back on her. She does not notice her first warning. She simply dismisses her maid's cheeky response. If one interprets this on the subjective level, it means that with a positive mother complex this kind of innocence that "does not notice" the darkness has the upper hand – a kind of "inability to notice." And this is always the case if one has not struggled with one's own darkness. One then falls into the hands of such people on the outside. The more one knows one's own evil and darkness ... One does not need to live it out, but one is aware that it is there within oneself. Everyone has it. And one should at least see where it is within oneself and know that it is there. And if you keep an eye on it or do not repress it, the devil within, so to speak, warns you of the devil in other people. For of course, the devil smells the devil.

I still know how, in my youth – and probably like all women at some point in their life – I had to wrestle terribly with jealousy. And when, for example, I caught sight of myself in the mirror when I was in a fit of jealousy, I noticed that I had a particular kind of look about me. I cannot describe it to you – but it was most disagreeable! And believe it or not, to this day if a woman is jealous I can see it in her eyes, but only because I recognize it in myself. It is that look one gets! I only have to glance at a woman and I see it in her eyes, but only because I had to wrestle with my own devil and recognize him for what he is – only because of this can I see it. If I had not had this experience, I would [have remained] naive and would, for example, trust women who were jealous of me, and be constantly disappointed by them. That is just how it is.

One can only have some kind of protection from, or deal with, the devil outside of oneself if one knows one's *own* pitfalls. And this is one of the great advantages that one attains from the very disagreeable process of getting to know one's own pitfalls. You can protect yourself. Your own devil smells the devil in others and can alert you. But if you repress your own devil entirely, he can show you nothing. And then you go about in the world like an innocent lamb being betrayed by everyone, or you are tricked in some way. This is why repressing one's shadow is such a catastrophe. And it is also why Jung emphasized how important it is to see one's own shadow. It is of vital importance to see one's own shadow.

And thus we see how the innocent child [in this fairy tale] realizes nothing and turns her back on this cheeky woman and leans over the stream. One has the feeling one could give her a push and she would not have a clue about what had happened. If we take this on a subjective level, it means that the princess has no connection whatever to the dark side. Her mother did. She had this evil handmaiden as a servant at her court. But her daughter has no connection to the darkness and, in this sense, she is not up to life. Which is why she thirsts for the water of life. Those who are too good are not up to life.

If one reads the stories of the saints, one sees that few lived to be more than seventy years old. The holier one is, the earlier one dies. If you want to live, sooner or later you have to integrate some darkness, for you cannot live without using your elbows. And thus, this means that the princess is too good. She is cut off from the water of life. And then she thirsts for the water of life. But the condition [for receiving it] is – the arrival of darkness! One cannot remain pure and live – you cannot have your cake and eat it, too. If you want to live, you are necessarily confronted with the problem of darkness. …[13]

The Old King at the Royal Court

So now the handmaiden mounts the horse, Falada. And the princess mounts her maid's miserable horse. And this is how they ride to the king's court. And once they arrive, the handmaiden immediately climbs the steps as "the princess" and leaves the other girl with the horses below. But the old king looks out of the window and sees this very pretty maid ("maid" in inverted commas) and asks the royal bride who she is. And she says,

> "I picked her up on my way for a companion. Give the girl some work to do, so she won't stand idly by." However, the old king had no work for her, and knew of nothing else to say but, "I have a little boy who tends the geese. She can help him." The boy was called Kürdchen (Little Conrad)[14], and the true bride had to help him to tend the geese.

The old king makes a further appearance for at the end of the tale Little Kurt or Little Conrad tells him what the maid had said and what was going on at the court. And thus, finally, the truth comes out. In fact, this is hinted

13 Noise distortion on the tape renders the next few sentences unintelligible, apart from a few unconnected fragments.
14 In German "Kürdchen" or "Konrädchen," literally "Little Kurt" or "Little Conrad."

at here upon their arrival. Evidently, the king is suspicious. At the very least, the princess has drawn his attention. It would seem that this old king was a wise king who somehow has the right intuition, while the young king naively allows himself to be duped. Mention is always made of "the young king" and "the old king." Most often, the young one only becomes king when the old one is dead. So we must be dealing with a very wise king here if he is abdicating while still alive. This almost never happens in fairy tales. He voluntarily elects the young one to be king. Clearly this figure is an old wise man if he is capable of doing this!

This also shows why catastrophes are so often depicted in fairy tales. It is because the old king does not want to abdicate. As a result, he becomes devilish. If he were able to abdicate, if he could voluntarily resign and not become rigid in keeping his authority, then he would actually become wise, like the king in this story. He still rules at the end of the story. He saves the entire situation. He rules, as it were, behind the curtains with his wisdom – for the best. This also shows how the problem of the generations could better be solved. "The old king" is not just an image, a kind of supra-idea, that has become worn out and should withdraw. This same dynamic happens between the generations with the older generation clinging to their ideas and becoming rigid, unwilling to give in for reasons of power.

This fairy tale has some very rare motifs. Which is why it is such a beautiful fairy tale. An old king like this one here seldom appears for he has a positive influence from the background and he sees – probably because he has few difficulties in ruling and has time to look out of the window – the pretty maid and thinks, "I wonder what her story is." He feels sorry for her and thinks she does not belong in the kitchen where she is treated badly by the kitchen staff, being ordered around like Cinderella. And so he gives her a little job. It is very lowly work – she has to tend the geese. But it means she is far away from everything, and from the evil bride of the young king: she is out in nature. So in a very tender, clever way he saves the girl and surrounds her with favourable life circumstances. Thus, in the background of this collective situation there is, so to speak, a kind of wisdom at play, one that has been superseded and has already retired to the background, but helps the princess nevertheless.

The Horse, Falada

We shall not discuss Little Kurt now but later when we discuss tending geese. For right now a further tragedy ensues. The impostor bride suddenly asks the young king, whom she has apparently married, to fetch the slaughterer to slaughter the horse, Falada, that she had ridden because it had annoyed her on the journey.

> *In truth, she was afraid that the horse might tell how she had behaved toward the king's daughter. Thus it happened that faithful Falada had to die. The real princess heard about this, and she secretly promised to pay the knacker a piece of gold if he would perform a small service for her. In the town there was a large dark gateway, through which she had to pass with the geese each morning and evening. Would he be so good as to nail Falada's head beneath the gateway, so that she might see him again and again? The knacker's helper promised to do that, and cut off the head, and nailed it securely beneath the dark gateway.*

And together with Little Kurt and the geese she went through the gateway the next morning and as she passed through it, she said, *"Alas, Falada, hanging there!"* And the head replied, *"Alas, young queen, passing by./ If this your mother knew,/ Her heart would break in two."* *"Then they went still further out of the town"* and so on. This is repeated several times. And it is partly the reason why finally her story is revealed, for, as we shall hear, Little Kurt later tells the king what is said every day and that the horse's head always addresses her as *"young queen."*

Thus, we must now look at this motif of the talking horse. This is a very Germanic motif. And this is, indeed, a German fairy tale and a rare one at that. Only in German fairy tales does this motif appear. For the ancient Germans, horses were sacred animals – as Tacitus writes.[15] This is why it is still taboo to eat horse meat today – except in military service,[16] where it is camouflaged with a sauce. Horse meat is as edible as cow meat. So it is a purely religious taboo that still exists amongst us. People say it is disgusting to eat horse meat. But it is not true. It is simply a food taboo that is based upon a religious idea.

---

15 Cornelius Tacitus, *Germania*, edited and translated into German by Gerhard Fink (Düsseldorf/Zürich: Artemis and Winkler, 1999), p. 21.
16 Much laughter from the audience.

Horses were the sacred animals of Wotan. And Wotan rode upon his eight-legged horse, Sleipnir, and is often portrayed as a horse himself. Thus he was, in fact, identical with Sleipnir. His sons were called "Hengist" and "Horsa." "Horsa" is the English word "horse" and "Hengist" is the German word "Hengst" [stallion]. In certain old skaldic songs, he was called "Hross-harsgrani," and this means "Horse Beard."[17] And the devil also inherited his cloven hoof from Wotan. So Wotan is a horse god or the horse itself. The horse and he are identical. And accordingly horses were sacred to the Germans. According to Tacitus, it was common to let horses run free in certain oak groves.[18] Seers and priests tried to predict the future from the whinnying of the horses. The Germans used the whinnying of horses in the same way that the Greeks tried to find out the will of the gods or what the outcome of a battle might be from the rustling of the oak trees of Dodona, or from the flight path of birds. And quite uniquely, they nailed horse skulls to trees and used them as an oracle.

Using the head as an oracle generally, not just of a horse, is an exceedingly widespread archetypal motif. For example, the head of Orpheus continued to sing and to speak as an oracle after he had been beheaded. In the Middle Ages, Pope Sylvester II (d. 1003) had a head that spoke to him in oracles.[19] In C.G. Jung's essay on *Transformation Symbolism in the Mass* there is a whole collection of these oracle-talking heads.[20] The Sabians – a Gnostic-Arabic sect of the Middle Ages – even sacrificed blonde young men whose heads underwent special preparation so that they could be used as an oracle afterwards. It was said of the Knights Templar that they used the head of Baphomet as an oracle that told them secret wisdom, etc. So it is a widespread mythical idea. The idea behind it is always that the head is,

---

17 *Handwörterbuch des Deutschen Aberglaubens* [Dictionary of German Superstition], edited by E. Hoffmann-Krayer and Hanns Bächtold-Stäubli, vol. 6 (Berlin/Leipzig: Verlag Walter de Gruyer, 1934/1935), column 1610-1613; see also Martin Ninck, *Wodan und der Germanische Schicksalsglaube* [Wodan and the Nordic Belief in Destiny] (Jena: Eugen Diederichs Verlag, 1935), p. 21.
18 Tacitus, *Germania*, p. 21.
19 C.G. Jung, "Transformation Symbolism in the Mass." In: *Psychology and Religion: West and East*, vol. 11 of *The Collected Works of C.G. Jung*, translated by R.F.C. Hull (Princeton: Princeton University Press, 1969), § 367. Pope Sylvester – his former name was Gerbert of Reims – was one of the greatest savants of his time, and well known as a transmitter of Arabic science.
20 Ibid., § 365-369 and § 373; see also C.G. Jung, "The Visions of Zosimos." In: *Alchemical Studies*, vol. 13 of *The Collected Works of C.G. Jung*, translated by R.F.C. Hull (Princeton: Princeton University Press, 1968), § 95.

so to speak, the seat of the spirit. This is why many primitive peoples bury their deceased parents or ancestors without great ceremony somewhere out in the field, but keep the head with them at home. In this way, the ancestral spirits live with them. The Romans placed little statues of their ancestors – the "lares" and "penates" – in their homes, specifically over their ovens. These were the spirits of their dead forbearers in the form of small holy figures. This is, if you like, the continuation of the more primitive practice of keeping the corpses of their deceased relatives at home. Originally, the Romans also buried the corpses of the deceased in the earth beneath their homes in order to keep them close by. Later they buried only the corpses of their deceased children under the well-trodden earth of their home, and for the others they put up these little figures into which the ancestral spirits could go. This was their ancestral cult. There are African tribes who still preserve the prepared heads of their dead ancestors.

The head represents the essence of a person, that which survives after death. Because of its round form, it is also a symbol of the Self. It is, so to speak, a symbol of the immortal part of man. It symbolizes what is immortal, what remains spiritually after death. Which is why the heads of the deceased were kept at home. And this was then transferred onto animals. When the princess wants to keep the head of Falada, then it is, so to speak, the essence of Falada's soul, or, as I would prefer to say, his spirit. The fact that the spirit of Falada speaks through the head just as it did when he was a horse is also evidence of this.

So what does Falada the horse mean psychologically? It is a gift from her mother. It is a talking horse and is therefore an especially valuable magical horse that the mother gives the girl. As we saw earlier, this would mean this positive instinctual basis, or being connected to one's instincts, that a positive mother complex instils in a woman. On the other hand, this horse Falada obviously has a close relationship to the realm of the spirit. It is a masculine creature. In some versions it is called Valentine, which is clearly a masculine name. The princess refers to the horse as "he" and not "she" so it is clearly a masculine horse.[21] And now we must recall that in the first kingdom the king, the princess's father, had died. Thus, it is my conjecture

---

21 In German, von Franz says, „Die Königstochter sagt ja auch: 'Falada, der du hangest' und nicht 'die du hangest.' Es ist also ein männliches Pferd." As relative pronouns in English do not distinguish gender, I have tried to express the meaning of what she said with my formulation of this sentence. (Translator's note)

that Falada is, in a manner of speaking, the spirit of this no-longer-present dead king.

Psychologically speaking, it is like this: when a spiritual world view dies, it means it is no longer being used, or no longer exists in the heads of people – in their conscious awareness. But where does a worldview go when it disappears from consciousness? It falls into the unconscious. It simply goes back to where it once came from. And this has a very strange effect. When a worldview has been historically superseded and, as a result, becomes unconscious again, it is not simply a matter of it "vanishing" and a return to the status quo, but it also has a sort of civilizing effect upon the unconscious. It remains in the unconscious as a sort of spirit of the unconscious. So one can say that when some aspect of culture that was once lived by people disappears, it has not by any means disappeared. It has had a cultivating effect upon the unconscious.

I do not have any documents about it, but I would bet that, for example, one could find traces of the Christian religion in the unconscious of a modern Russian. In Russia today, Christianity has been almost stamped out. This "king" no longer exists. It is a dead king, or a king that has been dethroned. This way of looking at the world no longer exists in Russia. But, as stated earlier, what has once existed exists forever and remains. It does not simply cease to exist. It leaves traces in the unconscious. Up until now, I have not analysed a convinced communist from Soviet Russia. But I have analysed someone from a different country behind the Iron Curtain – a convinced materialistic atheist. His unconscious is full of Christianity. ... He is so young that he did not live through the olden days and he grew up in the new system. He believes Christianity is an old historical bygone superstition and views it as he does any other primitive superstition – at least in his conscious life. But in his unconscious, the Christian culture is present. He has a certain spirituality, a certain European Christian spirituality within him.

If one were to analyse a person from a different cultural circle – let's say a Korean – one would certainly not find a layer of Christianity in their unconscious. These things are, to some extent, local and historical. But the big problem is how to explain this in biological-genetic terms? And thus, we land at the question as to whether or not acquired characteristics can be inherited. Is this possible? I do not dare to go out on a limb here. This problem has many thorns. But what one can say is that it is like this in dreams. But as to how these things get into people's unconscious and whether they are inherited or not are open questions. Fifteen years ago, one would not even have dared to say or ask such a thing. Lamarck[22] had been abandoned and only Darwin was valid.[23] There was no such thing as inherited, acquired characteristics. But according to the latest discoveries – that are heavily under attack from fanatical Darwinians – the whole question has been thrown open again. Especially the genetic substances, the deoxyribonucleic acids and the ribonucleic acids, apparently carry information. Everything in research is shifting right now and we therefore cannot say much about it. We have to leave it up to the geneticists to do more research into this.

From the psychological standpoint, we can only say that we do not know how these things are passed on, but that they are present in the unconscious. A lost culture does not disappear: it remains in the unconscious and somehow then appears in dreams. Thus one can say – and this is why I dare to speculate – that the horse, Falada, is, as it were, the spirit of the princess' father. The dead king appears as spirit in the horse, as a positive fatherly figure. It is not speculation to connect him to Wotan who was a divine living horse. This means that the horse Falada symbolizes a pre-Christian pagan father spirit. This would mean that the princess now lives in accordance with an earlier deeply instinctual, cultural and historical spirit that is emerging from the depths of the unconscious. This is typical of a woman. When a woman has a relationship to spirituality, it is most often a relationship to the spirit of nature, to a natural spirit, and not to some computer spirit, but rather to what one would call the natural inspiration of the unconscious. The princess now lives in accordance with this spirit and it is in him that she confides her suffering.

The word "Falada" is a problem. Bolte and Polivka have written about it.[24] But it does not give much insight. Curiously, the name "Falada" appears in the Old French Song of Roland (11th century) where it is called "Veillantif." In a version of the Song of Roland from 13th century[25] Roland's horse is called "Valentich" and in a version from the 12th century[26] it is referred to as "Velentin." In the work of Reinolt von Montalban there is a horse called "Valentin" and in the poem "Willehalm" by Wolfram von Eschenbach

22 Jean-Baptiste Lamarck (1744-1829).
23 Charles Darwin (1809-1882).
24 Johannes Bolte and Georg Polivka, *Anmerkungen zu den Kinder- und Hausmärchen der Brüder Grimm* [Notes to the Brothers Grimm's Fairy Tales], 2 vols. (reprint Hildesheim/New York: Georg Olms Verlag, 1982), vol. 2, pp. 273ff.
25 *Rolandslied des Strickers* [Stricker's Song of Roland].
26 *Rolandslied des Pfaffen Konrad* [Conrad the Priest's Song of Roland].

(1160/80 to approx. 1220) and in a work by Ulrich von Türheim (1195-1250) William of Orange has a horse called "Volatin," "Valatin" and sometimes "Valantin." In an earlier edition of this fairy tale, the name "Folle" is given.

> *"Oh, Folle! There you are, hanging! – O beautiful girl! There you are, going. If your mother knew of this, her heart would burst into sticks and stone."*[27]

"Folle" is simply a word for "foal." I think it probable that "Falada" actually means "Folleda, hanging there," being derived from "Folle, there you are, hanging" ("Folle, da du hangest"). The "da" in German got added to the "Folle." But it is a strange word. Bolte-Polivka, who are otherwise very erudite and know all the explanations, found out nothing and nor could I. I tend to think it could mean "Folle." But that does not really lead anywhere either. If the name "Falada" is derived from the horse in the Song of Roland, it would simply mean that it is a heroic horse from a bygone era.

The Goose Girl

After the princess had spoken to the horse's head,

> *… they went still further out of the town, driving their geese into the country. And when they came to the meadow, she sat down and unbound her hair, which was of pure gold. Conrad saw it, was delighted how it glistened, and wanted to pluck out a few hairs. Then she said: "Blow, wind, blow,/ Take Conrad's hat away,/ And make him chase it,/ Until I have braided my hair,/ And tied it up again." Then such a strong wind came up that it blew Conrad's hat across the fields, and he had to run after it. When he came back, she was already finished combing and putting up her hair, so he could not get even one strand. –* He always wanted to pluck out her golden hair. *– So Conrad became angry, and would not speak to her, and thus they tended the geese until evening, and then they went home.*

When she was at the gate the next morning, once again she said, *"Alas, Falada, hanging there!"* This took place every day. And Little Kurt's anger grew until he finally went to the old king and said, *"I won't tend geese with that*

27 J. Bolte and G. Polivka, Anmerkungen zu den Kinder- und Hausmärchen der Brüder Grimm [Notes to the Brothers Grimm's Fairy Tales], p. 274.

girl any longer." The old king then asked, "*Why not?*" "*Oh, because she angers me all day long.*" And he went on to describe how she talks so strangely to the head of an old dead horse. And he cited what she said. And he told how she could summon up a wind so that his hat would fly away, forcing him to run after it. Of course he omitted to say that he had wanted to pluck out some of her hair.

And now the old king's interest in the girl grew and he hid in a bush on the goose meadow to see for himself and he sees the whole scene unfold, and with Little Kurt as the mediator, the whole thing has a happy ending. A rascal like this who rehabilitates the queen, who has been suppressed or chased off into the forest, can be found in many fairy tales. There is a fairy tale called "Hans Wunderlich" in the volume of German fairy tales, *Deutsche Märchen seit Grimm.*[28] In this story a princess is vilified and cast out and she goes into the forest. There a young colourful boy appears, with lots of colourful feathers and hair, and he calls her "mother." This colourful chap plays all kinds of tricks and does all kinds of magic with the result that his parents make peace with each other and in this way he redeems his mother. There are various fairy tales in which a rascally boy figure redeems a queen.[29]

The figure of a young boy plays a large, and most often a positive, role in feminine psychology. In women's dreams, a young boy most often represents taking the initiative or her enterprising aspect. While a grown man, or the old wise man, symbolize more her spiritual aspect, a young boy symbolizes a practical, enterprising approach to life – in its positive sense. This is why women often dream of young boys.

Little Kurt, however, wants to pluck some strands of hair from her head. And this would mean he wants to have an influence upon her thoughts, or control her thoughts. Hair symbolizes one's thoughts. Hair is simply what grows randomly out of one's head. And one projects onto this not one's conscious thoughts, but rather one's unconscious thoughts and fantasies. The things one thinks without really wanting to – that is what hair symbolizes. In older interpretations, one reads that hair had a sexual meaning. This

---

28 Paul Zaunert and Elfriede Moser-Rath (eds.), *Deutsche Märchen seit Grimm* [German Fairy Tales since Grimm] (Düsseldorf/Köln: Eugen Diederichs Verlag, 1964), „Hans Wunderlich", pp. 31-40; see also the interpretation of this fairy tale in: M.-L. von Franz (previously H. von Beit), *Symbolik des Märchens* [Symbolism of Fairy Tales], vol. 1, p. 749-753.

29 J. Bolte and G. Polivka, Anmerkungen zu den Kinder- und Hausmärchen der Brüder Grimm [Notes to the Brothers Grimm's Fairy Tales], vol. 2, p. 236, footnote 2.

has to do with the story of Samson and Delilah.[30] After Samson's hair had been cut off, he was without any strength. Thus, the Freudian psychologists always connected hair to sexuality. This was then always copied. ... It is, however, a Freudian interpretation that finds no validation elsewhere.

That a person's strength is diminished if one cuts their hair is true. But it is a spiritual castration. It means that if one takes away someone's free thoughts and their permission to think freely, then one takes away their power. Amongst the Germanic peoples, for instance, only the free men and the noblemen were permitted to have long hair. Bonded farmers had to keep their hair short. This was a way of saying, "You are not entitled to think your own thoughts. *We* may think, and we may believe and we have mental freedom, but you have only to do your work and not think for yourself." And this is why I am very much in favour of long hair – of the freedom of thought. ...[31] It is demonstrative and it means, "I want to have freedom of thought; I want to be free to think whatever I choose to think." And why may they not? But hair, as I said, is also unconscious thoughts or dream thoughts or daydreams. Hair is an expression of all these things.

The princess has golden hair. And golden hair is a sign for that which has to do with the sun, for one's sun nature. The hero prince, the king and so on, all have golden hair. The princess' golden hair is [therefore] something like a natural sun crown. This is her royal, noble manner. One could say that she has majestic, noble, even queenly thoughts. And Little Kurt wants to control or take these thoughts away from her. This means that as positive as this rascal is, he should not be meddling with her hair! For this would mean she would begin to think up little intrigues, little tricks to play on people, in order to rehabilitate herself. But then her story would become calculated. It would not simply unfold. The princess would have played, as it were, with ideas about how to make things happen. And this would be beneath her dignity; it would be a break with her royal nature.

There are women, for example, who have little patience to bear a difficult situation. They then fall prey to their "rascally animus" and get up to some mischief. For example, they drive their husband's car into the ground, or something like that, something that is an unconscious rascally trick, in order to demonstrate their dissatisfaction with the unbearable situation.

30 Judges 16:4-31.
31 A great deal of laughter in the audience makes what follows inaudible. Marie-Louise von Franz was referring here to the time of the hippies and to the fashion at the time, also amongst men, to have long hair.

And this is, in fact, beneath the dignity of a grown woman, for she should be conscious. If she has resistances towards her husband, she should find a means and a way to tell him so directly, rather than driving his car into the ground. In our Jungian terms, this is also an animus that in situations like this just makes something happen to draw attention to the situation.

The princess resists this urge. She does not allow herself to get involved. Even though she is suffering, she upholds her majestic dignity and precisely because of this the rascal then does the right thing. He tells the king the whole story and thereby brings the truth to light, without the princess playing any tricks. It would have meant breaking her oath for she had sworn before God that she would say nothing. An oath is, after all, a religious affair – something that one cannot, and may not, break. And if the princess had secretly thought that Little Kurt might do something to help her ..., then she would have broken her oath behind her own back. But this is not what happens. She steers Little Kurt away. She communicates with Falada. And she is like a wind goddess for she can summon the wind. This, too, shows her connection to the spirit of nature, to the natural divine spirit. So the princess remains true to a religious attitude – religious in the sense of "being completely obedient to an inner spiritual law." She plays no tricks and lets the rascally boy be who he is, as it were, in her presence. She is not angry with him, but only causes his hat to blow away so that he has to run after it. But she prevents him from interfering with her spiritual aspect, with her natural queenly crown – her golden hair. And as this upsets Little Kurt, he does just the right thing. He goes to the old king and tells him everything that happened. Actually, at this point one should give a whole new lecture on feminine psychology. Instead of doing so, I recommend that you all go to Miss Barbara Hannah's lecture at the Jung Institute on feminine intrigue. In English, its title is "On Women's Plots." You can then get all the science on this problem. It would take too long here.[32]

One of women's biggest problems is that, in quiet moments and in half-conscious daydreams, they like to make plans for the future, plans that they then help along a little with their left hands in order to realize them. Put bluntly, this is called intrigue. But there are many in-between forms that one cannot directly label as an intrigue. It is a kind of wishful thinking that one just helps along a little bit. This is one of the great catastrophes – on the one hand of the feminine shadow, but the animus also gets involved – for

32 Barbara Hannah, *The Problem of Women's Plots in "The Evil Vineyard."* Guild Lecture, nr. 51 (London: The Guild of Pastoral Psychology, 1948).

very often by doing so, women destroy their entire destiny. The worst thing about this is that often they plot to achieve something for they feel they deserve it, but they cannot wait for it to come to them naturally. One often sees a woman who intuitively realizes she has the chance of getting a man, or a job, or something that she would like to have. And because she intuitively notices this, or is made aware of it, she begins to lend it a hand with her intrigues and ruins it all in the process.

It is the same in analysis, but one must first notice [the intrigue] – most people defend themselves fiercely before admitting to themselves that they do this. So firstly, one has to notice that it is being done, and then one has to sacrifice it. Most often this requires a larger surgical operation. It has been my experience, however, that when a woman is able to sacrifice her plotting, she gets what it is she was after, like a gift from heaven. If she had gone on with her plots, she would most probably not have got what she was after. It is most strange how this works sometimes. I recall often saying, "You see? Because you made this sacrifice, it has now been given to you." Of course, one may not say, "If you make this sacrifice, you will get what you want." That would not be sincere, and it would not be a true sacrifice. That would again be calculating. Many do this. They have heard about it, or have experienced it already themselves, and make a sacrificial gesture the next time; they perform the whole sacrificial ritual and think about it all the time. But to really sacrifice something in a way that it is completely gone is very, very difficult. If one [projects] a wishful fantasy onto a man, or onto some other concrete situation, to completely sacrifice it as if it were cut away and thrown into water often requires a devilish struggle. But if one makes the sacrifice, if one can really resist this great temptation of one's feminine nature to "*corriger la fortune,*" to "help things along," it then comes to one as if by itself, as if the energy that had been invested into plotting suddenly turns one's fate around.

This is what happens here. The princess does not allow Little Kurt to touch her hair. This means she does not allow the trickster, the rascally boy, to interfere with her inner world. And so he goes and tells the king the whole story. If he had been able to get a hold of her hair, he would not have done this. I do not know what he would have done with her golden hair, but if he had got it he would have had nothing to complain about and he would not have gone to the old king. But, because he did not, he goes to the old king and tells him about the strange things that have been going on.

The goose girl has been talking to this dead horse's head, and she has been magically conjuring up the wind.

> *The old king ordered him to drive his flock out again the next day. As soon as morning came, he himself sat down behind the dark gateway, and heard how the girl spoke with Falada's head. Then he followed her out into the country and hid himself in a thicket in the meadow. There he soon saw with his own eyes the goose-girl and the goose-boy bringing their flock, and how after a while she sat down and took down her hair, which glistened brightly. Soon she said, "Blow, wind, blow,/ Take Conrad's hat away"* – and so on – *while the maiden quietly went on combing and braiding her hair, all of which the king observed. Then, quite unseen, he went away, and when the goose-girl came home in the evening, he called her aside, and asked why she did all these things.* – He senses something. – *"I am not allowed to tell you, nor can I reveal my sorrows to any human being, for I have sworn under the open heaven not to do so, and if I had not so sworn, I would have been killed."*

The geese are an interesting motif. Why is it precisely geese that she has to tend? This was the old king's idea and the fairy tale is indeed called "The Goose Girl." Geese are also connected to Wotan. So once again we land in this territory. We have just had St. Martin's Feast Day.[33] And on St. Martin's Feast Day, a goose is slaughtered. In ancient times, geese were offered as a sacrifice to Wotan, and after Christianity spread, it was transferred to St. Martin's Feast Day. And thus we have St. Martin's goose. Bonded farmers at that time often had to deliver a goose to their master. Later, farmers had to give their village priest a goose on this day. This is all from pagan times. So the goose is an animal connected to Wotan.

In the Mediterranean region, the goose is connected to Aphrodite. There are images on beautiful old vases and cameos of Aphrodite riding through the air on a goose. The goose is also connected to the goddess of fate, Nemesis. The gander played a significant role in Egypt. It laid the great sun egg. As a gander, the all-powerful god Atum laid a golden egg out of which the world came forth and this is why he is also known as the "Great Cackler," or the "Great Gander." In ancient India, the goose was connected with the "hansa swan." … Domesticated geese walk in wonderful formation, like a procession. They march along in a very military fashion. And it is curious

---

33 St. Martin's Feast Day is on November 11th.

how wild geese fly in a very distinct triangular formation. All of this has made the goose a fascinating animal to man. In other words, the way animals behave – their famous *pattern of behavior* – that we recognize today in all species and impresses us so greatly when we study their behavior, was recognized by man long ago in the behavior of geese – namely, that animals have rituals and that their lives are highly ritualized.

This is why it was always a goose that behaved in a ritualistic way that did something that otherwise only humans do, for example, the way they gather in such a military-like formation. And this is why flying wild geese were a symbol of the Tao, for the secret powers that govern fate, in China. In the *I Ching or Book of Changes,* in hexagram 53 "Development" "The Gradual Progress" of the sixth line it is written, "The wild goose gradually draws near the cloud heights. Its feathers can be used for the sacred dance." And in the commentary it is written, "...like the flight of wild geese when they have left the earth far behind. There they fly, keeping to the order of their flight in strict formation. And if their feathers fall, they can serve as ornaments in the sacred dance pantomimes performed in the temples."[34] By flying in these strict formations, geese display, as it were, the lines of fate of the Tao, and a wise man can determine what they are from the flight of the geese. And then of course you know of the geese on the Capitoline hill that saved Rome.[35] Here, too, geese are clairvoyant; they express the will of the gods and behave according to secret spiritual laws. This has always made them fascinating. It is as if geese have a spirit and this is what enables them to create formations. This is how man viewed it in earlier times. And even though the word goose is used as a swearword, it is actually a bird of wisdom, specifically the sacred wisdom of nature.

So the old king orders that the princess should become the goose girl. This means that she must tend to and care for spiritual instincts or the spirit of nature. This is what the king orders her to do. And she does so with great commitment and this prevents her from getting mixed up in any of Little Kurt's rascally tricks. The princess must, as it were, take care of the spirit of nature without any ulterior motives and without any thought for personal gain. This is analogous to a natural religious attitude. Translated into our modern times, it would mean, for example, that one simply pays attention

---

34 *I Ching or Book of Changes*, The Richard Wilhelm Translation rendered into English by Cary F. Baynes (London: Arkana, Penguin Books, 1989), p. 208.

35 According to legend, in 387 B.C. the holy geese in the town of Capitoline saved Rome from being conquered by the Celts.

to the unconscious and to unconscious signals and one's dreams, rather than using intrigue in order to get out of some difficulty. It means that one says, "I submit to being led by my own inner spirit." This is what it would mean in our modern language.

The Iron Stove

And thus the king who had arranged it all arrives and wants her to tell him her story. But she may not. He becomes increasingly insistent and she repeatedly refuses. Finally, he has a good idea:

> *"If you will not tell me anything, then tell your sorrows to the iron stove there,"* *and he went away. So she crept into the iron stove, and began to cry sorrowfully,* *pouring out her whole heart. She said, "Here I sit, abandoned by the whole* *world, although I am the daughter of a king. A false chambermaid forced me* *to take off my royal clothes, and she has taken my place with my bridegroom.* *Now I have to do common work as a goose-girl. If this my mother knew, her* *heart would break in two." The old king was standing outside listening by the* *stovepipe, and he heard what she said. Then he came back inside, and asked* *her to come out of the stove. Then they dressed her in royal clothes, and it was* *marvelous how beautiful she was.*

So now all has been revealed. The goose girl becomes queen and the evil handmaiden is punished.

This is the motif of the oven confession, a motif that one also finds in Swiss legends. It is a fact that pipes conduct sound. One can also overhear things from the pipes of central heating. In Nazi Germany, for example, listening through pipes was used as a means of spying. They also used audio spying equipment, but stovepipes were also used to spy with. So it is an old trick to tell an oven something and the whole world can listen in. If the princess had discovered this, it would again have been an image of some trick, of her using her cunning. But it was the old king's idea. The old king told her to tell her story to the oven.

Here we see again how the princess absolutely refuses to be false or to betray anyone. This is why I believe this fairy tale is primarily an image of the task of the feminine, of not allowing oneself to be duped, but rather to stick to one's genuine feeling. This is, as it were, *the* great heroic deed. At no point, not even now when it would be so necessary to defend herself against the evil cunning of the handmaiden, does she allow herself to be ensnared. But the old king may resort to such a trick. He may. In his case, it is not a betrayal of feeling. He is not under oath. He is free to cook up such a scheme.

And now we come to the end of the fairy tale that has repeatedly led to shocked commentaries. At the wedding feast of the prince and princess, the old king asks the handmaiden *"what punishment"* she thinks *"a person deserved"* who has behaved in the manner of the handmaiden. And the false bride who does not realize that he is referring to her says,

> *"She deserves no better fate than to be stripped stark naked, and put in a barrel that is studded inside with sharp nails. Two white horses should be hitched to it, and they should drag her along through one street after another, until she is dead."* – And it continues, – *"You are the one," said the old king, "and you have pronounced your own sentence. Thus shall it be done to you."*

Such a cruel execution of the evil one has led certain modern readers to feel outraged. Such horrific punishment could hurt children etc. But children have enormous pleasure when an evil principle is radically wiped out. They do not experience this as squeamishly as adults do. Children also have a much better sense of things like this not being taken too literally, but rather they grasp its symbolic meaning.

But if we consider what this ending might mean psychologically, I would say that there are certain destructive – absolutely destructive – pathological psychic tendencies. They live within the shadow realms of us all. I do not mean pathological in the psychiatric use of the word. I simply mean it is so evil that one can only refer to it as being a sick kind of evilness. And this exists in all of us; up until now, I have found traces of it in everybody. And it is utterly destructive. It is completely wrong to be sentimental about these things. We have things within us to which we can only respond with, "Enough!" Some people, especially those who have some degree of education in psychology, use psychology to defend their own evil aspects. They say, "Yes, that is a shadow that needs to be integrated within, and it is a part of my whole personality." In this regard, I say to myself, "Yes, many dark sides are a part of one's whole personality. We cannot know just how many there are. But there are always sides to which the only healthy reaction, the individuation instinct in man, so to speak, is to say, "That's enough!" One must totally eliminate such sides.

And this is expressed symbolically here. Of course, evil never dies. In the next fairy tale there will also be perhaps a handmaiden, a witch or an impostor bride at work. She is an eternal figure, an eternal power within the human soul. But the end of the fairy tale means that her evil doing comes to a complete halt. This is what it means symbolically. And thank God there is such a thing. Thank God that what is evil within us, what makes us sick, what has a destructive effect can, in fact, totally stop. In psychological terms, this is what we mean when we speak of a healing. When something destructive totally and definitively ceases to have an effect, this is the process of healing. And this is why, from a symbolic point of view, we can say that such satanic punishment of evil is absolutely correct. We have such things within us. For example, if a person has the tendency – let's use a primitive example – to drink or to lie, then the only thing to do is to once say, "That's it! It's over now!" This would mean, "completely annihilating it." Such a tendency must be completely annihilated, and one may not say, "Oh, but it has a very nice side." No! "That's it! It's over!"

And then the whole situation transforms. This is why compassionate sentimentality in raising children or in psychotherapy is inappropriate. And it is typical that fairy tales that are about feminine psychology are about this issue, for women often have the wrong kind of sympathy, both with themselves and with others. And it is again this distortion of one's feelings. It is a very great danger. If one is clear about one's feeling, one can adopt a clear attitude, even a radical attitude. One cannot do this in respect to the evil in others. But towards the evil within oneself, it is the correct approach.[36]

36 Translated from German by Alison Kappes-Bates, Wädenswil, Switzerland.

Regine Schweizer-Vüllers

"He struck the rock and the waters did flow"

The alchemical background of the gravestone of Marie-Louise von Franz and Barbara Hannah

Introduction

Many people, from all over the world, visit Jung's grave at the graveyard in Küsnacht (plate 2, p. 226). They look at the gravestone, read the names, read the inscriptions on the stone. They think about it and – possibly – bring home something into their daily life, most likely mediated by one of the inscriptions, for instance "primus homo de terra – terrenus" on the right side of the stone and "secundus homo de caelo – caelestis" on the left side. "The first man is from the earth – earthly, the second man is from heaven – celestial."[1] Whatever it is, for whatever reason people may come and however personal the encounter at C.G. Jung's grave may be, we can assume that the stone conveys a message, a message from eternity as we can say. The stone itself becomes a messenger between the visitors and the life and work of C.G. Jung, a legacy that he has left to us.

Not far away from C.G. Jung's family grave at the cemetery of Küsnacht also lies the grave of Marie-Louise von Franz and Barbara Hannah (plate 3, p. 227). The gravestone with the names and the dates of the births and deaths of the two women consists in its upper part of a fourfold circle. When looking closer one can read on its left and right side the inscription: "Percussit petram et fluxerunt aquae," "he struck the rock" or "the stone,"

---

1 Paul, 1 Cor. 15:47. Biblical references are from The New Oxford Annotated Bible: New Revised Standard Version with The Apocrypha, edited by Michael D. Coogan (Oxford: Oxford University Press, 2010).

maybe also "he broke the stone" – "and the waters did flow." After the death of Barbara Hannah in 1986 Marie-Louise von Franz ordered this stone.[2] But when it was delivered one could see a small mistake above on the left side. At first sight Marie-Louise von Franz was angry about this, but later she remarked, that this little mistake would be just right since to wholeness belongs also incompleteness.[3]

Thus, the stone should express something whole. When people place stones on the graves of the deceased it generally symbolizes something eternal or divine, namely "that which, in human beings, survives death" as Marie-Louise von Franz herself has written.[4] Within the same context she described the stone as "an age-old symbol for the eternal, the enduring in man, from which he draws the strength he needs for life."[5] And at another place she says that the stone would be "a symbol of the inner god in man."[6] The gravestone of Marie-Louise von Franz and Barbara Hannah could express all this as well. For me it holds a very mysterious and also fascinating message. And I will try to convey parts of this message in what follows.

Now, the message is expressed on two levels, on one side through the inscription and on the other through the fourfold divided circle or the mandala. First I will look at the mandala. Only at the end I will come to the inscription on the stone with its Latin text, to its biblical but also, and more intensively, to its alchemical background.

When some time ago, by chance, I discovered that the fourfold circle on the gravestone of Marie-Louise von Franz and Barbara Hannah is identical with a well-known alchemical "picture," from a certain alchemical treatise I was fascinated by this discovery and started to translate the alchemical text from Latin into German. The depiction itself seems to be rather small and unimpressive (picture 1).[7] But it contains and represents the whole alchemical opus, which – as the accompanying text says – reaches by far beyond the individual human being or the alchemist and his endeavors. The alchemical treatise is called *Tractatus aureus Hermetis*, meaning *The*

---

2 Thus she created it by herself or together with Barbara Hannah some time before.
3 I am grateful to Alison Kappes-Bates, who told me of this.
4 Marie-Louise von Franz, *C.G. Jung. His Myth in Our Time*, translated by William H. Kennedy (Toronto: Inner City Books, 1998), p. 220.
5 Ibid., p. 219.
6 Ibid., p. 231.
7 Picture 1: The depiction in the *Tractatus aureus* with the accompanying text.

golden treatise of Hermes. There one finds the picture in the seventh and final chapter.[8]

Picture 1: *Tractatus aureus*, page 442

C.G. Jung mentioned the little depiction several times in his works, for instance in the last chapter of *Aion*, also in his article on Zosimos, as well in *Psychology and Alchemy* and at the beginning of *Mysterium Conciunctionis*.[9] Depicted is a circle with seven letters, fourfold divided. In the middle one

8 Jean Jacques Manget (ed.), *Bibliotheca chemica curiosa*, vol. 1, Geneva 702, p. 442 r; also Lazarus Zetzner (ed.), *Theatrum chemicum*, vol. 4, Strassburg 1659, p. 699.
9 C.G. Jung, *Aion. Researches into the Phenomenology of the Self*, vol. 9/2 of *The Collected Works of C.G. Jung*, edited and translated by Gerhard Adler and R.F.C. Hull (New York: Pantheon Books, 1959), § 377f; also *Psychology and Alchemy*, vol. 12 of *The Collected Works of C.G. Jung*, translated by R.F.C. Hull (Princeton: Princeton University Press, 1968), § 167, footnote 44; also "The Visions of Zosimos." In: *Alchemical Studies*, vol. 13 of *The Collected Works of C.G. Jung*, translated by R.F.C. Hull (Princeton: Princeton University Press, 1967), § 113ff; also "Paracelsus as a Spiritual Phenomenon." In: *Alchemical Studies*, CW 13, § 185f; also *Mysterium Coniunctionis*, vol. 14 of *The Collected Works of C.G. Jung*, translated by R.F.C. Hull (Princeton: Princeton University Press, 1970), § 8-12.

sees a small circle with a bigger A. It represents – as the accompanying text says – the alchemical vessel. This vessel has, as the text explains, a certain name. It is called pelican.

Often the alchemists gave their vessels names according to their form. And the pelican was always depicted so that his neck and his long beak describe a circle (picture 2).[10] But when the alchemical vessel is called pelican, it is not only this round form or circle that is addressed. Also addressed is a dynamic motion, a process, that proceeds with circling, circulating or rotating within itself. This circular motion is important. It is caused by a fire or by a source of heat beneath the alchemical vessel.

Thus, just imagine the circle, that is the mandala on the gravestone of Marie-Louise von Franz, fourfold divided with the small circle in the center, thereto the seven letters (picture 3). I assume one can recognize that the stone at the cemetery in Küsnacht corresponds to the illustration of the alchemical vessel, that is the pelican in the *Tractatus aureus*. And as I mentioned, the illustration represents not only the alchemical vessel, in which the alchemical process takes place, but also the process itself, that is its dynamic motion. Yes, this little depiction represents – we will come to this later – the beginning and the aim of the whole alchemical work, the opus. "One is the stone, one the medicine, one the vessel, one the method, and one the disposition."[11] This sentence comes from the beginning of the *Rosarium philosophorum* and quite well gives expression to my opinion of what the gravestone of Marie-Louise von Franz and Barbara Hannah represents.

Of course, equating the picture of the pelican in the *Tractatus aureus* with the circle or mandala of the gravestone of Marie-Louise von Franz and Barbara Hannah is a hypothesis. But this hypothesis seems reasonable to me and I will, on trust that it fits, build upon it in my interpretation. Thus in the following, we will look firstly at the pelican, that is the bird and its symbolic meaning, then we will look at the depiction in the accompanying

---

10 Picture 2: Depiction of the pelican respectively the alchemical vessel: Johannes Rhenanus, *Solis e puteo emergentis sive dissertationis chymothechnicae libri tres*, Frankfurt 1613; corresponds to picture B7 in C.G. Jung, *Alchemical Studies*, CW 13 (following p. 152).

11 C.G. Jung, *Psychology and Alchemy*, CW 12, § 404, footnote 12; Joachim Telle (ed.) *Rosarium philosophorum. Ein alchemisches Florilegium des Spätmittelalters* [Rosarium philosophorum. An alchemical Florilegium of the late Middle Ages], facsimile reproduction of the first edition Frankfurt 1550, vol. 1 (Weinheim: Verlagsgesellschaft Weinheim, 1992), p. 5.

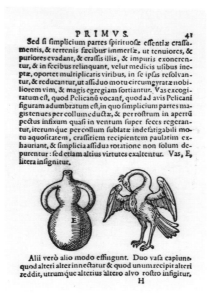

Picture 2: The Pelican and the alchemical vessel

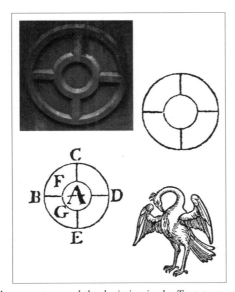

Picture 3: The gravestone and the depiction in the *Tractatus aureus* combined

text in the *Tractatus aureus*, as well as some alchemical pictures. In the last part I will look at the inscription on the gravestone. Possibly both levels cover the same mystery, one in the form of an "image," the sculpture, the other in form of a text, the inscription.

The Legend of the Pelican

Pelican is the name of the alchemical vessel that is depicted in the *Tractatus aureus*. With this name a certain form of the distillation apparatus is addressed as we have seen. But the alchemical vessel was never only a technological instrument. What the alchemists saw and experienced in their vessel were their own, inner psychic processes. Thus the alchemical vessel, in which the processes took place, became something psychic or alive, in any case something of highest value for them.

One can compare it with the chalice or the plate for the Host in the rite of the catholic mass. Both are vessels as well, in which a transformation takes place. Earthly substances, bread, water, wine are transformed into divine substances in order to be given later to men. Believers bind themselves to and become one with the divine. But the vessels in which the process of transformation of the substances takes place, the chalice or the patena, are holy objects, precious and made of gold and silver. During ordinary times they are kept at a special place, the tabernacle, which is carefully locked. The tabernacle also is a vessel and often is created like a little house. The divine substances are living beings dwelling within this house.

Now, often one can see on the tabernacles the depiction of a pelican, which sits in its nest and opens its breast with its beak, in order to restore its young offspring to life with the blood that flows out of its heart.[12] Since the earliest Christian centuries the pelican was understood always as an allegory of Christ. Christ allowed himself to be wounded and sacrificed himself while hanging on the cross. His blood was shed in order to bring new life to men, with the meaning of new spiritual life. In the same way the pelican sacrificed its blood for its dead offspring, which according to the legend, had been killed before, either by a snake or by their own parents. After three days of mourning, it says in the *Physiologus*, the pelican tears

12 For the following see Christoph Gerhardt, *Die Metamorphosen des Pelikan. Exempel und Auslegung in der mittelalterlichen Literatur* [Metamorphoses of the Pelican. Examples and interpretations in the literature of the Middle Ages] (Frankfurt/Bern/Las Vegas: Verlag Peter Lang, 1979), p. 137 and pp. 160-162.

up its breast with its beak and thus with its running blood brings the dead young birds back to life again.[13] Therefore we find depictions of the pelican not only on tabernacles. Often the nest with the bird and the little offspring also can be seen either under or on the foot of the cross,[14] or above the cross on the vertical beam. Thus the cross becomes a tree for the bird and his nest (plate 4, p. 228).[15]

The symbolic representation of the pelican, that, alongside Christ on the Cross, sacrifices itself for its offspring, led in the middle ages to the idea that the long beak of the pelican, with which the bird injures itself was identified with the Holy Lance of Longinus. This lance inflicted the fourth and strongest wound, namely the wound to the side of the suffering Christ, out of which according to the Bible ran blood and water. In the middle ages, especially in the writings of the mystics, the Lance of Longinus and the wound to Christ's side always were interpreted as an arrow of love, and respectively, according to the words in the *Song of Songs*, as a wound of love: "You have ravished my heart, my sister, my bride, you have ravished my heart with a glance of your eyes."[16] Likewise the pelican could become a symbol for a human being in a deep love, who wounds him- or herself and opens the breast or the heart in his or her love to God but also to another human being since the pelican appears in the songs of the troubadours as well. Therefore the pelican that injures itself as well as the wound and the running blood symbolize love, longing, desire. It is a love that violates, annihilates, even kills, but which leads to new life as well. The dead offspring are restored to life again.[17]

---

13 *Physiologus. A Medieval Book of Nature Lore,* translated, with an introduction by Michael J. Curley (Chicago: The University of Chicago Press, 2009), pp. 9f.

14 See for instance the cross in the pilgrimage church in Hergiswald, Switzerland with the pelican and the nest under the cross. In: Dieter Bitterli, *Der Bilderhimmel von Hergiswald* [The pictures on the ceiling of the church in Hergiswald] (Basel: Wiese Verlag, 1999), p. 39. To the right and left of the nest one can read: "Factus sum pelicano solitudinis," "I became the pelican in its solitude," in accordance with Psalm 102:6 "Similis factus sum pellicano solitudinis," "I am like a pelican in the solitude."

15 Plate 4: Christ on the tree of life; on top the pelican with his offspring. *Psalter of Robert de Lisle,* ca. 1310, Ms. British Library, Arundel 83 II, fol. 125 v; for more examples see Chr. Gebhardt, *Die Metamorphosen des Pelikans* [The Metamorphoses of the Pelican], pp. 17-19 and pictures 2-6.

16 Song of Solomon 4:9.

17 In one of his songs the German mystic Angelus Silesius (1624-1677) describes the blood of the pelican as "rose-colored blood."
"Ach ja, ach du vergeust dein Rosen-farbnes Blut
Gleich wie ein Pelican für seine Küchlein thut...

The pelican as a symbol quite decisively represents a process of transformation, in which love is the driving force. The bird represents injury, annihilation or even death. But also the pelican represents renewal and resurrection. I would like to mention here, at this moment, the life of Marie-Louise von Franz and also of Barbara Hannah. Surely both women oriented their whole lives to such a transforming love, which leads to wholeness. Both had placed this love as a focal point at the center of their lives and probably sacrificed a lot for it. And so it is meaningful that the pelican – although hidden and symbolical, but still – appears on their gravestone.

The Pelican in Alchemy

Earlier I have compared the alchemical vessel with the chalice and the patena in the Catholic mass. But the comparison is not quite correct. Indeed, in both places transformation takes place. Both places are connected with living substances. But when the unknown author of the *Rosarium philosophorum* says: "One is the stone, one the remedy, one the vessel, one the procedure and one the disposition" then the hermetic vessel is much more than a concrete item or a concrete apparatus. Beyond that it is something psychic, meaning a psychic realm or a psychic state. Actually the vessel represents the alchemist himself. The alchemist as a normal human being, through his endeavour to create a vessel for his substances, he himself becomes a vessel. In any case it seems that the act of establishing, building, finding and saving such a space or a vessel in and of itself becomes a medicine or a remedy.

The alchemist Gerhard Dorneus (1530/34-ca.1584) said that the alchemical vessel has to be built from the squaring the circle.[18] Squaring the circle, as we know, is an impossibility. It can be accomplished only approximately,

Ists dis du süesser Gott, ists dis mein Pelican?
So fülle doch mein Hertz und Seel darmit gantz an,
Und wandle mich in dich."
[Alas, oh well you waste your rose-colored blood/ As does the pelican for his little chick.../ Is this, is this you, sweet God?/ Is this my pelican?/ Thus fill my heart and soul with it quite whole and alter me in you.] Chr. Gebhardt, *Die Metamorphosen des Pelikans* [The metamorphoses of the Pelican], p. 93. This reminds one at the rose-coloured blood of the alchemists and their idea that in the last days the "putissimus homo," a "most pure" respectively a "most true" man will appear on earth. He will exude a healing and redeeming tincture or the rose-coloured blood. C.G. Jung, "The Philosophical Tree." In: *Alchemical Studies*, CW 13, § 383-391.

18 C.G. Jung, "The Visions of Zosimos." CW 13, § 115.

never completely. Therefore building the vessel is as difficult or – more precisely – impossible as creating the stone or the healing tincture. C.G. Jung describes very well what is about it psychologically. He says:

> It is essentially a psychic operation, the creation of an inner readiness to accept the archetype of the self in whatever subjective form it appears. Dorn calls the vessel the *vas pellicanicum* and says that with its help the quinta essentia can be extracted from the prima materia. The anonymous author of the scholia to the "Tractatus aureus Hermetis" says: "This vessel is the true philosophical pelican, and there is none other to be sought for in all the world." It is the lapis itself and at the same time contains it; that is to say, the self is its own container.[19]

"It is ... the creation of an inner readiness to accept" – or literally "to host," "to receive" – "the archetype of the self," Jung wrote. Obviously this inner readiness is not naturally or self evidently given to us in our concrete, reality based, earthly life. We have to create it, namely as something solid and stable, not as something that disappears when faced with every little disturbance. Without feeling, without devotion, without love it is not possible. Thus when the pelican becomes the symbol for the alchemical vessel, when through its love for its dead offspring it sacrifices itself in order to revive them back to life with its blood, then it seems to me that this bird represents an image for the right attitude or the right spirit of the alchemist in relation to his work or his opus. It was C.G. Jung's explicit concern to demonstrate that the alchemical process corresponds to the process of individuation.[20] As expressed in psychological language the pelican, in a general way, would represent the right attitude towards the process of individuation, the "inner readiness" as Jung put it, to become a vessel for the self. Or as we could also say, to become a solid and reliable vessel, in which God or the Divine can dwell in us.

We have seen that in the Christian context as in alchemy the pelican represents transformation and renewal, as well as death and resurrection.

19 Ibid.
20 C.G. Jung, "The Psychology of the Transference." In: *Practice of Psychotherapy*, vol. 16 of *The Collected Works of C.G. Jung*, translated by R.F.C. Hull. (Princeton: Princeton University Press, 1966) § 531: "This almighty taskmaster is none other than the self. The self wants to be made manifest in the work, and for this reason the opus is a process of individuation, a becoming of a self." See also: C.G. Jung, "The Philosophical Tree." CW 13, § 393.

Now, in alchemy the transformer is not Christ, the Son of God who came into this world without sin. Nor is it the believing man who strives to follow this God. In alchemy it is the earthly man that is changed, the inferior man, the man who is linked with the earth and with the body. And when I say "man," I mean the greater man or woman in us, not just our personal ego. On the gravestone of C.G. Jung we can read: "Primus homo de terra – terrenus," "the first man is from the earth – earthly." Actually this is Adam. Adam is the first man. Also he is the terrestrial man. We all share with him through our shadow, our body or our affective and emotional life. It is important that we don't identify with him or her, but know that this inferior man in us is something bigger than we. He also is a God. In alchemy it is Mercurius. C.G. Jung called him the spirit of the unconscious. At first he appears as overwhelming darkness, as shadow, chaos or *massa confusa* in the alchemical work. This material, this psychic state wants to be transformed. It is that *prima materia* out of which according to the words of Dorneus the *quinta essentia* can be extracted by the help of the "vas pellicanicum." Dorneus says "by the help of the vessel." Thus the vessel, the "vas pellicanicum" is not just a container or a box. It is something active and alive. It mobilizes something. It generates that out of the primordial chaos, through a rotating and circulating process of distillation something of an utmost psychic value, namely the *quinta essentia* will be extracted. This means, it becomes conscious and it can be experienced.

And what this actually means I will try to explain in the following passage.

The text in the *Tractatus aureus*

As mentioned above the mandala on the gravestone of Marie-Louise von Franz and Barbara Hannah corresponds to the depiction of the alchemical vessel or the "pelican" in the *Tractatus aureus* (picture 3). Preceding this little depiction is a longer text, in which the author tries to explain "the mystery of the pelican."[21] As it is the case with most of the alchemical texts it seems confusing at first. But I think the interpretation of the text can help to understand better the extraction of the *essentia quinta* and with this also the pelican and the mandala with its seven letters.

---

21 The text, discussed in the following, corresponds to page 442 r, see picture 1.

But to begin with I should say some words about the *Tractatus aureus* in general. It is a special text. It consists on the one hand of quotations, which are attributed to the great guiding figure of the alchemists, namely Hermes Trismegistos and on the other of so-called *scholia*. These are shorter respectively longer commentaries to these quotations.[22] The Hermes quotations are very old. They go back to an Arabic source. Thus they are Latin translations from Arabic.[23] Now, the commentator, who explains extensively these quotations, is an unknown alchemist from France, obviously a follower of Paracelsus, who lived in the 16th or at the beginning of the 17th century.[24]

This unknown alchemist begins now in the course of the seventh and last chapter to explain what the "great and difficult mystery of the pelican" really means. Initially he speaks of the "ardently desired blue or celestial colour" that should appear in the vessel that is locked with the "seal of Hermes."[25] However this "seal of Hermes" is not wax or resin or cork, clay or even paste, but a certain firm "dispositio naturae." The word "dispositio" means arrangement or order. However C.G. Jung translates it also as "disposition."[26] Likewise a certain "natural order" or "disposition according to nature" shall close the philosophical vessel. I think with this a psychic conduct is meant, an attitude which holds things within, just "sealed" as long as this "ardently desired blue or celestial colour" appears. Strangely enough this blue colour which must be a dark, even almost a black blue,[27] is

---

22 Jean J. Manget (ed.), *Bibliotheca chemica curiosa (Bibl. chem.)*, vol. 2, pp. 400-445; also L. Zetzner, *Theatrum chemicum*, vol. 4, pp. 592-705. Under the title *Septem tractatus seu capitula Hermetis Trismegisti, aurei* one can find the quotations of Hermes without the *scholia* in the composite manuscript *Ars Chemica*, vol. 1, pp. 7-31.

23 C.G. Jung, "Paracelsus as a Spiritual Phenomenon." CW 13, § 184, footnote 66: "The 'Tractatus aureus' is of Arabic origin, but its content dates back to much older sources. It may have been transmitted by the Harranite school." According to Telle the history of the *Tractatus aureus* "is unknown." "Profound inquiries are missing." Joachim Telle, *Alchemie und Poesie* [Alchemy and Poesy], vol. 1 (Berlin: Walter de Gruyter, 2013), p. 233f and footnote 41.

24 In the composite manuscript of Manget the year of publication is 1608 (p. 401). Bachmann / Hofmeier say that the tractatus since 1566 was printed "several times." Manuel Bachmann and Thomas Hofmeier, *Geheimnisse der Alchemie* [Mysteries of Alchemy] (Basel: Schwabe Verlag, 1999), p. 68.

25 *Bibl. chem.*, vol. 1, p. 442 r.

26 C.G. Jung, *Psychology and Alchemy*, CW 12, § 404, footnote 12; see above p. 96.

27 The Latin word *Cyaneus* corresponds to the Greek *kyanos* and means a dark blue, also the dark metal flow or the blue glass flow, ultramarine. This is why I do not use here the English translation "cerulean" in C.G. Jung's *Mysterium Conciunctionis*, CW 14, § 11, which indicates more a shining blue colour.

equated with the blood of the pelican, by which it revives its dead offspring back to life. The text says:

> Finally, there will appear in the work that ardently desired blue or celestial colour, which does not darken or dull the eyes of the beholder by the healing power of its brilliance, as when we see the splendour of the outward sun. Rather does it sharpen and strengthen them, nor does he… slay a man with his glance…, but by shedding of his own blood he calls back those who are near to death, and restores to them unimpaired their former life, like the pelican.[28]

Thus the blood of the pelican must be something like a "spiritual blood," a kind of a spiritual-psychic substance, which appears so to say in the nocturnal depth of the inner sky. Through its brilliance, that is through something shining it effects healing. The brilliance does not darken the sight of the beholder as the sun does, but sharpens and strengthens it and calls back to life, that which is near to death.

Here I think of the light of the feminine wisdom in the unconscious. And so this "ardently desired blue or celestial colour" would represent an understanding and knowing that comes from *Sophia* or *Sapientia*, healing and consoling and by this calling back to life. "*Sophia* is endlessly consoling," Marie-Louise von Franz once said. Therefore the blue colour and its brilliance must express a healing and consoling factor of most precious psychic value. And strangely enough in this text it is equated with the pelican and its blood. The text continues:[29]

> Namely, one says of the pelican, that she tears up her own breast with her beak, which is curved like a circle, and moistens her own dead offspring with the running blood and thus restores them back to life. Therefore the alchemists have a certain distilling apparatus, which shows the round form of this circle of the pelican. But one must remind the researcher of the true art concerning the pelican, that a great and difficult mystery was hidden within her by the philosophers. Thus as the pelican is a living bird and not dead, the philosophers also demand living bodies for their work and will not accept dead bodies, but spiritual ones and gifted with the highest plenitude of life forces. Namely, as the

28 *Bibl. chem.*, vol. 1, p. 442 r; also C.G. Jung, *Mysterium Coniunctionis*, CW 14, § 11.
29 *Bibl. chem.*, vol. 1, p. 442 r; my translation, except it is mentioned especially.

blood running out of the breast restores life to the dead fledgling, so does the greenness of our red lion awaken life that lies dormant in the dead and dark bodies of the metals and restores them to their former splendour and brilliance. And as finally the blood does not flow out until a circle or an orbit is made by the pelican herself before – "for when she applies her beak to her breast, her whole neck with the beak is bent into the shape of a circle"[30] – so the artifex is not able to call forth the true and tincturing blood of the lion, unless first occurs "the circulation of spirits" or the "circular distillation"[31]...

Two things are compared with each other, the pelican, who tears up its breast with its beak in order to bring back to life the dead fledglings and the alchemical vessel for distillation, which shows the same round form as the neck and the beak of the bird. However, when the text says: "But one must remind the researcher of the true art concerning the pelican, that a great and difficult mystery was hidden within her by the philosophers," then it is not clear if the author speaks about the pelican as a bird or if he speaks about the vessel, which shares the same name as the bird. It seems to be clear that a secret is hidden in this vessel, a "mysterium." And this secret concerns the bodies in the vessel, their transformation from dead bodies to living ones. These dead bodies in the vessel are also called "dead and dark bodies of the metals." Thus, the text deals with the transformation of metals. This transformation seems to be a great mystery. What does this mean?

The Transformation of the Metals

In alchemy each of the seven metals or ores, that is tin, copper, lead, iron, gold, silver and quicksilver, are attributed to the seven planets.[32] It is even said, that the planets with their rays of light constantly weave the metals or ores within the earth by circling around the earth. Psychologically the planets in heaven symbolize eternal constants of human personality. We can say, that Saturn, Mars, Venus, Luna, the moon and so on, are archetypal powers, which eternally determine human life. They are gods or divinities in heaven. But the metals, that belong one each to the planets, are their

30 C.G. Jung, *Mysterium Coniunctionis*, CW 14, § 8, footnote 40.
31 C.G. Jung, *Psychology and Alchemy*, CW 12, § 167, footnote 44.
32 Marie-Louise von Franz, *Alchemy. An Introduction to the Symbolism and the Psychology* (Toronto: Inner City Books, 1980), p. 220.

earthly equivalents. On a practical level – and now I refer to Marie-Louise von Franz's interpretation in her book *Alchemy*[33] – this means: when you fall in love with someone, a man or a woman, then Venus in her earthly aspect, namely as living psychic copper, manifests in your life. Or when you are overwhelmed by a huge negative emotion, tortured by a fury or hatred to someone, than "Mars has fallen into matter" as von Franz puts it.[34] Thus the whole problem of aggression then appears in the other person in a disturbing way. In other words, the relationships between the planets in heaven and the metals on earth have something to do with the process of projection.

But what does it mean now when in our text the metals are called "dead and dark bodies," in which lies dormant some kind of life, which is described as "spiritual" and "gifted with the highest plenitude of life forces"? What are or who are these dead bodies in the vessel? Maybe it seems paradoxical, but seen psychologically this means a situation when we are caught in projections, that is, when we experience Mars or Venus or some other planets as earthly, material metal bodies. They "have fallen into matter." In such a situation our whole libido flows outwards to the outer world. Our surroundings are completely alive, highest psychic values are experienced on the outside, but accordingly the metal bodies within us, within our psychic vessel are dead since the whole psychic energy or libido flows to the outside. For instance this can mean, that a beloved person, to whom we are very deeply connected emotionally, suddenly in a dream appears as deceased, that is, the unconscious says he or she has died. Such a dream psychologically means that everything that the beloved person represents in us, all these psychic values are dead. And it is important to bring these values back to life, similar to the alchemist who has to revivify the dead metal bodies in his vessel.

Therefore, this "great and difficult secret," about which the text speaks, would mean to revivify the dead psychic life in us or – expressed in psychological language – to retract projections which are fixed on the outside and to bring into consciousness inner images and contents, that are hidden within the projections. Marie-Louise von Franz describes very well that this is not at all an easy thing and that it needs a lot of time.[35] It can be a process over many years, a distillation process, which has to be performed

33 M.-L. von Franz, *Alchemy*, p. 220.
34 Ibid., p. 221.
35 Ibid., p. 222.

again and again, in which the initially dead bodies in our psychic vessel are transformed into "spiritual bodies," "gifted with the highest plenitude of life forces." Such a withdrawal of projections would mean that Venus or the living copper in us more and more has the effect that we feel replete and alive. Similarly, Mars or the living iron in us transforms more and more into a positive and creative energy and so on. This often repeated process of distillation, that means this patient work on the disturbing projections, repeated over and over again, finally allows – provided that everything goes well – the unification "of all the autonomous, collective components of the personality into an inner whole."[36] This inner wholeness is the aim of the alchemical process. It is the lapis or the healing medicine, the tincture or the quintessence. It is also the solid and indestructible vessel, that – as the alchemists hoped – even endures death.

Now, the text speaks about the "greenness of the red lion." It awakens the metals to life. And this greenness or *viriditas* of the red lion is compared with the blood of the pelican, which runs out of her breast. Blood means psychic life. The *Aurora Consurgens* says: "For the seat of the soul is in the blood, as Senior saith."[37] Now, according to our text, when the pelican wishes to bring her offspring back to life, she must first form a circle or become a circle. In addition the alchemist can only "call forth the true and tincturing blood of the lion" – which is equated to the greenness or *viriditas* – when the "circulation of the spirits" or "the circular distillation" previously has taken place. For me, this "circulation of the spirits" represents thoughtful pondering, circling, rotating, contemplating, recollecting, reflecting and studying in the way of the pelican, that is in a loving or related attitude or approach. The *distillatio circulatoria* has to take place in the spirit of the pelican, that is with Eros.

But what is the red lion and what is his greenness? I think we may identify the red lion as a most powerful desire or most intensive, fierce libido. The lion is the king of the animals. He is an animal full of power. The forces that he represents are fiery and of the strongest nature. We have seen that when such an intensive desire is directed to the outside – and that is the normal condition at the beginning –, then the metal bodies in the vessel are dead. But they should become alive, which means to become "spiritual." And as an alternative to "spiritual" we also can say "psychic" or

36 Marie-Louise von Franz, *Aurora Consurgens. A Document attributed to Thomas Aquinas on the Problem of Opposites in Alchemy* (Toronto: Inner City Books, 2000), p. 235.
37 M.-L. von Franz, *Aurora Consurgens*, p. 85; also M.-L. von Franz, *Alchemy*, p. 244.

"soulful." And for this transformation of the dead substances or bodies into something psychic or living the greenness, that is the *viriditas*, is needed.

In the fifth chapter of *Mysterium Coniunctionis* we find a short text out of the *Uralt Chymisches Werk* of Abraham Eleazar from 1760, in which a completely dark female figure, calling herself Shulamith asks, or better cries, for redemption. This black Shulamith corresponds to the beloved woman in the Song of Songs. But seen alchemically it is the *massa confusa* in the vessel, those black substances, which long to be transformed and redeemed. Thus, the *massa confusa*, this black unredeemed product of transformation is a living creature. Again and again she calls desperately for her beloved till finally she says about her:

> What shall I say? I am alone among the hidden; nevertheless I rejoice in my heart, because I can live privily, and refresh myself in myself. But under my blackness I have hidden the fairest green.[38]

"But under my blackness I have hidden the fairest green." C.G. Jung comments on this in really wonderful words. He says:

> It is the state of someone who, in his wanderings among the mazes of his psychic transformation, comes upon a secret happiness which reconciles him to his apparent loneliness. In communing with himself he finds not deadly boredom and melancholy but an inner partner; more than that, a relationship that seems like the happiness of a secret love, or like a hidden springtime, when the green seed sprouts from the barren earth, holding out promise of future harvests. It is the alchemical *benedicta viriditas*, the blessed greenness, signifying... the secret immanence of the divine spirit of life in all things. "O blessed greenness, which generatest all things!" cries the author of the *Rosarium*.[39]

Thus the alchemical *viriditas* means the exhilarating experience of a divine spirit of life in all things. Initially it is an inner experience that occurs "in communing with himself" as Jung says or – according to our text – in the process of the *destillatio circulatoria*, which, as in the spirit of the pelican, only can take place in an uttermost carefully locked vessel. The alchemist Johan Daniel Mylius (1585-ca.1628) describes the *viriditas* as a "virtue of

38 C.G. Jung, *Mysterium Coniunctionis*, CW 14, § 622.
39 Ibid., § 623.

generation," that God "breathed into all created things."[40] This "virtue of generation" is, according to Mylius, the *anima mundi*, the "Soul of the World."[41] This means, that the *viriditas* corresponds to a vital spirit or a living power which at the beginning is experienced in deep introversion, within the inner or psychic realm, but which also extends to outer nature and even to inorganic mater.

In 1939, while working on his lectures on the *Spiritual Exercises* of Ignatius Loyola and at the same time preparing his book *Psychology and Alchemy*, C.G. Jung had a vision.[42] I saw, as he said "bathed in bright light at the foot of my bed the figure of Christ on the Cross." It was "extremely distinct," he continues "and I saw that his body was made of greenish gold. The vision was marvelously beautiful, and yet I was profoundly shaken by it." C.G. Jung recognized, that the vision wanted to show him something important, namely "the analogy of Christ with the *aurum non vulgi* and the *viriditas* of the alchemists" and that he had experienced "an essentially alchemical vision of Christ." He continues:

> The green gold is the living quality which the alchemists saw not only in man but also in inorganic nature. It is an expression of the life-spirit, the *anima mundi* or *filius macrocosmi*, the Anthropos who animates the whole cosmos. This spirit has poured himself out into everything, even into inorganic matter; he is present in metal and stone. My vision was thus a union of the Christ-image with his analogue in matter, the *filius macrocosmi*.

The *destillatio circulatoria* or the Circling of the Spirits

Now, the *viriditas* in our text is very closely connected with the red lion. She even corresponds to the blood of the lion, with "the true and tincturing blood of the lion."[43] Psychologically this means, that just in the fiercest and greatest torturing emotions and affects lie the vital germs of a future experience of the *viriditas*. It is an enlivening, inspiring, fulfilling divine "virtue of generation" "in all created things" as Mylius says, which means also within

---

40 Here the translation follows the original German text.
41 C.G. Jung, *Mysterium Coniunctionis*, CW 14, § 623.
42 In the following Aniela Jaffé (ed.), *Memories, Dreams, Reflections by C.G. Jung* (London: Fontana Press, 1995), pp. 236f.
43 See above, p. 105.

us, given that previously – and I refer to the text – "the circulation of spirits or the circular distillation" has already taken place.[44] In order to clarify the connections once more: "the true and tincturing blood of the lion," that is the manifestation of the *viriditas* in our text is equated with the blood of the pelican, which before has torn up its breast with its beak. An enormous sacrifice is connected with this process along with an equally great distress. Since the pelican has lost its fledglings, it means the whole meaning of its life has been lost. In such a situation to tear up one's own breast or heart, means to give up all fixed concepts and also all hardening in order to be really open for such a circulation process within; in order to devote oneself with an open heart so to speak to this purifying, distilling and transforming process.

Let us come now to this "circulation of spirits" or to the "circular distillation." The anonymous author of the text continues:

> ... so the artifex is not able to call forth the true and tincturing blood of the lion, unless first occurs the "circulation of spirits or the circular distillation," "that is the outside should set in motion to the inside, the inside to the outside," likewise the lower upwards and the upper downwards, so that the outside and the inside, the lower and the upper all come together in one circle and you no longer recognize, "what was outside or inside, or lower, or upper: but all would be one in one circle or vessel." For this vessel is the true philosophical pelican, and no other is to be sought in all the universe. And without this all false alchemists work in vain.[45]

Looking more closely at this circling, rotating motion of exchange, it seems to be clear that the aim of all this motion is the "true philosophical pelican," that is the alchemical vessel as a stable inner realm. Nevertheless the motion is not going in just one direction, not only toward the inside. And even if it seems to be clear as well that the aim is something psychic or spiritual – sought are "living spiritual bodies" – it is not only a process of sublimation that is demanded. The motion goes up and down or back and

---

44 As an example see C.G. Jung's own experience. He realised, that in his emotions important inner images are hidden. Whenever he succeeded to find the constellated images, "the unrest or the sense of oppression vanished." C.G. Jung, *Memories*, p. 212.
45 *Bibl. chem.*, vol. 1, p. 442 r; see also C.G. Jung, *Psychology and Alchemy*, CW 12, § 167, footnote 44; also C.G. Jung, "The Visions of Zosimos." CW 13, § 115.

forth. The outside should not only come to the inside, the inside should come as well to the outside. And the lower should not only brought to the upper, the upper should also be brought down to the lower. This means that it is not only introspection that belongs to the process of individuation. We must not only look to our inner world. Sometimes it is also necessary to be confronted with the outer world; to be confronted with concrete reality and with other people in order to become truly conscious of certain disturbing projections. Of course, such a confrontation can be shameful. We will get ourselves into hot water. Also, what we have understood as a psychological fact within us – this would be something on a higher or conscious level – this should be confronted again and again with "the lower," in other words with our concrete physical and psychic reality. Does, what I have discovered or what I have brought to a conscious level, does this resist the concrete reality or is it necessary to look at the problem once again on a deeper level?

The aim of the whole process is "that all come together in one circle." This means, that everything becomes a whole. Connected with this is a transformation. Since when everything – and with this the primordial "massa confusa" is meant – has become so much one, that one can no longer recognize "what was outside or inside, or lower or upper," then the initial separated or even dissociated psychic parts within us have become one firm wholeness, namely the circle of the pelican. And with this also the vessel is built, "the true philosophical pelican," about which is said, that "no other is to be sought in all the universe." For the alchemists the stone, the lapis, the healing tincture and the vessel are various representations of one and the same mystery.[46] In psychological language it is the self, the impercievable wholeness of men. Marie-Louise von Franz speaks of "the goal of individuation," of "images of supreme value" in this context. When during the process of individuation of an individual such images appear[47] they represent "a kind of mid-point or center in which the supreme value and the greatest life-intensity are concentrated."[48] They cannot be distinguished from images of God in the various religions. They are images of the self or of the divine inner man. Marie-Louise von Franz continues:

46 "One is the stone, one the medicine, one the vessel..." See C.G. Jung, *Psychology and Alchemy*, CW 12, § 404, footnote 12.
47 For instance as castle, four-square city or garden, four-petalled flower, as star, crystal, stone, light, vessel.
48 M.-L. von Franz, *C.G. Jung. His Myth in our Time*, p. 73.

The experience of this highest end, or center, brings the individual an inner certainty, peace and sense of meaning and fulfillment, in the presence of which he can accept himself and find a middle way between the opposites in his inner nature. Instead of being a fragmented person who has to cling to collective supports, he now becomes a self-reliant whole human being who no longer needs to live like a parasite of his collective environment, but who enriches it and strengthens it by his presence. The experience of the Self brings a feeling of standing on solid ground inside oneself, on a patch of inner eternity which even physical death cannot touch.[49]

I think that after these words we can understand better our unknown author of the text when he almost exaltingly proclaims: "For this vessel is the true philosophical pelican and no other is to be sought in all the universe." And subsequently, in order to make it really clear to the reader what he means, he offers the image of the mandala with the seven letters as an example of this miraculous vessel. He says: "But in order that these things are better understood, it had pleased us to attach the following figure" (picture 4) and than he explains:

A is the inside as it were the origin and source from which the other letters flow, and likewise the final goal to which all others flow back as the rivers flow into the ocean or into the great sea. B.C.D.E. These four letters signify the outside, C.F. the above, E.G. the below. All these letters together in their wholeness A.B.C.D.E.F.G. clearly signify the hidden magical Septenary. At another place we have spoken about it in detail,[50] so that it is superfluous to say more about it here.[51]

---

49 Ibid., p. 74.
50 Namely in the second chapter of the text; *Bibl. chem.*, vol. 1, p. 418 l.
51 *Bibl. chem.*, vol 1, p. 442 r and p. 443 l; also C.G. Jung, *Mysterium Coniunctionis*, CW 14, § 9.

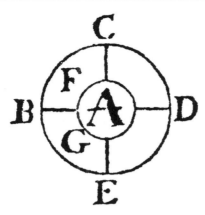

Picture 4: The alchemical vessel as a mandala

What we can see here is a mandala with seven letters. The letters are not evenly distributed. The outer letters prevail. As the author explains they flow like water out of a well to the outside. The well is in the middle the little circle with the A. The four outer letters shall now circulate with the two others, the above and the below (F and G) as long as they all have been flowed back into the center "as in the ocean or in the great sea." One might see expressed in this mandala the whole of human life as well as the individuation process of the individual. Indeed human life is a continuous cycle of repeated unfolding to the outside world and return to the source at its innermost being.

Now, the four outer letters of the mandala indicate that this unfolding to the outside or extraversion prevails and the goal, namely the return to the center lies ahead. All letters should flow back into the inner circle as the rivers return to the great sea. Therefore the center is both, the source or well, from which everything emerges and the ocean or the sea to which everything will go. In one way it is small and restricted yet at the same time it is infinitely large and open. As ocean or sea it expresses the infinite in us, the "limitlessness of the unconscious" as C.G. Jung puts it in *Memories, Dreams, Reflections*. It can only be experienced when we are "bounded to the utmost" as Jung says:

> The greatest limitation for man is the "self"; it is manifested in the experience: "I am *only* that!" Only consciousness of our narrow confinement in the self forms the link to the limitlessness of the unconscious. In such

awareness we experience ourselves concurrently as limited and eternal, as both the one and the other. In knowing ourselves to be unique in our personal combination – that is ultimately limited – we possess also the capacity for becoming conscious of the infinite, but only then![52]

Therefore it seems, that the return the middle or to the inside, into the small circle of one's own, unique essence is the unalterable precondition of the eternal, the timeless and the unlimited in us, of the encounter with the self. In this context Marie-Louise von Franz speaks about the "shut chamber of the heart" or the "secret source of life."[53] Here in this center, where we are unique, lies also the secret of our entity, the mystery of *what* we are and not *who* we are. Also the source of all our creative impulses or unexpected creative reactions lays here. Marie-Louis von Franz expresses it very beautifully when she says: "… for ultimately the individual is a unique and closed system, a unique thing which centres round a… source of life."[54]

In this sense the mandala with the seven letters on the inside would express the entire, individuated personality, who as "a unique and closed system… centres round a source of life." This source of life is Mercurius.[55] It is the little circle in the middle with the A. Mercurius with all its opposites is, as C.G. Jung writes, an image for the mystical experience of the artifex during his work. "As such he represents on the one hand the self and on the other the individuation process and, because of the limitless number of his names, also the collective unconscious."[56] Here in this text he is called "septenarius," "hidden magical Septenary." This "living seventh" contains – actually as does the eight – all the other letters as a whole in itself, however on a new level that is transformed and inside. Mercurius, we could say, is the beginning of the process, the source of life. Out of it everything is initiated. He is the process itself, which here leads over various levels. But he is the goal as well, namely the eight, by containing within himself all the remaining seven letters together in anew form.

---

52 A. Jaffé (ed.), *Memories, Dreams, Reflections by C.G. Jung*, pp. 357f.
53 M.-L. von Franz, *Alchemy*, p. 159.
54 Ibid., pp. 159f.
55 See C.G. Jung, *Mysterium Coniunctionis*, CW 14, § 9. Here Jung compares the little circle in the middle with the picture of the fountain of Mercurius in the *Rosarium philosophorum*. He quotes also from the first chapter of the *Tractatus aureus*, where Mercurius is depicted as a rotating circle in a square (*Bibl. chem.*, vol. 1, p. 408 r).
56 One of these names is "mare nostrum." C.G. Jung, "The Spirit Mercurius," CW 13, § 284, footnote 1.

It is striking how much the mandala in the *Tractatus aureus* resembles the front face of Jung's stone in Bollingen (plate 5, p. 229). We can see two circles as well, a small one and a bigger one. Here also the bigger circle is divided fourfold, however diagonally. Between the lines of the text we can find the six signs of the planets: Sun and Jupiter on the left side, Venus and Luna (the moon) on the right, Saturn and Mars above and below. But in the middle we can see the depiction of a small little man or a child with a lamp. On his coat is chiseled the astrological sign of Mercurius. As the text says, this little figure represents Telesphorus, the companion of Asclepios, the God of healing. Telesphorus denotes "the one who brings completeness" or "the one who guides to completeness." According to the text, that Jung had chiseled into the stone he is the divine child, the puer aeternus, who brings the new light and points to the future. The inscription reads:

> Time is a child – playing like a child – playing a board game – the kingdom of the child. This is Telesphoros, who roams through the dark regions of this cosmos and glows like a star out of the depth. He points the way to the gates of the sun and to the land of dreams.[57]

Telesphoros, the one who completes or the one who guides to the final goal, the divine child and the carrier of the new light, all this is closely tied to Mercurius and thus to the little circle with the A in the middle of the mandala in the *Tractatus aureus*. Only two details are different. On Jung's stone in Bollingen all notations are assembled inside the bigger circle, not outside. This points to a wholeness, which in the *Tractatus aureus* is mentioned only as a goal. Also the whole circle is framed and limited by a square. The square points to the earth and represents realization. Thus Jung's stone in Bollingen with the circle in the square would indicate, that a potential wholeness (the circle) has become a true reality in a human being, namely in C.G. Jung.

Let us come back to the seven letters in the circle or to the mandala in the *Tractatus aureus*. These letters should not simply be identified with the seven planets although this would be stand to reason. The anonymous author specifically chose letters although he just as easily could have chosen the signs of the planets. Furthermore these letters do not represent schematic signs. They are symbols. The Greek word for letter is *stoicheion*. But *stoicheia*

---

57 A. Jaffé (ed.), *Memories, Dreams, Reflections by C.G. Jung*, p. 254.

is also the word for the four elements, fire, water, air and earth. In antiquity the elements were Gods. Similarly, the 24 letters of the alphabet signify divine forces, eternal elements of meaning. In this context Marie-Louise von Franz speaks of "emanations of light."[58] Thus the seven letters in the pelican circle signify divine beings, "eternal entities" or archetypal patterns. Take for instance the four outer letters. Here one can think of the four cardinal points of the compass or the four elements, or the four functions, sensation, thinking, feeling and intuition. All of these are patterns depicting how man can behave towards his or her environment and also towards the inner world. But as stars in heaven they contain something resembling light, sparks of light. This means that each of these letters represent a divine power that conveys meaning.

All these seven letters should now be in a circling motion or a circulation, linking together in "one circle or vessel," that is to say to "the true philosophical pelican." In relation to the process of individuation this means, that the individual human being with its many differing, opposing, even dissociating psychic parts, which can push at one time from the inside, at another time from the outside, should become a circle or vessel by moving with a steady and patient "rotating circulation." In the little depiction of the *Tractatus aureus* the circle or the vessel are a mandala. "The mandala signifies the human or divine self," Jung writes in *Aion*, "the totality or vision of God."[59] It is an image of God. It represents the Godhead as a wholeness, which at the same time is the middle and the center. Gerhard Dorneus says "that nothing is more like God than the centre." For the center "cannot be grasped, seen, or measured." It "occupies no space." Therefore the center is "the nature of God."[60] Thus, in the center of a mandala dwells God. Here this is Mercurius, the spirit of the unconscious. He is the source, he is the sea. He is the stone, he is the circle. He is the alchemical vessel and the pelican. He is the whole alchemical work.

With this I come back to the gravestone of Marie-Louise von Franz and Barbara Hannah (plate 3, p. 227). What can we see here? We see the alchemical vessel, depicted as a mandala. It is called pelican, thus it means love, wound, sacrifice and new life. We see the beginning and the aim of

58 M.-L. von Franz, *Aurora Consurgens*, p. 330: "Hence, in alchemy, the stars were considered to be the twenty-four letters of a golden alphabet in the heavens, the 'heavenly crown' which unites all things."
59 C.G. Jung, *Aion*, CW 9/2, § 379.
60 C.G. Jung, "Paracelsus as a Spiritual Phenomenon." CW 13, § 186.

the alchemical process, as it is described in the *Tractatus aureus*. We can see also the center of this mandala, the little circle in the middle. In the middle of the mandala dwells the Godhead. According to the text of the *Tractatus aureus* this is Mercurius. This means that on the gravestone in the cemetery of Küsnacht we see a mandala in the center of which dwells Mercurius, the spirit of the unconscious. It is the spirit to whom Marie-Louise von Franz and Barbara Hannah committed their whole lives.

Alchemical Pictures of the Pelican

Before we come to the inscription of the gravestone I will look at three alchemical pictures depicting the nest with the pelican and its fledglings. The first (plate 6, p. 230) stems from a commentary of the *Aurora Consurgens*[61] and represents the work with the metals in the earth.[62] Two male figures in capuchin coats, maybe dwarfs or kabirs, one pictured in a red garment and the other clothed in a grey-blue are engaged in extracting the metals out of the earth. They are working with a blue-bladed pickax. Thus they are engaged in a psychic or spiritual procedure. To the right and high on a steep rock one sees the nest with the pelican and three fledglings eagerly opening their beaks. The pelican has positioned his neck and his beak into a circle. This refers to the alchemical process and the circling circulation or distillation. Obviously digging the metals out of the earth and working with the metals belong to this process, as it is described in the text of the *Tractatus aureus*.

The second picture (plate 7, p. 231) stems from the so-called *Alchemy handbook of the country doctor and surgeon Ulrich Ruosch from Appenzell*.[63] Indeed, it is a hand or pocket booklet. It is only 8 cm high and 6 cm wide. Obviously the country practitioner had put it in his pocket while traveling to his patients in the South of Germany or in the region of St. Gallen and the Lake Constance. In the middle part of this work one finds a series of

---

61 M.-L. von Franz, *Aurora Consurgens*, p. 5.
62 Plate 6: The work with the metals. *Codex Rhenovensis*, 15th century, Central Library Zurich, Ms. Rh. 172, p. 25. Under the picture, the title of the following, Chapter 29: "De qualitutibus singulorum metallorum," "From the natures of the single metals."
63 Plate 7: Rudolf Gamper and Thomas Hofmeier (eds.), *Das Alchemiehandbuch des Appenzeller Wundarztes Ulrich Ruosch* [The alchemy handbook of the country doctor and surgeon Ulrich Ruosch from Appenzell] (Basel: Schwabe Verlag, 2002), p. 37 (in the original p. 47 r). Ulrich Ruosch lived in the 17th century. The little booklet is in possession of the family Ruosch in Appenzell up to the present day.

twelve pictures illustrating the alchemical process. Each picture shows a vessel in front of a landscape. In the vessel one can see a liquid and also an astrological sign. At the top of the vessel appears a symbol representing the stage of the process. These stages are named: solution, putrefaction, fixation, multiplication and so on. In addition other texts can be seen.

The vessel with the pelican is the eighth in the series. In contrast to the other pictures it has no title. Thus it seems to be something special. The pelican and his chicks are white. One can see the sign for Luna, the moon. Striking is the blue color of the liquid in the vessel. I think this eighth picture indicates that a kind of goal already has been reached. This goal is connected with the moon, also with the feminine, and with the appearance of the white color in the *opus*. The stage of the *albedo* is indicated. C.G. Jung calls the *albedo* "the silver or moon condition" and "the first main goal of the process."[64] It is the moment when the *prima materia*, the dark primary matter in the *opus* has been washed often enough, cleansed and distilled and now has lost its blackness so that the whiteness can appear. Marie-Louise von Franz understands this as a true withdrawing of the disturbing and torturing projections. One no longer falls back into the old complexes. She writes: "As soon as a projection is *really* withdrawn a sort of peace establishes itself – one becomes quiet and can look at the thing from an objective angle."[65] To the stage of the *albedo* belongs the condition that one maintains a certain distance. On remains a little bit above things so to speak. Still, it is not quite yet the complete goal of the alchemists. Therefore C.G. Jung writes, that the "silver or moon condition" should increase to the "sun condition," that is to the *rubedo*. In other words, according to the *destillatio circulatoria*, which is expressed in the alchemical symbolism of the pelican, the process has to proceed further. The accompanying text speaks on behalf of this understanding. It runs:

Dieser pelican jetzt thuet/ helfen seinen jungen mit dem bluot/ doch sterben sie wider gar gern/ uf das sie werden zum Morgenstern.

---

64 C.G. Jung, *Psychology and Alchemy*, CW 12, § 334.
65 M.-L. von Franz, *Alchemy*, p. 222. She says: "One can look at the specific problem or factor in an objective and quiet way and perhaps do some active imagination about it without constantly becoming emotional, or falling back into the emotional tangle. This corresponds to the *albedo*."

[Now, this pelican does help/ his chicks with his blood/ but soon they will likely die/ in order to become the morning star.]

Therefore the next image in the series, number nine, illustrates the continuation of the process. Its emblem is the sign of Venus and it has as its symbol the six-fold morning star. The liquid in the vessel is red.

The third picture brings us to the picture series of the *Rosarium philosophorum*. It is the seventh picture in the second half of the series. Its title is *perfectionis ostensio*, which means "depiction of the completion" (plate 8, p. 232).[66] It shows Mercurius as a crowned hermaphrodite, male and female. He stands triumphantly on a dragon-like snake with three predator-like heads. This would be the *prima materia* in its primary state. In his right hand he holds a chalice with three snakes, in his left hand a single snake. This suggests the axiom of Maria Prophetissa,[67] which indicates, that a wholeness is achieved. In addition, the garment with the four colors of the alchemical process also represents wholeness. However, in his brief reflection upon this picture C.G. Jung additionally points to some sinister or ambivalent aspects, for instance the bat's wings or the green lion at the back of Mercurius.[68] Also the number eleven – the eleven flowers on the sun tree – is rather ambivalent. In the Christian context it was attributed to the devil.[69]

On the right side of the picture we can see the pelican with his three offspring in the nest. It illustrates, as C.G. Jung remarks the *destillatio circulatoria*. This indicates that with this picture the process of transformation is not yet completed. The process continues. The hermaphrodite cannot be the goal. Psychologically it means wholeness, but one that is unconscious, namely an unconscious fusion or mergence of the feminine and the masculine, not a union, in which the conscious human being, man

66 Plate 8: *Rosarium philosophorum,* Library canton St. Gallen, Switzerland, collection Vadiana, Ms. 394 a, picture 17. See Rudolf Gamper and Thomas Hofmeier, *Alchemische Vereinigung. Das Rosarium Philosophorum und sein Besitzer Bartlome Schobinger* [Alchemical union. The Rosarium Philosophorum and its owner Bartlome Schobinger] (Zurich: Chronos Verlag, 2014), p.65.
67 "One becomes two, two becomes three, and out of the third comes the One as the fourth." See C.G. Jung, *Psychology and Alchemy,* CW 12, § 209.
68 See C.G. Jung, *Alchemical Studies,* CW 13, picture B2 (following p. 152).
69 There are thirteen suns in corresponding depictions, for instance in C.G. Jung, *Alchemical Studies,* CW 13, picture B2 or in J. Telle, *Rosarium philosophorum,* vol. 1, p. 166. Also this number is ambivalent in the Christian context. Thirteen can mean Christ beside the twelve apostles, but also Judas who betrayed Jesus. Redeemer or betrayer, the thirteenth can be both.

or woman unites with the masculine or the feminine of one's own soul. In fact the picture series of the *Rosarium* does not end with this picture. Three others follow. The following picture, number eight, shows a green lion, which swallows the sun indicating a new *nigredo*. But the last two pictures, the ninth and the tenth of this second series of the *Rosarium*, both represent a kind of resurrection. One picture shows the redemption of the feminine in the figure of the *assumptio Mariae*, that is the assumption of Mary. The other depicts the redemption of the masculine in the figure of Mercurius, who like the resurrecting Christ leaves his grave.[70] In both pictures the masculine and the feminine are transformed and also redeemed, but they are also separated. The transformation or redemption leads up to heaven, as well as to the spiritual realm, which perhaps puts it back into a Christian context. One feels that this cannot be the end or the final goal.

The medieval alchemists did strive for the coniunctio of the opposites of the masculine and the feminine. But as C.G. Jung in his work "The Psychology of the Transference" pointed out, they got stuck in a kind of concreteness, that is, in a projection onto the concrete. In this context Jung speaks of "the immaturity of the alchemist's mind."[71] In the process of the individuation of modern man the hermaphrodite never appears as an "image of the goal" as Jung observed. Instead, images of wholeness appear in the form of mandalas, that is as a circle or a square. "Such images," Jung wrote, "unite the opposites under the sign of the *quaternio*, i.e., by combining them in the form of a cross, or alternatively they express the idea of wholeness through the circle or the sphere."[72]

Maybe we sense now, why C.G. Jung took so seriously this inconspicuous depiction of the alchemical vessel in the *Tractatus aureus*, this fourfold divided circle, the mandala with the seven letters and why he mentioned it several times in his writings. It is rather seldom that one finds such a mandala as an image of the goal in the alchemical scriptures. It seems as if at that time the unknown author of the *Tractatus aureus* already had a premonition of future psychic developments, which only took place some centuries later.

---

70 The inscription under the picture reads: "After much and many suffering and pain/ I am resurrected, clarified and loose of all blemish." See J. Telle, *Rosarium philosophorum*, vol. 1, p. 191.
71 C.G. Jung, "The Psychology of the Transference." CW 16, § 533.
72 Ibid., § 535.

The Inscription on the Gravestone

"Percussit petram et fluxerunt aquae," "he struck the rock" or "he broke the stone," "and the waters did flow." As I mentioned earlier, the gravestone of Marie-Louise von Franz and Barbara Hannah features two layers – the sculpture, the fourfold divided mandala as well as the inscription. Now when we come to the inscription the question is posed, how can one approach this particular phrase? One possibility would be to look at its historical, religious and also mythological aspects. In this case it would mean to have a look at the famous verse in the second book of Moses.[73] Moses had guided the Israelites out of Egypt through the Red Sea and into the desert. But soon the people began to complain and to quarrel. They were thirsty for they had no water. The distress was so great that it is said: "So Moses cried out to the Lord." And the Lord, Yahweh, spoke to him and said: "Go on ahead of the people, and take some of the elders of Israel with you; take in your hand the staff with which you struck the Nile, and go. I will be standing there in front of you on the rock at Horeb. Strike the rock, and water will come out of it, so that the people may drink."[74] One can see, here, it is God himself, it is Yahweh, who demands Moses to strike the rock. This differs from a second passage, namely in the fourth book of Moses, in which almost the same directive is given.[75] Again, the Israelites were querulous, since they were in need of water. Again Moses invoked the Lord. But this time the Lord directed Moses: "Take the staff, and assemble the congregation... and command the rock before their eyes to yield its water." But Moses, so enraged by the rebellious crowd, shouted to the people: "Listen, you rebels, shall we bring water for you out of this rock?" And he took his staff, struck the stone two times and the waters started to flow. Thus, the miracle appeared again. But Moses was punished severely by the Lord for this display of self-will or for this outburst of emotionality. He was not permitted to enter the Promised Land. He could see it, but he could not enter it. He was sentenced to die before he could reach this goal, the ultimate goal of his life.

These are the two biblical accounts, that underlie the inscription on the gravestone and certainly it could be meaningful to study them in an effort

---

73 Exodus 17:5-7.
74 Later the rock at Horeb was named "massa," which means "temptation" and "meriba," which is "strife" since the Israelites quarreled with God.
75 Numbers 20:1-13.

to understand them psychologically. But there is yet another possibility as well. Namely, we can look into the works of Marie-Louise von Franz. We can look into her own books, to see if somewhere appear the biblical verses, or the image of the rock that was struck, out of which the waters began to flow. Then we can take a look at what she herself has written about it. Actually, in her translation and commentary on the alchemical work *Aurora Consurgens* – and Marie-Louise von Franz herself considered this her most important book – indeed this image appears three times and at three different places, each appearance revealing a slightly different meaning. To give a brief explanation, the *Aurora Consurgens*, which means "Rising aurora" or "Rising dawn," consists of twelve chapters altogether. The last seven chapters are so-called parables, which are allegorical stories or similes.

Literally the Latin phrase on the gravestone appears only once, namely in a footnote at the beginning of the second parable, which is entitled "Of the Flood of Waters and of Death, which the Woman both brought into the World and put to Flight."[76] It is a very dark chapter. Now, if one reads and carefully follows the footnote, one discovers a surprising source from where Marie-Louise von Franz became acquainted with this phrase. It does not at all come from the second or fourth book of Moses, but rather originates from Psalm 77, verse 20. Indeed, in Psalm 77, the phrase is related to the miracle which occurred at the rock in the desert. Nevertheless it has its own context. The second place the account of Moses is mentioned in the *Aurora Consurgens* is found in the fifth parable.[77] It has the title: "Of the Treasure House which Wisdom built upon a Rock." This time the Latin text of the *Aurora* differs strikingly from the inscription on the gravestone in Küsnacht. However here Marie-Louise von Franz discusses most extensively the image of breaking the rock or stone. Finally, the third place is located in the sixth parable[78] with the title: "Of Heaven and Earth and the Arrangement of the Elements." Here, the Latin text closely resembles the inscription on the gravestone.

I will now look at these three places in the *Aurora Consurgens*, each time connecting them with the commentary of Marie-Louise von Franz. And by doing so I hope to better understand the inscription and its alchemical background. The *Aurora Consurgens* is a medieval alchemical treatise, attributed to St. Thomas Aquinas (ca. 1225-1274) as his last work. As Marie-Louise von

---

76 M.-L. von Franz, *Aurora Consurgens*, pp. 66f, footnote 2.
77 Ibid., pp. 102f.
78 Ibid., pp. 126f.

Franz has described, it is a visionary and ecstatic text, which suggests that it comes from a man, who has experienced a breakthrough of the unconscious in a most earthshaking way. And now, through the process of his writing this man attempts to understand his experience. Marie-Louise von Franz assumes that the author actually was St. Thomas Aquinas and that the text originated immediately before his death.[79] Taken as a whole the seven parables of the second part of the *Aurora* describe a process, which begins in the outermost darkness and confusion, in the *nigredo*, and slowly leads to the light and to the *albedo* or to the "rising dawn of the morning."[80] But also, each parable in and of itself depicts a progression, an *opus* on a small scale, which begins in the darkness in order to end with a prospect of hope. The whole text describes a kind of circling, a spiral circulating, always on a new level. In this way the author of the *Aurora* tries to comprehend his experience, namely the breakthrough of the unconscious, and attempts to connect it with his worldview.

Of the Flood of Waters and of Death, which the Woman both brought into the World and put to Flight (2nd parable)

The second parable begins with a flood or an inundation. But it is not the author who is inundated. Rather it is a feminine figure, who he calls *Sapientia Dei*, that is the Wisdom of God. Speaking about herself this divine feminine figure says:

> When the multitude of the sea shall be converted to me and the streams have flowed over my face...[81]

And as a footnote to this line Marie-Louise von Franz quotes exactly the phrase that we can read on her gravestone: "Quoniam percussit petram et fluxerunt aquae et torrentes inundaverunt," "because he struck the rock, and the waters gushed out, and the streams overflowed."[82] In her commentary she points particularly to the expression "multitude of the sea." According

---

79 In regard of dating the text, Marie-Louise von Franz wrote: "I myself incline to date it to the middle or second half of the thirteenth century." See *Aurora Consurgens*, p. 24.
80 M.-L. von Franz, *Aurora Consurgens*, p. 215.
81 Ibid., pp. 66f.
82 Ibid., p. 66, footnote 2.

to Isaiah[83] the expression refers to "the pagans dwelling by the sea," or in other words to the barbarians. They have fallen in. In the Christian context, generally the sea represents an alien, dangerous, even devilish-demonic power. Thus, the sea can be called the "diabolical sea." And the pagan nations living close to the sea refer to people who "have given themselves to the devil."[84] Thus what happened here to the author of the *Aurora* or to his anima was a breakthrough of the "pagan parts" of his own psyche, a not at all harmless emotional or barbarian invasion caused by the collective unconscious.

Now, to this concussion belongs also the experience of fight, bloody slaughter and triumph. The anima, which before has been overwhelmed by the waters of the sea, suddenly appears almost like the Indian Goddess Kali, when she says:

> ... and [when] the arrows of my quiver are drunk with blood and my presses are fragrant with the best wine and my barns are filled with the corn of wheat.[85]

With this a raving is expressed, a terrifying outburst of ferocity, blood, rage and drunkenness. From Avicenna comes the saying that the *nigredo* "signifies the victory or domination of the female."[86] But just in this – and now I quote – "hostile, emotional outbreak of the 'divine' element, utterly destroying the world of consciousness"[87] lies the hidden germ of a future new life, of a light that comes out of the darkness as Christ, but which actually corresponds to the *Filius philosophorum*, the redeemer of the alchemists. The text says:

> ... and [when] the bridegroom with the ten wise virgins hath entered into my chamber and thereafter my belly hath swelled from the touch of my beloved and the bolt of my door hath been opened to my beloved,... and [when] a light hath risen up in darkness and the Sun of Justice hath

---

83 Isaiah 60:5.
84 M.-L. von Franz, *Aurora Consurgens*, p. 245.
85 Ibid., pp. 66f.
86 Ibid., p. 247. In a woman's psyche probably it will be different. There the *nigredo* signifies "the victory and the domination" of the male.
87 Ibid., p. 247.

appeared from heaven, then the fullness of the time shall come when God shall send his Son, as he hath said.[88]

Thus, the inundation and the gushing waters are not only destructive, but also fertilizing and vitalizing. The experience of the *nigredo* can mean both death *and* new life. This is the meaning with which at first we should understand the inscription on the gravestone: "He struck the rock and the waters did flow." But it has to be mentioned as well, that in verse 20 of psalm 77, from where the inscription literally originates, by the word "he" it is not Moses that is meant, but rather Yahweh, the Lord. The meaning of the inscription related to this text therefore should read: "He," that is God, the Lord or Yahweh, "struck the rock and the waters did flow."

Of the Treasure-House which Wisdom built upon a Rock (5th parable)

Wisdom hath built herself a house, which if any man enter in he shall be saved and find pastures, as the prophets beareth witness: They shall be inebriated with the plenty of thy house...[89]

This is, how the fifth parable begins. What does this house of Wisdom or this treasure house represent? Alchemically speaking it is the *lapis*, the stone as an utmost highest value, but psychologically it is an image of the self. In her commentary to this sentence Marie-Louise von Franz quotes a text from the Arabic alchemist Alphidius:

Know, my son, that this knowledge is in a certain place and that this place is everywhere. The place is the four elements, and they are four doors, which if thou wouldst know I say firstly that they are four stations, four corners, four ends and four walls... This is the treasure-house in which are treasured up all sublime things[90]... The house in which these treasures are is closed with four doors and they are locked with four keys, each door having one... Know therefore, my son, that he who knows one key and knows not the rest shall open the doors of the house with his key, but he shall not see the things that are in the house, for the house has a surface which stretches far out of sight. Therefore each door

88 Ibid., pp. 67-69.
89 M.-L. von Franz, *Aurora Consurgens*, p. 101.
90 Literally "all things in their essence."

must be opened with its own key, until the whole house is filled with light, then anyone may enter and take of the treasure.[91]

Thus one needs four keys in order to approach the house of Wisdom. Psychologically, as Marie-Louise von Franz writes, this corresponds to the "psychic process for realizing the self by means of all four functions of consciousness."[92] She continues this thought in a footnote, in order to say, that the surface "leads to endless looking," if the house is opened with only *one* key. This "may refer to the psychological danger of using only *one* function to 'unlock' the unconscious. Fascinated by thinking, feeling, intuition or sensation (fact-collecting), one sees only the 'surface' and not the whole house," that is built "by an inner fixation."[93]

"Wisdom hath built herself a house…" Thus, the building of this house refers to a consolidation or realization of psychic wholeness. Marie-Louise von Franz speaks about the "coagulation of the lapis"[94] But the architect of that house is not the human Ego. It is God or better his wisdom. She is the builder. It means that the building or constructing of the treasure house of Wisdom is a renewal in the self. Here we can observe processes of transformation which indicate that God him- or herself wanted to be experienced and comprehended in a new way. For this he needed a human being, namely Thomas of Aquino, in order to transform in him.

What this means becomes clear when one looks at the images, in which the treasure house of Wisdom is described. This house is of the highest value imaginable. "Its walls and streets are of purest gold, and its gates gleam with pearls and precious stones."[95] One day in its courts are better than thousand others.[96] But whoever opens the treasure house will "face to face and eye to eye… look upon all the brightness of the sun and moon."[97] With this the mysterium of the union of sun and moon is addressed. And Marie-Louise von Franz shows very beautifully that the conjunction of the two divine lights actually is the new God image and that looking at it "face

---

91 Ibid., pp. 314f.
92 M.-L. von Franz, *Aurora Consurgens*, p. 315.
93 Ibid., footnotes 3 and 5.
94 Ibid., p. 316.
95 Ibid., p. 105.
96 Ibid., p. 101.
97 Ibid., p. 105.

to face" conveys something solid and eternal, a "feeling of immortality,"[98] "an inalienable experience upon which the whole future man is founded."[99]

Now it is strange that in the midst of this almost hymnic description of the house of wisdom and its treasures, suddenly the following passage appears:

> ... for it [the house] is founded upon a sure rock, which cannot be split unless it be anointed with the blood of a most fine buck-goat or be smitten three times with the rod of Moses, that waters may flow forth in great abundance, that all the people both men and women drink thereof, and they shall neither hunger nor thirst any more. Whosoever by his science shall open this house shall find therein an unfailing living fount that maketh young, wherein whoever is baptized, [he] shall be saved and can no more grow old.[100]

This inner image received from the unconscious by the author of the *Aurora Consurgens* brings us back to the inscription on the gravestone of Marie-Louise von Franz and Barbara Hannah. It is not easy to understand. Actually, this "sure rock," on which the house of wisdom stands, is something indescribable. It is the foundation of the house and at the same time it is the house of wisdom itself. But as an "unfailing living fount" it is also something within the interior of the house. It is the *lapis philosophorum*.[101] It is a paradox, that on the one hand this rock or house, that is the *lapis*, is described as of the highest value and on the other hand as something that should be opened or also split open, either by the rod of Moses – we will come to this later – or by "the blood of the most fine buck-goat." In the middle ages the buck or the he-goat belonged to the devil and in antiquity he was the animal of the god Pan. The blood of the buck represents libido, concupiscence and greediness, sensuousness, desirousness, but also warmness, sympathy, love. The blood is the "soul of the goat" and symbolizes as such the animal man in us or – as von Franz describes it – "an animal and emotional factor in man."[102] This also should be included in the process since the text says that within the house an "unfailing living fount

98 Ibid., p. 323.
99 Ibid., p. 340.
100 Ibid., p. 103.
101 Ibid., p. 323.
102 Ibid., p. 324, also p. 327.

that maketh young" can come forth. Paradoxically, the hard rock and the "blood of a most fine buck-goat" belong together as steadfast and spiritual firmness on the one side, and as liveliness as well as an enlivening substance on the other. Both are aspects of the *lapis*. Both are aspects of the self. In her book on *Alchemy* Marie-Louise von Franz speaks to this as follows.

> It is a very great paradox that liquid – the unformed water of life – and the stone – the most solid and dead thing – are, according to the alchemists, one and the same thing. That refers to those two aspects of the realization of the Self: something firm is born beyond the ups and downs of life, and at the same time is born something very living which takes part in the flow of life, without the inhibitions or restrictions of consciousness."[103]

Of Heaven and Earth and the Arrangement of the Elements (6th parable)

With this we come to the sixth parable that is entitled: "Of Heaven and Earth and the Arrangement of the Elements." Actually what is described here is an "alchemical world-creating process."[104] The alchemists often compared their alchemical work with God's work of creation. When we read in Genesis: "... the earth was a formless void and darkness covered the face of the deep, while a wind from God swept over the face of the waters,"[105] then this primordial chaos, this "formless void and darkness" in the depth resembles the *massa confusa* in the vessel of the alchemist. During the process or the *opus* this should transform into an ordered wholeness or into the union of the *lapis*. Like God the Creator, the alchemist also creates a new world. And in the sixth parable of the *Aurora Consurgens* this new world is described as the "new earth." Psychologically we can say, it is a matter of a new understanding of the divine aspect of the earth.

Initially the earth is only one of the four elements, fire, water, air and earth. But the earth as the fourth element is the one, which contains and constitutes all the others. The earth is the "mother of the elements." Out of this earth as the fourth element emerges the new cosmos. But according to the text the earth is also the *Sapientia Dei*, the Wisdom of God. This

103 M.-L. von Franz, *Alchemy*, p. 174.
104 M.-L. von Franz, *Aurora Consurgens*, p. 339.
105 Genesis 1:2.

means that she represents the divine feminine figure who had encountered the author of the *Aurora* in his vision, that had deeply shocked him.[106] Now, the creation of the new world or of the new earth, this birth, is preceded by a process of dying and of death. The end of the world or even an apocalypse occurs. The text says: "For from the earth are the elements separated by dying, and to it do they return by quickening, for what a thing is composed of, into that must it be resolved."[107] As far as the elements are living components or building blocks of the world, their death means a destruction of the world, psychologically seen as an extinguishing of the conscious ego-personality. Several times, Marie-Louise von Franz compares the experiences that Thomas of Aquino must have had before his death with an outburst of psychosis.[108] But in the unconscious exists also some kind of psychic order. It seems, that such an ordering principle existed also within Thomas of Aquino and therefore such a new order could "built itself up again out of the chaos"[109]. A new earth or a new cosmos, a new highest value emerged. I think we can even say, that this is a new image of God. In this image the new earth appears as God himself. Marie-Louise von Franz writes: "... the author... puts the earth in the place of God... This earth itself is the risen Christ and the divine mystery – indeed, it is God himself."[110]

But it is "at the same time the ordinary mortal man,"[111] even the human body. The earth is both, divine and human. It is even – according to the text of the *Aurora Consurgens* – the divine word,[112] meaning that this alchemical earth is a divine spirit. It is the Divine Wisdom as Christ is the Wisdom. But instead of coming from above, from heaven, this spirit comes from below out of the darkness.

Now, having concluded this introduction, we can look at the third text, where the *Aurora Consurgens* speaks about the concussion or the splitting of the rock, as well as the water that begins to flow. We can find this at the end of the sixth parable. Here it is said:

---

106 Therefore Marie-Louise von Franz calls her an "Anima-Wisdom-figure" (p. 340).
107 M.-L. von Franz, *Aurora Consurgens*, p. 342.
108 Ibid., p. 342.
109 Ibid., p. 342.
110 Ibid., p. 353.
111 Ibid., pp. 353f.
112 Ibid., pp. 127 and 353: "... because it upholdeth all things by the word of its godhead."

The earth, since it is heavy, beareth all things, for it is the foundation
of the whole heaven, because it appeared dry at the separation of the
elements. Therefore in the Red Sea there was a way without hindrance,
since this great and wide sea smote the rock and the (metallic) waters
flowed forth."[113]

"Therefore in the Red Sea there was a way without hindrance." This way
is the first bit of dry land, the first emergence of the new earth from the
abyss of the sea. For the alchemists the Red Sea was equivalent to the mysterious "divine water" or the "water of the art." This water always was both,
corroding, poisonous, killing, as well as vivifying, enlivening, healing. In
the Christian context the Red Sea was the baptismal water, "the baptism
reddened by the blood of Christ, in which our enemies... are drowned."[114]
Now strangely enough the text says, that this "great and wide sea" smote
or broke the rock – referring to the rock at Horeb – "and the metallic
waters flowed forth." While in the fifth parable the blood of the buck goat
is equated with the staff of Moses, here it is the Red Sea. "This great and
wide sea" splits the rock, that means, it is identified with the rod of Moses.
Marie-Louise von Franz explains this paradox as following:

> The rod symbolizes an orienting factor which is contained in the "water"
> of the unconscious and which, like the magic staff of Hermes, causes
> sleep and waking, rouses to life or leads the way into death.[115]

This "orienting factor" in the unconscious is a great mystery. The unconscious seems to have something like its own will and its own direction or
tendency. When we speak of the "spirit of the unconscious" or "the autonomous psyche," then we think of this autonomous "will" or of this orienting
tendency of the unconscious. The rod of Moses, which we encounter in
the fifth and in the sixth parable, corresponds to the staff of Mercurius or
Hermes, the Caduceus with the double snake. And Mercurius is the spirit
of the unconscious. It is this spirit who strikes or splits the rock and who
causes the waters to flow. Thus, when the stone or the rock opens it is not
the work of man. Above I mentioned that the inscription on the gravestone

---

113 M.-L. von Franz, *Aurora Consurgens*, p. 127.
114 C.G. Jung, *Mysterium Coniunctionis*, CW 14, § 256. Literally it should read: "The
      ardent red baptism through the blood of Christ."
115 M.-L. von Franz, *Aurora Consurgens*, p. 355.

of Marie-Louise von Franz and Barbara Hannah only once appears literally in the *Aurora Consurgens*, namely in a footnote at the beginning of the second parable and that it corresponds to verse 20 in psalm 77. According to the context I translated this verse as following: "He, God, Yahweh, struck the rock and the waters did flow." Now after we have had a look at the other passages in the text, we can translate anew and more precisely. The rod of Moses, which apparently is mentioned in the fifth and in the sixth parable, and also the "blood of the most best buck-goat," which Marie-Louise von Franz described as the warm, human, life-affirming, also libidinous aspect of the human personality, indicates the figure of Mercurius. Therefore we may translate: He, Mercurius, this *spiritus rector* of the alchemical work and thus of the process of individuation, "struck the rock, and the waters did flow," "percussit petram et fluxerunt aquae."

Summary

Now I return to the beginning of these reflections and to C.G. Jung's gravestone at the graveyard in Küsnacht (plate 2, p. 226). Although I read the inscription on the stone I have not gone into it. "Primus homo de terra – terrenus, secundus homo de caelo – caelestis," "the first man is from the earth – earthly, the second man is from heaven – celestial." What does this inscription signify? To be sure it refers to Paul's first letter to the Corinthians.[116] Thus it seems to be clear that the first man refers to Adam, the earthly-physical man and the second to Christ, the heavenly-spiritual man. This phrase however, also appears in Alchemy. In *Mysterium Coniunctionis* C.G. Jung reveals that the alchemist Blasius Vigenerus[117] mentioned this phrase in Paul's letter strangely enough in order to connect it with the four "elements... circular in their arrangement." In his commentary on 1. Cor. 15:47 Vigenerus writes:

> For the elements are circular [in their arrangement], as Hermes makes clear, each being surrounded by two others... Man, therefore, who is an image of the great world, and is called the microcosm or little world... has also his heaven and his earth. For the soul and the understanding are his heaven; his body and senses his earth. Therefore, to know the

---

116 Paul, 1 Cor. 15:47. Paul says: "The first man was from the earth, a man of dust; the second man is from heaven," meaning Christ as the second man.
117 He has written *De igne et sale*, in: *Theatrum chemicum*, vol. 6, pp. 1-39.

heaven and earth of man, is the same as to have a full and complete knowledge of the whole world and of the things of nature.[118]

Writing about this C.G. Jung referred to the mandala. "The circular arrangement of the elements in man is symbolized by the mandala and its quaternary structure."[119] This brings us back to the gravestone of Marie-Louise von Franz and Barbara Hannah (plate 3, p. 227). Here also we see a mandala with a quaternary structure. Earlier, when looking at the mandala with the seven letters in the *Tractatus aureus* (picture 4), we discussed that the four elements represented the foundation of psychic wholeness. Fire, water, air and earth symbolize the archetypal fundamentals of our human consciousness. They connect us with the world, with the inner world, the microcosm and with the outer world, the macrocosm.

But at the same time, as Vigenerus says, we are both, heaven and earth. Both dwell within us. Thus we consist of psychic building stones or specific aspects of a great wholeness in the beyond. But how can we ever bring together these great and eternal polar opposites in us in order to experience the feeling of a firm and stable wholeness? How can the first man, the man made of earth, Adam or Eve, in us and the second man, the heavenly man become a whole? How can heaven and earth really come together in us to make us whole?

The alchemists had an image for this. They spoke of the rotation and circulation of the stone through the four elements. The highest value, the self must realize itself in us again and again, each time on a new level. Therefore again and again this highest value must be divided, destroyed and broken. We see this depicted beautifully in the three passages within the text of the *Aurora*. Firstly in the second parable: here a tremendous breakthrough of the unconscious occurs, an inundation of dark, pagan, even demonic manifestations. Thus the rock or the stone is broken. But also the text speaks of the "light in the darkness" and of a promise of a new life out of this dark flood. In the fifth parable the author of the *Aurora* speaks of "the blood of a most fine buck-goat." It should break the rock or the stone. Obviously the warm, lively, even animal-like or instinctive strength of soul-forces shall become the foundation of the new highest value. This is the "treasure house of wisdom." In the "treasure house of wisdom" the *hierosgamos* of sun and moon comes to pass. And Marie-Louise von Franz

---

118 C.G. Jung, *Mysterium Coniunctionis*, CW 14, § 554.
119 Ibid., § 556.

writes, that the *visio Dei,* that is the "vision of God... – the hierosgamos of sun and moon[120] – was itself the rock, that is, an inalienable experience upon which the whole future man is founded."[121] Finally the sixth parable: here a new earth is born and out of the depth of the Red Sea emerges a new way. The rock of Moses is so powerfully shaken, that out of it the waters begin to flow. Here I understand the rock as a value that needs to be transformed. Possibly here the rock alludes to the *homo primus,* the first man, who should become transformed into the second man.

Immediately after this passage the text goes on to speak about the first and the second Adam. The first Adam is composed of "corruptible elements" and consequently must decay necessarily. But the second Adam is formed out of "pure elements" and thus will enter eternity. About him the text says: "Therefore what is composed of simple and pure essence, remaineth for ever."[122]

I think here we may compare the first and the second Adam of the *Aurora* with the first and second man inscribed on C.G. Jung's gravestone. "The first and earthly Adam," that is the physical man, consists of four elements, but of a composition "that might easily disintegrate."[123] Therefore he is corruptible. The second Adam however emerges only gradually "from the circulation of the four." He is, according to Marie-Louise von Franz, the fifth, the quintessence. In him the opposites are contained, the masculine and the feminine as well as all the other qualities, going "beyond the opposites."[124] The second Adam is the inner man. He can be male and female, the royal bridegroom and the *Sapientia Dei,* the Wisdom of God. He is of "simple and pure essence" and thus eternal. At the end of the sixth parable therefore it is said:

> He that hath ears to hear, let him hear what the spirit of the doctrine saith to the sons of the discipline concerning the earthly and the heavenly Adam, which the philosophers treat of in these words: When thou

120 The English translation here is not good. It reads: "... and it is psychologically possible that the vision – the *hierosgamos* of sun and moon – was itself the 'rock'." One can see that the translator does not understand the intention of Marie-Louise von Franz and tries to trivialize her words.

121 M.-L. von Franz, *Aurora Consurgens,* p. 340.

122 Ibid., p. 357 and p. 360.

123 Ibid., p. 360.

124 Ibid.

hast water from earth, air from water, fire from air, earth from fire, then shalt thou fully and perfectly possess our art.[125]

I think that both the inscription on the gravestone of C.G. Jung and the inscription of the gravestone of Marie-Louise von Franz and Barbara Hannah "percussit petram et fluxerunt aquae," "he struck the rock and the waters did flow," represent one and the same eternal mystery. They point to and circle around the mystery of the *coniunctio*, the uniting and becoming one with the divine essence in life and also at life's end, in death. They suggest a continual renewal in this world and in the beyond.[126]

LXXVI. Figur.

Picture 5: "Revivifying": Sol and Luna rise from the fountain, on the left the pelican
(Stoltzius von Stoltzenberg, *Chymisches Lustgärtlein*, Frankfurt 1624)

125 Ibid., p. 360.
126 The author thanks Judy Dowling cordially for her great help with the translation into English.

Tony Woolfson

"I came across this impressive doctrine"
Carl Gustav Jung, Gershom Scholem, and Kabbalah

> You are a Kabbalist.
> Why do you say that?
> Because you accept the reality of evil.[1]

Note to the reader

While it is easy to imagine that all Jewish Kabbalists were mystics, fascinat-ed by the mystery of God's Creation, Jewish mystics were not necessarily Kabbalists. It is often hard to distinguish the Kabbalah from the Jewish Mystical tradition more generally. Many renowned Rabbis throughout the centuries were just as observant of the ritual practices of what became known after the Enlightenment and Emancipation of the 18th and 19th Centuries as Orthodox Judaism as they were learned in the esoteric and mystical teachings of Judaism, such as the Kabbalah. The significance of the East European Hassidic movement in its more recent manifestations dating from around 1750, and which continues to this day, for example, in the prominence of Lubavitcher Hassidim and in the widespread interest in the mystical tales of Rabbi Nachman of Bratislava, demonstrates that unity of Jewish orthodox ritual and Jewish mystical practices. In what follows the reader should note that there is often no clear distinction to be made between Kabbalah and Jewish mystical practices generally. Perhaps they might all be subsumed under the one term, the Jewish spiritual tradition, somewhat in the sense intended by C.G. Jung in his advice to the reader of

---

1 A man dreamt that a female figure told him this (personal communication).

his *Answer to Job*, where he insists on the importance of both physical and psychical truths.[2]

Prelude: In the Beginning and With the Beginning

The world view of the Kabbalistic tradition and the analytical psychology of Jung start from the same mythological place, and the common denominator of both is an alchemical view of the world.

Commenting on the ritualistic dismemberment of a sacrificial victim, the division of baptismal waters into four parts, or indeed the idea of the four functions of consciousness in his typology, Jung reminds us that, "the purpose of the operation is to create the beginnings of order in the *massa confusa*." In Jung's analytical psychology this means, "the reduction to order, through reflection, of apparently chaotic fragments of the unconscious which have broken through into consciousness."[3]

The goal of the *opus* is to extend consciousness and, in psychological and spiritual terms, to bring order out of disorder. While a stone will always remain a stone or a physical body a physical body, the goal of the alchemists was always to *extract* the spiritual out of the material. Psychologically, we can experience so much in our lives, but the responsibility we have is to find the holy and the spiritual in all those experiences.[4] A religious life always involves transforming habits and rituals into sacrifices which literally make sacred or whole. At the end of the *Book of Job*, God tells Job's friends to give their offerings to Job who will make the ritual sacrifices on their behalf; that is because Job has spoken of Him "the thing that is right" and because his suffering has been accepted as a true sacrifice and, therefore, as truly sacred.[5]

Nothing like a simple linear ascent from the darkness of matter to the light of spirit is ever possible. Sometimes we have to descend or apparently regress in order to move forward or ascend. Another apt image of the

---

2 C.G. Jung, *Answer to Job* (1951), in: *Psychology and Religion: West and East*, vol. 11 of the *Collected Works of C.G. Jung*, translated by R.F.C. Hull (Princeton: Princeton University Press, 1969), § 553.

3 C.G. Jung, "The Visions of Zosimos" (1944), in: *Alchemical Studies*, vol. 13 of *The Collected Works of C.G. Jung*, edited and translated by Gerhard Adler and R.F.C. Hull. (Princeton: Princeton University Press, 1967), § 111.

4 I am grateful to Gotthilf Isler for this formulation.

5 The Book of Job, 42:7-10; all Biblical translations are from the 1611 King James Version.

possibility of following a natural gradient toward wholeness is the spiral: "The spiral moves away from the original place to another, yet it always returns to the same place but just a fraction above; always moving away and always coming to the same." Jung called this "sameness, non-sameness."[6]

The Kabbalistic equivalent of the *massa confusa* or the *prima materia* of alchemy is the cosmic catastrophe that is said to have occurred at the beginning of creation and by which it is imagined that evil entered into the world as a separate entity. The received tradition of the Kabbalah has as its goal, therefore, the repair and restoration of the shattered primal unity of the world. The Hebrew words for that repair are *tikkun olam*, meaning repair of the world. A very original contemporary rabbi has translated *tikkun* as politics, meaning, of course, politics as ethical actions, not as the selfish pursuit of power.[7] We will see below that Jung calls the "cosmic responsibility" of sharing with God in that co-evolutionary work of repair the "impressive doctrine" bequeathed to us by Isaac Luria, the Safed Kabbalist.

Jung starts, then, with an image of primordial events and happenings, the *massa confusa* or *prima materia* of alchemy. These psychoid imprints are universal and timeless, because they emerge from the bottomless depths of the collective unconscious. They are instinctual and spiritual, infra-red at the physical end and ultraviolet at the spiritual end of the spectrum,[8] physical and psychical. Jung holds that there is a guiding principle operating in each of us and in the world as a whole, the principle of the objective psyche and of the Self, indistinguishable, says Jung, from a God-image.[9]

The way of the Self involves our approaching the numinous, which Jung calls "the real therapy,"[10] and which requires insight, courage, and action. It is a profoundly religious task to find the way we are meant to follow. As Saint Matthew said, "For many are called, but few are chosen."[11] That may be because the task before us is always profoundly difficult and at times

---

6   *Visions. Notes of the Seminar Given in 1930-1934 by C.G. Jung*, edited by Claire Douglas (Princeton: Princeton University Press, 1997), p. 243.

7   Lawrence Kushner, *The Book of Words* (Woodstock, Vermont: Jewish Lights, 1993), pp. 83-86.

8   C.G. Jung, "On the Nature of the Psyche" (1955), in: *The Structure and Dynamics of the Psyche*, vol. 8 of *The Collected Works of C.G. Jung*, translated by R.F.C. Hull (Princeton: Princeton University Press, 1969), §§ 413-414.

9   C.G. Jung, "The Spirit Mercury," in: *Alchemical Studies*, CW 13, § 289.

10 C.G. Jung, *Letters*, selected and edited by Gerhard Adler in collaboration with Aniela Jaffé. Translated by R.F.C. Hull, in two volumes (Princeton: Princeton University Press, 1973), 20 August 1945, vol. 1, p. 377.

11 Matthew, 22:14.

dangerous. As Jung says, "We must not underestimate the devastating effect of getting lost in the chaos, even if we know that it is the *sine qua non* of any regeneration of the spirit and the personality."[12]

Picture 1: An alchemist's laboratory, 1595

Probably more than anyone else in modern times, C.G. Jung has made of alchemy a respectable field of study.[13] Jung recognised in the alchemical process of seeking to extract spirit from base matter that the gold is in the proverbial shit, as we might call it. An adult university student of mine very excitedly told me, "I dreamt I was stirring the shit!" Similarly, an analyst, most likely Fraser Boa who edited the book in which the dream is related, dreamt in his final year of training in Zurich that, "The hand of God is in the shit."[14] Gershom Scholem, indisputably the greatest scholar of Jewish Mysticism in the last Century, wrote, "The core of all alchemy, however understood, is the transmutation of base metals into gold, the highest and

12 C.G. Jung, *Psychology and Alchemy*, vol. 12 of *The Collected Works of C.G. Jung*, translated by R.F.C. Hull (Princeton: Princeton University Press, 1968), § 96.
13 Picture 1: An alchemist's laboratory. Heinrich Khunrath, *Amphitheatrum Sapientiae Aeterna* [Amphitheatre of Eternal Wisdom], Hamburg 1595, reproduced in Manuel Bachmann and Thomas Hofmeier, *Geheimnisse der Alchemie* [Secrets of Alchemy] (Basel: Schwabe Verlag, 1999), p. 166.
14 Dr. Marie-Louise von Franz in conversation with Fraser Boa, *The Way of the Dream* (Toronto: Windrose Films, 1988), p. 337.

most noble metallic element."[15] As we said above, the parallel to this in our personal lives is the religious work, the *opus*, of disentangling the mass of unconscious forces in order to find the gold in the proverbial shit, the good in the evil, and the light in the darkness. Put another way, the God-image within may be striving to lead us to what Jung calls a "relationship" or "correspondence" with God, which Jung says is *"in psychological terms, the archetype of the God-image."*[16]

The alchemical emphasis was always on extracting the spirit in matter, and the Kabbalistic endeavour had exactly the same goal. According to Gershom Scholem, "there is a structural relationship between the ascension from the lowest to the highest levels of the Kabbalistic Tree of Life and al-chemical steps involved in the refining of the philosophical gold according to a mystical view of the *ars magna*, the 'Great Art.'"[17]

What do we find at the beginning of Biblical creation in Genesis? *Massa confusa.* The Hebrew words, *Vehaaretz hayitah tohu vebohu*, "And the earth being unformed and void, with darkness over the surface and a wind from God sweeping over the water,"[18] are variously understood to mean chaotic, dense, dark, murmuring, and terrifying. The psalmist said, "Deep calleth unto deep ..."[19] Subterranean waters and primeval oceans roil and storm. Submerged volcanoes erupt. There are whales, sharks, aquatic dinosaurs, sea monsters, and the Leviathan of the *Book of Job*, not to mention the cosmic enormity of more recent historic revelations at places like Mount Sinai. As the Biblical God rhetorically asks Job,

> Have you penetrated to the sources of the sea,
> Or walked in the recesses of the deep?[20]

In the extraordinarily extensive study he undertook of alchemy, published in *Collected Works* Volumes 12, 13, and 14, C.G. Jung was obviously enor-mously interested in the Kabbalistic ideas and symbols that he encountered. He must have known all about the Kabbalistic Tree of Life by 1944 when

---

15 Gershom Scholem, *Alchemy and Kabbalah*, translated by Klaus Ottmann (Putnam, Connecticut: Spring Publications, 2006), p. 20.

16 C.G. Jung, *Psychology and Alchemy*, CW 12, § 11 (Jung's emphasis).

17 G. Scholem, *Alchemy and Kabbalah*, pp. 40-41.

18 Genesis, 1:2; c.f., also, Avivah Gottlieb Zornberg, *The Murmuring Deep: Reflections on the Biblical Unconscious* (New York: Schocken Books, 2009).

19 Psalms, 42:7.

20 The Book of Job, 38:16.

he was very seriously ill and experienced a vision of himself in the *Pardes Rimonim*, the Orchard of Pomegranates, at the mystical wedding of *Tifereth*, Majesty, and *Malkhuth*, Kingdom. To this we will return below.

In the first instance Jung learned about Kabbalah from reading 16th and 17th Century alchemical texts, like Christian Knorr von Rosenroth's, *Kabbala Denudata*. In *Mysterium Coniunctionis*, Jung refers repeatedly to such Kabbalistic symbols as Adam Kadmon, the Anthropos or Primordial Man, the *Sefirot* and the *Sefirotic Tree of Life*, and the mystical union of *Tifereth* and *Malkhuth*, the mystical masculine and feminine.

Just as alchemy was considered an obscure and unscientific body of thought until Jung more or less resurrected it from that obscurity, Kabbalah, the core of the Jewish spiritual and mystical tradition, was also considered beneath serious consideration in newly rational, modern Jewish circles. The person that single-handedly began to rescue the Kabbalah from that obscurity was of course Gershom Scholem, close friend from his intellectually precocious Berlin youth of another uniquely brilliant literary Jewish scholar, Walter Benjamin. What an irony of history it is that in New York less than two years before the visitation upon Poland of the Panzer Tank and Stuka Dive-Bomber, which heralded the attempted complete destruction of European Jewry, Gershom Scholem delivered the scholarly lectures that were published in 1941 as *Major Trends in Jewish Mysticism*,[21] thereby inaugurating the contemporary study of the timeless wisdom of the Kabbalah.

It is also an irony of history that in Berlin in 1922 the young Gershom Scholem went to see a well-known Jewish scholar, the aged Rabbi Philip Bloch:

> Bloch gave me a very friendly reception – as a young colleague, so to speak. "After all, we both are *meshugga* [crazy]," he said. He showed me his Kabbalistic collection, and I admired the manuscripts. In my enthusiasm I said, quite naively: "How wonderful, Herr Professor, that you have studied all this!" Whereupon the old gentleman replied: "What, am I supposed to read all this rubbish, too?" That was a great moment in my life.[22]

---

21 Gershom Scholem, *Major Trends in Jewish Mysticism* (New York: Schocken Books, 1961).
22 Gershom Scholem, *From Berlin to Jerusalem: Memories of My Youth* (New York: Schocken Books, 1980), p. 150.

Incidentally, in his short study, *Alchemy and Kabbalah*, Scholem mentions that, "Twenty years ago [in 1957] a friend and I paid an unforgettable visit to the wonderful mystical library of Oskar Schlag in Zurich."[23] Oskar Schlag was "one of the most gifted mediums of the twentieth century," and one of the founders in Zurich in the late 1940's of the Hermetic Society, of which both Carl and Emma Jung were for a time members. Oskar Schlag's home in Zurich has been turned into a museum, where the 26,000 volumes of his collection are housed.[24]

First Interlude: Wet and Dry

Those two giants of Twentieth Century scholarship, Carl Gustav Jung and Gershom Scholem, actually had rather a low opinion of each other. There was first of all the very tricky matter of the allegation made against Jung of his having some kind of sympathies with the Nazis, the subject of a famous letter Gershom Scholem wrote to Aniela Jaffé in May 1963. Scholem told her that he was first invited to come to Eranos in 1947 but was uncertain whether or not he should accept the invitation because he had "heard and read a number of criticisms of Jung's behaviour." He consulted Rabbi Leo Baeck, the spiritual leader of German Jewry who was imprisoned in Theresienstadt for much of the war and who knew Jung. Leo Baeck said he must go to Eranos and told Scholem of his own initially very testy *Auseinandersetzung*, or confrontation, with Jung just after the war in the course of which Jung said that, yes, he had *ausgerutscht*, or slipped up (the original German means something potentially dangerous) in his earlier understanding of apparently progressive elements in the rise of Nazism. On the basis of that reconciliation between Jung and Baeck, Gershom Scholem accepted the invitation to come to the Eranos gathering in 1949 and he remained associated with Eranos for almost thirty years.[25] There he presented the remarkable historical researches into Kabbalah that were subsequently

---

23 G. Scholem, *Alchemy and Kabbalah*, p. 87.

24 Hans Thomas Hakl, *Eranos*: *An Alternative Intellectual History of the Twentieth Century*, translated by Christopher McIntosh with the collaboration of Hereward Tilton (Montreal and Kingston, Canada: McGill-Queens University Press, 2013), pp. 93-95.

25 Gershom Scholem, *A Life in Letters, 1914-1982*, edited and translated by Anthony David Skinner (Cambridge, Massachusetts and London: Harvard University Press, 2002), letter of 7 May 1963, pp. 393-394.

published as the indispensable, *On the Kabbalah and Its Symbolism* and *On the Mystical Shape of the Godhead.*[26]

Picture 2: Gershom Scholem at Eranos in August 1951

At Eranos, Scholem's views clashed diametrically with Jung's. Although he obviously highly valued the opportunity to present his historical researches into Kabbalah at the intimate annual conference in Eranos of fellow German-speaking scholars, Scholem made no concessions to the ethos at Eranos, set by Jung's presence.[27] In fact, as late as 1964 Scholem still felt "sceptical" concerning the "riddle" of Jung and Nazi Germany in general and Jung's published views in particular, for example, his 1936 essay on "Wotan," the tone of which Scholem still found "ambivalent" concerning Nazism.[28] Scholem described himself as an historian of religious ideas with an expertise in the history of Jewish mysticism. He was interested in the constancy of historical change, not in any archetypal, *unchanging* character

26 Gershom Scholem, *On the Kabbalah and Its Symbolism*, translated by Ralph Mannheim (New York: Schocken Books, 1969), and *On the Mystical Shape of the Godhead*, translated by Joachim Neugroschel (New York: Schocken Books, 1993).
27 Picture 2: Gershom Scholem at Eranos in August 1951.
28 G. Scholem, *A Life in Letters, 1914-1982*, pp. 405-406; c.f., C.G. Jung, "Wotan" (1936), in: *Civilisation in Transition*, vol. 10 of *The Collected Works of C.G. Jung*, translated by R.F.C. Hull (Princeton: Princeton University Press, 1964), pp. 179-193.

of the phenomena, in other words, he was uninterested, for example, in what Marie-Louise von Franz, following Jung, has said was necessary to interpret fairy tales, amplifying and comparing motifs, and collecting parallels between motifs.[29] We can see from Jung's letters how interested he was to find parallels between Jewish and Christian Kabbalah. On the other hand, we can see in Scholem's work, *Alchemy and Kabbalah*, that he wanted to determine whether Christian borrowings from Jewish Kabbalah accurately represented the Kabbalah, which he found they mostly did not. In one case Scholem found, "a deformation or transformation, if not transmutation of the Jewish Kabbalah into something purely Christian."[30]

In letters to third parties Jung and Scholem spared few words about each other. To Morton Smith in December 1950 Scholem wrote that he refrained at Eranos from "psychological excursions,"

> But I felt that much could be done in this field by someone with a sound philological training and not given to the more extreme forms of psychoanalytical fantasies for which I cannot arouse much sympathy. I feel that much of the amateurish character of psychological researches into the History of Religion, especially of the Freudian and Jungian brand, is caused by the lack of a sound philological basis for their contentions.[31]

Perhaps that explains why, after the publication of Jung's *Answer to Job*, Gershom Scholem held a seminar at the Hebrew University in Jerusalem with the title, "Der liebe Gott als Patient von Jung."[32]

As this concerns a fundamental difference between the two scholars, we need to understand what is really at stake here. In October 1937 Scholem wrote a letter to Salman Schocken, founder of the renowned Schocken publishing house in New York, in which he came close to expressing his own credo:

> Certainly, history may seem to be fundamentally an illusion, but an illusion without which in temporal reality no insight into the essence of things is possible. For today's man that mystical totality of "truth,"

29 Marie-Louise von Franz, *The Interpretation of Fairy Tales* (Boston: Shambhala Publications, 1996), p. 43.
30 G. Scholem, *Alchemy and Kabbalah*, p. 97.
31 G. Scholem, *A Life in Letters, 1914-1982*, p. 351.
32 [The beloved God as Jung's patient] I thank René Malamud (d. 2015) for this information.

whose existence disappears particularly when it is projected into historical time, can only become visible in the purest way in the legitimate discipline of commentary and in the singular mirror of philological criticism.[33]

Paradoxically, therefore, the "mystical totality of truth" can only become visible in the form of its projections into historical time, there and then and here and now, to be unearthed, recovered, and transmitted through the infinitely painstaking researches of commentators like Professor Scholem. Through the historians' painstaking commentaries and researches we might begin to approach that "mystical totality of truth." If that diurnal task seems at all mundane, of this world alone, not so, writes Scholem in a 1939 letter to Theodor Adorno:

> What is remarkable about every rational form of mysticism lies in the relation between tradition and experience ... Jewish mysticism, in its very name, points to this relation; for *Kabbala*, in German, translates as "tradition" and not "*Ur*-experience." From the outset the Kabbalists, including the greatest visionaries among them, always – and with awesome energy – affirmed that their insights were a species of commentary.[34]

Gershom Scholem was perfectly willing to acknowledge that Jewish Kabbalists and Christian alchemists shared a common source in the Old Testament, but he simply saw no necessity, "to resort to the more far-reaching psychological hypothesis of archetypes of the soul, as developed by C.G. Jung in his respective works."[35]

There is no agreement whatsoever between the Jewish historian and the non-Jewish psychiatrist on the subject of an influence working both ways between Jewish Kabbalah and Christianity. In October 1966 James Kirsch wrote to Gerhard Adler that he had asked Scholem whether there were

---

33 Quoted Anson Rabinbach, "Introduction" to *The Correspondence of Walter Benjamin and Gershom Scholem, 1932-1940*, edited by Gershom Scholem, translated by Gary Smith and Andre Lefevere (Cambridge, Massachusetts: Harvard University Press, 1989), p. xxxi.

34 G. Scholem, *A Life in Letters, 1914-1982*, p. 300.

35 G. Scholem, *Alchemy and Kabbalah*, p. 41; it is interesting that Walter Benjamin spared no words when writing to Gershom Scholem in a slightly different context of his desire to wage "an onslaught on the doctrines of Jung, especially those concerning archaic images and the collective unconscious," letter of 2 July 1937, *The Correspondence of Walter Benjamin and Gershom Scholem 1932-1940*, p. 197.

any signs of a "deep occupation of the Jews with Christ and the Christian mystery." Scholem answered that, "there was nothing concerning Christ or the Church."[36] As we shall see, for Jung that was tantamount to complete nonsense.

Picture 3: The *Sefirotic Tree* from Moses Cordovero, *Pardes Rimonim*, 1592

Here we must briefly discuss the central importance in the Kabbalistic universe of certain divine entities which are usually portrayed as a Tree of Life, the *Sefirotic Tree*. The Kabbalists portrayed the revelation or emanation of God's energy as forming a Tree of Life, symbolically understood as having ten *Sefirot*.[37] *Sefirot* is the plural of the Hebrew word *Sefirah*, which has many meanings, including these: "Sayings, names, lights, powers, crowns, qualities, stages, garments, mirrors, shoots, sources, primal days, aspects, inner faces, and limbs of God."[38] The *Sefirot* symbolically represent, therefore, what are considered to be primal aspects of God's Being, imaginally understood. The ten *Sefirot* are usually depicted as ten circles arranged in the shape of a tree.[39] The tree as a Tree of Life is of course a universal archetypal symbol,

36 Letter of 11 October 1936, quoted *The Jung-Kirsch Letters, The Correspondence of C.G. Jung and James Kirsch*, edited by Ann Conrad Lammers, translated by Ursula Egli and Ann Conrad Lammers (New York: Routledge, 2011), p. 153.

37 G. Scholem, *Major Trends in Jewish Mysticism*, p. 13

38 G. Scholem, quoted Harold Bloom, *Kabbalah and Criticism* (New York: Continuum, 1999), p. 26.

39 Picture 3: Diagram of the ten *sefirot* from Moses Cordovero, *Pardes Rimonim*, Krakow 1592. The ten *sefirot,* one inside another, are composed of the initial Hebrew letter of each *sefirah* starting with the first *sefirah* Kether, that is, crown and ending in the middle with the M for *Malkhuth* or *Shekhinah*.

enormously important in Jung's *opus*. Energy is imagined to flow upwards, downwards, and horizontally between the ten *Sefirot*. For example, on the horizontal level there has always been an imagined tension between two opposing aspects of God's Being, *Hessed*, Loving-kindness, and *Gevurah*, Judgement. Observant Jews ritually pray that God's loving-kindness will prevail over His tendency for stern judgement.

Energy is imagined to flow down from the three purely spiritual and unknowable *Sefirot* at the top, *Kether*, *Chochma*, and *Binah*, Crown, Wisdom, and Understanding. Energy emanates down to the ever more concrete, material, and human, called *Malkhuth*, Kingdom, the source of God's immanence in nature, the energy which is the closest and most accessible to us humans here below. Going the other way, the *Sefirot* represent stages in the ascent of the soul from the material to the spiritual and divine plane of existence. Jung has written, "*Kether*, the crown, corresponds to the upward growing root of the Tree of the *Sefiroth*."[40] This refers to the image of the archetypal Tree of Life as an Inverted Tree with its roots "in the air,"[41] or in heaven. An analysand of Jung's depicted the Tree as growing simultaneously upwards and downward.[42] A story is told from around a century ago of another kind of inverted tree:

> Preparations were underway for a Christmas party in the Paris apartment of G. I. Gurdjieff when the Master himself came in, approached the decorated Christmas tree, and insisted that the decorations be removed from the tree and that it be hung upside down from the ceiling with the roots upwards.

Returning to Jung on the subject of the *Sefirotic Tree*, in 1952 James Kirsch wrote to Jung asking what role Christ and the Christian mystery play in the Jewish psyche. Jung wrote back:

> I can call your attention to the extraordinary development in the Cabbala. I am rather certain that the *Sefirotic Tree* contains the whole symbolism of a Jewish development parallel to the Christian idea. The

---

40 C.G. Jung, *Mysterium Coniunctionis* (1955-6), vol. 14 of *The Collected Works of C.G. Jung*, translated by R.F.C. Hull (Princeton: Princeton University Press, 1963), § 18.
41 Ibid., § 37.
42 C.G. Jung, "The Philosophical Tree" (1954), in: *Alchemical Studies*, CW 13, Figure 6, § 311; cf., C.G. Jung's discussion of other examples from Kabbalah, Hindu mythology, Christian Mysticism, and Alchemy, ibid., § 410-414.

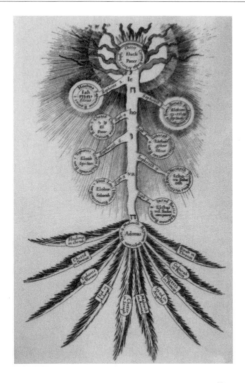

Picture 4: The *Sefirotic Tree* as Inverted Tree[43]

characteristic of a Jewish development parallel to the Christian idea. The characteristic difference is that God's incarnation is understood to be a historical fact in the Christian belief, while in the Jewish Gnosis it is an entirely pleromatic process symbolised by the concentration of the supreme triad of *Kether*, *Chochma*, and *Binah* in the figure of *Tifereth*. Being the equivalent of the Son and the Holy Ghost, he is the *sponsus*, the spouse bringing about the great solution through his union with *Malkhuth*. This union is equivalent to the *assumptio beatae virginis*, the Assumption of the Blessed Virgin [by Pius XII in 1950], but definitely more comprehensive than the latter as it seems to include even the extraneous world of the *Klipot* [This refers to the vessels that shattered in the primal cosmic catastrophe,

43 Picture 4: The *Sefirotic Tree* as inverted Tree. Robert Fludd, Utriusque cosmi maioris, vol. 2, Frankfurt 1621, reproduced in Alexander Roob, *The Hermetic Museum. Alchemy and Mysticism* (Cologne: Taschen Verlag, 1997) p. 318.

thereby bringing the reality of evil into the world]. Professor Scholem is certainly all wet when he thinks that the Jewish Gnosis contains nothing of the Christian mystery. It contains practically the whole of it, but in its unrevealed pleromatic state [pleromatic is the Gnostic term purporting to describe the spiritual universe as the abode of God and of the totality of the Divine powers and emanations].[44]

Carl Jung was clearly a lot more willing to call himself a Kabbalist than Gershom Scholem was to call himself a Jungian! Professor Scholem had already dismissed "psychological excursions," as he called them in the 1950 letter quoted above, of "the Freudian and Jungian brand" for their lack of professional philological scrutiny. The key question here is epistemological, having to do with what it means to say that we know something. Scholem says that we can know from the historical record what happened, where it happened, and when it happened. To some degree Scholem belongs to the long tradition of commentators on the received tradition of the Word ascribed to God Himself, even if Scholem himself as a modern academic would not embrace the creedal tradition, as such. As we noted above, Jung relies on a kind of ahistorical, associative, and amplificatory way of knowing, involving a search for parallel expressions of basic universal truths. That is what knowledge of the archetypes gives us. In contrast to Scholem's philological scrutiny, therefore, Jung adduces the Christian mystery as present "in its unrevealed pleromatic state," hardly likely ever to satisfy the Jerusalem Professor.

Jung's writing, in English, "Professor Scholem is certainly all wet when he thinks that the Jewish Gnosis contains nothing of the Christian mystery," is really quite amazing, given that calling someone *wet* only entered the English language in the 1930's. "Wet" was of course popularised in the very nasty British Conservative Party in-fighting in the 1990's when the "Iron Lady," Margaret Thatcher, called the less hard-core Conservatives under John Major, "wet." Calling someone "wet" is highly insulting. And what did Scholem lack the courage to do? He simply would not and could not accept that "practically the whole" Incarnation of Christ and the validity of the Holy Trinity, supplemented in our time (1950) in the Beatification, the *Assumptio Mariae*, the ascension of the Virgin Mary to a place in the new Quaternio of Catholic symbolism, was all "contained" in the Jewish Gnosis, "but in its unrevealed pleromatic state."

44 *The Jung-Kirsch Letters*, letter of 18 November 1952, pp. 143-145.

It is impossible fully to develop this thorny issue here. For two millennia very strong feelings have been constellated concerning Christian attempts to assimilate and convert Jewish people, forcibly or peacefully, to Christianity. A small but telling example is Jung's own copy of a 17th Century anonymous version of Christian Knorr von Rosenroth's, *Kabbala denudata*, "Kabbalah revealed," the full title of which can be translated, "An Outline of the Christian Kabbalah, that is a Hebraizing Accommodation to the doctrine of the New Covenant, useful for the Forming of a Hypothesis for the Conversion of the Jews."[45] To put it mildly, it was hardly the norm in bygone centuries to ask the Jews if they actually had any desire to convert to Christianity!

It is easy to overlook just how introverted and completely self-referential Jewish people first of all had to be when confined to the ghetto. Ghettoes keep the outside world out as well as the inside world in. Obviously Jews have been forcibly reminded throughout their history, even long after their Emancipation in Western Europe from the ghettoes, of the desirability of living lives apart. For the most part, then, it is simply self-evident that the answer to James Kirsch's question to Gerhard Adler in 1966, concerning "a deep occupation of the Jews with Christ and the Christian mystery," could only be a resounding, "No!" The culture of the Jews has completely ignored everything about Jesus, yes, in the sense of deliberately choosing simply not to spend a moment considering Him and His life, especially as it has involved accepting the impossible dogma that He is the Son of God. No wonder Carl Gustav Jung and Gershom Scholem were like two ships passing each other in the night! For Jung, Christ is a "highly numinous figure."[46] To which, if he said anything at all, Scholem might answer, "Well, you may think that, but I don't trust your sources, if there are any, for saying that."

Second Interlude: "Now a mystic, now a prophet, now a critic."[47]

Their incompatibilities aside, however, there are clear parallels between these two subject matters, Carl Jung's *opus* and Kabbalah. Gershom Scholem may have found no evidence of an influence of Christian Mysticism on

---

45 Ibid., editor's citation at p. 144, footnote 39.
46 C.G. Jung, *Answer to Job*, CW 11, § 663.
47 G. Scholem, diary entry of 24 July 1919, quoted in *Lamentations of Youth, The Diaries of Gershom Scholem, 1913-1919*, edited and translated by Anthony David Skinner (Cambridge and London: Harvard University Press, 2007), p. 6.

Jewish Mysticism, but he certainly accepted the importance of Renaissance humanists like Johannes Reuchlin from Germany and Pico della Mirandola in Florence, who called the Kabbalah "the eldest and deepest wisdom of mankind." According to Scholem, Pico della Mirandola was the first Christian to take a "deep interest" in the Kabbalah[48] and he began to introduce the Kabbalah into the world of the Florentine circle around Marsilio Ficino.[49] As an historian of religious ideas Scholem certainly discussed the very clear Neoplatonic or Gnostic influences in Kabbalah. For him this had nothing to do with the notion of a collective unconscious and everything to do with philology and history.

Gershom Scholem was just as interested as Carl Jung, however, in the mythological underpinnings of religious belief. After all, Scholem wrote that, "The price of God's purity is the loss of His living reality. For the living God can never be subsumed under a pure concept."[50] It is hard to imagine Jung's finding fault with that statement. Not being himself a religiously observant Jew Gershom Scholem knew that Kabbalistic visions were best understood as myths and wrote that, "Kabbalists strove from the very first to anchor the ritual of Rabbinic Judaism in myth by means of a mystical practice."[51] In other words, they did not seek to establish a rabbinic grounding for their myths, which was the hitherto traditional way. Much more significantly, Gershom Scholem tells us that Kabbalah was the "vengeance of myth."[52] Instead of what Jung called dogma and creed and a second order formalism of belief and observance typical, for example, of the great twelfth Century rationalist Jewish scholar Moses Maimonides,[53] the Kabbalists produced stories and myths. Behind that general remark, Gershom Scholem's amazing statement about the "vengeance of myth" recognises that there is always a tension, dialectical but not necessarily always oppositional, between the tendency to a rigid codification of ritualised practices and efforts that are always being made to breathe new life into the old texts. As Marie-Louise von Franz says, "If one can still read such a revealed text or religious experience with the eyes of the soul, then it still

---

48 G. Scholem, *On the Kabbalah and Its Symbolism*, p. 62.
49 G. Scholem, *Alchemy and Kabbalah*, pp. 85-86.
50 G. Scholem, *On the Kabbalah and Its Symbolism*, p. 88.
51 Ibid, pp. 132-133.
52 Ibid., p. 99.
53 C.G. Jung, *Psychology and Religion* (1938/1940), CW 11, especially § 9, 75, and 76. Moses Maimonides formulated the "Thirteen Articles of Faith," each of which begins, "I believe with perfect faith that ... " They are basic tenets of Jewish Orthodoxy.

conveys life and the original meaning, and then the effect of petrification does not occur."[54] That is precisely what Gershom Scholem spent his whole adult life doing and we are the beneficiaries of it.

Although Gershom Scholem described himself as merely a commentator and an historian of Jewish Mysticism, he was far more than simply an "objective" academic. He actually had much in common with Jung in welcoming a dialectical tension between individual creative spontaneity and tradition. Just as Jung has been called a mystic,[55] so we find a 1919 diary entry by the brilliant young Scholem in which he says that the task of the creative individual, "now a mystic, now a prophet, now a critic," is to "uncover new messianic dimensions in [each] respective generation."[56] Those exact words could have been applied to Carl Gustav Jung at various points in his long life. One difference between them, perhaps, is that the Jewish professor was seasoned in the long-established Jewish art of covering up the sometimes too obvious traces of one's presence. Irony serves that purpose; so does hiding oneself in the texts, which Scholem acknowledged that he did, similar to an artist like Botticelli's placing himself into the crowd scene in his master work, "The Adoration of the Magi."[57]

In actual fact, the ever religiously observant rabbis had always warned against any attempt to understand the Kabbalah literally. The texts were to be analysed as a whole, but only by means of what have been called "hints and allusions."[58] Hints and allusions appear so far to have been quite enough, for the Kabbalists gave themselves astoundingly free rein and license in re-imagining and re-formulating anything and everything Biblical in sometimes startlingly strange ways.[59] The Kabbalists produced

---

54 Marie-Louise von Franz, *Individuation in Fairy Tales* (Dallas: Spring Publications, 1977), p. 57f.

55 See, for example, Aniela Jaffé, *Was C.G. Jung a Mystic and Other Essays* (Einsiedeln: Daimon Verlag, 1989), and Gary Lachtman, *Jung the Mystic* (New York: Jeremy Tarcher/Penguin, 2010).

56 Quoted Anthony David Skinner, "Introduction," Gershom Scholem, *Lamentations of Youth, The Diaries*, p. 6.

57 Ibid., pp. 4-5. Josef Weiss, Scholem's star pupil, made the comparison which Scholem accepted as valid.

58 Rabbi Aryeh Kaplan, "Introduction" to the 12th Century Kabbalistic text, *The Bahir, Illumination* (York Beach, Maine: Samuel Wiser, 1989), p. xix.

59 Wondrous examples of amplifying canonical texts are to be found in the 13th Century mythopoeic fantasies of the *Zohar*, albeit the *Zohar* was intended as Biblical commentary.

what has been called the "official theology of the Jewish people,"[60] but whereas the Holy Office ordered Giordano Bruno burned at the stake and Galileo confined for years under house arrest, and whereas the Dominican mystic Meister Eckhart died while still under investigation for heresy, there never has been a Jewish Holy Office to charge the Kabbalists with heresy and the Kabbalists "never really became a separate domain of spiritual life outside the religious tradition."[61]

We cannot know exactly what effect the historical catastrophe of the total destruction of the Jewish presence in Spain in 1492 and in Portugal in 1508 had in the next decades on Isaac Luria and the other Safed Kabbalists such as Moses Cordovero, his teacher, and Chaim Vital, his most important disciple. Gershom Scholem says that Kabbalism underwent a "complete transformation."[62] Isaac Luria has been called "extraordinarily original" and perhaps the "only visionary" among all the Kabbalists.[63] Scholem calls the doctrine of *tzimtzum*, meaning concentration or contraction, one of the "most amazing and far-reaching conceptions ever put forward in the whole history of Kabbalism," even if it was not entirely original to Isaac Luria.[64]

For the emanations of the first part of creation to take place the Godhead has to be imagined as voluntarily withdrawing Its totality and contracting into Itself to make a space for creation to begin. That is what is meant by *tzimtzum* or contraction. This can also be imagined as a single white line of light within the total circle of light of the Divine presence. If the contraction can be imagined as an inhaling, or an intake of breath, then we can imagine that the first exhalation, or breathing out, of creative Divine energy or emanation was so strong that the vessels or shells, the *klipot*, were overwhelmed by that energy and a cosmic catastrophe thereby ensued, the *shevirah*, or shattering of the vessels. That is how evil is conceived to have entered the world as a separate and independent reality, not as something involving men and women in the first instance, but as inherent in some way in the Godhead and in the process of creation itself. That is the meaning of

60 Rabbi Adin Steinsaltz, quoted in *Essential Judaism* (New York: Pocket Books, 2000), p. 402.
61 Rabbi Adin Steinsaltz, "Afterword," in: Herbert Weiner, *9 ½ Mystics, The Kabbala Today* (New York: Collier, 1992), p. 385.
62 G. Scholem, *Major Trends in Jewish Mysticism*, p. 244.
63 H. Bloom, *Kabbalah and Criticism*, p. 39.
64 G. Scholem, *Major Trends in Jewish Mysticism*, p. 260.

"the great dialectical leap" Luria made beyond the teachings of his teacher, Moses Cordovero.[65]

This acceptance of the reality of evil may be equivalent to the amazing statement Jung reportedly made when asked how he could live with the knowledge that he had recorded in his *Answer to Job*. He said that, "I live in my deepest hell, and from there I cannot fall any further."[66] Jung was referring to the reality of evil inherent in the dark side of the God-image, to the opposites within the God-image itself, and to the enormous responsibility we assume in trying to follow the will of God.

The true originality of Isaac Luria's Kabbalistic myth lies in its denial of a one-sided idea of creation simply progressing out from the Creator. As Harold Bloom says, "Reality for Luria is always a triple rhythm of contraction, breaking apart, and mending, a rhythm continuously present in time even as it first punctuated eternity."[67] "Mending" is *tikkun olam*, the repairing, restitution, and salvation of the world, undertaken by individual humans. In Isaac Luria's meaning, *tikkun* involves religious acts of a meditative character, acts carried out with conscious Intention, or *kavannah*, which bring us closer and closer to the Divine in Devotion, or *devekut*. Gershom Scholem writes that *tikkun* involves, "the restoration and reintegration of all things to their original condition because the Divine plan has been hindered on an ontological level by the breaking of the vessels and on a human level by Adam's fall."[68]

A fifteenth Century alchemical image beautifully portrays the first man, Adam, the universal man, the fallen man, fallen into matter from which the alchemical task is to redeem him by extracting the spirit in the matter.[69] From the dead body succumbing to decay at the bottom of the retort, "the mercurial soul, the spirit, the tincture is extracted."[70] In what Scholem calls, "a great myth of exile and redemption,"[71] Lurianic Kabbalah imagined that Adam's human task was to remove from himself all the "fallen sparks" that were still in exile consequent to the shattering of the vessels and to put them

65 H. Bloom, *Kabbalah and Criticism*, p. 37.
66 Quoted in Marie-Louise von Franz, *Jung: His Myth in Our Time* (Toronto: Inner City Books, 1998), p. 174.
67 H. Bloom, *Kabbalah and Criticism*, p. 39.
68 Gershom Scholem, *On the Mystical Shape of the Godhead*, p. 242.
69 Picture 5: Adam, the first man and the alchemical *opus. Miscellanea d' Alchimia*, Italy 15th Century, reproduced in A. Roob, *Alchemy and Mysticism*, p. 307
70 Gerhard Dorn, *Theatrum chemicum* (1602), quoted A. Roob, *Alchemy and Mysticism*, p. 307; cf., C.G. Jung, *Psychology and Alchemy*, CW 12, § 357f.
71 G. Scholem, *On the Kabbalah and Its Symbolism*, p. 117.

in their proper place. But Adam failed to do that, and his fall corresponds on a human level to the ontological level of the shattering. Consequent to the fall and the expulsion from Eden, God's feminine Presence, the *Shekhinah*, also went into exile, and in consequence the sparks of her presence must be redeemed.[72] The Kabbalists affirmed as an article of faith, however, that in order to redeem Adam we must scrupulously follow the Laws of Moses,[73] which is obviously a much more creedal imperative than anything Jung had in mind.

Picture 5: Adam, the universal man

Taken together, the great threefold myth of exile and redemption, involving the contraction, *tzimzsum*, the shattering of the vessels, *shevirah*, and the repair of the world, *tikkun*, is both profoundly conservative, as the conscious intent is "to restore our days as of old," in the words of a Jewish daily prayer, and profoundly revolutionary, as it is the ethical responsibility of each and every individual to contribute in some way to repairing the world. Jung found most exciting the prospect of our repairing the world as a co-evolutionary task with God, about which he wrote in English to the Reverend Erastus Evans in February 1954:

72 Ibid., p. 115
73 Gershom Scholem, *On the Possibility of Jewish Mysticism in Our Time and Other Essays*, edited and with an Introduction by Avraham Shapira. Translated by Jonathan Chipman (Philadelphia: The Jewish Publication Society, 1997), pp. 12-14.

Christ is most decidedly not the whole Godhead as God is "hen to pan" [The One, the All]. Christ is the Anthropos that seems to be a prefiguration of what the Holy Ghost is going to bring forth in the human being. … In a tract of the *Lurianic Kabbalah*, the remarkable idea is developed that man is destined to become God's helper in the attempt to restore the vessels which were broken when God thought to create a world. Only a few weeks ago, I came across this impressive doctrine which gives meaning to man's status exalted by the incarnation. I am glad that I can quote at least one voice in favour of my rather involuntary manifesto.[74]

Jung's involuntary manifesto recalls the fact of a mortal man, Job, being unjustly punished for something he clearly did not do, at the behest of Satan, the "Adversary," who goaded the Godhead Yahweh-Jehovah into testing His servant, the God-fearing Job. It also recalls the fact of Job's enduring and surviving the suffering unjustly visited upon him, which results in the elevation of the man Job to a truly amazing place:

The new factor is something that has never before occurred in the history of the world, the unheard-of fact that, without knowing it or wanting it, a mortal man is raised by his moral behaviour above the stars in heaven, from which position of advantage he can behold the back of Yahweh, the abysmal world of "shards."[75]

In consequence, the Answer to Job has to be Yahweh-Jehovah's incarnating in His son Jesus Christ and the sacrifice of the Crucifixion. That is what Jung means by the importance of the Incarnation, but what is really significant is that evolution now means co-evolution, where the humans have to live with the double aspect of the light and dark sides of the Deity, and where, as we move and transform in consciousness, we help the Creator also to become more conscious. For that purpose man, being destined to play a part in the Divine drama, *must* receive the Holy Spirit.[76]

The wonderful idea of our conscious choices helping God to become conscious, an aspect of what the Kabbalists called *tikkun*, repair, runs

74 C.G. Jung, *Letters*, vol. 2, 17 February 1954, p. 157.
75 C.G. Jung, *Answer to Job*, CW 11, § 595.
76 C.G. Jung, "Letter to Père Lachat," 27 March 1954, *The Symbolic Life*, vol. 18 of *The Collected Works of C.G. Jung*, translated by R.F.C. Hull (Princeton: Princeton University Press, 1980), § 1551.

through Jung's thinking, from as early as 1929 in this exciting letter to Walter Corti:

> God wants to be born in the flame of man's consciousness, leaping ever higher. ... One must be able to suffer God. That is the supreme task for the carrier of ideas. He must be the advocate of the earth. God will take care of himself. My inner principle is: Deus *et* homo. God needs man in order to become conscious, just as he needs limitation in time and space. Let us therefore be for him limitation in time and space, an earthly tabernacle.[77]

In a very important 1956 letter to Elined Kotschnig Jung describes what we can call the co-evolution of man and God, "The significance of man is enhanced by the incarnation. We have become participants of the divine life and we have to assume a new responsibility, viz. the continuation of the divine self-realisation, which expresses itself in the task of our individuation."[78] What an amazing insight, that through our individuation we are responsible for Divine self-realisation.

Finally, of the many examples of this theme, here is a short extract from Jung's amazing "Late Thoughts," at the end of his *Memories, Dreams, Reflections*:

> In the experience of the self it is no longer the opposites "God" and "man" that are reconciled, as it was before, but rather the opposites within the God-image itself. That is the meaning of divine service, of the service which man can render to God, that light may emerge from the darkness, that the Creator may become conscious of His creation, and man of himself.[79]

It is exciting to learn that before Isaac Luria or Carl Gustav Jung invoked what has been called a co-evolution of humans and God, around the year 1200 Menahem Recanati, whose work on a Kabbalistic interpretation of the commandments was much read, wrote that, "those who perform the ritual lend stability, as it were, to a part of God Himself, if it is permitted

---

77 C.G. Jung, *Letters*, vol. 1, 30 April 1929, pp. 65-66.
78 C.G. Jung, *Letters*, vol. 2, 30 June 1956, p. 316.
79 Aniela Jaffé (ed.), *Memories, Dreams, Reflections by C.G. Jung*, translated by Richard and Clara Winston (New York: Vintage Books Random House, 1989), p. 338.

to speak in this way."[80] We might say that ritual action represents and calls forth divine life if, that is, we are able to extract the spiritual content from the concrete aspects of the ritual. This is similar to Jung's saying, in "The Psychology of the Child Archetype," that, "Religious observances ... serve the purpose of bringing the image of childhood, and everything connected with it, again and again before the eyes of the conscious mind so that the link with the original condition may not be broken."[81]

A renowned 18th Century Hasidic rabbi reminds us that the work has to be continued and renewed, just as we try to live with conscious intention and presence:

> This is how we must interpret the first words in the Scriptures. "In the beginning of God's creation of the heavens and the earth." For even now, the world is still in a state of creation. When a craftsman makes a tool and it is finished, it does not require him any longer. Not so with the world!
> Day after day, instant after instant, the world requires the renewal of the powers of the primordial world through which it was created, and if the power of these powers were withdrawn from it for a single moment, it would lapse into chaos.[82]

Postlude: A Marriage Made in Heaven?

Throughout his entire working life we can see that Carl Jung was concerned with "the coming into being of what is essentially human, the *emergence of human consciousness.*"[83] As we know, Jung found in alchemical symbolism deep resonances to his own work, especially in the idea of the reconciling and union of opposites in a sacred marriage, the *hieros gamos.* Jung writes:

---

80 G. Scholem, *On the Kabbalah and Its Symbolism*, p. 125.
81 C.G. Jung, "The Psychology of the Child Archetype" (1951), in: *The Archetypes and the Collective Unconscious*, vol. 9i of The *Collected Works of C.G. Jung*, translated by R.F.C. Hull. (Princeton: Princeton University Press, 1968), § 275.
82 Rabbi Simha Bunam of Pzysha (d. 1827), quoted Martin Buber, *Tales of the Hasidim* (New York: Schocken Books, 1995), p. 259.
83 *Children's Dreams. Notes from the Seminar Given in 1936-1940 by C.G. Jung.* Edited by Lorenz Jung and Maria Meyer-Gass, translated by Ernst Falzeder with the collaboration of Tony Woolfson (Princeton: Princeton University Press, 2008), p. 367 (emphasis in the original).

For the principal pair of opposites is the conscious world and the unconscious world, and when the two come together, it is as if man and
woman were coming together, the union of the male and the female,
of the light and the darkness. Then a birth will take place. Therefore in
alchemy the *Lapis philosophorum* [the Philosopher's Stone], which is the
reconciling symbol, is often characterised by the union of the male and
the female.[84]

In order to bring about what he called the union of the conscious world
and the unconscious world, Jung, like the Alchemists and the Kabbalists,
emphasised the extraction of spirit from matter.

In the Jewish mystical tradition, the indispensable energy required for
that process is that of the *Shekhinah*, God's female Presence in the world.
This aspect of the divine is imagined to have been in exile since the sin
of Adam's fall. Ever since then good and evil have been confounded in
the realm of the *klipot*, the vessels which had already shattered under the
pressure of energy emanating from the Godhead. According to Lurianic
Kabbalah, whenever we fall into sin this shattering of the vessels is repeated,
the holy is tainted with the profane, and the *Shekhinah* remains endlessly in
exile, imagined as Biblical Rachel's weeping for her children, the Children
of Israel in exile.[85] In *Mysterium Coniunctionis*, Jung equates the Kabbalistic
Shekhinah with, "the prima materia in its feminine aspect,"[86] and calls her
the Widow.[87] As Christian Knorr von Rosenroth says, "This is Malchuth
when Tifereth is not with her." The widowed *Shekhinah* is also called the
Orphan, so deep is the sadness and so symbolic is the *Shekhinah* of the
"underlying feminine principle."[88]

We might say that, just as God contracts Himself to make space for
Creation to commence, so the loss of His *Shekhinah* symbolises the part
of God Himself that is exiled from God. For the Kabbalists, redemption
hinges on the reunion of God and His *Shekhinah*. The Kabbalists held that
every religious act should be accompanied by the formula: This is done
"for the sake of God and His *Shekhinah*."[89] That is why the Kabbalists
always stressed the vital significance of the smallest details of the law and

84 C.G. Jung, *Visions Seminar*, vol. 1, p. 574.
85 G. Scholem, *Major Trends in Jewish Mysticism*, pp. 279-280.
86 C.G. Jung, *Mysterium Coniunctionis*, CW 14, § 14.
87 Ibid., § 18.
88 Ibid.
89 G. Scholem, *On the Kabbalah and Its Symbolism*, p. 108

the ritual,[90] and why the goal of prayer is to bring about that love between *Tifereth* and *Malkhuth*. The *Zohar* even understands the prayers symbolically as preparing the *Shekhinah*, the in-dwelling presence, just as one prepares a bride for marriage with her beloved, and the bringing of that marriage to fruition.[91]

Jung, too, was well aware of this powerful mission: "In this wicked world ruled by evil, *Tifereth* is *not* united with *Malkhuth*. But the coming Messiah will unite the King with the Queen, and this mating will restore to God his original unity."[92]

Jung himself experienced the Kabbalistic vision of the sacred marriage, or *coniunctio*, between *Tifereth* and *Malkhuth*. It was in 1944, the year in which Jung broke his foot followed just ten days later by a very serious heart attack. He hovered between life and death for three weeks, and only for an hour late at night was he able to eat the food the nurse, whom he imagined to be an old Jewish woman, brought him. During that hour he experienced truly awesome visions. He writes that the old Jewish nurse was with him in the *Pardes Rimonim*, the mystical Garden of Pomegranates, where the Kabbalistic wedding of *Tifereth* and *Malkhuth* was taking place. Or the mystical wedding of the ancient sage, Simeon ben Jochai, was taking place. Jung writes: "At bottom it was I myself: I was the marriage. And my beatitude was that of a blissful wedding."[93]

In receiving such a numinous vision when he was so seriously ill, Jung must have come as close as can be imagined to an experience of the fullest individuation and the most complete integration imaginable of all the psychic components in his being. Masculine and feminine were united, as were the masculine and feminine aspects of the Godhead. This was truly an awesome vision.

A sacred marriage is also the subject of an exquisitely bittersweet story attributed to Rabbi Eizik of Kallo, an Hasidic master who lived in Hungary in the 19th Century. It is called *The Sabbath Guests*:

Two Hasidim arrived in the city of Kallo on the eve of the Sabbath and sought out the famed hospitality of the Rabbi of Kallo. The visiting

90 Adin Steinsaltz, "Afterword," in: Norbert Wiener, *9 ½ Mystics*, p. 387.
91 Lawrence Fine, *Physician of the Soul, Healer of the Cosmos* (Stanford, California: Stanford University Press, 2003), pp. 224-225.
92 C.G. Jung, *Mysterium Coniunctionis*, CW 14, § 18.
93 A. Jaffé (ed.), *Memories, Dreams, Reflections by C.G. Jung*, p. 294.

Hasidim greatly anticipated spending the Sabbath in the company of the renowned Rabbi.

Soon everyone had gathered together to celebrate the Sabbath, and all looked forward to the righteous one, the *Tzaddik*, for the sign to welcome the Sabbath Queen, the *Shekhinah*, and bring in the Sabbath. But the *Tzaddik* did not stir. Not a single muscle moved. Every eye remained on him, yet he seemed detached, in deep concentration.

The visiting Hasidim were startled at such behaviour, for everyone knew that the Sabbath candles must be lit no less than eighteen minutes before sunset. Could the Rabbi have lost track of time?

All at once there was a knock at the door, and a couple came in. The young man was dressed in a white robe, as was worn in Safed where it was told that each Sabbath evening the Holy Ari, Isaac Luria, and his disciples donned the white robes of Sabbath purity and re-birth before going out into the fields to greet the Sabbath.

The young woman, who was also wearing white, was hauntingly beautiful, with very dark eyes, her head covered with a white scarf. The *Tzaddik* rose, at the same time signalling for the Sabbath to begin. The Hasidim began singing *Lecha Dodi* (the Kabbalistic song of welcome to the Sabbath bride, the *Shekhinah*, composed in the 16th Century in Safed, and still sung every Sabbath evening in the synagogue), as the Rabbi of Kallo greeted his guests. He treated them with every kindness, paying as much attention to the woman as to the man. This already greatly upset the visiting Hasidim, but they were guests and there was nothing they could do.

After the meal the Rabbi of Kallo rose and said: "This couple have come here to be wed this day. And I have agreed to marry them." Now these words were a deep shock to the visiting Hasidim. Why? – it is forbidden to marry on the Sabbath. And so they began reciting Psalms to themselves, to protect them from the proposed desecration of the Sabbath. At that moment the Rabbi turned to the two Hasidim and addressed them. He said, "Of course, the consent of everyone present is necessary if the wedding is to be performed. Please tell us if we have your consent." And there was almost a pleading tone in his voice.

Now it is one thing to witness such a desecration, and quite another to participate in the performance oneself. But the two Hasidim did not dare turn down the *Tzaddik* to his face, so they each dropped their eyes and continued reciting Psalms, and a great fear was in their hearts.

At last, when the Hasidim raised their eyes, they saw that the couple were gone. The Rabbi of Kallo was slumped in his chair. For a long time there was silence. At last the Rabbi said:

"Do you know who they were?"

Each of the Hasidim shook his head to say no. And the Rabbi said:

"He was the Messiah. She was the *Shekhinah*, the Sabbath Queen. For so many years of exile they have sought each other, and now they were together at last, and they wanted to be wed. And, as everyone knows, on the day of their wedding our exile will come to an end. But that is possible only if everyone gives his full assent. Unfortunately, you did not, and so the wedding could not take place."[94]

The story surely says it all: as consciousness dawns of the dreadful ascendancy of the minutiae of creedal observance over the beauty of spontaneous experience there is the terrible feeling of having just missed the boat -- and what a boat! A sacred marriage made in heaven to be consummated here on earth. How sad that the pious Hasidim are all too obviously the earthly representatives of the legalistic God of the Jewish dispensation, apparently themselves unable to imagine that out of the *materia* of the *Shekhinah* there could emerge that union of the earthly and the spiritual realms.

How easy it is to be wise after the event, however, and to forget the enormous achievement and the enormous difficulty of the *opus*, of aspiring to an inner and outer sacred marriage, not to mention restoring to the Divine His and Her archetypal unity.

Epilogue

In the end, as in the beginning, it is all about words, all about stories. Carl Gustav Jung, the "witch doctor" of Küsnacht as he was known locally, spent his life collecting dreams, his own and other people's. He even offered "small rewards" to the Elgonyi tribespeople in Kenya if they brought

94 Re-told by Howard Schwartz in, "The Quest for the Lost Princess," Edward Hoffman, ed., *Opening the Inner Gates, New Paths in Kabbalah and Psychology* (Boston: Shambhala, 1995), pp. 30-31. For some reason that I have been unable to discover, Howard Schwartz's version is quite different from that in *Rabbi Eizik, Hasidic Stories about the Zaddik of Kallo* (Cranbury, New Jersey: Associated University Presses, 1978), pp. 37-40. A resonant story being a resonant story, I have retold Howard Schwartz's version with some minor variations.

him their dreams, but by 1925 the rationalist ethos of the British colonial administration had so infected the tribespeople that they told Jung dreams were no longer needed, "because now the English knew everything!"[95]

And at almost exactly the same time, Gershom Scholem, the idealistic and brilliant young scholar, left his past in Berlin behind and made *aliyah* (emigrated) to Palestine, where he spent the rest of his scholarly life until his death in 1982 as an increasingly renowned Professor at the newly established Hebrew University in Jerusalem. There he more or less single-handedly collected centuries of wild and crazy stories in the mystical tradition of Judaism, stories of a time immemorial when there was a *Presence*, and then came *the Absence of a Presence*, and *the Presence of an Absence*, stories which until the modern rationalist times were known to everyone, stories which by their own account helped so many Jewish people to endure the centuries and centuries of exile from the Promised Land; stories of how the men used to go out into the fields surrounding Safed of a Friday evening just before sunset to welcome in person the Sabbath Bride, *Shekhinah-Malkhuth*, and how they sang the hymn of welcome, *lecha dodi*, "Go, my Beloved, to meet the Bride, let us receive the face of the Sabbath… " And the men wore the white robes of Sabbath purity and rebirth while at home their wives, each one an *eishet chayil*, a woman of valour, prepared a Sabbath feast fit for the Sabbath Bride and Groom, and the wives lit the two Sabbath candles, symbolic of the holy Sabbath *coniunctio*, no less than eighteen minutes before the going down of the sun, upon which everyone entered the temple in time that is the Sabbath, God's gift to the Israelites, which they are commanded to "remember and to keep holy," whereas in fact, everyone knows that the Sabbath kept the Jews at least as much as the other way round.

Although Professor Jung[96] found God in his own and other people's dreams, some of the stories he told were simply too far-fetched for certain inhabitants of the stories like the Jews who, unlike the Elgonyi tribespeople that said dreams were no longer needed, have in fact survived more than two thousand years of dispersion, exile, tragedy, and triumph not by ever taking up arms but by telling and re-telling their own collective dreams and stories. Many of the stories are about losing and finding, and about homelessness

---

95 A. Jaffé (ed.), *Memories, Dreams, Reflections by C.G. Jung*, p. 265.
96 "I'll tell the Professor – he won't be a moment." Thus did Ruth Bailey, Jung's secretary, tell Eugene Rolfe on 15th December 1960 that his eagerly awaited appointment with Jung at Seestraße 228 in Küsnacht was about to begin. Eugene Rolfe, *Encounter with Jung* (Boston: Sigo Books, 1989), p. 195.

and rootlessness, so much in fact that long before contemporary experiences of displacement and homelessness these Jewish People became known as Eternal Wanderers. There even arose an infamous Mediaeval story, with no basis in fact, in which the curse of being doomed to wander endlessly was laid on the head of the Jew in Jerusalem that supposedly refused to give Jesus water to drink as he bore the cross to Calvary.

That story might have been known to the renowned photographer Roman Vishniac, who in the year 1938 was commissioned to travel from the New Country to record for the last time Jewish life in the Old Country, because everyone could tell it was soon to end, and he created timeless images of what posthumously was called a "vanished world." One day the photographer was walking down a street in Cracow, shabby, wintry, slushy, and cold, when he encountered a tall, bearded, obviously rabbinical old man who was dressed in the Hasidic fashion, and the photographer bethought himself to ask him how long he had been wandering (see plate 9, p. 233).[97]

"From the beginning" was his answer.

Although Roman Vishniac did not ask the Talmudic scholar what he meant, we can surely say that those are archetypal wanderings.[98] As indeed are the kinds of spiritual quests undertaken by C.G. Jung throughout his long life, during one of which he says, "I am a wandering beggar."[99]

And almost simultaneously Professor Scholem responded with alacrity to an invitation from a Jewish Institute in New York to lecture for the first time in English on what he had unearthed from fifteen years spent sifting, documenting, and interpreting the many centuries of a mythological Jewish universe existing parallel to the universe of the minutiae of prescribed daily observances. So far had the New World, symbolised in the tradition of the new, evolved from the earlier times when mythology was ever-present in

97 Roman Vishniac, Hasidic man, wearing a *shtreimel* [fur hat] on the Sabbath, Kazimierz, Krakow, ca. 1935-1938.
98 Roman Vishniac, *To Give Them Light*, Preface by Elie Wiesel, edited by Marion Wiesel (New York: Simon and Schuster, 1993), p. 133. Years later, Roman Vishniac and Gershom Scholem came to know each other well, and in the Roman Vishniac Archive in New York City there are photographs of Gershom Scholem taken in Switzerland in the late 1970's by Roman Vishniac (Susan Carlson, Curatorial Assistant at the International Center of Photography, New York, personal communication).
99 C.G. Jung, *The Red Book – Liber Novus*, edited by S. Shamdasani. Translated by M. Kyburz, J. Peck, S. Shamdasani (New York: W.W. Norton & Company, 2009), p. 316.

daily practises, that the research findings of Professor Scholem, published as his *Major Trends in Jewish Mysticism*, effected a revolution in the study of those arcane old texts and inaugurated what today has become the respectable and fashionable interest in Kabbalah, even to the wearing of Kabbalistic charms by people like the songstress Madonna, and to the highly questionable practise of selling "Kabbalah Water" in plastic bottles at the world-wide network of Kabbalah Centres set up by the American Rabbis Berg.

And so Gershom Scholem found his way to Eranos in 1949, and he showed up nearly every year until 1978, and he was as esteemed as Henry Corbin and Mircea Eliade for his erudite presentations on religion. We are the beneficiaries of those presentations and invaluable essays. And there was not exactly a love at first sight between Professor Scholem and Professor Jung, although there are obvious parallels between the alchemical dream-time of the psychologist and the mythological dream-time of the Jewish spiritual tradition.

C.G. Jung had his own purpose in mind, truly a fascinating one, concerning an alternative story of the God of the Old Testament, of His dark and suppressed side which He did not recognise, and of how, consequent to the suffering unjustly visited upon Biblical Job in order to prove a point against his own God's self-doubt, He incarnated into a human being just as the human being spiritualised into a creature Divine, and the Cross was where they met, at which point the answer to Job is given.

And Gershom Scholem has to tell C.G. Jung that the Jewish People have never had any interest in this archetypal theme of the significance of the Incarnation by God in His Son.

For his part, Professor Scholem had to admit what we mostly all know, that the world of the Kabbalists is not in fact our real world at all, and just as the Kabbalah is concerned with belatedness, as we always arrive on the scene *after* the primal Catastrophe, *after* the Shattering of the Vessels, we can and must at best try to restore our place in the Divine scheme as it used to be and indeed help God in the restoration of His unity. On the importance of that *opus* both Professors are in complete agreement. Scholem knows that we moderns have also arrived on the scene belatedly, because for the most part we simply cannot embrace the fundamental tenet of the Kabbalists, as believing and observant Jewish people are expected to do.

The fundamental tenet of Jewish faith concerns the presuppositionless world of *torah min hashamayim*, of Torah from Heaven, the archetypal world of the Hebrew God who communicated and communicates still to those faithful who are able to accept, declare, and believe the sacred words that are sung in the synagogue whenever the unrolled Torah scroll is held up for all present to see, that the Torah now in their hands is the same one that God transmitted to Moses. And those are the words which all Kabbalists felt beholden to restore in all their primal numinosity.

Most of us are unable or unwilling to inhabit that archetypal world and live accordingly, and so in 1963 Gershom Scholem gave a public lecture entitled, "On the Possibility of Jewish Mysticism in Our Time." And the answer he gave was, it is not possible, because we cannot live with the reality of *torah min hashamayim*, Torah from Heaven.[100]

But we can keep telling our personal and shared stories, which we do, and there can be a startling numinosity in such telling and re-telling.

For Gershom Scholem in New York in 1938, faced with the historical inevitability of yet more tragedies befalling the Jewish People, what matters is to retrieve and preserve whatever we can of the past triumphs and tragedies. And so he concludes his path-breaking lectures on Jewish Mysticism with a story he heard from the Nobel Prize winning Hebrew novelist and story-teller, S. J. Agnon, who must have heard it at some point after it was published in Warsaw in 1906 in a collection of tales about a famous Galician Hasidic Rabbi, Israel of Rishin:

> When the founder of modern Hasidism, the Baal Shem Tov (1700-1760), had a difficult task before him, he would go to a certain place in the woods, light a fire, and meditate in prayer – and what he had set out to perform was done. When a generation later Dov Baer the Maggid, or Teacher, of Mezeritz was faced with the same task he would go to the same place in the woods and say, "We can no longer light the fire, but we can speak the prayers."
> And what he wanted done became reality.
> A generation later Rabbi Moshe Leib of Sassov had to perform this task and he too went into the woods and said, "We can no longer light a fire, nor do we know the secret meditations belonging to the prayer, but we do know the place in the woods where it all takes place."
> And that was sufficient too.

100 G. Scholem, *On the Possibility of Jewish Mysticism in Our Time and Other Essays*, pp. 14-19.

But when another generation had passed and Rabbi Israel of Rishin felt called upon to perform the task, he sat down in his golden chair in his castle and said, "We cannot light the fire, we cannot speak the prayers, and we do not know the place, but we can tell the story of how it was done."

And the story teller adds that telling the story was sufficient unto the fullness thereof in this case too.[101]

To the writer of these words there befell an exquisite co-incidence concerning just this story. I was travelling in a train from Geneva to Zurich in September 1995 when I first read this story. And I thought how appropriate a summation it is of the history of religion from direct experience to the experience of talking about the events without being able actually to be historically present at them, not to mention from direct experience to the experience of denominational religions as only petrified, dogmatic, and very boring, and I thought I must tell the Hasidic story in lectures on Judaism that I was preparing for the Jung Institute in Küsnacht. That evening I opened a wondrous volume of poetical, mystical, and spiritual Jewish writings from the beginning until now, and there right on the opening page was the very same story.

When Gershom Scholem was still a young man, he realised that a creative individual needed to be "now a mystic, now a prophet, now a critic," a realisation surely applicable also to C.G. Jung, and Gershom Scholem obviously remembered those words in 1938 when he concluded his lectures on Jewish Mysticism, because even after re-telling the story of the special fire, the special place, and the special prayer, all obviously aspects of the Divine Presence, he pronounced these final fateful words,

> To speak of the mystical course which, in the great cataclysm now stirring the Jewish people more deeply than in the entire history of Exile, destiny may still have in store for us – and I for one believe that there is such a course – is the task of prophets, not professors.[102]

After the Catastrophe Gershom Scholem came to Eranos on the Lago di Maggiore and delivered the first of those astounding lectures that are so fundamental to our understanding of Kabbalah as the mythology of the

101 G. Scholem, *Major Trends in Jewish Mysticism*, pp. 349-350, slightly adapted.
102 Ibid., p. 350.

Jewish People, and there, with the realities both of the Six Million and the founding in 1948 of the State of Israel foremost on people's minds, he concluded his presentation on Kabbalah and Myth with a similar profession of faith in the continuity of that mystical course experienced by the Jewish People "in the struggle and victory of these last years," and which now provides an opportunity "to fulfil its encounter with its own genius."[103]

It is more and less difficult for Jewish people to tell stories about their way of life without at some point needing to consider their own shared historical experiences. There can come a point when memory no longer only redeems us but, so to speak, holds us captive in the complexes constellated by a very emotionally charged history. That may be why the world renewed Yiddish writer, Isaac Bashevis Singer, once said that, "Jewish people remember too much." And the burden of remembering so much must explain why an old kibbutz resident who faithfully attended every community meeting finally broke years of silence and very, very hesitantly managed to speak boldly:

"I am against Jewish history!"

Gershom Scholem spent his entire adult life studying Jewish historical experience in the context of texts that are available to us, and to some extent, therefore, his scholarly works are inseparably linked with that experience.

No such profound links can be found between C.G. Jung and Swiss-Protestant experience, or Swiss 20th Century experience. Naturally, Jung was a very Swiss sort of person and there is to some degree a predictable context to some of what he said and did, such as we find in his volume of essays on the 1933-1945 time, *Essays on Contemporary Events*. There is also to a certain degree a professional medical context in which he so brilliantly worked as a medical psychologist, as he often described himself.

In the context of mysticism and alchemy in general, and the Kabbalah in particular, however, C.G. Jung's experience was often in a way heretical and always unashamedly and uniquely personal. Not for him any need or desire to place his experiences in the context of an identity like that held all his life by Gershom Scholem.

For Professor Jung, what matters is that each and every one of us tells the story that is uniquely his and hers, not somebody else's, be that a parent, a partner, or an authority figure of some kind. And what matters is that each

---

103 G. Scholem, *On the Kabbalah and Its Symbolism*, p. 115.

and every one of us lives the reality of evil without judgement and without projecting the shadowy aspects of ourselves onto convenient Others. In other words, we must not "succumb to either of the opposites."[104]

One reason C.G. Jung is so important, even in the context of studying Jewish Kabbalah, is that he lived and experienced so deeply whatever he studied and learned in his long life. Jung has bequeathed to us the experiences of a profoundly mystical human being. At the end of *Liber Secundus* of the *Red Book*, for example, he writes,

> The touchstone is being alone with oneself.
> This is the way.[105]

In oldest age C.G. Jung must have spent so much time alone with himself that he came very close to those darkest fears that beset us as we approach death. In an amazing letter, hand-written in November 1960, the Zurich Professor unburdened himself to an English theologian, Eugene Rolfe, one of whose books he considered a "ray of light" at a very difficult time. In particular, Jung considered himself to have failed where it mattered most:

> I have failed in my foremost task, to open people's eyes to the fact, that man has a soul and that there is a buried treasure in the field and that our religion and philosophy is in a lamentable state.[106]

C.G. Jung was very well aware of how hard it is to live between the opposites. In full awareness of the opposites facing St. Paul, he saw him as the apostle, "directly called and enlightened by God," and as a "sinful man unable to pluck out the "thorn in the flesh." And a lyrical summation follows at the very end of his *Answer to Job*:

> That is to say, even the enlightened person remains what he is, and is never more than his own limited ego before the One who dwells within him, whose form has no knowable boundaries, who encompasses him on all sides, fathomless as the abysms of the earth and vast as the sky.[107]

*

104 A. Jaffé (ed.), *Memories, Dreams, Reflections by C.G. Jung*, p. 330.
105 Jung, *The Red Book – Liber Novus*, p. 330.
106 The letter is reproduced in full in Eugene Rolfe, *Encounter with Jung*, pp. 157-159.
107 C.G. Jung, *Answer to Job*, CW 11, § 758.

Was Carl Gustav Jung a Jewish Kabbalist? No.
Was Carl Gustav Jung a Christian Kabbalist? Maybe.
Was Carl Gustav Jung a Kabbalist? Of course!
How so?
Because he accepted the reality of evil.[108]

108 This essay is a revised version of a lecture presented at the Psychology Club in Zurich in November 2014.

C.G. Jung

A Discussion about *Aion*

Psychological Society of Basel, 1952

Preliminary remarks of the editors

The following article contains a previously unpublished discussion with C.G. Jung, recorded on 25 January 1952 at the Psychological Society of Basel, which was founded in 1933. The president at that time, Margret Ostrowski-Sachs, was the initiator. She was the wife of the well-known Russian-German mathematician, Alexander Ostrowski, and a student of C.G. Jung. As a member of the Psychology Club of Zurich, she was very close to Jung. After his death, she published her notes from various conversations with Jung in her book, *From Conversations with C.G. Jung.*[1]

Jung had agreed to answer questions related to his work, *Aion: Researches into the Phenomenology of the Self.*[2] This work concerning the psychic background of the "Christian aeon" originally appeared in 1951 in volume 8 of Psychologische Abhandlungen [Psychological Treatises],[3] together with a contribution by Marie-Louise von Franz, on the passion of Perpetua,[4] in which she outlined the psychological transition from antiquity to Christianity. Jung's work emerged from his deep concern about the estrangement of Europeans from their cultural-historical roots. During these years, Jung was occupied with his principal

1 Margret Ostrowski-Sachs, *From Conversations with C.G. Jung* (Zürich: C.G. Jung Institute, 1971).
2 C.G. Jung, *Aion: Researches into the Phenomonology of the Self*, vol. 9/2 of *The Collected Works of C.G. Jung*, edited and translated by R.F.C. Hull (Princeton: Princeton University Press, 1968).
3 C.G. Jung, *Aion: Untersuchungen zur Symbolgeschichte mit einem Beitrag von Marie-Louise von Franz* (Zürich: Rascher Verlag, 1951).
4 Marie-Louise von Franz, *The Passion of Perpetua. A Psychological Interpretation of her Visions*, edited by Daryl Sharp (Toronto: Inner City Books, 2004).

work, *Mysterium Coniunctionis*.[5] He wrestled with the sixth and last chapter, "The Conjunction." Apparently he was only able to complete this when he had thoroughly reappraised the Christian self symbol in *Aion*.

Wherever possible, the editors have retained Jung's lively speaking style. Only where necessary for clarity were small changes carried out. These are indicated by brackets []. Omissions, and places in which the recording was unintelligible even after repeated listening, are indicated by periods... Passages that are actually intelligible, but make no sense in context, are omitted and indicated by parentheses (...). The section headings have been added by the editors.

We are grateful to the Foundation for the Works of C.G. Jung for permission to publish this document for the first time as part of the volume marking the hundredth anniversary of the Psychology Club.

*

Margret Ostrowski-Sachs (president of the Psychological Society of Basel): Members and honored guests, this evening we have the very special pleasure of welcoming Professor Jung; he, whose name is most often mentioned in our circle; whose works are most often quoted. [We are glad] that we dared [to ask him]. At our suggestion, Professor Jung has agreed to a discussion evening about *Aion*.

In presenting our questions to you, we want to become clear about several important points and correctly visualize them. Because whoever speaks about the spirit and content of an age [aion] must not only be familiar with the intellectual history of two millennia but also have already gained for himself a standpoint that is actually anchored outside of this age. He must have gained a certain distance from the events and feeling content of this age in order to be able to assess from the psychological perspective the symbols and the transformation of symbols and their meaning over the last two millennia. And now, this evening, when we present our questions, we must be clear that these very questions push at the boundary of this aion, into areas that perhaps have been problematic more than once for all of us, into questions, into problems, which for some of us are still sacrosanct realities. We are also clear that we are treading on delicate terrain, because it concerns an area where knowledge and intuition meet. However, when one writes such a difficult book, one must also risk that the questions are

---

5   C.G. Jung, *Mysterium Coniunctionis*, vol. 14 of *The Collected Works of C.G. Jung*, translated by R.F.C. Hull (Princeton: Princeton University Press, 1970).

correspondingly difficult (laughter). And if it is all right with you, I would propose that we now move on to the discussion.

C.G. Jung: Yes, yes. I am ready.

Good evening, Ladies and Gentlemen.

By way of introduction, I want to express my thanks, especially to your honorable president, for the friendly reception you have given to me and my wife this evening. I am therefore completely ready to launch myself into the discussion. I hope you will ask your questions fearlessly, in the knowledge that I am myself conscious of what difficult things I have written and what audacious things I have said in this book. The big difficulty, as you will have seen, lies in the fact that I have occupied myself here with a figure [Christ], which as the president rightly said, is for many people a sacrosanct quantity. However, in this regard I must say that there are also many others, who are likewise good people as well as very good citizens, who do not find such a figure sacrosanct. Because, you know, as soon as we think about something, then we actually offend it, and quite frankly I cannot see why we shouldn't think about such things. So, that is my standpoint. It may be a blasphemous standpoint, but I have a better impression of God. He has given me a certain intellect, and he will not have given me this for nothing. So if I don't use it then I don't see at all why he made the effort to equip me with such an intellect.

These days, there are too many people who can't simply believe, aren't there? They have to understand it. I am one of these people. Above all things, I can't believe anything at all. Either I know something, and then I don't need to believe it, or I don't know it, so why should I then believe it? Just so! So please ask me your questions now.

Question: ... In *Aion*, you write: "I have therefore suggested that the term 'psychic' be used only where there is evidence of a will capable of modifying reflex or instinctual processes."[6] On the other hand, in the new edition of *Psychological Types*, it says: "I regard the will as the amount of psychic energy at the disposal of consciousness."[7] From this, one would have to conclude that only consciousness, not the unconscious, is assigned to the psychic realm. Despite this, we do classify the unconscious as psychic too, although consciousness is not present in it. How can we explain this?

6 C.G. Jung, *Aion*, CW 9/2, § 3.
7 C.G. Jung, *Psychological Types*, vol. 6 of *The Collected Works of C.G. Jung*, translated by H.G. Baynes and R.F.C. Hull (Princeton: Princeton University Press, 1971), § 844.

C.G. Jung: Do you mean that acts of will begin in the unconscious?

Question: No. I refer to the first definition in *Aion*, where you write that the term "psychic" is used only "where there is evidence of a will capable of modifying reflex or instinctual processes," that is, where the reflex and instinctual processes may be changed by the will. And on the other hand, in *Psychological Types* you now define the will as the energy available to consciousness. From this one would have to conclude that only consciousness, not the unconscious, is classified as psychic. Despite this, we do classify the unconscious as psychic too, although it has no conscious will.

C.G. Jung: Yes, yes, of course.

Question: Although it has no conscious will? How can we explain that?

The Unconscious as Psychic Function

C.G. Jung: That is a difficult, complicated matter, which naturally I have treated only superficially here. I have covered that extensively in my essay, "The Spirit of Psychotherapy."[8] There, I have established how we ought to interpret the psychic conceptually, namely as that sphere in which the will is able to alter instinctual processes. So the will arises from consciousness; that is a function of consciousness; otherwise it is no will, only a drive. It doesn't follow, however, that the unconscious is not psychic, because the unconscious is influenced in large part by the will. I don't say "compelled" or "directed," rather "influenced," because we know that the conscious attitude exerts a curious constellating effect on the unconscious contents, in that in consequence, the constellation of the unconscious is essentially altered through a particular psychic attitude. Otherwise the unconscious would have no biological justification to exist.

However, it has the right to exist as a potentiating function, and it compensates – occasionally even complements – conscious events. Of course, this is only valid insofar as the unconscious occupies an appropriate area in the sphere of the personality. Fairly certainly, however, it stretches far

---

8   C.G. Jung, "The Spirit of Psychology," trans. R.F.C. Hull, in: *Spirit and Nature, Papers from the Eranos Yearbooks*, ed. by Joseph Campbell (Princeton: Princeton University Press, 1954), vol. 1, pp. 371-444. A later, revised and augmented version appears as "On the Nature of the Psyche." In: *Structure and Dynamics of the Psyche*, vol. 8 of *The Collected Works of C.G. Jung*, edited and translated by Gerhard Adler and R.F.C. Hull (Princeton: Princeton University Press, 1970), § 343-442.

beyond, and there our criterion for "psychic" stops anyway. Then of course we know no more: is it an organic compulsion, or is it some life occurrence not necessarily of a psychic nature.

To give an example, take the archetypes as ideas. Of course they are either contents of consciousness, or they originate in that intermediate twilight zone between the unconscious and consciousness. Or, they are even more remote, as a priori forms of human spiritual functioning and are therefore in a state of absolute irrepresentability, about which nothing more can be said.[9] Then you can only say they are just occurrences, about which we can no longer say with certainty that they are psychic. We have no empirical basis; they are transcendental; they transcend consciousness. That means, the true formal preconditions of our psychic events are fundamentally transcendental in nature.

Or, you could also say, they are only hypotheses, which however have a certain right to exist, since we know that our psychic events are to a large extent a priorily arranged. They are somehow ordered, and this order doesn't come from the conscious image or from conscious intention.

Question: In *Aion* you write:

> As I have shown, the alchemical fish symbolism leads direct to the *lapis*, the *salvator*, *servator*, and *deus terranus*; that is, psychologically, to the self. We now have a new symbol in place of the fish: a psychological concept of human wholeness. In as much or in as little as the fish is Christ does the self mean God. It is something that corresponds, an inner experience, an assimilation of Christ into the psychic matrix, a new realization of the divine Son, no longer in theriomorphic form, but expressed in a conceptual or "philosophic" symbol. This, compared with the mute and unconscious fish, marks a distinct increase in conscious development.[10]

How does this conscious development appear today? Could you say something about parallel images and events of people today, compared, for example to what was revealed by the fate and visions of Perpetua in that time? And then, conscious development also means to overcome the Heimarmene. Could conscious development overcome the harshness of a

9 See C.G. Jung, "On the Nature of the Psyche," CW 8, § 417.
10 C.G. Jung, *Aion*, CW 9/2, § 286.

fate like Perpetua's? Does the archetypal time problem always manifest in some form as outer fate? And then I would like to know, to what kinds of consequences does the discovery of synchronicity as a principle of acausal connection lead?[11] How is the new that arises through the conscious development of the synchronicity principle reflected in the transformation of humans and the god image?

C.G. Jung: ... That is... (audience laughter)... You must tell me, what I should actually answer. For heaven's sake, that's a whole mountain range! You must extract one question that I can answer.

Question: Perhaps, if you can give us a parallel from the present time to what the visions of Perpetua represent for the time of transition to the Age of Pisces.

The Compensating Function of the Unconscious

C.G. Jung: That is a very banal manifestation. You can observe such visions and images accompanying our contemporary events in every analysis. For example, the dreams dreamt during and after the war, which contain an entire mass of symbolism, which of course I can't enumerate completely. These exhibit a compensatory character throughout, just like the visions of the holy Perpetua. Those visions compensated a time very different from today. Completely different psychic necessities existed then, and today, with our very different conscious situation, other compensations are of course required.

Question: [recording interrupted]

The Chthonic Spirit in Alchemy

C.G. Jung: Once again, that is an enormous wide-ranging question. I would have to present the entire mass of casuistry. I'm not ready for that and would need to have my notes by me. At most, I can illustrate with the strange approach of alchemy. That is to say, alchemy is medieval nature philosophy, which used a large amount of fantasy material – that is, visionary and also

11 C.G. Jung, "Synchronicity: An Acausal Connecting Principle." In: vol. 8 of *The Collected Works of C.G. Jung*, edited and translated by Gerhard Adler and R.F.C. Hull (Princeton: Princeton University Press), § 816-968.

dream material. As the alchemists themselves say, occasionally the *hydra theion* – that is, the divine water, or the *aqua permanens*, would be revealed to them in dreams. They also write fantasy stories – these famous parables – in which they try to describe the process somehow. And what they describe there is an individuation process, expressed in modern language. Now there, in that time, the unconscious compensation busied itself with preparation for the age of natural science, and there was then a decline, so to say, of material that was expressed through the symbol of Mercurius. That is a real chthonic spirit, who is in the last instance that *serpens*, that serpent, who resides in the center of the earth. That would be the deepest point. This idea is circulated in ever clearer form during the course of the Middle Ages until the end of the 17th century. And that is the form of the lapis, which arises out of exactly this snake, and out of this dragon, and the lapis is then made parallel with Christ.

Is the lapis put in place of Christ, or is the stone actually Christ, or does it stand next to Christ? One often doesn't know. It is expressed most clearly in the words of Henricus Khunrath, who lived in the 16th century. He said that Christ is the *Salvator microcosmi*, the healer of men, the saviour of humanity. The stone, however, is the *Salvator macrocosmi*; it is the redeemer of the cosmos.[12] With that, something was added to the Christian point of view that was, one can naturally say, implicitly available to Christian doctrine. For example, if you think of St. Paul, who speaks of the *Apo-katastasis panton*,[13] of the world of creation that sighs with us in bondage, which through Christ would also be redeemed. But, anyway, that refers to animated creation; he doesn't talk about minerals, for instance. But the alchemist also includes minerals, because the minerals are also diseased. They are *leprosa* – they have leprosy. So the entire creation is stained by the *peccatum originale*, by original sin, and must be redeemed from this curse.

This happens through this *Salvator macrocosmi*, who, however, does not descend from the spiritual sphere above, as in Christianity; rather he comes up from the depths. He is initially a snake, a dragon or other nasty animal – an evil spirit, sometimes the devil himself, and he plays mischievous pranks

12 C.G. Jung, "The Visions of Zosimos." In: *Alchemical Studies*, vol. 13 of *The Collected Works of C.G. Jung*, translated by R.F.C. Hull (Princeton: Princeton University Press, 1964, § 127; "The Philosophical Tree." CW 13, § 384; Heinrich Khunrath, *Vom hylealischen Chaos der naturgemässen Alchymiae und Alchymisten* (Graz: Akademische Druck- und Verlagsanstalt, 1990).

13 The expression means *complete restoration*. For *Apokatastasis*, see 1 Cor. 15:25-28 and Rom. 16:27.

on the alchemists. He hinders them in their work, bedevils their apparatus, or makes them fall asleep when they should stay awake in order to stir up the fire – or other such games.

...and the Triumph of Materialism

Those are all beliefs of the alchemists. They developed their redeemer concept out of this form, out of this mischievous figure, therefore from a kind of nature creature. And here he climbs up from below, quite in contrast to the Christian view, and unites the below with the power of above, *vis superiorum*, and then returns with this combined strength to earth. And they say that his strength, *vis eius integra est*, therefore his power, his might, is then completely united, when he changes again into earth. Now that is the opposite of spiritualization; it is materialization. As you can see, it already anticipated the developments of the scientific era and materialism, and that almost three hundred years earlier. It is a reaction of spiritless nature to the pure pneumatic spiritualization of the Christian world view. So that is an example of this compensation.

Now, naturally, the people who conceived this philosophy didn't live in our time. In our time we say we have already overcome... the age of scientific materialism. Of course that is not true; rather, now we are right in the middle of it. You see, there are currently isolated individuals who have overcome this rubbish, but that doesn't mean that this nonsense proclaimed from above doesn't quietly continue to grow in the depths within the common people. As they have ascertained statistically, for ordinary truths, it takes about twenty years until the tram conductor, the craftsman and the factory worker know something about it. So this scientific materialism now celebrates a great triumph to an outrageous degree. We must not give ourselves over to the idea that scientific materialism might be overcome, there is no question of that. We are stuck in it, and consequently, we now have a completely different conscious condition today from, for example, the medieval nature philosophers.

The Answer of the Unconscious

On the one hand, we have the living impression of pneumatic Christendom, that is, the Christian world view, while on the other hand, we have scientific materialism; and that is this well-known conflict between faith and knowledge which we are in. And now the question here is what is the unconscious doing *now*? What drives it now? Yes, as always it makes dreams and visions, and they are currently really very interesting. To again give an example, the result of this is the entire mandala symbolism, with which you are already familiar. That is very clear. There are such uniting symbols, which join the pneumatic with the chthonic and somehow bring them into balance. However, it is no longer the case that there is only an above and a below, but now [there is] also a right and a left. Therefore the unity completes itself in a *quaternio* and in a fourth that for ages has already been extremely meaningful.

Philo Judaeus[14] said that the number four is the most meaningful number. However, at that time no real conflict was understood by that, except that they assumed that the elements didn't have a good relationship to each other. They fought one another – they were enemies. The number of elements is a primeval *quaternio*, like the four temperaments, the four seasons, the four cardinal directions and so forth. These are simply the four components of a holistic unity. However, today the opposition within a *quaternio* is generally understood; namely, that there is an above and a below, and a right and a left, whereby the right and the left mediate, to some extent, between above and below, or the above and below mediate between right and left.

Such mandalas come about spontaneously, which of course most people haven't known. Thus they believe that I have been telling people that they should now draw mandalas; that would be good for psychic hygiene. One draws a mandala! Of course that is calculated rubbish. These things arise completely spontaneously. For instance, I've seen mandalas of children whom I didn't know personally – children of people I also didn't know – who under especially difficult psychic circumstances have begun to draw mandalas quite spontaneously, in order to quiet themselves, to bring order to the chaos in which they lived. It is an ordering symbol *par excellence*, and so nowadays, in our truly chaotic situation, the unconscious tries to bring order based on this very old archetype of the four. With this, I want to make you aware that these fours are not something equivalent; rather, *threes* are equivalent. *One* always makes an exception: it is double, or it is ambiguous, it is uncertain.

14 Philo of Alexandria, Jewish philosopher and theologian of the first century CE. He was the most important representative of Hellenistic Judaism.

Even H. G. Wells,[15] in his fantastic stories, got it completely right, of course without having any idea of these things. Perhaps you know his little story, *The Time Machine*.[16] There is this motor that runs not only through space but through time, so that when one sits on it one can travel to the future, or when one reverses the lever, one travels backwards in time. And the characteristic of this machine, he wrote, lies in the fact that it has four columns [rods]. Three of these are plainly quartz columns; one, however, vibrates so that one never sees clearly. That is the three and the one.[17] That is also an old principle of nature philosophy going back to Alexandrian times, that the one that joins to the three has a difficult form – an ambiguous, double form.

The *Assumptio Mariae*

Now I can give another example that has triggered general horror and many protests. Even the English archbishops were roused from their repose, specifically by the *Assumptio Mariae*. There comes a fourth to the court of the Trinity. Yes, of course, speaking purely dogmatically, she is no goddess, she is only 99 percent goddess, but she is at least *coredemptrix* [co-redeemer] and the dispenser of mercy, and so forth. She is the bride of the bridegroom. At any rate, one would certainly have to be something of an old-fashioned conservative if one wanted to claim that the woman *eo ipso* would be below the man. However, if one is even a bit modern one accepts they are equivalent. Therefore we must assume that the bride, who is raised to the heavenly bridal chamber, is equal to the groom. That is the practical conclusion that generally has been drawn for the last thousand years. Therefore Mary isn't in the... [unintelligible] but she is the fourth. And now, where is the vibrating now, where is the unclear in Maria? One indication is that she is the great interceder for sinners, so she has a special understanding for people of the dark, and then – I scarcely dare to say this – she is also a woman. It is the typical difference between female and male psychology,

---

15 Herbert George Wells (1866-1946).
16 Herbert George Wells, *The Time Machine: An Invention* (UK: William Heinemann, 1895).
17 Compare C.G. Jung, "Flying Saucers: A Modern Myth." In: *Civilization in Transition*, vol. 10 of *"The Collected Works of C.G. Jung*, edited and translated by Gerhard Adler and R.F.C. Hull (Princeton: Princeton University Press, 1970), § 738.

the same old story: someone calls from the balcony, "Three cheers for that little difference." (laughter)

Or, in the Middle Ages, if you for example go back to the Maria symbolism of the alchemists, that is, to the symbolism of the feminine, there you find very strange things. Take Eve, for example, the role of Eve. Of course, she is a special case. In short, the feminine is the number two. Therefore the number two is characteristic for Eve. The number three is masculine; it is characteristic for the man. That's why the devil has... for whom the number two is absolutely characteristic, because he is the doubter; he was made on the second day of creation, on Monday, on the day of the moon, and on *that* day, God did not say that what he had made was good, but on all of the other days he said it.[18] These people [the alchemists] emphasize that. This also explains why the devil initially caught Eve, and then, through Eve, Adam.

There you see the profound scepticism of these old rulers toward feminine nature! These things are a little unfamiliar, but they are traditionally in the air. And when the English archbishops and other theologians get upset about it – about this new dogma – [there are] good reasons for it.

What happens when a feminine being joins the masculine Trinity? Well then a *quaternio* arises; then you get precisely this crossing [Durchkreuzung][19]. Then our Christian world view is no longer a purely patriarchal matter; now a matriarchal element enters into it. She is the *regina coeli*. She is absolutely imperative. She is *mediatrix* and *coredemptrix*. You can receive no mercy unless the mother gives it to you, since Christ gives no mercy; he only produces mercy, but the mother confers it. And that is strict church doctrine.

Now for Protestantism, of course that naturally means a problem of the first order. You see, currently the situation is like this: the Catholic church has successfully established a *quaternio* by crossing the male line, the patriarchal line, with that of the matriarchal one. It's a stroke of genius, so to say, a symbolic one. But Protestantism is still a male religion, exclusively a male religion like Mithraism,[20] and it has long been said that Mithraism really only declined because all the women transferred to the cult of the

---

18 C.G. Jung, *Mysterium Coniunctionis*, CW 14, § 238.
19 The German expression alludes to the cross, that is, to the crucifiction of Christ.
20 Compare C.G. Jung, "Answer to Job." In: *Psychology and Religion: West and East*, vol. 11 of *The Collected Works of C.G. Jung*, translated by R.F.C. Hull (Princeton: Princeton University Press, 1969), § 753f.

Great Mother, while the men went to the men's club, namely to Mithras, where women were not admitted. Women had another religion; they had a goddess.

Maria, the Mother of God

In Catholic countries nowadays, Maria is immensely popular, precisely because, as *sous-entendu*, she is a goddess. The first great step to the *Assumptio* was [taken at] the Council of Ephesus.[21] In Ephesus the great mother goddess – Artemis-Astarte in Asia Minor – ruled, and in every town Maria was declared as *theotokos*, as Mother of God, by which she was transported into the vicinity of the gods. In this fifth century, this *transitus* legend arose – the *Assumptio* legend – from which the entire *Assumptio* movement actually dates. But that is a Gnostic-influenced tradition consistently rejected by the church, which however, had already gained so much ground that, one can say, the whole thing was already settled a thousand years ago. One need not get excited about it anymore. But that is an example of how it works today: from the unconscious through the mandala and relevant symbols; in the Catholic church through the *quaternio* of the divine figures.

So please, always remember, don't misquote me if you talk about it. In church doctrine, Maria is no goddess, although she is 99 percent one. Maria is not prayed to, rather she is worshipped. It is called *timētai hē María* when she is worshipped, but no genuflection [*proskynesis*] is made before her, one doesn't throw oneself on the floor in adoration. Go to the Catholic church once and see for yourselves what the practice is! There are I don't know how many Maria prayers and hymns, which differ not at all from any invocation. One can invoke Christ with the same words, or the Holy Ghost; one just changes the names. The church has already long blurred these distinctions and has proven very clever regarding the Maria cult. Now the pope has gone and caught the entire clergy in their own trap, in that he said, well all right then, in that case she is also God.

In any event, there is tremendous opposition [to the new dogma of the *Assumptio Mariae*] within the Catholic church. They are all shocked to death by the consequences. Of course it has enormous consequences. I can't go into all of them, but that is just one example. Yes, I mean the archetypal time problem, which manifests in psychological phenomena,

21 Council of Ephesus, 431 CE.

which of course don't exist for all those people who don't observe anything psychologically. And then, as you have seen, there are also occurrences having outwardly historical form, which are such facts. For example, the *declaratio solemnis* of the *Assumptio*; that is such a case.

In this context, I would rather not go into the question of synchronicity. Should this problem arise in connection with astrology, then I could perhaps say something about it.

Quaternity as a priori Formation

Question: [unintelligible]

C.G. Jung: Whatever the image of the quaternity is, is of course a psychic matter. The image is conscious, but the formation, the a priori formation of a quaternity – that touches on something. It doesn't simply come out of the air or from nothing; rather it touches on a transcendental foundation, on an unconscious basis, about which we can say nothing.

That is the unknowable archetype as such, whose nature I have also described as *psychoid*, in order to have a word for it. I call the *psychoid* a "quasi-psychic," but we know nothing about it.[22] It is completely obscure and it is an ordering factor. It is therefore not something from conscious tradition. Naturally, in no way do I [wish to] deny conscious tradition. Obviously there is conscious tradition; there is a migration of myth and all that. However, in cases where really nothing of that kind can be perceived, there are completely spontaneous quaternity phenomena. They simply exist just as there are blossoms that are five-petaled and six-petaled and so forth; so there are also these *quaternios* with humankind. That is a fact of nature like a blossom. There is absolutely no apparent reason why there should be five- or six-petaled, seven-petaled and nine-petaled and I don't know how many. We would say it is purely accidental. But it is a fact.

On Good and Evil

Question: [female voice; partially unintelligible]... I find it enormously disturbing that the Trinity becomes a quaternity either through the devil or through Maria – that is, through the woman.

22 Compare C.G. Jung, "On the Nature of the Psyche," CW 8, § 367f.

C.G. Jung: Yes, yes.

Question: And now the pair of them are so near to each other that – one finds this hard to accept – one can amplify one [the devil] with the other [Maria, woman]. Can one then speak of the same qualities?

C.G. Jung: So it would seem.

Question: Just now you said that Maria is actually raised up through materialism?

C.G. Jung: I haven't said that, the church has said that. She has experienced this hope; however, I am not convinced.

Question: [Is it really true] that the Christian view of materialism is evil?

C.G. Jung: Yes, for the church.

Question: But if that is now also psychologically true, then...

C.G. Jung: No, it only seems so. You must not forget that for every pneumatic religious form, the opposing chthonic obviously is the evil enemy. That is the dark, the other, that to be fought against. And if you now assume that nothing is so dark that there isn't a little good in it somewhere, and that perhaps the pneuma is equally not as wonderful as one thought, then of course the situation is completely different. What we call "devil" is maybe not quite so devilish after all. It is simply dark in contrast to the light. Yes, the light can work just as destructively as the dark and vice versa. All is relative.

For example, should doubt arise in someone's mind about the goodness and splendour of the spirit, yes, then the opposing dark "unspirit" [das dunkle Ungeistige] is maybe quite positive! So, now we come a little bit closer to the specific value of the feminine nature, because for the man, the pneumatic standpoint, which today we call the intellectual standpoint, is obviously *the* right thing: sense and reason and knowledge, and so forth. However, that is really not so terribly positive; it can have quite abominable consequences, as we have seen often enough. And by contrast, the dark is then suddenly very agreeable and much less dangerous. In this respect, for example, the Mother of God is quite a positive symbol for the dark side of our psyche.

In this respect, the Chinese are much more balanced than we are. We Europeans are always a little bit crazy. We are somewhat unbalanced; we are a nervous affair in comparison to the Chinese spirit. In China, it's quite a different case – much more matter-of-fact – just two principles. *Yang* is the pneumatic principle: that is, the light, the dry, the fiery, the south side of the mountains, the dragon. *Yin* is the dark, the nocturnal, the moist, the north side of the mountains and the tiger, a nocturnal predator.[23] *Yin* is just as good as *yang*, but it is different... Whoever says only *yang* is good – well of course he has the tiger against him; and should anyone get the idea that the tiger is the only right one, he has the dragon against him. And that's how we are in Europe.

Now the entire situation changes as soon as you change your premises. The premise of the absolute good of the spirit is of course connected to the Christian weltanschauung. God is spirit and is *the* good, while evil is a *me on*, a non-being.[24] So even the very substance is taken from the other side. There is *only* the good, and when there is something bad, then it is always attributed to humankind. In this process, the church is oblivious to what she thereby does to a person. Quite simply, she promotes him to [the status of] a divine adversary, who then has the power to ruin the beautiful world play [Weltspiel] of the good Lord. That is something so precious, so costly, that, as is well known, God even had to kill his own son, in order to compensate this evil. However, we cannot assume that the person would be worthless. Yes, these are the psychological consequences; that's how it appears.

The Irrepresentability of the *Mundus archetypus*

Margret Ostrowski-Sachs: You speak of the paradoxical character of the self, which like all archetypes has a light and a dark aspect. However, you add that this should in no way convey that the self "is anything like as contradictory in itself." It is quite possible that the "frightening figures may be called forth by the fear which the conscious mind has of the unconscious."[25] What psychology can convey about the archetypes through scientific research therefore doesn't grasp the last realities, rather only their

23 Compare Marcel Granet, *Das Chinesische Denken* (München: Deutscher Taschenbuch Verlag, 1963), pp. 86ff.
24 For *me on*, see C.G. Jung's letter to Father Victor White of 31.12.1949 in: C.G. Jung, *Letters*, vol. 1, selected and edited by Gerhard Adler with Aniela Jaffé, tr. R.F.C. Hull (London: Routledge and Kegan Paul, 1973), pp. 539ff.
25 See C.G. Jung, *Aion*, CW 9/2, § 355: "It is quite possible that the seeming paradox is nothing but a reflection of the enantiodromian changes of the conscious attitude which can have a favourable or an unfavourable effect on the whole."

image in the souls of humankind who still live in the grip of consciousness and unconsciousness. Do you now assume that, behind the images of the archetypes as we know them, another world stands that actually exists? Does that world also transform? Or do only the archetypal images that people have of this world transform?

C.G. Jung: Of course that is also a question that greatly exceeds my capacity. I can say nothing at all about it. I can only say that I am of the opinion that these images are based on something. The archetype of the quaternity is based on something. It points to something. However this something is completely unknown to us. If we say there should be something, we form, so to say, a hypothesis about it: for example, behind a *quaternio* is something. Of course this hypothesis constructs an existence, a hypothetical existence, which one could say, would be a kind of background world [Hinterwelt]. That would be a *mundus archetypus*, as the scholastics have called it. Of course, we can't say that a transcendental, hypothetical object is either an existence nor a non-existence. We can't say anything about it at all. Because if we could say something about it with validity, then the object would be immanent – it would no longer be transcendental. Somewhere we encounter the same unknown, about which we can decide nothing further. The question is only: is this hypothesis nonsense or not? Is it arbitrary or not?

Modern physics has supplied us with a host of examples where we can see that certain things simply cannot be visualized any more; or one can only visualize them through contradictions... We can be fairly sure that the essence of light per se is a unity and not a duality, although we express the nature of light through the study of waves and particles. But it is actually a unity. This is a no-nonsense hypothesis; that is even highly likely. And that is exactly how it is with the archetypes. We don't actually know what they are. Experience shows us it is like this: just as every person has a good and a less good side – that is to say, a shadow – every self is a transcendental object, because it cannot be experienced as whole. It is a hypothesis. But as a hypothetical essence, one can only presuppose that it gives rise to light and dark manifestations.

Therefore, were one to use the language loosely, one could say that the self has a positive and a negative side; it consists of *yang* and *yin*, although this statement is in no way possible for a transcendental object. Just as the nature of light is something unified, so the nature of the self is also something unified. But for our purposes, it appears to be separated. It appears like this, and it appears like that, because we cannot perceive anything without discrimination. So, if something is completely unified, (...) it casts no shadow, because there is nothing different from it, and if nothing is there that is different from it, how can we say something about it anyway? For example, if you are totally alone in the world – if *one* person is alone in the world, he never knows that he is a human being; he can say nothing at all about himself. He doesn't know what kind of being he is. He can only know it insofar as he can be distinguished [from others]. Something that cannot be distinguished is no subject for observation. It's the same with all these archetypal principles. Nothing can be said about their true nature.

On the Differentiation of the Dark Principle

Margret Ostrowski-Sachs: You speak about the transformations that occur in the God-image and in the myth of an age, and how consequently they reshape to new meaning. In *Aion* you point out the transformation from Leviathan to Behemoth and to Christ.[26] Does that accord now with the following scenario: in paradise the image of the godhead was still unambiguous – therefore still a unity, so in the heavenly condition. With the Fall, caused by the appearance of the serpent, it was split into light and dark aspects. Through the widening of consciousness, the serpent, or its corresponding sea monster, the Leviathan, was also split into Leviathan and Behemoth. Behemoth would in this case be a warm-blooded animal – one with a negative aspect. It no longer lives in the sea, but rather on land, near to people.

In this respect, therefore, the Behemoth would be between the godhead above the clouds and the evil in the water. Therefore that which is less evil and closer to humans, and consequently closer to God, prepares that psychological content that would be depicted in the Age of Pisces in the figure of Christ – as that same Christ who is man and god, [and who] represents the mediation between humankind and God. Consequently humankind would be reconciled with God. However, because a piece of the original God-image always remains split off in Leviathan, it would probably be the work of the coming age to integrate this split-off piece of the God-image remaining in the water. Would that now be the work that is confronted, so

26 C.G. Jung, *Aion*, CW 9/2, § 181-185.

to say, during the struggle with [Auseinandersetzung] and integration of the shadow? Would this work also be to raise up the Leviathan?

C.G. Jung: Yes, this matter is also rather complicated. I have indicated here that Behemoth and Leviathan – these are two characteristic animals that in a certain sense characterize the *natura res*. Originally, it has only to do with a serpent. In the Ugaritic texts from Ras Shamra, which go back very far to the third millennium before the birth of Christ, there is a serpent, the serpent *Ltn*. So that is Leviathan, and already there, in a passage about this serpent, a second one is distinguished, and this distinction can be found again in Isaiah, with the quick-moving serpent and the coiled serpent.[27] Therefore these two serpents indicate that the idea of this chthonic primal being, of this Leviathan, eventually splits. That means the concept is differentiated. It is a symbol containing contradictory natures. With the serpents in Isaiah, one doesn't see that yet; one also doesn't see it with the serpents in the Ugaritic texts. But then, in the later tradition, one sees that beside the Leviathan is a Behemoth, namely a buffalo. And these two are now hostile to one another, because there comes a great battle between Leviathan and Behemoth at the End of Days. They are both mortally wounded in this battle; then they serve as food for the devout. There are very amusing stories in which the Leviathan is salted by the dear Lord as food for the righteous in paradise.

With this differentiation of the darkness, the first millennium after Christ prepares itself, in that a compensation is in the offing in the unconscious precisely there, in that time when a complete split in consciousness exists between the light pneumatic and the chthonic world of darkness. In this compensation, this differentiation of the original Leviathan is now continued, and is carried on in alchemy as the two animals fighting each other: the motive of the two fighting animals, the two dragons – the winged dragon and the wingless dragon – in direct relation to Isaiah. Or, they are two lions, a male lion and a lioness, who fight each other; or it can be a unicorn and a stag, or a wolf and a dog, and so forth. Therefore, this already very old differentiation is now carried further. And now we see how in alchemy, this dragon fight differs from the transformation of the dragon; that is, the [alchemical] symbolization goes beyond that of the Jewish tradition. Behemoth and Leviathan come to an end; they are slaughtered, salted, or else consumed immediately on the Day of Judgment as a eucharistic meal,

27 Isaiah 27:1.

and with that, the whole story ends. It began already in antiquity with the killing of the dragon; however, in the Middle Ages, the thing developed further. The two devour each other, so to speak, or it is a dragon that bites its own tail, through which a transformation then develops.

In this way then, a completely new redeemer concept arises. However, it is in no way true, for instance, that out of this Behemoth (which is closer to God, so to speak, because it lives in the mountains) the Christ figure arises. Rather, it is the *lapis philosophorum*, the *filius philosophorum*, that arises from it. That is already a prelude to the later development of the first and second millennia after Christ. You see, the tension between Christ and the devil is in consciousness! The figure of Christ is anticipated in a completely different way; it is anticipated in Egypt. That is the dying and resurrecting god of the Near East. It goes back to the fifth millennium before Christ, to the figure of Osiris. That is a pure pneumatic figure, while the differentiation of the Leviathan is actually already forming compensation for the pneumatic principle from pre-Christian times, because the pneumatic principle became predominant with Greek philosophy approximately during the time of the Greek Golden Age, when the ancient gods had already reached their end. They had already been discredited in the time of Homer; so already seven to nine hundred years before Christ they had in large part forfeited their credit owing to their all-too-human qualities [Allzu-Menschlichkeit].

The Jewish and Christian Concepts of God

C.G. Jung: Dr. Reichstein asked another question, which essentially amounts to why the Jews at that time couldn't accept Christ.

Of course, one can give various answers to this question. But since we are now talking about symbols, one could say, taking a subjective view, that a highly probable reason is this: Old Testament theology has a god concept, the Yahweh god concept, which is morally neutral. That means – I haven't said it quite right: Yahweh is a guardian of justice and is himself unjust. He sins against his own commandments, which he issued on Mt. Sinai. That is a fact you can recognize from the Old Testament. It was a problem at that time, and for long afterwards in Orthodox Judaism, how one could come to terms with this splitting or conflict within Yahweh.

For example, there are stories from the later tradition, or even a prayer, in which Yahweh – as I have already cited in *Aion*[28] – is beseeched to make somewhat more use of his good qualities, instead of his evil ones. He is so bad tempered that when he has an attack, he must even hide his righteous under his throne [Stuhl] so that he won't destroy them, when he bludgeons all the others to death. That is an amoral god concept, or a conflicting god concept. Now that gradually intensified with the history of justice. We still have the *Book of Enoch*, which was written about one hundred years before the birth of Christ. Here we already have a quite clear expression of a tendency to have a guardian of justice on the heavenly court. That is the Son of man. The Son of man was sent as an advocate, so to speak, for humankind at the heavenly court, in order to persuade Yahweh to act more or less fairly. That was an expression of a certain rebellion against this incessant amorality... You have probably all heard that Christianity suddenly fell from heaven in the year "such and such"; of course that is a world history falsification. Nothing is historically so prepared as Christianity.

So the *Book of Enoch*, was of course frequently read in the time of Christ, and Christ quite certainly knew it. Everything of significance is in it. And then, we have the Christian Reformation, which was at the beginning a Jewish affair. You can see that clearly in the synoptic Gospels. Christ, that is, Jesus of Nazareth, was a Jewish reformer. His teaching was clear: God is good. He is a loving father who loves people and doesn't want to destroy them. That was then a clear answer to this old problem. Now one can easily imagine the Jewish theologians of that time had their Yahweh god concept, and they were not going to be convinced by anything else. Try saying something to today's theologians, and you will see what you are up against. There is nothing to be done about it; that's the way it is, and that's how it was back then too. In a certain sense, they were even right, because we have to say, if God is really good, it is hard to explain how Belsen and Auschwitz could have come to pass. I would certainly say that.

I could never agree with the viewpoint *omne bonum a Deo, omne malum ab homine* – all good comes from God, and all evil comes from humankind. Good God, that would mean that all humans would be as great as God, because evil is almost on a level with good! It's already almost a miracle if for once something good happens. Usually, everything goes to the devil, no? And evil is such an enormous force, even dogmatically, that God

28 Ps. 89:34ff. Compare C.G. Jung, *Aion*, CW 9/2, § 169.

himself was compelled to become human, in order to see justice done for
once. That wouldn't have been necessary, were it not for the existence of evil
and were it not a very serious matter. He [God] always tries to take revenge
on the erring, instead of once tweaking his son, that is Satan, by the ears.
That doesn't occur to him; he is always left in peace and on the sidelines,
while people are penalized. How could humans, who are so stupid – aren't
they? – so suggestible; who can boast to each other about every fraud; how
then [could they] resist the father devil when he comes? That is completely
hopeless. And the good devil is one of the sons of God who has the ear of
the father. Yahweh doesn't hesitate for a moment to torment relentlessly his
loyal servant and slave, Job, without the slightest reason, simply because he
made a bet with the devil, with his own son.

There you see this conflict; of course it is utterly intolerable. And Christ
tried to carry out a reformation in order to achieve an exclusively good
God-concept. That happened under Greek influence of course. To the
Greek way of thinking, this Yahwistic idea of God was simply impossible.
One couldn't reconcile that. Even the devout Jews couldn't do it. There is a
story by Ibn Esra that goes: There was an old Spaniard, a wise religious man,
who was never able to read the Eighty-ninth Psalm, because he found it too
difficult. What's written in the Eighty-ninth Psalm? Yahweh's betrayal of
David! He swore to David by his own holiness that he would keep his covenant, but he didn't keep it. The ancient Jews, and of course, especially the
theologians, took note of that. And because of that, they couldn't simply
give way when a reformer arrived... If one thinks about our reformers, for
instance, Calvin,[29] if someone held a slightly different view, it cost him his
head or got him roasted. And if he had someone beheaded, and the execu-
tioner didn't strike accurately and had to hack off the head slowly, then, as
Calvin wrote to Antistes Bullinger,[30] it would be a *providentia specialis* of the
Lord that it took a little longer, in which case it was totally all right. Yes,
that is our Calvin. The *theologicus* is no small thing. And of course this was
also true at that time.

---

29 Johannes Calvin (1509-1564), Swiss reformer in Geneva.
30 Heinrich Bullinger (1504-1575), Swiss reformer and antistes of the Reformed Church
   of Zurich.

The Transformation of God

Question concerning Satan and Job: Is it not possible to imagine that when this, so to say, had happened to God that he would have been hoodwinked by Satan?

C.G. Jung: That did indeed happen to him. At some time or other there were a few occasions when such things happened to him that he regretted afterwards. I mean, he really rued it.

Question: Didn't that bring about a transformation?

C.G. Jung: Yes, that is another question: What kind of God transformation resulted from that? We see this even in Christianity. This transformation of God occurred there, much to the horror of the Jewish theologians. But it was one of them who invented this idea of transformation. It was made in their own family. Christ was a Jew, don't forget. But that was already predestined. That had to happen like that. Because the great danger was, that in the clash with the Greek spirit, Yahweh would have simply gone under – an unbearable thought. That's why all the Greek gods went to the devil, because they were so immoral. It had to happen just like that.

Now, you also asked what that has to do with the Age of Pisces. So, it is in the Age of Pisces that a one-sided position arises. There are two fish, which oppose each other in parallel, according to this prophecy – it is a symbolic prophecy. So according to this prophesy, one can see in the heavens how the first fish, the East Fish in whom the precision of the equinox first appears, is vertical, with its head towards the north pole. And the second fish is horizontal. In between is a commissure. The millennium falls into this commissure. We are now in the sphere of the second fish, that is the Antichrist, who was also already evangelically foretold. But in the end, these are really astrological predictions. Christ's rule lasted a thousand years, then [the rule of the Antichrist] began.

Shortly after the millennium, in 1015, the first signs of a new religious idea appeared, namely, that not God but the devil had created the world.[31] So now the thing gets turned around. Why didn't the Orthodox Jews go along with this development? That's easy to explain: out of conservatism! In addition this view was in their opinion definitely false. One had to reckon that Yahweh, being of unsound mind, could not be relied on. There

---

31 See C.G. Jung, "The Fish Symbol of the Cathars," in: *Aion*, CW 9/2, § 225-238.

would be no justice from him. Job already expresses this idea (what a superb thought!): "I know that an advocate lives in me" who will help to counter God.[32] That is to say, God himself against God. That shows the split clearly. But this advocate would later become the Son of man, the guardian of justice.

In Judaism, as you already know, a trinity concept developed in the Kabbalistic tradition. This idea appeared in the figures of Tifereth, Malkhuth and the Shekhinah, who must be separated and reunited again. Thus an age-old Greek sibling myth is invoked, namely, that of Uranos and Thetis, who don't sleep with each other anymore, and consequently the world is in a bad state. So this is your typical bridal pair; it is the couple that should unite the opposites. Therefore, at the End of Days, when the Messiah comes, the heavenly wedding takes place. These are now typical Christian ideas, which have pushed through uninfluenced by Jewish Orthodoxy, but these are in actual fact real Christian thoughts.

Within esoteric lore, the Jews went along with Christianity, but only the initiates knew that. The others knew nothing about it. Now there is still a strong opposition to the Kabbalistic tradition within Jewish Orthodoxy. In Judaism, this Kabbalistic tradition occupies the place of alchemy in Christianity. Alchemy is a secret knowledge, which collided with the orthodox view and consequently could only eke out a bare existence in the darkness. Yes, well for instance, with our psychology we also had to live, so to say, in the catacombs, while the academies and other well-meaning authorities were in power. Yes, then even I would have been burned at the stake a long time ago. I would have been roast beef. Thank God, in this respect the times have changed to some extent.

From the Age of Pisces to the Age of Aquarius

Margret Ostrowski-Sachs: Does the same tendency that you attribute to the Age of Pisces, namely the transformation in each half of life to an opposite attitude, also hold true for the individual in whose horoscope the sign of Pisces predominates?

C.G. Jung: You need only look at the astrological character of Pisces. On the one hand, Pisces is very unfavourable. For ages it has been *voraces* and so forth, that is, gluttonous and greedy in every respect. It even appears

---

32 C.G. Jung, "Answer to Job," CW 11, § 567.

in Christianity as the *concupiscentia mundi*. On the other hand, it is very spiritual. And that shows the possibility of enantiodromia. Such is the Pisces character: on the one hand, a tendency to become wishy-washy, lost in the waters of the unconscious, that is, in the *pelagus mundi*, in the sea of sin and of the world; on the other hand, a flowing up to heaven with the reversed River Jordan. That is the astrological Pisces character. I have much too little experience in this respect to say more about this, but it wouldn't surprise me in the least if, when examining a typical Pisces case in the first half of life, we were to find: the midnight cat, they say, is quite a saint by day [jung im Bett, alte Betschwester] – something like that.

Margret Ostrowski-Sachs: I have another question. Can we assume that, in the Age of Aquarius, a collective symbol for that which stood behind the figure of Christ will again arise? Or will the future symbol only be encountered in individually experienced form?

C.G. Jung: Well, as far as Aquarius is concerned, if I wanted to say something there, I would have to resort to raw speculation. Actually, there are clues in the history of symbols, namely… no, I can't reveal the whole arcanum! (laughter in the audience) These historical symbol matters are extremely interesting. I only want to draw your attention to it. I couldn't do it anyway without a constellation chart where we could look at the zodiac with the *paranatellonta*,[33] together with the rising sign. Of course, constellation charts play a large role, but I only want to call attention to one.

Above Aries is a triangle, the so-called Triangulum. Andromeda is located above the first fish of Pisces. Perseus is in front of the triangle. Perseus, the great hero, frees Andromeda. Andromeda is the virgin who was bound to the rock for the dragon. She is located above the first fish. Something completely different lies above the second fish: a pneumatic symbol, Pegasus, indicated by a large square. The underlying sign, next to Taurus, is *cetus magnus*, the great whale, the Leviathan, extending exactly to the end of the second fish of Pisces. There he comes to an end, and the sphere of the Southern Fish, *piscis austrinus*, begins. The Southern Fish is a small fish – while the Leviathan is a sea monster – and Aquarius must pour him water, the *hydropoe*. The water from Aquarius flows exactly into the mouth of the fish in the constellation below.

---

33 *Parantellonta astra*, literally "together rising stars." The concept comes from astrology and refers to the relationship between two heavenly bodies that are found at the same time either on the horizon or on the meridian.

From the perspective of symbol history, that is extremely interesting. When you look at a star chart you can see everything. You can consider what it might roughly mean. Here we have the triangle, more or less heralding Christianity. Then comes the first fish, with the Virgin, the sun woman [Gestirnsweib][34] above it. Then we have the square, with the second fish below it. These are very interesting symbols. Therefore, this would fit with my expectation, that if archetypes really exist, then of course they are projected onto the stars. They are always projected onto the distance because in us they are so remote; we are far away from them. They are projected onto what is furthest away, and people have quite naively given them a name without knowing why, from this unconscious stance. There was no recognition, no knowledge, rather a doing; they called them something and venerated them as such.

Ritual – Past and Present

With primitive peoples,[35] things were always first done and then thought about. In this respect I saw very interesting things with my primitive people in Africa: they performed clearly meaningful rites, without knowing the meaning of them – without ever having known it. So the ethnologists say, there you see how primitive these people are; they don't even know what they're doing. Do you know what I say then? "My dear professor, now we are going on an expedition to Zurich." And now we walk up the Zurichberg and knock at a villa.[36] An educated man, a mister so-and-so, lives there. And we ask him, "Look here, we are two ethnologists, and we want to study the curious religious practices prevailing in this country, as well as the religious mythological ideas. Would you please tell us what kind of mythological ideas you have, and what religious practices you follow?" Then Mr. Meier will say, "Well, you've come to the wrong address. I have no – but that's ridiculous. We have no mythological ideas on the Zurichberg and most certainly no religious practices. For that, you must go to the Catholic church, but not to me." We retreat, somewhat embarrassed, and then I go back there

34 Revelation of John 12,1: "a woman clothed with the sun, and with the moon under her feet, and on her head a crown of twelve stars."
35 Owing to its present pejorative implications, this word is no longer used to refer to the archaic peoples. What follows here shows clearly that Jung was against this meaning of "primitive." The editors have retained this word in order to keep as close as possible to Jung's text.
36 The Zurichberg is the richest and most fashionable section of the city of Zurich.

with my colleague at Christmas. The tree stands in the house with lights on it, with golden globes, suns, stars, apples and I don't know what else. Then my friend says, "Now here is a rite after all. That is a fine thing that you are doing here, Mr. Meier, but you told us that you had no mythological ideas."

"What? I don't have any!"

"Yes, but what are you doing there, then?"

"Well, that's a Christmas tree."

"What is that, then? What is a Christmas tree? Why are you doing that? What is Christmas?"

"Well, that is the celebration of the birth of Christ."

"Yes, but what does the fir tree have to do with the birth of the Lord Jesus?"

Absolutely nothing at all, no scriptural authority! There's nothing in the *depositum fidei* about a Christmas tree, and there's nothing for a long time afterwards either.

So what is Mr. Meier doing then? Well, he is doing something without knowing what a Christmas tree is. Now we know it. But few people do know what it really is.

So we behave exactly like primitives, and pardon me, that is not the only case. The next time we visit Mr. Meier, we go in spring, at Easter. At that time this gentleman is occupying himself with rabbit idols and is practicing an atrocious fertility rite involving coloured eggs. Well, that is the Kore being sought. Yes, the lost goddess is sought. These rabbit idols are disguised and really made of chocolate, aren't they? That is also an abominable rite, because they gobble up their own gods! Just imagine it! Mr. Meier has never considered that we can enjoy the gods as food, because he was no longer raised Christian. Yes, you see, we are amazed that they consume the corn god, or some such, in Central America, but nobody thinks that that could have anything to do with us, not in the remotest.

Now, you see we are exactly like the primitives: we do these things without knowing what we are doing. Humanity was always like that, and so man named the stars. And where did these names come from? From his soul, from that which he had in himself – that is what he expressed. And so, from what is in us, we make a Christmas tree. We don't know what we are doing, because we act unconsciously. We are preformed, we are predetermined. The unconscious spirit is more present than we are. And only much later do we reflect on it, if we ever begin to reflect on it at all. It's really quite amazing how much one never thinks about, isn't it? But that's the way it is.

Yahweh's Covenant with the People of Israel

Question: [unintelligible]

C.G. Jung: There is also the issue of being chosen, isn't there? That simply means, one is obligated to Yahweh, that is, to the worship of God. The people of Israel are the wife of God, and they would commit adultery were they to adopt a new idea, that is, an idea that God may be only good. That is adultery; that is forbidden. The law must be observed. But, as we said, later this Christian development will be taken up in Judaism without external influence. However these are really only archetypal ideas anyway. One cannot claim that Tifereth has anything to do with Christ. The idea of Malkhuth or the Shekhinah, that is quite genuinely Jewish.

Question: Won't thereby the mediating figure be a priori eliminated?

C.G. Jung: Yes, of course, because it won't be recognized that an individual requires an advocate. He is just vulnerable, as vulnerable as a woman is to her husband. She is simply married to him, she must obey. It's a purely patriarchal idea. She has no rights. It is no contract, because with Yahweh no contract is possible. He considers contracts worthless, as with David, who had a covenant with him. That was treated like a scrap of paper. Under these circumstances, the idea of a mediator could not of course be accepted. But it was taken up in the form of Tifereth. That is a mediator between Kether, Chochma, and Binah (the trinity), and Malkhuth. Tifereth also stands exactly in the middle of the sefirotic system.

Mercurius

However, he [Tifereth] actually has more parallels to the figure of Mercurius than to Christ. Mercurius is an extremely strange figure, isn't he? In classical times he is already called *Hermes tre unus*, Hermes the triple one. Therefore, *Hermes Trismegistos*, the thrice great, is of course, in dubious proximity. He is an *ambiguus*; therefore he is very questionable.

He is called *utriusque capax*; he is capable on both sides. *Cum bonis bonus, cum malis malus* – good with the good, evil with the evil. He is a figure who is much more comparable to this amoral God, but who is also much more in the realm of human beings. That's why the Hassidic religion is a very spontaneous religion, which of course, is influenced by the original Kabbalistic tradition. There, there is an immediate experience of God and also a profound knowledge of religious experience, which can only be found through a Meister Eckhart or an Angelus Silesius.

Projection

Question: [unintelligible]

C.G. Jung: I mean, of course, there is something right about this compensatory relationship between Jewish and Christian psychology. It is indubitably so, that they each project the shadow on the other. However, that is inevitable. That is exactly the same as when, for example, you have whites and blacks together in a social context. That is exactly the same. Or Indians and Europeans together; there we immediately have a compensatory relationship. Here projections are merrily reciprocated, and each one is grateful to be free of his shadow. That's why we read detective novels. It is an extremely pleasant occupation. There, one always knows who did it. It would be terrible if we didn't know it! Then one might arrive at the conclusion that it was oneself.

Margret Ostrowski-Sachs: Ladies and Gentlemen, in the introduction to this discussion, it was pointed out that one is only called to write about an age in an immanent sense if one has already detached oneself from its content and acquired a standpoint *au dessus de la melée* [above the fray]. We have had this confirmed this evening. In order to talk about the Age of Pisces, one ought not to be a Piscean, but rather one must be an Aquarian, perhaps even a cautious Aquarian, who doesn't tell us too much about the Age of Aquarius yet.

Dear Professor Jung, you sensed our interest and our involvement, from our questions and from our pleasure in your visit, and actually from the entire atmosphere of this evening. I would like to hope that you also feel our gratitude for everything that you have always given us.[37]

37 Translated from German by Joan Allen Smith, Küsnacht, Switzerland.

Murray Stein

Jungian Psychology and the Spirit of Protestantism

Introduction: C.G. Jung, a Protestant

In the globalized world of the present day, analytical psychology is read, taught, and practiced worldwide, and thus far this school of depth psychology has been able to grow and flourish in all cultures that are at least moderately receptive to modernity. Only in regions where modernity has not taken hold, or where strict and traditional religious authorities are in control of culture, or where respect for the individual's human rights is negligible, do its empowering ideas receive a hostile reception. Moreover, liberal religious people of all denominations, whether Christian, Jewish, Moslem, Hindu, Buddhist or other, have been able to pick up the ideas of analytical psychology and place them side by side with their religious practices and beliefs without creating a severe conflict. Conservative religious people, on the other hand, even in areas of the world that are largely modern and secular in their social organization and governance, are suspicious of depth psychology in all its forms and tend to reject it and stay away. This rejection is due to the obvious fact that psychoanalysis and analytical psychology are products of modernity and carry modernity's secular attitudes in their core beliefs and visions of the human.[1] Modernity and conservative religions have been and continue to be sworn enemies of one another.

This nearly universal reception of analytical psychology on the part of people who identify with the values of modernity does not, however,

1 Peter Homans has examined the social origins of psychoanalysis and made this point convincingly in: Peter Homans, *The Ability to Mourn: Disillusionment and the Social Origins of Psychoanalysis*, (Chicago: The University of Chicago Press, 1989) and Peter Homans, *Jung in Context: Modernity and the Making of a Psychology* (Chicago: The University of Chicago Press, 1995).

preclude us from asking the question of what it owes to its cultural origins in Swiss Reformed Protestantism and to what extent and in what ways Jung's own personal Swiss Protestant cultural background cast an influence over his psychological theory and the subsequent shape and content of the field of analytical psychology.[2] As a science and as a form of clinical psychoanalysis, analytical psychology is thoroughly modern and neutral with respect to religious belief of any kind, but its early history and above all the Swiss Reformed cultural background of its founder, C.G. Jung, are deeply rooted in the Protestant Christian tradition. This may be a reason why Protestant people and cultures may find Jungian psychology to be more comfortably compatible with their other cultural attitudes than do others. They can feel an immediate affinity with it and can respond to it – especially to its "spiritual" side –more fully and enthusiastically than do others. This would be a complement to Freud's now famous words in a letter to Karl Abraham: "Please be tolerant and do not forget that it is really easier for you than it is for Jung to follow my ideas, for in the first place you are completely independent, and then you are closer to my intellectual constitution because of racial kinship, while he as a Christian and a pastor's son finds his way to me only against great inner resistances."[3]

Freud had a clear picture of Jung's native Swiss Protestant cultural make-up and foundations, and the differences between Freud's Jewish background and Jung's Protestant Christian background were not trivial items among the several causes that drove them to a parting of the ways. Their story is a story not only of the clash of individual geniuses but also of a clash of cultures. Freud's roots were Jewish, Jung's were Christian. This did not keep them from trying to transcend their cultural differences for the sake of science, but in the end they failed to achieve the desired result not only, or even primarily, because of religious differences (to which neither of them was ideologically committed in any explicit fashion whatsoever) but because of differing philosophical commitments having to do with the limits of rationality and the scientific enterprise. The difference in their respective relationship to their background traditions, I would argue, was the critical point. Freud was more consciously distant from his Jewish

2 For a thorough review of the works written on the Jewish background of Freud's psychoanalysis, see D.B. Klein, *Jewish Origins of the Psychoanalytic Movement* (Chicago: University of Chicago Press, 1985). In this essay, I am similarly exploring the influence of Jung's Protestant Christian background on his depth psychological theory and practice.

3 P. Homans, *The Ability to Mourn*, p. 36.

religious background (or perhaps more defended against its intrusions into his conscious activities) than Jung was from his Protestant tradition. Jung's roots remained sunken deeply in Protestantism whereas Freud had laid down strict commitments to the positivist scientific worldview of his time and took little positive notice of his forebears' spirituality. Freud was a critic of religion; Jung was an interpreter of religion with an open attitude toward its value as a resource for psychological wholeness and well-being.[4]

As a personal aside, my own introduction to Jung came about in a Protestant Christian worship service while I was a student at Yale University. One Sunday morning the guest preacher at Yale's Battell Chapel was the Rev. Dr. Thayer Green, a Jungian analyst from New York and a former Protestant chaplain at a nearby college. The theme of his sermon was the problem of evil and the dark side of God, a suitable topic for the mid-1960s in America, convulsed as the country was by the civil rights movement and the war in Vietnam. He used Jung's *Answer to Job* as a reference and quoted from it extensively. For me, this was without question the most exciting and memorable sermon I had ever heard in this Protestant church, which was justly famous for the liberal theology of its ministers whose fiery social action sermons stirred many to march for civil rights in America and to oppose the unjust war in Vietnam. To my quite uninformed mind at the time, Jung's thought and the theology of liberal Protestantism seemed to fit together hand-in-glove. Jung's ideas could be preached in church! Jungian

---

4   It may seem paradoxical that there have been so many prominent Jewish Jungian analysts and authors in the century of analytical psychology's history. As Jung himself noted, most of his patients were either Protestant or Jewish, while few were Roman Catholic. See C.G. Jung, "The Symbolic Life." In: *The Symbolic Life*, vol. 18 of *The Collected Works of C.G. Jung*, translated by R.F.C. Hull (Princeton: Princeton University Press, 1976), § 608-639. Modern Protestants and Jews have something in common, more perhaps than either group has with the other Christian traditions (Roman or Orthodox). Jung attributed this to the similar problem modern Jews and modern Protestants have with their religious traditions. As a result of modern ways of thinking, they have left them behind, except sentimentally or formally, and are therefore in search of a new kind of access to spirituality, which they find in Jung's approach to symbols and the unconscious. Prominent Jewish Jungian authors like James Kirsch, Erich Neumann and Gerhard Adler wrote extensively on their own religious traditions from a Jungian perspective and adapted Jung's Protestant Christian spiritual journey to their own cultural styles and needs without great difficulty. Unlike Freud, whose commitment to positivist science and strictly rational thinking precluded anything smacking of "mysticism," these were modern Jews in search of a new form of spirituality, and Jung's breakthrough proved to be of assistance for them. Their numerous and profound contributions to analytical psychology have, in turn, been greatly responsible for the field's continuing vibrancy and robust growth.

thought and Protestant theology were of a piece, or so it seemed to me at the time.[5]

Given this churchly entry into analytical psychology, I want to take special care not to exaggerate the importance of Jung's Protestant Christian heritage in his overall *oeuvre*. It would be absurd to claim that Jung's thought and the field he founded are limited to a Protestant Christian Weltanschauung. However, at the risk of stating the obvious, it remains important to recognize that the founder's cultural background and his intellectual antecedents were heavily weighted with Protestant thought and cultural attitudes.

In a late and highly personal reference of this foundation, Jung wrote to Henry Corbin in a letter dated 4 May 1953: "Schleiermacher really is one of my spiritual ancestors. He even baptized my grandfather... The vast, esoteric, and individual spirit of Schleiermacher was a part of the intellectual atmosphere of my father's family. I never studied him, but unconsciously he was for me a *spiritus rector.*"[6] This reference to the great Protestant theologian, Friederich Schleiermacher (1768-1834), is especially relevant because of what he specifically stood for and still means for modern Protestant theology. The attitude toward religious faith and theology that he forged for himself as he broke out of his pietistic religious upbringing and for which he became justly famous we can see distinctly reflected in Jung's life and writings. Eric Sharpe, in his essay in *The Routledge Companion to the Study of Religion*, says of Schleiermacher's theological views: "...to Schleiermacher, the heart of religion was to be found, not in rules and regulations, hierarchies, hassocks and hymnbooks, but in the individual's experience of (or sense of) and dependence upon a power infinitely greater than his own."[7] Two features are of critical importance in this modern Protestant formulation of the centrepiece of the religious attitude: the centrality of the individual and not a community (a church), and the sense of dependency on a greater power

---

5   Years later, while studying for my doctorate at the University of Chicago under the guidance of Peter Homans, I discovered that the relation between Jung's writings on theological themes and his attitudes toward Christianity are not entirely compatible, although there are many overlappings. I published the results of this research in: M. Stein, *Jung's Treatment of Christianity – the Psychotherapy of a Religious Tradition* (Wilmette, IL: Chiron Publications, 1985).

6   C.G. Jung, *Letters*, vol. 2, selected and edited by Gerhard Adler in collaboration with Aniela Jaffé. Translated by R.F.C. Hull (Princeton: Princeton University Press, 1975), p. 115.

7   E.J. Sharp, "The Study of Religion in Historical Perspective," in: *The Routledge Companion to the Study of Religion*. J.R. Hinnells (ed.), (London: Routledge, 2005), p. 35.

(again, not upon the church but directly upon God). What Jung did a century later was to transcribe this feeling – the individual's sense of dependency on "a power infinitely greater" – directly into secular psychology and give it a central position in his depth psychological framework.

In Jung's psychological view, the center of human consciousness – an individual's "ego" – is critically dependent upon the powers of the unconscious in the form of the complexes and archetypes, and ultimately on the self, for its stability, its prosperity and its very continuing existence as a conscious subject. As Schleiermacher came to sense a radical dependence upon God, so Jung felt such dependence upon the central agent of power and organization in the psyche, the self. People who study Jungian psychology are predictably given to acknowledging this as bedrock psychological reality. *Vocatus atque non vocatus, deus aderit* – "whether called upon or not, God will be present," the saying carved over the entrance to Jung's house, is another expression of this same feeling. Schleiermacher would have felt right at home there.

Jung absorbed this recognition of dependency on a higher power from the strong Protestant atmosphere in his family and in the general religious and cultural milieu of Basel, his hometown throughout the formative years of his early and university education. We are all dependent on God, he would have thought, and He can cross our path at any time and cause severe disruptions or good fortune. All things that happen are *Deo concidente*! This became a favorite expression of Jung's. In his autobiography he recalls the now famous incident of being forced to imagine God defecating on the cathedral in Basel and destroying it. God was behind this thought, he concluded. His own child's ego would not have come up with such a monstrous fantasy, he was sure. It was a divine visitation. A child's mind, as well as an adult's, is subject to divine intervention![8]

It should be noted that the Protestant tradition, out of which Jung came, was a liberal and not a conservative one. "The vast, esoteric, and individual spirit of Schleiermacher was a part of the intellectual atmosphere of my father's family," he writes to Corbin. The atmosphere was not rigidly fixed on principles of belief and conduct and on theological principles and doctrines. In fact, from Jung's description of his parson father, Paul Jung was if anything rather casual about doctrine. For Jung, as for Schleiermacher, the essence of the religious person was a feeling of dependence on God, not

8 Aniela Jaffé (ed.), *Memories, Dreams, Reflections by C.G. Jung* (London: Fontana, 1995), pp. 35-36.

dependence on a community of belief, on churchly rituals or on customary religious practices. A later addition to this perspective on the religious came to Jung through the work of Rudolf Otto, another Protestant Christian theologian, whose book *Das Heilige* [*The Idea of the Holy*, in the imperfect English translation] brought the term *numinosum* into the discussion of religious experience and gave Jung a handy adjective for describing the feeling people have when they experience archetypes [the "gods" of the collective unconscious]. Jung was very attracted to Otto's work and to his notion that numinous experience is the ground of all religions. The experience of the Holy (the *numinosum*) lies at the base of Jung's psychology of religion and also at the core of his approach to psychotherapy.[9]

To take Jung's identity as a "protestant" one step further, one can note that, linguistically defined, a "protestant" is someone who "protests," especially against authority. This was the term applied to the great 16th Century Reformers – the German Martin Luther (1483-1546), the Swiss Ulrich Zwingli (1484-1531) and the French John Calvin (1509-1564). They protested vigorously against the authority of the Roman Catholic Church in regulating religious practices in Christendom and based their theology and their conception of the church on the Holy Scriptures and not on churchly tradition. They boldly scraped away centuries of accumulated ritual, structure and imagery, and they sought to return the faithful to a pristine version of Christianity as it was practiced in the first century. What came into being as a result of the struggles against Papal and priestly authority was a vision of the singular individual, standing alone before God without clerical mediation, supported morally (to a limited extent) by a community of believers but not dependent upon them or on anyone else for securing a conviction of salvation and redemption. Religious life became a private affair, transacted strictly between the individual and God. The Protestant was prepared to defy authority for the sake of an individual interpretation of Scripture. Self-reliance and thinking for oneself became hallmarks of the Protestant character. Nevertheless, a Protestant of course remained a faithful Christian out of respect for and adherence to Biblical revelation, and therefore was one for whom the figure of Christ and the notion of *imitatio Christi* were critically important for life and for the attainment of

---

9   See: Murray Stein, "On the Importance of Numinous Experience in the Alchemy of Individuation," in: A. Casement & D. Tacey (eds.), *The Idea of the Numinous* (London and New York: Routledge, 2006).

ultimate meaning. Jung takes this line of thinking to its logical conclusion in his highly protestant late work, *Answer to Job.*

A Protestant is defined, then, by a readiness to protest against external authority and a tendency to think independently, a person for whom autonomy and individuality are highly prized traits and belong to the ideal character. One can see this character profile clearly in Jung's relationship with Freud. It was precisely around the issue of authority that their relationship came unglued.[10] Jung's critical thinking led him to conclusions that went against the thrust of Freud's leadership and his insistence on certain dogmas of psychoanalysis. When he published his independent (protestant) views in 1912, Freud's frosty reception initiated a rapid end to their personal relationship. Jung protested loudly against Freud's authoritarian attitude toward his fellow psychoanalysts, treating them like children,[11] and so went his own independent way. Their split looks like a kind of replay of the Protestant Reformation, with Freud in the role of Roman Pope and Jung taking the part of the militant Zurich Reformer, Ulrich Zwingli. To this day, there is an uneasy relationship between the two "churches," psychoanalysis and analytical psychology.

"The Protestant is left to God alone," Jung states baldly in "Psychology and Religion," his Terry Lectures at Yale University in 1937.[12] A Protestant Christian is a solitary individual and must stand alone before God and humanity: "For him there is no confession, no absolution, no possibility of an expiatory *opus divinum* of any kind. He has to digest his sins by himself;

10 See A. Jaffé (ed.), *Memories, Dreams, Reflections by C.G. Jung*, p. 158: "Freud's response to these words was a curious look – a look of the utmost suspicion. Then he said, 'But I cannot risk my authority!' At that moment he lost it altogether. That sentence burned itself into my memory; and in it the end of our relationship was already foreshadowed. Freud was placing personal authority above truth." George Hogenson, in his fine work, *Jung's Struggle with Freud*, examines the issue of authority in the relationship in great detail. George Hogenson, *Jung's Struggle with Freud* (Wilmette, IL: Chiron Publications, 1994).

11 In a letter of 18 December 1912, Jung writes to Freud: "You go around sniffing out all the symptomatic actions in your vicinity, thus reducing everyone to the level of sons and daughters who blushingly admit the existence of their faults. Meanwhile you remain on top as the father, sitting pretty. For sheer obsequiousness nobody dares to pluck the prophet by the beard and inquire for once what you would say to a patient with a tendency to analyse the analyst instead of himself. You would certainly ask him: '*Who's* got the neurosis?'" McGuire, W. (ed.), *The Freud-Jung Letters* (Princeton: Princeton University Press, 1974), p. 535.

12 C.G. Jung, "Psychology and Religion." In: vol. 11 of *The Collected Works of C.G. Jung*, translated by R.F.C. Hull (Princeton: Princeton University Press, 1969), § 86.

and, because the absence of a suitable ritual has put it beyond his reach, he is none too sure of divine grace."[13] This same emphasis on solitude and individuality is central to Jung's view of psychological development as he describes it in various writings on the individuation process and most dramatically in his account of his own experiences in *The Red Book*. Moreover, as I will show, the *imitatio Christi* was for Jung a fundamental metaphor for the individuation process. This combination of features in his thinking locates Jung solidly in Protestant Christian culture. While he ventured far beyond this cultural domain in his thinking, he never abandoned it. It retained its grip on him, and he used it as a touchstone. Here lay his roots.

Jung's "Way" as Revealed in *The Red Book* – The Spiritual Journey of a Modern Protestant

Jung concludes the Second Book (*Liber Secundus*) of his spiritual journey as depicted in *Liber Novus* (aka *The Red Book*) with a dramatic flourish. After his long and exhausting sojourn in the netherworld, the narrator firmly seals its entrance closed with the words:

> Now shut, you bronze doors I opened to the flood of devastation and murder brooding over the peoples, opened so as to midwife the God. Shut, may mountains bury you and seas flood over you.
> I come to my self, a giddy and pitiful figure. My I! I didn't want this fellow as a companion. I found myself with him. I'd prefer a bad woman or a wayward hound, but one's own I – this horrifies me.

And then, after a brief reflection on the need to return to the Middle Ages (a stage of firm religious belief, a mythological stage of consciousness) and come forward into modernity with a new kind of personal development that would create a more adequate "I," a suitable and purified vessel that would be a "womb" for the birth of new life, the book concludes:

> The touchstone is being alone with oneself.
> This is the way.[14]

---

13 Ibid.
14 C.G. Jung, *The Red Book – Liber Novus*, edited by S. Shamdasani. Translated by M. Kyburz, J. Peck, S. Shamdasani (New York: W.W. Norton & Company, 2009), p. 330.

These resolute lines state an essential realization: the narrator recognizes decisively that he stands utterly *alone* and must face up to this psychological reality. *Scrutinies*, which follows immediately upon the conclusion of *Liber Secundus*, begins with an imaginative testing of this fundamental proposition: The narrator's "I" is examined minutely for all his character flaws, a rigorous self-interrogation and analysis of the ego and its shadow.[15] Afterwards, he is generously rewarded with the teachings of Philemon in his "Seven Sermons to the Dead." Philemon concludes his teachings to the unruly and unsatisfied Dead with a moving affirmation of transcendence for the individual human soul. Individuals may be utterly alone and must stand before God as such, but they have an eternal home symbolized by a star. When the spirits of the dead hear this Seventh Sermon, they are content and make their way out of time into eternity.

Could Jung have composed *The Red Book* had he not been a Protestant Christian? I believe not. The core presuppositions of Protestant Christianity provided the essential ingredients necessary to undertake the type of inner journey that Jung engaged in during his self-exploration at mid-life, which resulted in *Liber Novus*. In a letter to the Swiss Pastor Walter Bernet, Jung reflected:

> Always Paul's experience on the road to Damascus hovered before me, and I asked myself how his fate would have fallen out but for his vision... Yet this experience came upon him while he was blindly pursuing his own way. As a young man I drew the conclusion that you must obviously fulfil your destiny in order to get to the point where a *donum gratiae* might happen along. But I was far from certain, and always kept the possibility in mind that on this road I might end up in a black hole. I have remained true to this attitude all my life.
>
> From this you can easily see the origin of my psychology: only by going my own way, integrating my capacities headlong (like Paul), and thus creating a foundation for myself, could something be vouchsafed to me or built upon it, no matter where it came from, and of which I could be reasonably sure that it was not merely one of my own neglected capacities.[16]

---

15 In the German, Jung uses the word *Prüfstein* (in the English "touchstone"). The third section of *The Red Book*, titled *Scrutinies* in English, is *Prüfungen* in the German, which would normally be translated as "Tests."

16 C.G. Jung, *Letters*, vol. 2, 13 June 1955, pp. 257-258.

The experiences described in *The Red Book* constituted for Jung the psychological equivalent to Paul's transformation on the road to Damascus and his subsequent vocation, "the point where a *donum gratiae*" ("gift of grace") befell him. Reading between the lines of this letter to Pastor Walter Bernet and of many other of Jung's writings now that *The Red Book* has been published, one finds countless direct and indirect references back to the period in his life of which he says in *Memories, Dreams, Reflections*: "The years when I was pursuing my inner images were the most important in my life – in them everything essential was decided... the later details are only supplements and clarification of the material that burst forth from the unconscious, and at first swamped me. It was the *prima materia* for a lifetime's work."[17] The *donum gratiae* that came to him during this period was nothing less than his vocation.[18] This notion that the individual has a God-sent vocation is not peculiar to Protestantism, but it is certainly an important strand in the Protestant tradition.

The final result of this inner journey, too, was importantly shaped by Jung's Protestant Christian heritage, even though many other ingredients and influences are evident in the text.[19] As he said later in his Terry Lectures: "The Protestant is left to God alone... He has to digest his sins by himself... [but] if a Protestant survives the complete loss of his church and still remains Protestant, that is to say a man who is defenceless against God and no longer shielded by walls or communities, he has a unique spiritual opportunity for immediate religious experience."[20] Here Jung is speaking of himself and referring back to his experiences as recorded in *The Red Book*. As he says at Yale, this type of "immediate religious experience" is a precious option open to a Protestant like himself, which he exercised in spectacular form.

17 A. Jaffé (ed.), *Memories, Dreams, Reflections by C.G. Jung*, p. 199.
18 This is a reference to Ephesians 3:7 where Paul, writing to the church in Ephesus, declares the basis of his vocation of ministry to the gentiles: "Of this gospel I was made a minister according to the gift of God's grace which was given me by the working of his power." Revised Standard Version. In the Vulgate, which Jung is citing, the verse runs: "*cuius factus sum minister secundum donum gratiae Dei quae data est mihi secundum operationem virtutis eius.*" The "donum gratiae" is the gift of grace that brings a vocation to a person's consciousness.
19 With respect to the paintings and some of the influences that may have contributed to their style and content, see Jay Sherry's "A Pictorial Guide to The Red Book," in: *ARAS Connections: Image and Archetype*, 2010, Issue 1, www.aras.org
20 C.G. Jung, "Psychology and Religion," CW 11, § 86.

The Individuation Process as an *Imitatio Christi*

It is becoming ever more clear that Jung's Protestant background provided a key framework for his thinking about the central thematic in his *oeuvre*, the individuation process and its casting as a *spiritual* as well as a psychological development. In locating this idea about human development in close relationship to Jung's Protestantism, however, one should not try to pin him down exclusively to such a specific and localized set of assumptions. Rather, it is more accurate to consider how his concrete historical context provided a ready-made cultural and intellectual structure in which he could work out one of his own highly original psychological ideas (i.e., individuation) while at the same time recasting some of his religious tradition's fundamental teachings about the human condition and the nature of the relation of the human to the Divine.[21] One must look at this as a dialectical relationship between Jung's originality and his background religious tradition as a Swiss Protestant who grew up in the very lap of this deeply penetrating cultural context.

Jung was a Swiss Protestant formally, as was his family of origin. He grew up and came of age in Basel, Switzerland, an old and historic bastion of Protestant theology and religion and in the 20th Century the city of Karl Barth, the most influential Protestant theologian of his era. Jung's father was a pastor in the Swiss Reformed church, as were his maternal grandfather, Samuel Preiswerk (1799-1871), and six of his uncles; he was baptised and took communion in it; he was married in it, and he is buried in the cemetery in Küsnacht/Zurich. While he was certainly highly critical of this particular manifestation of Christianity (in a sense, he protested against Protestantism, which makes him a double-Protestant) and felt himself to be an outsider to it in many ways,[22] as in some respects he felt

21 This view is in accord with Peter Homans, *Jung in Context*, where he writes: "Jung sought to revitalize contemporary culture, which – he believed – had lost its anchorage in the past, by re-linking that culture to its past (especially the mythic past) with the assistance of depth psychology, and he worked within the assumptive world of Christian humanism" (p. xliii). It should be remembered that the father of Christian humanism, Erasmus, was a fellow Basler who lived there during the Protestant Reformation, and also that Jung as a teenager found the famous Delphic oracle *vocatus atque non vocatus deus aderit*, which he later posted above the doorway to his home in Küsnacht, in a volume of classical writings edited by Erasmus. The importance of Basel culture on Jung's attitudes and thinking is also underscored by Jay Sherry in his *Carl Gustav Jung – Avant-Garde Conservative* (New York, Palgrave: Macmillan, 2010).

22 See A. Jaffé (ed.), *Memories, Dreams, Reflections by C.G. Jung*, pp. 36 ff., for example. Many passages in the autobiography show his negative views of the Swiss Reformed church.

about Christianity in general,[23] he did not publicly or privately repudiate it, nor decisively distance himself from it, nor identify with other cultural or religious options that might have been open to him. Rather, he remained located within its cultural orbit, albeit somewhat uneasily at many points in his life, and worked out his life story within this context. Moreover, as I see him, Jung was a Protestant in more than name only as I am trying to show in this essay.[24] Already in his youthful Zofingia Lecture, "Thoughts on the Interpretation of Christianity,"[25] he shows his colors as a theological thinker with passion for a strong vision of Christ as a transpersonal (metaphysical) Power and Presence, not merely a memory or a theological concept. His undergraduate lecture has the zest and rhetorical passion of a Kierkegaard or a Nietzsche.

I am most particularly interested here in exploring the connection and deep continuity between Jung's concept of individuation and his highly unusual interpretation of *imitatio Christi*. Running already through the entire *Liber Novus* is this specific version of *imitatio Christi*, and it re-appears in many of his later writings and centrally in the very late and most theological of all his works, *Answer to Job*, where he gives it the name of *Christification*. Only a liberal Protestant of Jung's type could have come up with such a novel and original rendition of this familiar Christian theme of discipleship.

The individuation process occupies the center of Jung's mature thought about psychological and spiritual development, especially as this pertains to adulthood and to what he referred to as the second half of life. In Jung's vocabulary, the term individuation covers the whole spectrum of human development, which can be divided into several important stages, but at its core is the goal of a "union of opposites," that is, the integration of conscious and unconscious aspects of the adult personality. This integration constitutes a *realization of the self*, the goal of the psyche's entelechy. How does this psychological idea of individuation link up with the religious

---

23 See Murray Stein, *Jung's Treatment of Christianity*, especially Chapter 3, "On the Relationship between the Doctor and Patient." Also Murray Stein, "Introduction" to *Jung on Christianity* (Princeton: Princeton University Press 1999); and Part I: "Jung's Relationship to Christianity."

24 I am appreciative of the work of Andreas Schweizer, who persuasively linked Jung to Luther in many important respects in his paper: A. Schweizer, "Fare hin mit deim geist an galgen! Martin Luther und C.G. Jung," in: *Der Mensch und sein Widersacher*, E. Hornung und A. Schweizer (eds. 2003), Eranos 2001-2002.

25 C.G. Jung, "Thoughts on the Interpretation of Christianity, with Reference to the Theory of Albrecht Ritschl," in: *The Zofingia lectures*, (Princeton: Princeton University Press, 1899/1983), pp. 89-111.

notion of *imitatio Christi* and therefore with the Christian culture into which Jung was born, grew up and lived his entire life?

The Imitation of Christ by Thomas a Kempis is a familiar medieval classic, a book of devotion highly regarded by Roman Catholics and Protestants alike. Underscoring the value of deep introspection and the development of interiority as the centrepiece of spirituality, it has been widely used in monastic settings and as a meditational book by many Christians. Its main effect is to lead the deep reader into identification with the life of Christ, who serves as a model of spiritual perfection. A work given high priority by Jesuits and attributed with evangelical power by John Wesley, it has served Christians of all denominations over centuries in their devotional lives and spiritual development.

Interestingly, the notion of *imitatio Christi* is probably a version of the earlier Jewish idea of *imitatio Dei*, which originates in a commandment in Leviticus 19:2: "Speak to all the congregation of the people of Israel and say to them: You shall be holy, for I the Lord your God am holy." Christians believe that Christ – as the Son of God – shows the way to achieve fulfilment of this commandment, and this leads directly into the idea known as *imitatio Christi*. By achieving a state of identification with Christ (i.e., God) and therefore sharing in His Holiness, the human may approach the state of Divinity and even realize a kind of deification, albeit on the human level. In the Orthodox tradition, this is called *theosis* and is considered the highest purpose of human existence.

Jung's own personal experience of "deification" – a primary source for his later understanding and elaboration of the notion of individuation – is recounted and reflected upon in the 1925 Seminar he gave at the Psychology Club in Zurich.[26] In the published *Liber Novus*, we now have the full description of this remarkable spiritual moment. What we find in the original text is an account of a deeply emotional vision of and encounter – indeed identification – with the crucified Christ:

> I see the cross and Christ on it in his last hour and torment – at the foot of the cross the black serpent coils itself – it has wound itself around my feet – I am held fast and I spread my arms wide. Salome draws near. The serpent has wound itself around my whole body, and my countenance is that of a lion.

26 C.G. Jung, *Analytical psychology – notes of the seminar given in 1925*, W. McGuire, (ed.). (Princeton: Princeton University Press, 1925/1989), pp. 92-99.

Salome says: "Mary was the Mother of Christ, do you understand?"

I: "I see that a terrible and incomprehensible power forces me to *imitate the Lord* in his final torment. But how can I presume to call Mary my mother?"

S. "You are Christ."

I stand with outstretched arms like someone crucified, my body taut and horribly entwined by the serpent: "You, Salome, say that I am Christ?" It is as if I stand alone on a high mountain...[27]

When Jung cast a reflective glance back on this transformative experience with his students and followers at the Psychology Club in Zurich in 1925, he linked it explicitly to the individuation process: "In this deification mystery you make yourself into the vessel, and are a vessel of creation in which the opposites reconcile."[28] Here we see that he directly identified individuation as the process of uniting the opposites within oneself with a powerful imaginal experience of *imitatio Christi*. For Jung, the symbol of the crucified Christ clearly operated as a transformational symbol in and through which, in a mystical experience of identification, he was made momentarily into a "vessel of creation in which the opposites reconcile."

Traditionally, the phrase *imitatio Christi* has been used by Christians in a different way altogether, namely to describe and to encourage a life of pious service to others, self-sacrifice, and deep prayer. The stories about Jesus in the Gospels are taken as the model: Jesus was a "suffering servant," who taught his disciples to pray and gave up his life for others, and his disciples are to do likewise. In other words, they are to imitate him by modelling their behaviour on his. Occasionally, *imitatio Christi* is associated with mystical states of union with Christ – similar to what Jung experienced – and with receiving physical signs of identity with the Crucified such as *stigmata*. *Imitatio Christi* is what many of the saints of the Roman Catholic Church are known for and what they accomplished *par excellence*, which is why they are recognized and beatified.

While the experience Jung describes in *Liber Novus* resembles the traditional pattern in some respects, he nevertheless came to interpret *imitatio Christi* in quite a different sense. In my view, he adapted the traditional idea of following and imitating Christ to a modern, post-creedal context

27 C.G. Jung, *The Red Book*, p. 252 (Italics added).
28 C.G. Jung, *Analytical Psychology*, p. 99.

and thereby brought it into a psychological context that does not require or even strongly imply an experience of Christ or any sort of Christian faith. In this sense, he universalized the idea and made it applicable to people of other cultures and religious backgrounds as well as to modern, secularized, agnostic people, while retaining the more traditional Christian version for himself.

Imitatio Christi and Christification as Archetypal Processes

In Jung's rendition, the *imitatio Christi* means finding a "personal myth" and living it fully, honestly, and to the bitter end if need be. Just as Jesus found his myth in an identity as Son of Man (or Son of God), so modern individuals must find a myth within their own psychological experience that will carry them as far as possible toward the goal of meaning and wholeness. In *Answer to Job*, Jung calls this "Christification of many."[29] This means, finding a "living symbol" that most fully captures for oneself the relation between the ego and the self and carries within it a transcendental reference. This is the equivalent, or parallel, to Jesus of Nazareth, who as an ego personality – as a son of the carpenter Joseph and his wife Mary – found in his identity with Yahweh, the Father, the Lord God Almighty of the Bible, a myth and an identity that connected ego and the transcendental aspects of the self for him.

How does one do this in modern, secular, post-creedal times? First of all, it is *not* done, according to Jung's model for the modern person, by looking nostalgically backward to collective entities (such as the Church or other mythologically-based institutions) and expecting them to provide a symbol for developing the ego-self connection through rituals of initiation and divinization by, for example, giving a new name to those who choose to enter religious life. This is the normal and usual path in strong symbolic religious traditions, where the individual participates in a collectively affirmed structure of belief and ritual practice and thereby gains access to the archetypal foundations that this tradition rests upon. (In Mithraism, for example, there were seven stages of initiation and divinization available to wholehearted participants, who in the end reached a full level of identity as incarnated deities.)

---

29 C.G. Jung, *Answer to Job*, CW 11, § 758.

Instead of this traditional path, Jung recommends to the individual a completely different and uniquely individual one: Go within, pay attention to dreams, contact the unconscious using active imagination, faithfully follow the images given to you with all your heart, and out of this inner work will emerge the necessary symbols for individuation and wholeness. (Here we see the Protestant emphasis coming through in Jung's attitude, wherein the individual must face God alone and digest his sins by himself. Initiation is an individual, inner enterprise.) From this practice, Jung teaches us, there will appear symbols that can transform identity and can lead to a process that is analogous to Jesus' experience of accepting his divine vocation, as he did at his baptism by John in the River Jordan. These transformational symbols, springing from within, i.e., from out of the depths of the archetypal layers of the unconscious, become the chief guides and motivators for individuation in life. They transform a mundane, secular ego life into a divine drama in which the image of the Divinity within (*imago Dei*) incarnates fully through thought, word, and deed.

In *Answer to Job* Jung writes that the transformation from the man, Jesus of Nazareth, into the symbolic Christ is not a one time occurrence. This was not a unique event in human history, as much theology in the Christian Church (less the Eastern Orthodox than the Western tradition, however) would have it. It is available to all individuating humans. As it was for Jesus, too, there are many temptations to leave this divine path and vocation – temptations to power, to money, to fame, to the pleasures of the flesh in all their variety. To lose oneself in the ten thousand things offered by the world – in "Maya" – is as much a temptation for moderns as for ancient men and women. So the challenge is to remain conscious of the symbols offered by the self and to return to the path indicated after one has inevitably drifted away from time to time. It is a path of meaning and a path of suffering, as it was for Jesus.

The cross symbolizes for the individuating person the pain and difficulty incurred when one takes up the vocation of uniting the opposites within oneself. Jung's positive assessment of the meaning of such suffering is strictly in line with the Christian notion that Jesus' suffering was meaningful and not an accident. Suffering did not make Jesus into a "victim" but into a hero of individuation. In the end, there is "victory" if one is faithful and true to the symbolic path offered by the self.

It can be claimed – and I would do so – that Jung's interpretation of *imitatio Christi* takes its meaning and extends it far beyond the strictly Christian context, making it applicable to everyone, no matter of what confession or religion or culture, who wishes to take up the *opus* of individuation. Jung universalizes the *imitatio Christi*, and so he breaks it free from its specific historical religious context. If people from completely different religious or cultural backgrounds – e.g., Japanese Buddhist, Indian Hindu, Chinese Taoist, African animist – enter into dialogue with the unconscious, recording and working with dreams, engaging in active imagination, withdrawing projections and integrating their contents, they will also receive symbolic images that can become the basis for an individuation process as described by Jung, for an *imitatio Christi* in the expanded, non-denominational sense of the phrase. The process is archetypal – i.e., universal and generally human – and not just an option limited to a special culture. Individuation is a process of psychological transformation that is archetypal. *Imitatio Christi* is therefore, for Jung, a Christian instance of an archetypal process. For Jung as a Swiss Protestant by origin, with deep roots in this culture, the phrase *imitatio Christi* was a personally meaningful expression indicating "the symbolic life."

There is, however, another and more theoretical sense in which individuation is archetypally based upon a pattern resident in the notion of *imitatio Christi*. In this reprise, it signifies ego development and the discovery and affirmation of a person's specific individuality and uniqueness as a singular human being.

Individuation as Jung conceived of it, progresses in three major stages or movements. It begins at birth (or already *in utero*), which is characterized by the psychological condition of unconscious wholeness. In this state, the original, inborn and innate self is pure potential and exists *a priori*, that is, prior to any differentiation, consciousness, or centralized awareness. It is diffuse; there is no ego, no definite "I." Out of this primal condition, there emerges over a period of time (35 years or so, all told – this is the "first half of life") a centralized ego, which in the course of development takes on a specific identity through processes of differentiation, identification and introjection and comes gradually into a sense of self that is unique and distinct. The distinction formed in this stage of development between "I" and "not I" is fundamental, and this pertains to both inner psychic contents and to the outer world of objects. In the third phase of individuation, a state of recovered wholeness becomes possible (but not inevitable), now in a conscious form, which integrates the conscious and unconscious elements of the personality through the activation of the transcendent function.

This, in barest form, is the outline of a lifelong individuation process as conceived by Jung. It takes place in three stages.

These three stages in turn correspond, in Jung's interpretation, to the unfolding of the Trinitarian Godhead in the Christian theological cosmos. Beginning with Yahweh as a representation of the original and whole but indefinite state of the Godhead (the Father), Christ (the Son) represents the development of the definite state of ego-consciousness within the Godhead in the form of a singular human being, which is then followed by the manifestation of the Holy Spirit as the agent working toward integration of the two, a symbol of the transcendent function. Individuation involves, in this three-part rhythm, essentially and centrally the process of "becoming definite" as its middle and therefore crucial development. This is the second stage of the individuation process, which is represented in the Trinitarian unfolding by the Son, Jesus Christ. The birth, development, and life of Jesus as a single human being are thus a representation of the constellation of the ego within the totality of the psyche as a whole.

Like Jesus in relation to the Godhead, then – and this is the *imitatio Christi* pattern within every individuation process – all human beings, no matter what their culture may be or their religious persuasion, become definite in relation to the preconscious self as they individuate. They declare themselves separate from their parents and other influences in the cultural world, they separate from the "shadow" (Satan, in Jesus' case) and other aspects of the unconscious (the anima or animus), they find a unique and individual identity and path in life, and in the end they have to confront consciously the parts of the self they have repudiated and rejected and integrate them into a new sense of psychological wholeness (integration of the separated opposites). The individuation process is a psychological version of the divine procession from Father to Son to Holy Spirit, from undifferentiated wholeness through differentiation and separation to conscious wholeness and reintegration. So the individuation process is *nolens volens* an *imitatio Christi* with the conscious ego in the position of the Second Person of the Trinity.

Two Vignettes, featuring Jung as a Protestant Teacher

In his scientific writings and occasional articles for popular magazines and journals, Jung almost invariably strikes the posture of physician and scientist, even if he is writing about art, literature or religion. This persona served him well for the purpose of advancing his ideas in professional and public domains and also for shielding him from attacks by unsympathetic critics who would claim that he was overstepping the bounds of his competence. Many of his papers begin with a kind of apology, in which he claims to be speaking as a psychiatrist and not as a… theologian, philosopher, literary or art critic or whatever the specialist subject matter at hand may be. However, in his private correspondence (as well as in a few works such as *Answer to Job, Memories, Dreams, Reflections,* the seminars at the Psychology Club and the ETH, and above all in *The Red Book*) he steps out of this persona to an extent and allows other features of his personality and his thinking to appear. In these works, he speaks his mind more freely and so reveals his private thoughts on many subjects along with his emotional reactions. In these pieces, his otherwise guarded private and personal thoughts and attitudes step more explicitly into the light, and we as readers can feel the difference, sometimes dramatically.

There were occasions, too, where he spoke to select audiences and friendly groups in a casual, spontaneous manner. Since he would have considered these remarks to be more or less off-the-record, he allowed himself to give freer rein to thoughts and feelings that were otherwise held more firmly in check. Also, the contexts stimulated him and drew out of him a particular kind of response. Here I will describe two such moments and cite them as indications of his intimate connection to the Protestant Christian tradition, which he usually held at arms length and often spoke of quite critically. In the two scenes I cite, we see the mature figure of Jung (he was in his early 60's) coming out as something of a reincarnation of his pastoral forebears, the Swiss Protestant preachers and clergymen that were in his lineage. On these occasions, he became charismatic in a quasi-religious sense, i.e., spontaneously inspired in the moment and by the audience he was addressing, and letting this spiritual intrusion into his normally rational and critical consciousness spill out all over his grateful audience. This is Jung the Protestant preacher unbound.

The First Vignette – Königsfeld, Germany 1937

In January 1937, Jung attended a conference held in Königsfeld, Germany with the title *An der Schwelle, Grundfragen der Seelenkunde und Seelenführung* ["At the Threshold: Fundamental Questions of Psychotherapy and Spiritual Direction"]. He had been invited by the organizer of the conference, Pastor Rudolf Daur, to come and express his views on psychotherapy and "the care of souls" to an audience made up of German pastors, religious counsellors and spiritual directors. Also present were members of the *Bund der Köngener*, originally a German youth organization with roots in the late 19th Century and organized under this name after WW I.[30]

It is important to note that Rudolf Daur (1891-1976), pastor of the Markuskirche in Stuttgart, had assumed the leadership of the *Bund* in 1933 after one of its founding members, Jacob Wilhelm Hauer (1881-1962), had been respectfully dismissed by the majority of the membership when he tried to take the organization in a direction better adjusted to the "Volkish" ideology emerging in Germany at the time and more in line with the ideas of National Socialism (Nazism). Hauer had for some years been distancing himself from the Christian church and now was busy founding his distinctly non-Christian "German Faith Movement" based on German mythology and Hindu philosophy. In a confrontation with Hauer in 1933, the majority of the membership of the *Bund* decided to affirm their Christian identity and not to forsake it by going in "Aryan" and "Volkish" directions with Hauer.[31] In this company, then, Jung had the opportunity to address a group of Protestant Christians who at the time were suffering considerable distress in the surging tide of Nazi evil flooding across their country. They were afraid that their churches in time would be washed away.

According to the Report, the audience in Königsfeld was thrilled that Jung would attend, and everyone was filled with excitement as they waited for his belated arrival. In his lectures there, Jung spoke without text or notes, and Rudolf Daur wrote the following report afterwards, published in the Report of the Conference:

> Was it not stirring to hear coming out of this mouth, from this independent and incorruptible man, that the Christ event has penetrated so deeply into the human soul, at least of Western people, that there is no going back or going around him? He [i.e., Jung] is a man who only wants

---

30 Before WW I, the members of what was to become the *Bund* were akin to Christian Boy and Girl Scout groups that would meet for weeks at a time in camps in the forests of Germany, its program built around intensive Bible study, hiking, swimming and so forth. Later as the *Bund*, this group matured into a movement of adult Evangelical Christians with liberal and ecumenical perspectives, which included Protestant pastors and spiritual directors.

31 For a full account of the history of the *Bund*, see H.-C. Brandenburg & R. Daur, *Die Brücke zu Köngen – Fünfzig Jahre Bund der Köngener*, 1919-1969 (Stuttgart: J.F. Steinkopf Verlag, 1970). On the decisive turning point in 1933-34, see especially chapter 8.

to serve the truth, who more than once has affirmed that he is prepared to burn all bridges behind him, who knows about the wisdom of the East and the revelations of the most diverse peoples and times, and who still believes in the future of Christianity, albeit a renewed, deepened, interiorized Christianity, which is however not at all an ahistorical, subjective enthusiasm but rather a fulfilment of what was announced and embodied by the Master from Nazareth, whose image with a few deft strokes became mysteriously alive and moving. This man even believes in the future of the Church, and he opened the eyes of more than one person to the most mysterious, almost forgotten and nowadays only superficially understood and valued treasures, symbols and images of the Church. What light falls on Luther's proclamation that the Christ is *peccator simulque Justus* ("at once sinful and righteous") when one recognizes the necessity of our shadow; how lively become the Biblical questions about God for whom 1000 years are but as a day through the deeper insight into the reality of the soul, which within the realm of time and space is almost irrelevant. What new and lively meaning the words "lead us not into temptation" in the Lord's Prayer take on when one hears the amusing yet very serious story from Jung's own childhood, that it is an arrogance of ego-consciousness to say that God can only be good. The *Deus absconditus*, the puzzling, incomprehensible but real God, is here made available to feeling or intuition more than in sophisticated Dogmatics. How simply and yet knowledgeably this man speaks on the meaning of true prayer, which is no longer just childish requests made to God, but rather a becoming free of the ego. How alive with colour and sound become words like "spirit" and "the journey to heaven and to hell" and stories like those of the first Pentecost when Jung interprets them or lets us overhear their linguistic and original meaning."[32]

From this fairly breathless report, we can see what a strong impression Jung made on his Protestant listeners and how his remarks struck deep chords of sympathy among them and encouraged them to continue their Christian mission in this toxic environment. He had the uncanny ability to inject new life into traditional and seemingly outworn symbols and theological ideas. He seems to have grasped the topics being discussed at the conference on a

32 Ibid., pp. 41-42. Translated by Murray Stein.

level far more profound than his listeners were accustomed to, and his words lit up the minds and the hearts in the room brilliantly. His remarks were inspirational, and they communicated his own personal understanding of the Christian faith as this had been worked out in extra-ecclesiastical circles (in his active imagination experiences, as described in *The Red Book*, in his analytical practice as reported by many patients, in his seminars at the Psychology Club and in other places). Here in Königsfeld, Jung obviously felt at home and comfortable among fellow Protestants like himself and easily found the pitch suited to the pastoral and youthful audience before him. He spoke as a Protestant Christian to fellow Protestant Christians who were threatened by the ghastly developments in the world around them, and his words gave them hope that their faith would prevail. This was the astonishing message coming from the famous Zürich psychiatrist, C.G. Jung.[33]

The Second Vignette – New York City, a Last Supper in 1937

The second occasion, similar to the first in some respects although the setting was entirely different, is mentioned in a letter to Jung from the New York Jungian analyst, Eleanor Bertine, dated November 2, 1937. The event she describes in this moving letter took place some nine months after the conference in Königsfeld (above). She speaks of a talk that Jung gave spontaneously to a group of friends and students in New York while en route back home to Switzerland following his Terry Lectures at Yale University. A farewell dinner for Jung was arranged by the Psychology Club of New York at the conclusion of a long and exhausting but also brilliantly successful trip. Always hungry for more, Jung's followers pleaded for a few final words before his departure for Europe the following day. These were to be Jung's last words uttered publicly in America. Two years later, WW II broke out, and Jung's health deteriorated thereafter so he would never return to America again. In her letter, Bertine describes the scene as follows:

> There you, C.G. Jung, began by saying you did not know what more you had to say to us, you had had to talk so much, etc. Then "It" began to break through you. It showed how the spirit had first appeared in the gods, then in the one God, *to Pan*, whence it moved to the Son of Man,

33 Jung has sometimes been mistakenly accused of favoring Hauer's German Faith Movement and his sympathies toward National Socialism. This vignette shows the opposite to be true.

one individual who had made his experiment fully, as we all must do, had made his mistakes, for to live is to make errors, but because he had lived utterly true to his best conviction, had won through to the body of the resurrection. This understanding of the man, Jesus, made him our brother, and the Christ, the Spirit, can live, no longer in one man for all, but in the unconscious of every man. And as "It" talked, Christ stood in the room in our midst, the word made flesh and dwelling visibly among us. But not this time as the one God-man who lives it for all, but as the quite human man who has realized Man, and so was able to awaken the Christ in those of his hearers who had ears to hear. To me that experience came in the utter devotion that unfurled to whatever It was that talked through you that night and claimed my deepest reverence and gratitude... It was not an experience of transference, but of the truth that lies back of transference.[34]

Bertine's letter catches the hushed tone of a special moment – for her a numinous experience, clearly – as Jung was delivering himself of some final thoughts to his closest friends in America at a kind of Last Supper. Others in the room took notes of the talk, and the event was later written up and published in the Club's report. The published version has Jung saying the following:

Jesus, you know, was a boy born of an unmarried mother. Such a boy is called illegitimate, and there is a prejudice which puts him at a great disadvantage. He suffers from a terrible feeling of inferiority for which he is certain to have to compensate. Hence the temptation of Jesus in the wilderness, in which the kingdom was offered to him. Here he met his worst enemy, the power devil; but he was able to see that, and to refuse. He said, "My kingdom is not of this world." ... The utter failure came at the Crucifixion in the tragic words, "My God, my God, why hast thou forsaken me?"...
We all must do just what Christ did. We must make our experiment. We must make mistakes... When we live like this we know Christ as a brother, and God indeed becomes man... then only does God become man in ourselves...

34 Unpublished letter, ETH Archives, Zurich.

And so the last thing I would say to each of you, my friends, is: Carry through your life as well as you can, even if it is based on error, because life has to be undone, and one often gets to truth through error. Then, like Christ, you will have accomplished your experiment. So, be human, seek understanding, seek insight, and make your hypothesis, your philosophy of life. Then we may recognize the Spirit alive in the unconscious of every individual. Then we become a brother of Christ.[35]

This is a perfect, succinct expression of Jung's view of the *imitatio Christi* for modern men and women. Bertine's words capture the spiritual aura circling about Jung, and they express his ability to evoke the spirit in a collective context. In this respect, he was an evangelist, a messenger, of the Divine. What is his message? *Imitatio Christi!* – that is to say, in Jung's post-creedal understanding: Follow your own personal myth as you discover it in your experience of the psyche, and never mind if it conforms to public opinion, to collective religious teachings received in your tradition, or to generally accepted cultural patterns. This journey will be your greatest treasure in life, possibly also your greatest burden and suffering, but it will carry you to your individuation's goal. This I regard as the faith of a modern, post-traditional, non-creedal Protestant.

Conclusion

One must absolutely and without question recognize that Jung outgrew and exceeded his Protestant cultural location enormously and in many directions. His research was scientific in the narrow sense of controlled experimentation in the early phases and in the broad sense of being empirical and grounded in publicly verifiable "facts" in the later phases. The theories he elaborated to account for the facts he uncovered in these researches were always and invariably stated carefully as "hypotheses" and not as doctrines, truths, or revelations. Nor did they rely on backing from other revelations of a divine origin. In other words, Jung was not a theologian in any traditional sense of the word, Protestant or otherwise. In addition, his researches extended into many areas of human knowledge that had nothing

---

35 W. McGuire and, R.F.C. Hull (eds.), *C.G. Jung Speaking: Interviews and Encounters* (Princeton: Princeton University Press, 1977). pp. 97-98.

to do specifically with religious thought, and so they were not restricted to Protestant Christian sources. Methodologically, he was a scientist.

In his inner life as well, he was in many ways not limited to Protestant themes and images. If we study his autobiography, *Memories, Dreams, Reflections,* and *The Red Book,* we find many psychic figures and images that are not specifically Protestant or Christian, but are rather linked to or derived from other sources – figures like Philemon, for instance, who is a wisdom figure that cannot be located in an exclusively Christian worldview; or Aion, the god of infinite time, which has its source in Mithraism and Zoroastrian religion; or Izdubar, a Babylonian hero/deity; or Phanes, an Orphic deity. These symbolic figures, which played a central role in Jung's identity and inner life, do not have their roots in Protestantism. Their sources are much older, broader, and mainly non-Biblical.[36]

So it would be a gross error to paint Jung as exclusively a Protestant Christian and nothing more complex than that. That said, there are important continuities between Jung's thought and attitudes and his Protestant heritage, especially with regard to the deep links between the individuation process and *imitatio Christi.* It is these that I have tried to elucidate in this essay. It is my hunch that Protestant Christianity was Jung's fall-back, default position upon which he relied in an intuitive and largely implicit way as he taught, analysed, wrote and lived his personal life. It is therefore important to keep this in mind as one studies Jung's works and appropriates his methods and attitudes for oneself.[37]

---

36 Sanford Drob has written a long and fascinating book in which he draws parallels between Jung's thought and Jewish mysticism, especially the Kabbalistic element in it. He shows quite convincingly that "as great as is Jung's acknowledged affinity to the Kabbalah, his unacknowledged relationship was even greater." Sandford Drob, *Kabbalistic visions: C.G. Jung and Jewish mysticism* (New Orleans: Spring Journal Books, 2010), p. 4. One can also draw similar parallels between Jung's thought and Chinese Taoist philosophy. All of which is to say that there are many important influences to be found in Jung's mature thought.

37 First published in: *International Journal of Jungian Studies* (London: Routledge, 2011), vol. 3, No. 2, pp. 125-143

Plate 1: Peter Birkhäuser, Sun of the Night (1970)

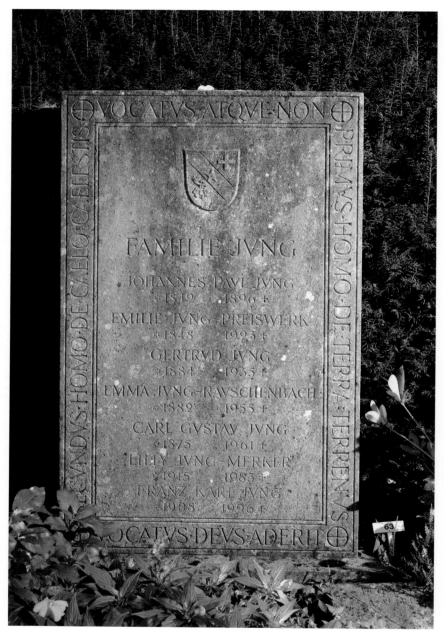

Plate 2: Gravestone of the Jung-Family at the Cemetery in Küsnacht

Plate 3: Gravestone of Marie-Louise von Franz and Barbara Hannah in Küsnacht

228

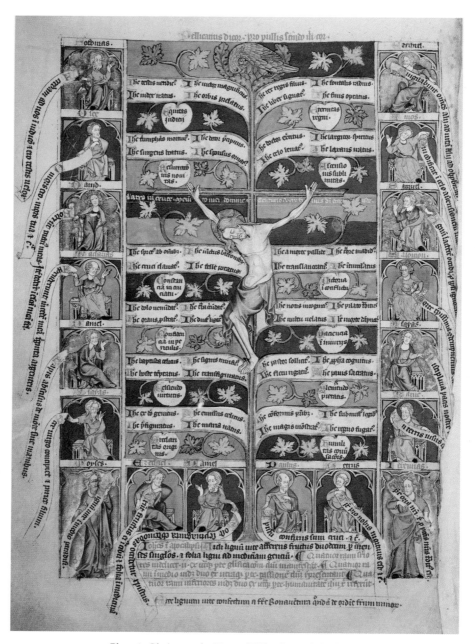

Plate 4: Christ on the Tree of Life, above the Pelican

Plate 5: C.G. Jung's Stone in Bollingen

230

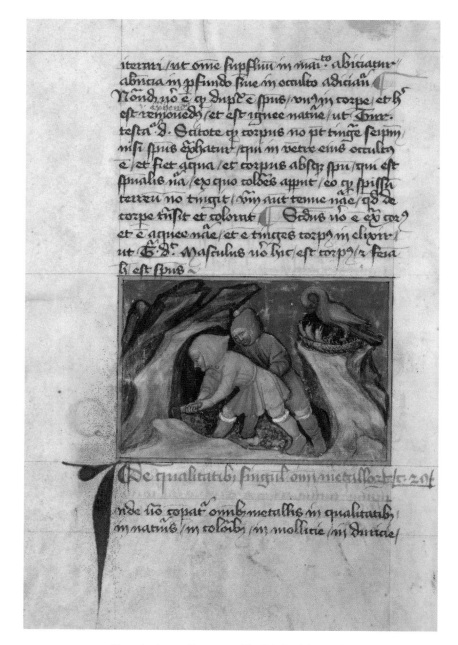

Plate 6: *Aurora Consurgens*, The Work with Metals

Plate 7: Pelican with the Fledglings, in the Vessel the Waxing Moon

Plate 8: Mercurius as Crowned Hermaphrodite with the Pelican

Plate 9: Hasidic Man in Krakow (ca. 1935-1938)

234

Plate 10: A Treasure Vase at Somi's Initiation Ceremony

Plate 11a: The Great Stupa of Sanchi

Plate 11b: Treasure Vases on the North Gate of the Great Stupa of Sanchi

236

Plate 12: *Śālabhañjikā* on the North Gate of the Great Stupa

Plate 13: The Goddess "Abundance" from Mathurā (2nd cent.)

238

Plate 14: The Birth of the Future Buddha (Nepal, 9th cent.)

Plate 15: The *Kandariya Mahadeva* Temple in Khajuraho, Madhya Pradesh (11th cent.)

Plate 16: The *Kumbum* of Gyantse, Southern Tibet (15th cent.)

Marianne Jehle-Wildberger

Stations of a Difficult Friendship
Carl Gustav Jung and Adolf Keller

Vocatus atque non vocatus deus aderit.[1]

The psychiatrist C.G. Jung (1875-1961) and the Protestant theologian Adolf Keller (1872-1963) corresponded with each other for fifty years.[2] Beginning in 1907, it continued until 1958 when Keller suffered a stroke and lost his power of speech. Few of Jung's friendships endured as long as the one with Keller. His contact with the Dominican priest Victor White[3] was of much shorter duration.

The exchange between Jung and Keller was most intensive during the years from 1909 until 1923, exactly at a particularly important time for Jung, as he had separated from Sigmund Freud, was in search of his own way, and was preparing the groundwork for his own theory. Carl Gustav Jung's *The Red Book*[4] originated during this time. The minutes of the meetings of the early psychiatrists' circle surrounding Jung (1909-1918) to which

1 *Vocatus atque non vocatus deus aderit* (Invoked or not invoked, God will be present.) Inscription, chiseled in stone, above the door of the house of C.G. Jung and onto the tombstone of the family tomb in Küsnacht. It is a quotation from the book *Adagia (Proverbs)* by Erasmus of Rotterdam. Jung had bought this book when only 19 years old. The verse goes back to the oracle of Delphi. Adolf Keller liked this maxim too.
2 See Marianne Jehle-Wildberger, *C.G. Jung und Adolf Keller. Über Theologie und Psychologie. Briefe und Gespräche.* An English translation of the book will be published at Princeton (ed. Philemon Foundation). See also Marianne Jehle-Wildberger, *Adolf Keller. Ecumenist, World Citizen, Philantropist* (Eugene Oregon/Cambridge: Wipf and Stock/The Lutterworth Press, 2013).
3 Victor White, Dominican father in England (1902-1960), exchanged letters with C.G. Jung between 1945-1960. See *The Jung-White Letters*, ed. Ann Conrad Lammers and Adrian Cunningham (London/New York: Philemon Series, Routledge, 2007).
4 Carl Gustav Jung, *The Red Book. Liber Novus*, ed. and introduction by Sonu Shamdasani (New York: Norton, 2009).

Keller, although an outsider, belonged, give evidence of their early, very close relationship.[5] As well, the archives of the still existing *Psychology Club*, which was founded in 1916, are an important source.[6] Only one single letter has survived from the first 23 years of their relationship. It was from Jung to Keller, dated 1915. It is a very revealing document![7]

After 1923 their contact became less frequent, which had to do with professional reasons on Keller's part. In 1943 their friendship grew again closer and they pursued an active correspondence. Only eight of the 81 available letters[8] were written prior to 1943. So, the existing letters were written primarily during their later years. These letters are of both psychological and theological value, and throw light on their personal relationship. During the entire time of their relationship, articles and books were published which, at least indirectly, provide insight into the ongoing discussion between these two friends.

C.G. Jung was numbered among the most renowned personalities of the 20th century. His understanding of the human soul and his innovative therapeutic method are still remembered. His significance for 20th century humanities remains uncontested, despite differing opinions. The opposite is true of Adolf Keller. Today, hardly anyone knows him, although he was highly esteemed as a parish minister in Zurich from 1909 until 1923, and afterwards as an internationally active ecumenist and as head of a charitable organization. He enjoyed during his lifetime an esteem similar to that of C.G. Jung.

Jung's and Keller's concern was mainly for people. Of interest is, although gifted and talented second level students, they both showed a dislike for mathematics. It was too abstract for them. While still a student, Jung expressed the opinion: "Without the psyche there would be neither

---

5 The author thanks Dr. Andreas Schweizer, president of the *Psychology Club Zurich*, for giving her the permission to read the typed records of the early circle around C.G. Jung 1913-1918.

6 Records of the general assemblies, the assemblies of the members and the sessions of the board of the *Psychology Club* as well as the printed yearbook.

7 As to Jung's letter of 1915 see below p. 250.

8 Most of the letters between Jung and Keller are stored in: Nachlass C.G. Jung, library of the ETH Zurich, HS 1056: 755ff. – All the preserved 81 letters are published in M. Jehle-Wildberger, *C.G. Jung und Adolf Keller*. 5 letters from Jung to Keller were already published in Carl Gustav Jung, *Letters*, selected and edited Gerhard Adler in collaboration with Aniela Jaffé. Translated by R.F.C. Hull, in two volumes (Princeton: Princeton University Press, 1973).

knowledge nor insight."[9] Jung's and Keller's life work had, in a narrow sense, a scientific side; both wrote numerous books, often with quotations. Yet they considered themselves practitioners. It was the living human being that interested them. They were concerned for his well-being. In particular, they were perceptive to a person's psychological distress. – Of great importance to both was the belief in a higher Force. For the theologian Keller this was obvious. But also for the psychiatrist Jung, this was of deep concern, which the inscription above the door to his house shows.[10]

Yet it was exactly in this matter that fundamental differences were to become evident. – What they shared in common was a remarkable interest in the world at large, a broad intellectual horizon, a knowledge of languages, a preference for everything English, as well as an unbelievable creativity and capacity for work.

Their years together in the *Society for Analytical Psychology* and the *Psychology Club* (1907-1923)

Both friends, as already mentioned, considered themselves to be religious. Jung, the son of a minister, experienced already as a youth, that his father, who followed an orthodox, literalist orientation of theology, preached from the pulpit a position which in the face of scientific developments, he could no longer ascribe to. Relatively young, he broke under the weight of this conflict.[11] His adolescent son, C.G. Jung, observed this conflict with deep dismay. As a medical student, he gave talks in his fraternity, the *Zofingia*, in which he took distance from the orthodox theology of his father.[12] He also rejected the liberal theology, which most ministers at that time accepted, because he believed it destroyed the biblical myths.[13]

For the rest of his life he held an aversion for he theological teachings of both schools. Nevertheless, he sympathized with mysticism and pietism because in these religious movements faith is interiorized and truly lived.[14] He advocated experience as the path to knowledge – and for the worth of

9   Aniela Jaffé (ed.), *Memories, Dreams, Reflections by C.G. Jung*, translated by Clara and Richard Winston (New York: Random House, 1965), p. 119.
10 See footnote 1.
11 A. Jaffé (ed.), *Memories, Dreams, Reflections by C.G. Jung*, pp. 214-216.
12 Carl Gustav Jung, *The Zofingia Lectures 1896-1899*, transl. Jan van Heurck, introd. Marie-Louise von Franz (Princeton: Princeton University Press, 1983), § 138.
13 Ibid., § 251.
14 Ibid., § 255.

the soul. Empiricism was important, not rationalism. And yet, he longed
for a prophet, a "messenger of God," who would lead Christianity onto the
right path.[15]

Adolf Keller, the son of a Schaffhausen village schoolmaster, like Jung,
came from a religiously conservative milieu. His mother's faith had a re-
laxed pietistic touch to it. Her heart-warming religiousness had a strong
influence on Keller. As well, he found his father's faith to be authentic.
He studied theology. The historical-critical interpretation of the Bible of
the liberal school to which his professors in Basel and Berlin belonged, at
first, disconcerted him. With time he accepted it. Mostly, he was impressed
by the experience theology of the Berlin professor Julius Kaftan. Upon his
return to Switzerland, he joined a group of theologians whose objective it
was to mediate between conservative and liberal theologies. He, too, longed
for a prophet who would bring an end to the unholy conflict between the
schools and would give a new impulse to theology.[16]

Keller's contact with Jung began about 1907, while he was a parish
minister in Geneva. He found the pastoral work of many of his colleagues
to be inadequate and wanted to learn more about the soul. Parallel to his
parish duties he studied psychology under Théodore Flournoy, who was a
professor at the University of Geneva – a scholar whom he highly regarded
and whom Jung admired as a fatherly friend. Jung wrote to Sigmund Freud:
"We have found a new friend in the Geneva Protestant minister Adolf
Keller, who already works proficiently in psychoanalysis."[17]

In 1909, Keller, now minister at St. Peter's in Zurich, was accepted,
although as theologian an outsider, into the circle of psychiatrists at the
Psychiatric Clinic Burghölzli. The circle had been formed in 1907. Jung,
who had initially been at this clinic working under the chief physician
Eugen Bleuler, opened his private practice in 1909 in his new house in
Küsnacht. Here he gathered several of his former colleagues, among them
Ludwig Binswanger. Also, Keller's university friend Oskar Pfister, minister
at the Blackfriars Church[18] in Zurich and interested in psychology, had the
privilege to participate in this group of psychiatrists. The discussions in this
round were lively and often controversial.

---

15 Ibid., § 138.
16 Keller to Leonhard Ragaz, May 1, 1924, archives of the State of Zurich, WI 103.2.
17 Jung to Freud, March 7, 1909, in: *Sigmund Freud – C. G. Jung: A Correspondence,* ed.
   William McGuire/Wolfgang Sauerländer (Zurich: Ex Libris 1974), letter 133.
18 Before Reformation Pfister's church had been the church of the Dominican fathers.

Picture 1: Congress in Weimar[19]

In 1911, the *3rd International Psychoanalytical Congress* took place in Weimar. Sigmund Freud, the patriarch of psychoanalysis, and C.G. Jung, whom he had appointed "Crown Prince," were the two dominating figures. The photograph shows them in the center of the group, standing next to each other. Adolf Keller, also at the congress, stands behind Jung to the upper right, recognizable by his moustache and pointed dark beard. Eugen Bleuler, Ludwig Binswanger and Oskar Pfister can be located in the lower left. Keller already anticipated the breach between the two stars. When in 1912 it came to that, he chose to stand by Jung, because he considered Freud's emphasis on sexuality as the cause of psychological disorders – although broadly defined – as too one-sided. Jung stood for a diversity of causes for psychological disorders and, furthermore, appeared to show more interest in religious phenomena than did his mentor. Théodore Flournoy also remained loyal to Jung. However, Oskar Pfister and Ludwig Binswanger seemed at first to hesitate.

After the breach in 1912, the discussions in the circle around Jung carried on as usual. The participants were still almost exclusively psychiatrists. Jung held most of the lectures and made numerous comments. He was the

19 M. Jehle-Wildberger, *C.G. Jung und Adolf Keller*, p. 28.

uncontested master. Nevertheless, other psychiatrists also presented talks. Open dialogue was cultivated.

At the time Carl Gustav Jung was working on his book *Symbols of Transformation*.[20] Keller recalled: "We experienced the development of the book... quite directly. The group had a revolutionary aspect, which expressed itself in a clear position of protest against society, tradition, and as well, theology and the church."[21] Jung gave Keller the proof sheets of the second part of the book to take with him on his honeymoon to Cairo in early 1912 (where Keller had taken up his first assignment as minister for the German community there). He was asked to verify detail issues in the museums and libraries, a clear vote of confidence!

Picture 2: Freud, Jung and Keller[22]

Keller was among the more active members of the circle around Jung. At the biweekly meetings there was always a lecture followed by a long discussion. The book, *Symbols of Transformation*, one of Jung's main works, constituted

---

20 Carl Gustav Jung, *Symbols of Transformation*, vol. 5 of *The Collected Works of C.G. Jung*, translated by R.F.C. Hull (Princeton: Princeton University Press, 1956).
21 Adolf Keller, *Aus meinem Leben*, typed, 1940, p. 59, in: private archive of the Keller family.
22 Detail from the cover of M. Jehle-Wildberger, *C.G. Jung und Adolf Keller*.

the most important topic of discussion in 1913.[23] It gave insight into the broad mythological realms of other cultures and religions. The theory of the collective unconscious and of archetypes took their beginnings therein. Ludwig Binswanger expressed his fundamental criticism to that. For other reasons, it came to a controversy between Oskar Pfister and Jung.

Keller eagerly asked questions regarding the book, was impressed but also expressed criticism. It bothered him that Jung equated the Greco-Latin Helios-Sol with the biblical divine light, and that he put the Persian Mithras on the same level as Jesus.[24] Indeed Keller, like Jung, was open to other religions. Such that, in 1936, he would participate in the conference of religions held in London to which Jews, Muslims, Christians, Hindus, and Buddhists came. Still, Jung's comparisons went too far for him.

Of importance is: From the very start, the topic of Christianity played a central role in the discussions between Jung and Keller. In the circle as a whole, the focus of course was on the treatment of people suffering from psychological problems. All the time, there remained the quiet hope that the breach with Freud would be mended. Jung explained in early 1913, that with regard to his relationship to Freud, it was "not about a schism, but rather about further development."[25] However, he continued, Freud explains neurosis as causal, he himself as in part causal, in part final. An introvert's neurosis should be addressed more likely as final, an extrovert's as causal. In any case, one should no longer ask exclusively where the neurosis comes from, but rather what is its purpose. Behind the neurosis is the question, which duty does one not want to fulfill, a duty that one has placed on one's self. Therefore, dreams should be read prospectively.[26] – Keller then wanted to know if every dream should be interpreted as prospective, because in his pastoral work, he frequently interpreted dreams. Jung replied, the objective of the unconscious needed to be uncovered, because it never deceives.

A year later, 1914, Jung held two lectures "On Dream Symbolism."[27] Now, he totally rejected Freud's theory about dreams. From his point of view, Freud neglected the manifest dream content. A dream has a tendency to balance out, and has as such a final (i.e. a target-oriented) function. For example, Freud would interpret a nightmare as the fulfillment of a wish,

---

23 Records of the *Psychologischer Verein* (1913-14) / *Verein für Analytische Psychologie* (1914-18), typed, in: *Psychology Club Zurich.*
24 Records *Psychologischer Verein*, 14 February 1913.
25 Records *Psychologischer Verein*, 31 January 1913.
26 Ibid.
27 Records *Psychologischer Verein*, 30 January 1914.

whereas, he, Jung, as the sign of a real danger. – Again here, Keller did not hold back with his questions. He requested more accuracy regarding Jung's explanation of introversion and extroversion: "If the distinction between the [two] types is so important, how does one make the distinction?"[28], he asked. The question is "very complicated," Jung said, and couldn't be answered definitively. But a few weeks later, he returned to Keller's question and gave an extensive, complex answer:

> Psychological phenomena are manifestations of energy. This energy we call in psychology libido, and is more or less… comparable to [Bergson's] élan vital… The concept of libido corresponds to the energy concept of conservation and transformation of the total sum of energy… With regard to [psychic] energy, there are various conditions, first the kinetic should be considered. The object is occupied, and thereby, has a temporary influence on the subject. This occupying energy arises however in the subject. Thus, the external world gets a greater emotional meaning, equivalent to extraversion… Compared to that, the introversion, where the internal maintains the upper hand…[29]

It becomes clear, that Jung was querying and everything was in progress. Keller was not only witness to the development of Jung's theory, but with his questions, prompted the formulation and specification of the new theory. He delivered his own substantial contributions to the discussion. In two lectures, he spoke on the French philosopher Henri Bergson, about whom he had currently published a book, and whose theses also interested Jung. The focus on psychic life was common to both Bergson and Jung, as it was for Keller. Jung's "libido" paralleled Bergson's "élan vital."[30] Jung expressed his approval of both lectures. After that, Keller lectured on three evenings about Théodore Flournoy's works.

In the summer of 1914, Jung came to the conviction that the break with Freud was definite. In a secret vote on the question, whether or not to maintain membership in the *International Psychological Congress,* fifteen of the group members voted no, going along with Jung, one abstained. Only Keller voted yes – a small indication, that despite his devotion to Jung

---

28 Records *Psychologischer Verein,* 24 October 1913.
29 Records *Psychologischer Verein,* 21 November 1913.
30 Adolf Keller, *Eine Philosophie des Lebens (Henri Bergson)* (Jena: Eugen Diederichs, 1914), 146 pages.

he maintained an independent position. Now Jung's circle was called the *Society for Analytical Psychology* – to differentiate from Freud's *Psychoanalysis* – or simply, the "Zurich Group." Some of the hitherto members withdrew, among them Ludwig Binswanger and Oskar Pfister. Apparently, neither had participated in the vote. Jung felt abandoned. He fell into a deep crisis. Keller was now the only theologian on his side.

At this point in time, Jung had just begun what he referred to as his scientific self experiment: In quiet hours, he let himself fall into the depths of his soul, in order to glean knowledge about the unconscious. What he experienced during his "nightly sea voyage" was both magnificent and dreadful. *The Red Book* gives testimony to his experience. It became the basis for his further work. Long kept in a safe, it was published in 2009 by Sonu Shamdasani. Along with its psychological importance, *The Red Book* has a high artistic value. – The process which Jung went through in his self experiment he called "Individuation." It is a way to "the Self," a self that is light and dark. Very few knew of Jung's experiment. One exception was Tina Keller-Jenny, Adolf Keller's much younger wife. Because she was shy and sometimes plagued by anxiety, she underwent depth-analysis with Jung, as one of his first clients. He permitted her, which only few were granted, an occasional glimpse into the emerging *Red Book*.

Tina Keller-Jenny,[31] who came from a similar upper class milieu, as did Emma Jung-Rauschenbach, and grew up overprotected, experienced her long years of therapy with Jung as painful, but in the end, healing. Already the mother of three children, she began to study medicine – against Jung's advice, who thought it unnecessary. However, she wanted to become an equal partner to her husband! This showed, that thanks to her studies, and of course the therapy with Jung, and the understanding support from her husband, her self-confidence grew tremendously. After completing her studies, she opened a practice in the spirit of Jung, but then emancipated herself partly from him. Together with Toni Wolff, a close associate of Jung, she developed a respiratory and dance therapy, having made the experience that not all psychological problems can be addressed through words. These two women were pioneers in the work they achieved together.

And now, that important first letter from Jung to Keller.

---

31 Tina Keller, *Wege inneren Wachstums für eingespannte Menschen. Aus meinen Erinnerungen an C.G. Jung.* Separatdruck zu Wendepunkt Nr. 5-7 (Erlenbach/Bad Homburg: Bircher-Benner, 197), and Tina Keller-Jenny, *The Memoir of Tina Keller-Jenny*, ed. Wendy K. Swan (New Orleans: Spring Journal, 2011).

Küsnacht-Zurich, 5 November 1915

Dear Friend!

Thank you very much for your Day of Prayer and Repentance sermon,
the beautiful words which I have taken into my heart. May I make a
small remark about your psychological process? Of course, under the
assumption, that I know, you couldn't have expressed it any differently
in your sermon.

You describe the process: Self-knowledge and Self-reflection – Revision
of Attitude – Brotherhood of Mankind. With this logical insight, I
agree. Why are human beings such fools as not to do this? They could,
by means of insight and will – as we have been doing to this day. In
reality, it doesn't go like that, but quite differently. Namely, this process
must be *lived* [i.e. long and intensively]: Then the following occurs:

I. Stage: Introversion: The individual's disengagement from society.
Due to the too strong common attitude, this does not work without
misunderstanding, animosity and hate = war.

II. Stage: Libido in the mother: Awakening of the archaic = psychosis.
Unleashing of highs and lows. An almost anarchistic situation, in any
case, dissolution of society to the highest degree (Dismemberment
motive).

III. Stage: Hatching: Mystical development and union, about which
I know too little, which I can sense rather than know. Because we
have not come that far in our own experience. The dismemberment of
the old is not yet completed. The isolation is awful. It has its start in
national isolation.

The task *in these times* is to preach the first stage: Guiding the person to
turn inwardly...[32]

Jung's comments need to be seen in reference to the First World War and to
his self experiment.

With regard to Stage I, he and Keller were in agreement. A person must
reflect upon himself, must face his shadow. In Jung's opinion, this stage
lasts a long time. He rejected every kind of superficiality. From Jung, Keller
learned how to authentically listen to his clients in a psychological situation. He termed his own first stage "Ploughing," i.e., to open up the soul.

32 Jung wrote the letter by hand. The original lies in: Sondersammlung der Winterthu-
rer Bibliotheken CHW, Ms Sch 153,9.

Playing a part in Jung's Stage II was the fact that the world, at that time, was falling apart, as well as his own nightly sea voyages, which were for him, in part, horrific. Keller understood Stage II differently than Jung: The "Ploughing" in Stage I was followed by "Sowing," i.e., the consoling promise of divine mercy, which then led to a "Renewal of Attitude."[33] How liberating this promise could be, Keller experienced in his pastoral work with prison inmates, which was part of his duties at St. Peter's.

In Stage III, Jung seemed to be groping. It wasn't yet clear. Nevertheless, he hoped for a positive development, a mystical union. – Keller, in his Stage III, "Brotherhood," meant concern for one's fellow human beings.

Keller's three steps come across as more optimistic than do Jung's three stages. But ultimately, Jung, too, hoped for healing, such as a participating responsibly in society. – In the 1915 letter, Jung described himself and Keller as introverted. Summarizing, it can be said, that Jung's letter reveals his arduous struggle to find an effective therapy. At this time, Adolf Keller and Oskar Pfister founded the beginnings of pastoral psychology, i.e., the application of depth psychology methods in pastoral counseling.

As pastor, Keller was very much in demand, of which Jung was aware. One day, he sent Edith McCormick-Rockefeller, co-founder of the *Psychology Club*, to Keller. Jung had been treating her for several years. During an entire year, Keller took the American lady with him on pastoral visits. He hoped, through the encounter with suffering, sick, or poor people, he could pull her out of her depression – with moderate success. But apparently, she greatly appreciated Keller and frequently slipped him some money for those in his care. – In later writings, Jung advocated cooperation between theologians and psychologists in the treatment of mentally ill people.[34]

In 1916, together with his wife Emma, Jung founded the *Psychology Club*[35] having responded to the suggestion of Harold and Edith McCormick-Rockefeller. Unlike the *Society for Analytical Psychology*, the *Psychology Club* was to be open to a broad general public. Therefore, Tina Keller-Jenny, who was a client of Jung, was admitted to the *Club*. She also took part in seminars which Jung offered within this setting. As in the *Society*, lectures and discussions were held in the *Club*. In addition, social events were hosted,

33 Also Oskar Pfister used the terms "ploughing" and "sowing" in his pastoral care!
34 Carl Gustav Jung, *"Psychotherapists or the Clergy"* and *"Psychoanalysis and the Cure of Souls"* in: *Psychology and Religion: West and East*, vol. 11 of *The Collected Works of C.G. Jung*, translated by R.F.C. Hull (Princeton: Princeton University Press, 1969), § 327-347 and 348-354.
35 See M. Jehle-Wildberger, *C.G. Jung und Adolf Keller*, pp. 56ff.

such as dinners, game and dance parties, as well as concerts. Keller, who was an accomplished pianist, played once at the *Club*.[36] Something of that kind would have been unthinkable in the *Society*.

Soon, a problem arose in the *Club*, which was brought to attention by Edith McCormick-Rockefeller, namely, the lax admission policy. This resulted in *Club* members with very different needs. This problem led to Tina Keller-Jenny's resignation, who found the discussion, at times, too shallow. Ultimately, even C.G. Jung and Emma Jung left the *Club*. Adolf Keller, however, persevered.

Subsequently, stricter conditions for participation were introduced, whereupon the renegades returned. The level improved. Often, external speakers were invited, among them Herman Hesse and Martin Buber.[37]

Keller held in the *Club* an entire series of challenging lectures, the first in 1918 on "The Gospel and Christianity."[38] His objective was to relate the findings of Analytical Psychology to the Gospel. Therein, he spoke of the individuation of Jesus: The life of Jesus, he said, signifies a "personal life to the fullest. The word became flesh and dwelt amongst us... It served to build inner strength in an individual and in the community, and puts before our eyes a complete, pure humanity in its perfect form."[39] Already in his youth, Keller continued, Jesus left home and family to go into the solitude of the desert, he withdrew himself from the collective pressure of public opinion, entered the temple with revolutionary defiance, and died companionless. "But his solitude does not imply drowning in the individuation process. In his experience of God, in the founding of a new spiritual community, he achieved a higher collectivity."[40] For Jesus, Keller said, it was about a genuine deliverance from mankind's inner bondage. The proposal of the individuation of Jesus was innovative and bold! Keller stood closer to Jung than ever.

In two further, unavailable lectures at the *Club*, Keller spoke about his two month trip through the USA (1919), and on "Ethics in Psychoanalysis"

36 Records of the *Psychology Club* of October 18, 1924. Keller presumably played Bach or Beethoven or Brahms or perhaps even all of them – he liked them very much.
37 M. Jehle-Wildberger, *C.G. Jung und Adolf Keller*, p. 60. Martin Buber spoke at the Club only once, on December 1st 1923, at the time of the presidency of Hans Trüb when Jung was absent from the Club.
38 The typescript of the lecture is in the archive of the *Psychology Club* in Zurich, under "manuscripts" folder M 12.
39 Ibid., p. 5. See John 1:14.
40 Ibid., p. 7.

(1920). Far-sighted was his lecture on "The Psychology of large mass events" (1924), which was based on his negative impressions of religious gatherings held in sport stadiums in the USA.[41] Finally, in 1947, urged by Jung, he spoke "About the Concerns of Dialectical Theology."[42] This new theology was articulated by Karl Barth during the First World War. At the end of the war, his *Epistle to the Romans*[43] was published, after which he became the focal point of Keller's debate with Jung.

First and foremost, it must be emphasized: Over many years, until around 1923, Jung and Keller and their families were very close. The Kellers were often invited to the Jungs' open house evenings in Küsnacht, and also privately – and vice versa, the Jungs were invited by the Kellers to the vicarage of St. Peters. Both couples had five children. Jung was godfather to Adolf's and Tina's third child, Margrit (1916-1997). Conversely, Keller was very much the family minister for the Jungs. He baptized Helene, Carl's and Emma's youngest child in the library of Jung's house at Küsnacht. He also performed the burial service for Emma's mother.[44] In their letters, Jung and Keller addressed each other simply as "Dear friend," which was uncommon at that time even among colleagues, and which Jung allowed only a small number of very intimate friends. His letters to Keller were always signed "Carl," a rarity of even greater value.

The Period of Transition and later years' correspondence

At the close of the First World War, Keller's life changed significantly. At first, this had to do with Karl Barth's *Epistle to the Romans* from 1919. Everyone was talking about *Dialectical Theology*. Keller was fascinated with it, although he considered Barth's saying "God is the Wholly Other" one-sided. Still, he saw in Barth, who at one time – in Geneva – had been his curate, the prophet he had been longing for. Barth's emphasis on a transcendent God stood in opposition to Jung's emphasis on God's immanence. For Keller, the two images were not exclusive.

---

41 M. Jehle-Wildberger, *C.G. Jung und Adolf Keller*, pp. 59f. A. Keller, *Ecumenist*, p. 51.

42 The summary of the lecture figures in the annual report of the *Psychology Club*, (Zurich: Buchdruckerei Fluntern, 1946/47), pp. 29f.

43 Karl Barth, *Der Römerbrief*, erste Fassung, 1919, GA vol. 16, (Zurich: TVZ, 1985). – See also: Frank Jehle, "Der junge Karl Barth," in: Frank Jehle, *Von Johannes auf Patmos bis zu Karl Barth*, (Zurich: TVZ, 2015), pp. 101-124.

44 See Jung to Keller, March 17, 1932, letter 3, in: M. Jehle-Wildberger, *C.G. Jung und Adolf Keller*, p. 130.

Picture 3: Adolf Keller, at the age of about 70[45]

Also, at war's end, a worldwide ecumenical movement came into being. Keller joined it and soon rose to one of its most important representatives. For this reason, in 1923, he gave up his pastorate at St. Peter's. Now working for the reconciliation of churches of the former enemies, he was constantly travelling. Moreover, he encouraged the founding of the *Swiss Federation of Protestant Churches,* and he built up an ecumenical organization to aid the damaged churches in Europe, the Inter-Church Aid (which was the forerunner of the HEKS[46]). Leading this organization became his main task. 1928 he moved together with his family to Geneva, the center of ecumenical Christianity. His contact with Jung had to be held at a minimum. Yet, he kept his membership in the *Psychology Club.*

At the beginning of 1933 Hitler came to power. Already at the end of the year, in his lectures at Princeton, USA, Keller warned about the developments in Germany. In his charitable organization, he immediately

45 M. Jehle-Wildberger, *Adolf Keller. Pionier der ökumenischen Bewegung,* p. 521.
46 HEKS = *Swiss Protestant Church Aid,* founded in 1946.

cared for the Jewish and so-called Jewish-Christian refugees who knocked on his door. Several times, he spoke up in their interest before government officials in Bern. As he wrote 1942, he personally had tended to 2'600 refugees. – Jung also recognized the destructivity of National Socialism, but in the first two or three years hoped, nevertheless, there would be a creative impulse. At the latest, in 1936, he took a decisive anti-national socialist position. His lectures in Yale in 1937, to a partly uncritical audience, give evidence to this. He too, in his – widely criticized – function as president of the international *General Physicians' Association for Psychotherapy* saved many Jewish physicians.[47]

During the Second World War, from 1943, Keller began to pass his diverse duties into younger hands. He wrote to Jung: "... once again one reaches out to people who share our fate and are still with us. You have been for us [for Tina and himself] one of these portentous powers, and I call you friend... I would like to see you more often, without encumbering you, in an encounter that is appropriate for apprentices of dying, and which is not concerned with things, thoughts, and people, but with grandeur et misère de l'homme, and with God Himself, just as He can be heard by everyone."[48] He wanted to encounter Jung as an equal. No other of Jung's correspondence friends dared make such a claim, apart from Freud. Jung, it seems, responded hesitantly to Keller's suggestion. Perhaps the reason is, that he was seriously ill at the time, or because he felt more attracted to the symbolism and the Mariology of the Catholic Church. That is why he anticipated more from discussions with Catholic rather than Protestant theologians. An example is the question of justification. Jung opposed the Lutheran rejection of "good works," which seemed to contradict his concept of individuation. Yet, Jung oversaw that the "sola gratia"[49] was an important doctrine not only of the Protestants, but also of the Roman Catholic Church. (He was going to learn this through his dialogues with the Dominican Victor White.) Incidentally, Jung saw himself explicitly as

47 C.G. Jung was not the president of the German branch of the society, as some people wrongly had claimed.
48 Keller to Jung, May 21, 1943, letter 12, in: M. Jehle-Wildberger, *C.G. Jung und Adolf Keller*, pp. 137f. – To "*grandeur et misère de l'homme*" see Blaise Pascal, *Pensées*, chapter II and III of part I.
49 Sola gratia (by grace alone). This principle of Reformation (and of classical Roman-catholic theology as well!) stands against people who tend to believe that it is possible to redeem themselves.

a Protestant, if as one on the extreme left, he even understood himself as a savior of Protestantism.[50]

The letters from 1943 forth are dominated by three themes: 1. The *Dialectical Theology*, 2. A dream of Keller's, 3. Jung's book, *Answer to Job*.

Regarding the first: Jung apparently did not understand what Barth intended with his theology. But, as mentioned above, in 1947 he let Keller lecture at the *Psychology Club* about *Dialectical Theology*. In the meantime, Barth had tempered his extreme theory on the transcendence of God. By then he reflected more and more on God's incarnation and on the Holy Spirit and in this respect on God's immanent aspect. Moreover, already in a sermon in 1914, he had emphasized: "For the soul is not a part of the person, but the whole person... When the soul is well, then the entire person is well."[51] At the same occasion he had spoken of the "Divine" in man.[52]

Conversely, although Jung never explicitly denied the existence of a transcendental God, he said – as did Barth – it cannot be demonstrated. For Jung, only the immanence could be experienced. Despite these similarities, and although both came from old Basel families, both belonged to the *Zofingia* fraternity, both were father's of five children, both had, besides a wife, a second woman at their side, and – above all – both were convinced of an almighty God, they consequently avoided each other – no doubt out of self-protection.

Keller tried, unsuccessfully, to bring them together. He was convinced that a synergy of their ideas would profit both of them and humanity in general. – Incidentally, at the 1964 national exhibition in Lausanne, a space was devoted to Swiss philosophers. Four were presented in more detail: Jean-Jacques Rousseau, Heinrich Pestalozzi, Carl Gustav Jung, and Karl Barth![53]

The second main topic that was dealt with, concerned a dream that Keller had had, in which Jung bought the idyllic Rhine valley near Rüdlingen, where Keller had spent his childhood. The valley is shrouded with mythical stories. According to Jung's interpretation, it now belonged to

50 Jung to Keller, March 1951, letter 31 in: M. Jehle-Wildberger, *C.G. Jung und Adolf Keller*, pp. 171ff.

51 Sermon of June 28, 1914 in Safenwil, in: Karl Barth, *Predigten 1914*, ed. Ursula and Jochen Fähler, (Zurich: TVZ, 1974), pp. 338-348, quotation pp. 440f.

52 Ibid., p. 342. – Compare Frank Jehle, "Karl Barths Predigt über Jakobs Kampf am Jabbok," in: Frank Jehle, *Von Johannes auf Patmos bis zu Karl Barth*, pp. 125-133.

53 *Philosophie in der Schweiz. Eine Bestandesaufnahme. Von Lambert (1728-1777) bis Piaget (1896-1980)*, ed. Martin Meyer, (Zurich/Munich: Artemis, 1981). – Pierre Corday, *Das Buch der EXPO*, (Bern/Lausanne: Hallwag/Payot, 1969/74), p. 116: "The theology is represented by an – old – text of the bible and by the books of Karl Barth."

him, while Keller maintained it belonged to both of them. Jung insisted on his competency as interpreter of dreams. Keller clung to his competency as the dreamer. – The argument swelled back and forth in several long letters. At first glance, they appear tiresome. Yet, it is worth the while to read them carefully. Because it is about their deepest personal relationship, as well as about the transcendence and immanence of God, more precisely, about revelation and natural theology.

Finally, Keller wrote, the prior imbalance of give and take between them needed to be corrected. "Nevertheless," so literally, "I am concerned with inwardly finding closure, intensively, with that which you personally and your work mean for me and the culture in general. And this significance is so great, wide and deep… When I look back on my life, and inwardly or in an autobiography, describe the potent influences, then you have your solid place, and that remains yours, even though I cannot put myself in the same seat, and you do not permit a greater closeness, although I often wished for it."[54]

Jung answered by return mail: "I would very much like to discuss with you on any topic, as I have few opportunities to talk to males. I have had some friends, but they have died. To talk with others, i.e., to talk so that one gets something out of it, is so difficult, because they cannot relate to my spiritual world, and thus feel asked too much of… For essentials, I am always available."[55] With regard to their correspondence about dream interpretation, Jung accommodated Keller, although probably he, Jung, was the one who was right. The two aging and lonely men needed each other. Not only Jung had lost most of his friends, so had Keller.

After the exchange of letters about Keller's dream, they had a long discussion in Bollingen in May of 1951. The central themes must have been God, therapy, and the relationship between theology and psychology. Apparently, as can be concluded from Keller's subsequent letter, the discussion was harmonious, even though they did not agree on certain key issues. However, they seemed to have accepted this. That day in Bollingen was very possibly the pinnacle of their relationship.

54 Keller to Jung, February 6, 1951, letter 25 in: M. Jehle-Wildberger, *C.G. Jung und Adolf Keller*, pp. 151ff.
55 Jung to Keller, February 12, 1951, letter 26, ibid., pp. 155ff.

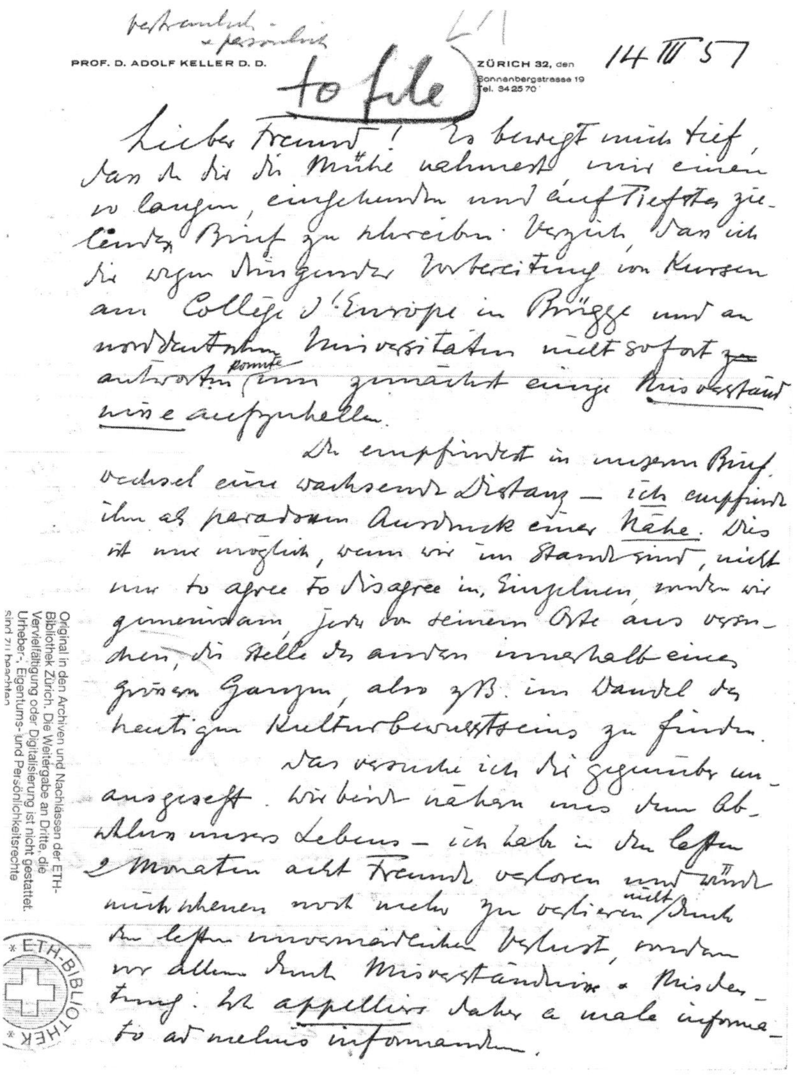

vertraulich – persönlich

PROF. D. ADOLF KELLER D. D. ZÜRICH 32, den 14 III 57
Sonnenbergstrasse 19
Tel. 34 25 70

to file

Lieber Freund! Es bewegt mich tief, dass du dir die Mühe nahmest, mir einen so langen, eingehenden und auf Tiefstes zielenden Brief zu schreiben. Verzeih, dass ich dir wegen dringender Vorbereitung von Kursen am Collège d'Europe in Brügge und an norddeutschen Universitäten nicht sofort zu antworten konnte, um zunächst einige Missverständnisse aufzuhellen.

Du empfindest in unserem Briefwechsel eine wachsende Distanz – ich empfinde ihn als paradoxen Ausdruck einer Nähe. Dies ist nur möglich, wenn wir im Stande sind, nicht nur to agree to disagree im Einzelnen, sondern wir gemeinsam, jeder von seinem Orte aus versuchen, die Stelle des andern innerhalb eines grösseren Ganzen, also z.B. im Wandel des heutigen Kulturbewusstseins zu finden.

Das versuche ich dir gegenüber unausgesetzt. Wir beide nähern uns dem Abschluss unseres Lebens – ich habe in den letzten 2 Monaten acht Freunde verloren und würde mich schämen noch mehr zu verlieren, nicht durch den letzten unvermeidlichen Verlust, sondern vor allem durch Missverständnisse & Missdeutung. Ich appelliere daher a male informato ad melius informandum.

Picture 4: Handwriting of Adolf Keller[56]

56 Letter 30, M. Jehle-Wildberger, *C.G. Jung und Adolf Keller*, p. 172.

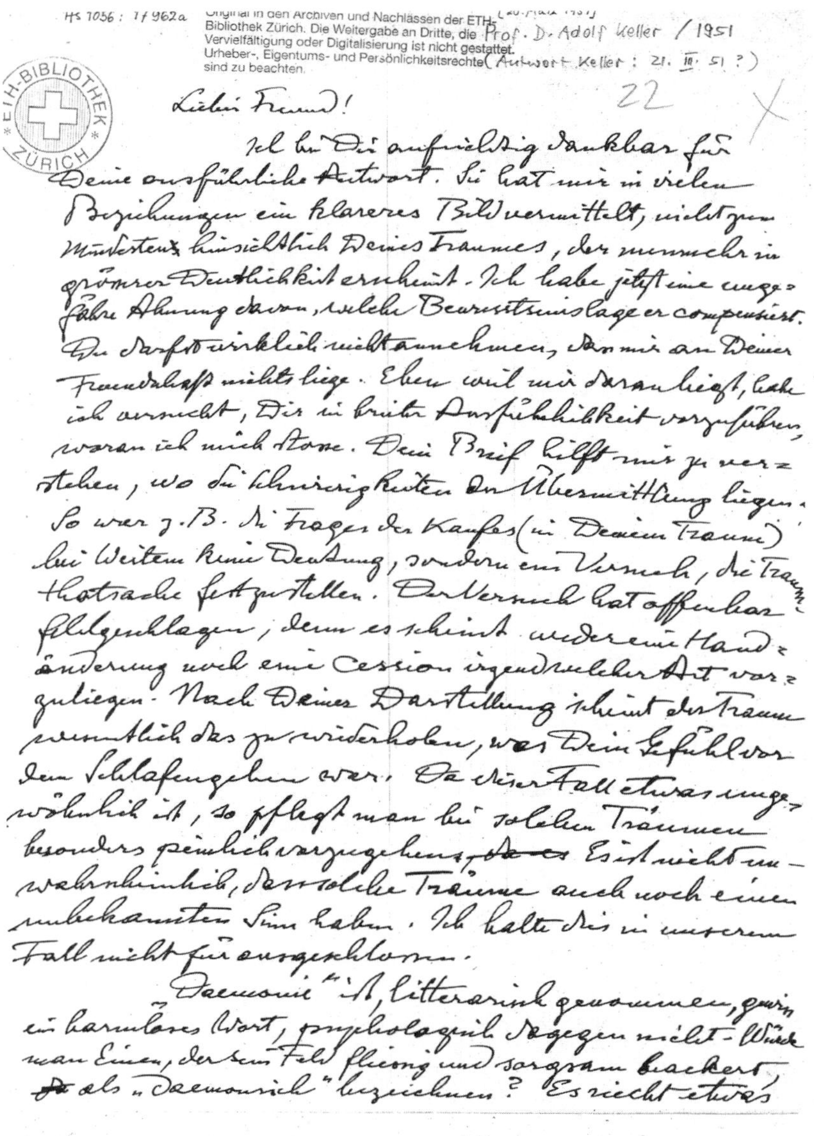
Hs 1056 : 11962a
Original in den Archiven und Nachlässen der ETH-Bibliothek Zürich. Die Weitergabe an Dritte, die Vervielfältigung oder Digitalisierung ist nicht gestattet. Urheber-, Eigentums- und Persönlichkeitsrechte sind zu beachten.
Prof. D. Adolf Keller / 1951
(Antwort Keller: 21. III. 51 ?)
ETH-BIBLIOTHEK ZÜRICH
22

Lieber Freund!

Ich bin Dir aufrichtig dankbar für Deine ausführliche Antwort. Sie hat mir in vielen Beziehungen ein klareres Bild vermittelt, nicht zum Mindesten hinsichtlich Deines Traumes, der nunmehr in grösserer Deutlichkeit erscheint. Ich habe jetzt eine ungefähre Ahnung davon, welche Bewusstseinslage er compensiert. Du darfst wirklich nicht annehmen, dass mir an Deiner Freundschaft nichts liege. Eben weil mir daran liegt, habe ich versucht, Dir in breiter Ausführlichkeit vorzuführen, woran ich mich stosse. Dein Brief hilft mir zu verstehen, wo die Schwierigkeiten der Übermittlung liegen. So war z.B. die Frage des Kaufes (in Deinem Traum) bei Weitem keine Deutung, sondern ein Versuch, die Traumthatsache festzustellen. Der Versuch hat offenbar fehlgeschlagen; denn es scheint weder eine Handänderung noch eine Cession irgendwelcher Art vorzuliegen. Nach Deiner Darstellung scheint der Traum wesentlich das zu wiederholen, was Dein Gefühl vor dem Schlafengehen war. Da dieser Fall etwas ungewöhnlich ist, so pflegt man bei solchen Träumen besonders peinlich vorzugehen. Es ist nicht unwahrscheinlich, dass solche Träume auch noch einen unbekannten Sinn haben. Ich halte dies in unserem Fall nicht für ausgeschlossen.

„Daemonie" ist, litterarisch genommen, gewiss ein harmloses Wort, psychologisch dagegen nicht. Würde man Einen, der sein Feld fleissig und sorgsam beackert, als „daemonisch" bezeichnen? Es riecht etwas

Picture 5: Handwriting of C.G. Jung[57]

57 Letter 31, M. Jehle-Wildberger, *C.G. Jung und Adolf Keller*, p. 173.

With that, the third topic: A few weeks after their meeting, Jung sent Keller the manuscript (resp. typescript) for his book in progress, *Answer to Job*.[58] He had thrown it down on paper within a few weeks after a feverish illness and apparent excitation. What instigated his writing, as he states in the introduction, were several of his patients who interpreted their mental suffering as a punishment from God. They struggled with God. – Jung noticed that the biblical Book of Job served as a paradigm for a God experience that was, at that time, widespread. He wrote *Answer to Job* specifically out of his experience as a physician. The book sprung out of his compassion for his patients. It was as if he recognized in them the innocent Job, who had lost his cattle, his family and his health, and had to endure Yahweh's wrath. Jung's accusation to Yahweh is harsh. He is a God who commits theft, murder, intentional bodily harm and breach of law. Nevertheless, this God, according to Jung, had a good side. However, darkness, that is to say the devil, is a part of him. Jung spoke of God's quaternity, as opposed to the trinity. Job was superior to Yahweh, and it is he who brings about a turn in the story.[59]

Keller's reaction was restrained. At first he expressed praise. But then he implied that Jung's description did not conform to Christian theology: "Could the religious motif of integration," he wrote, "that is, unity, contain the same religiously binding force as does the need for forgiveness, for personal community, for salvation...?"[60] He mentions the Holy Spirit "as the principle of becoming,"[61] by which he meant the transformation of the concept of God, which takes place in the Job story. Jung might want to reconsider his harsh comments about Yahweh. – The Dominican Victor White, whom Jung also let read the manuscript, pointed in a similar direction.[62]

Keller suggested to Jung that they meet for a private conversation, in which he presumably wanted to discuss his misgivings. Whether or not it came to that, cannot be determined. In comparison to the manuscript, the book,[63] which was published in 1952, was somewhat milder, possibly due to the objections of the two theologians. But long passages were still severe

---

58 A copy of the typescript is in the archive of the *Stiftung der Werke von C.G. Jung* in Zurich.
59 To the whole section see M. Jehle-Wildberger, *C.G. Jung und Adolf Keller*, pp. 114ff.
60 Keller to Jung, August 17, 1951, letter 42, ibid., pp. 186ff.
61 Ibid., p. 188.
62 Ibid., pp. 116f.
63 Carl Gustav Jung, *Antwort auf Hiob (Answer to Job)*, first edition (Zurich: Rascher, 1952).

and evoked pronounced criticism from both Old Testament theologians in Zurich at that time. The point of the biblical story of Job, they maintained, is the transformation of the concept of God, the overcoming of the archaic, avenging God. As well, Karl Barth, who had deliberated intensely on the biblical Job, came to the conclusion, Jung had misunderstood the biblical *Book of Job*.[64]

Nevertheless, the theologians were impressed that Jung addressed the topic of theodicy, the difficult question of the purpose of suffering, and what God possibly had to do with it. Jung's book prompted them to reflect. But Jung felt misunderstood by the theologians, probably also by Keller. In any case, there were fewer letters.

Another thing: In the introduction to *Answer to Job*, Jung states he was not able to write objectively, but needed to put into words his emotional subjectivity. This indicates *Answer to Job* was not only about his patients, but also had to do with himself. He wrote: "The memory of my father is that of a sufferer, who suffered from an Amfortas wound…"[65] Paradoxically, in *Answer to Job*, he assumed the same literalist understanding of the Bible which had broken his father. Jung's access to the Bible was intuitive. Indeed, in some places he makes clear, that the *Book of Job* in the Bible is about transformation of the concept of God, yet he wrote, contrary to his own custom, mostly simply "Yahweh" or "God." Keller commented in a later letter, it would have been better had Jung differentiated between God and the concept of God.[66] – Despite his reservations, Keller promoted the publishing of Jung's *Answer to Job* in the USA. But even the Bollingen publishing house which was specialized in Jung was not ready to publish Jung's new book as it feared negative responses.

As of 1955, the letters were more frequent. Seldom were they about existential questions. Jung's health became more fragile. The death of his wife, Emma, had affected him deeply. His letters were short. Keller's aging process showed in endlessly long letters, which were often repetitive. He reported about friends of Jung in California, who had now become his own friends; amongst them, the psychiatrist James Kirsch.[67] Keller often stayed

---

64 M. Jehle-Wildberger, *C.G. Jung und Adolf Keller*, pp. 122f.

65 A. Jaffé (ed.), *Memories, Dreams, Reflections by C.G. Jung*, p. 215.

66 Keller to Jung, July 12, 1957, letter 77, in: M. Jehle-Wildberger, *C.G. Jung und Adolf Keller*, pp. 246ff.

67 *The Jung-Kirsch Letters: The Correspondence of C.G. Jung and James Kirsch*, ed. Ann Conrad Lammers, transl. by Ursula Egli and Ann Conrad Lammers, Philemon Series, (London/New York: Routledge, 2011).

in California. It was here, in early 1958, that he suffered a stroke. Jung was deeply concerned. His last, moving letter closed with the sentence: "But at our age we have learned, intrepida mente, to look into the face of all manner of fates, and to leave to higher powers all that is good and helpful."[68]

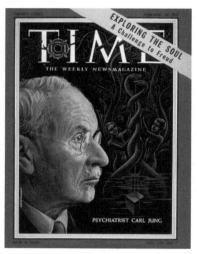

Picture 6: Cover of Time Magazine, February 14, 1955[69]

*

The conversation between Jung and Keller was the first of its kind. Jung and Keller were both highly sensitive persons. It had come to ill-feelings between them not only for objective reasons, but also for reasons of character, after which reconciliation always followed on its heels. But thanks to this sensitivity, they were able to be critical observers of the world, and perceive people's problems and vulnerability. Thus they became pioneers in the area of caring for souls, and seekers in search of a cure for the world. – Adolf Keller set a memorial to Carl Gustav Jung with his article for Jung's 60th

68 Jung an Keller, April 3, 1958, letter 81, in: M. Jehle-Wildberger, *C.G. Jung und Adolf Keller,* pp. 251f. – intrepida mente [with fearless mind].
69 M. Jehle-Wildberger, *C.G. Jung und Adolf Keller,* p. 203. See Keller to Jung, Los Angeles, February 12, 1955, letter 54, ibid., pp. 202ff. Jung had become not only wiser, but prophetic as well, and milder and sadder about the human condition, commented Keller.

birthday, titled *"Analytical Psychology and Religious Studies."*[70] He began with the sentence: "As one crosses the threshold of C G. Jung's home, the visitor is arrested by a Latin inscription carved in stone on the door lintel; it is from the Delphic oracle: vocatus atque non vocatus deus aderit." The article closes with the sentence: "But pastoral care will become a better guide to salvation and life if it strives for both: a better understanding not only of God but of the soul as well."[71]

70 Adolf Keller, "Analytische Psychologie und Religionsforschung" [Analytic Psychology and Religious Research], in: *Die Kulturelle Bedeutung der komplexen Psychologie,* ed. *Psychology Club* Zurich, (Berlin: Julius Springer, 1935), pp. 271-297. As appendix printed in M. Jehle-Wildberger, *C.G. Jung und Adolf Keller,* pp. 275-305.

71 M. Jehle-Wildberger, *C.G. Jung und Adolf Keller,* p. 305. The author thanks Carol Idone, St. Gallen, cordially for this English translation. This essay goes back to the lecture which the author gave at the opening of her book about C.G. Jung and Adolf Keller on October 23, 2014 at the *Psychology Club* in Zurich.

Hermann Strobel

Aloneness as Calling

Preliminary remarks of the editors

The following contribution is based on two lecture manuscripts of the author, who passed away in 2006. The text has been slightly revised for the publication. Subheadings as well as footnotes were added by the editors. We express our gratitude to Isabelle Strobel for permitting this publication.

*

C.G. Jung writes in a letter to Karl Oftinger, founder of the "Liga gegen den Lärm" [League Against Noise][1] in the year 1957:

> Noise protects us from painful reflection, it scatters our anxious dreams, it assures us that we are all in the same boat and creating such a racket that nobody will dare to attack us… It relieves us of the effort to say or do anything, for the very air reverberates with the invincible power of our modernity. The dark side of the picture is that we wouldn't have noise if we didn't secretly want it… If there were silence, their fear would make people reflect, and there's no knowing what might then come to consciousness. Most people are afraid of silence; hence, whenever the everlasting chit-chat at a party suddenly stops, they are impelled to say something, do something, and start fidgeting, whistling, humming, coughing, whispering. The need for noise is almost insatiable, even though it becomes unbearable at times. Still, it is better than nothing. "Deathly silence" – telling phrase! – strikes us as uncanny. Why? Ghosts walking about? Well, hardly. The real fear is what might come up from one's own depths – all the things that have been held at bay by noise.[2]

---

1 Karl Oftinger had asked C.G. Jung for a contribution to be published in a newspaper.
2 C.G. Jung, *Letters*, selected and edited Gerhard Adler in collaboration with Aniela Jaffé. Translated by R.F.C. Hull (Princeton: Princeton University Press, 1975), September 1957, vol. 2, p. 389f.

To me, Jung's observances about noise seem of importance, because of the problem that on one hand being alone with oneself can be at times so difficult while on the other hand, again and again we run after chatter, radio, television and media of all kinds without feeling fortified by it. The buzzing of today's world is indeed affecting every one of us more than ever. And so in regard of aloneness we could express this final sentence as follows: "What we try to keep away from ourselves by extroversion is in reality the fear to bear the silence of aloneness."

In this lecture it is not my intention to deliver concepts. I would prefer to circumambulate the problem of aloneness by examples, and ask questions regarding the statement that today aloneness has turned to something lacking any value. Maybe today especially, it is of value and importance to learn about aloneness.

What wants to break in

About sixty years ago during the war, when I had to stand guard alone one night, I experienced how disturbing it can be when one is alone. At that time there were good reasons to feel such disturbance. Standing on guard, I could expect an attack by the enemy at any time. In the dark of the night there was no possibility of seeing anything. At that time I did not help myself with the "whistling," "singing" or "coughing" of which Jung writes; these are not recommended for a sentinel standing on guard at war. In support of my courage against the dark aloneness I silently recited all the poems I could remember from my time in college; German, Latin or Greek ones. And suddenly I gratefully remembered my time as a student, when I had to learn by-heart such poems and how much of a burden that was to me at the time. That's how I helped myself to endure the sizzling silence of the night. Apparently it was not so wrong at all.

Perhaps you know the passage in the book *Shadow and Evil in Fairy Tales* where Marie-Louise von Franz describes her difficulties with aloneness.[3] She had read in C.G. Jung that the unconscious had especially been enlivened in the saints living alone in the desert and she decided to give this experience a try for herself. At the time she was still a young woman. So she made herself comfortable, all alone in a mountain hut high up in the

---

3 Marie-Louise von Franz, *Shadow and Evil in Fairy Tales,* Revised edition (Boston: Shambhala 1995), pp. 184ff.

mountains in wintertime, waiting for things to come. As long as she went down regularly to shop in the village and speak to the people, nothing happened.

> Finally I forced myself with only a pencil and paper to write down my dreams and possible fantasies, to sit the whole day and do nothing... and the first experience I had was that time began to drag! It dragged like Hell! I looked at my watch and it was ten o'clock. I sat and listened to the birds and the snow water dripping on the roof and thought I had sat an eternity, but it was only ten-thirty and not yet time to cook the spaghetti, and so on, forever... This got worse, but I stuck it out, and then the unconscious became alive because my mind got wandering on the idea that sometimes burglars got into such huts, especially escaped prisoners... That fantasy got me completely, and not seeing that it was just the thing I was looking for, I was absolutely panic-stricken. I took the axe for chopping the wood and put it beside my bed and lay awake trying to decide whether I would have the courage to bang such a man over the head if he came in... Next morning I thought that now I'd had it and must go home, but then I had a second thought and said, "But that was what I was looking for!"

In this moment Marie-Louise von Franz discovered the power of the *inner images* and what impact they can have on the outer reality. She encountered her own inner qualities and was afraid they could break in as "criminals" or "burglars" who could threaten the ego. She began to hold a dialogue with these "housebreakers" and to have a discussion with them, which in Jungian Psychology we call *Active Imagination*. Marie-Louise von Franz looked for the inner images and spoke to them as soon as they showed up, and this helped! She felt better, removed the axe and stayed in the hut without even locking the door. She writes:

> I could have stayed weeks more... I was even stupid enough, though I knew something of Jungian psychology, not to see that this burglar was the animus invading my territory... That experience taught me that loneliness piles up whatever you have in your unconscious, and if you don't know how to cope with it, it comes first in a projected form. In my case it was projected into the idea of a criminal, and if I had belonged to a layer of civilization which still believed in demons, then I would have

thought the Kurupira was coming or that the "It" from the mountains had thrown snow at me… Most people are not capable of standing such situations for a long time; they need the companionship of other people to protect themselves against "It."[4]

This "It" refers to aspects of the soul having stayed unconscious. One can be taken by their energetic potency; the emergent inner images in this process then appearing as real on the outside. It is not always easy to perceive a difference between such inner images and reality. If we don't succeed, the inner world can separate us from our surroundings, making us feel alone or lonely.

Alone with one's innermost being

In a letter dated February 1802 Johann Wolfgang von Goethe (1749-1832) writes to Charlotte von Stein:

One should not stay alone for so long, one is immersed in certain interests capturing all of one's spirit; and when one enters the world and meets friends, one realizes that on the outside there is no trace of what our inside is occupied with and at this moment one becomes aware of the impossibility to tie one's innermost being.[5]

When Goethe wrote this he was not literally alone, but embedded in a social network to a large extent determined by himself. He was considered the dominating figure of literary life in Germany in the first third of the nineteenth century. However in his letter to Mrs. von Stein Goethe describes that sometimes there is an innate difficulty in all deeper relationships. Whether concerning relationships with people or being intertwined with "one's innermost being"; each form of deepened dedication can lead to a mental state which brings about a feeling of aloneness as it emerges and can have an effect of estrangement from the social surroundings. What is experienced in the depths is at times not to be shared and thus not to be expressed. Such an experience of aloneness has to be differentiated from the

---

4 M.-L. von Franz, *Shadow and Evil in Fairy Tales*, p. 186.
5 *Goethes Briefe an Charlotte von Stein* [Goethe's letters to Charlotte von Stein], edited by Jonas Fränkel, vol. 2 (Berlin: Akademie-Verlag, 1960), p. 399.

reality of an actual state of aloneness. One can be overcome by it while in the midst of other people, as Goethe's example demonstrates.

The example given by Goethe about "interests" shows that something is at work between the perceiving ego of the observer, his internal unconscious and an outer object, be it a human being or some other element and that this "something" has a nature of its own and is alive. However it is dependant upon not staying with perception only; thinking, intuition and feeling, that is to say the whole human being, has to be animated. Sometimes one can be seized or even obsessed in the process.

In this state such people appear a "bit strange" to us. It seems as if learning is inevitable, asking of us the task of dealing with aloneness, of accepting as well as enduring our *otherness*. If we succeed there is little need to worry about staying alone with "one's innermost being." It is a fact that it works in a connecting way – as long as it remains alive and does not stagnate. Indeed it can bring about changes that we experience as painful. However in the end, these changes will lead to new connections again. It is all about turning our innermost interest towards the aloneness as something which demands our attention, if we don't want to risk experiencing, it is just as injuring or destroying.

Travelling in the mist

In a poem of Hermann Hesse (1877-1962) with the title *In the Mist* the state of aloneness is solely described as a problematic feeling.[6]

> Wondrous to wander through mists!
> Parted are bush and stone:
> None to the other exists,
> Each stands alone.
>
> Many my friends came calling
> then, when I lived in the light;
> Now that the fogs are falling,
> None is in sight.

---

6 Hermann Hesse, *Gesammelte Werke* [Collected Works], vol. 1 (Frankfurt a.M: Suhrkamp Verlag, 1970), p. 27.

Truly, only the sages
Fathom the darkness to fall,
Which, as silent as cages,
Separates all.

Strange to walk in the mists!
Life has to solitude grown.
None for the other exists:
Each is alone.

The lasting effect of the poem acts on the laconic, mind touching assumption that no one knows the other and everybody is alone and one cannot expect anything else but to be alone. Hermann Hesse connects this feeling with the conflict between "light" and "dark." One has friends as long as one lives "in the light." Darkness isolates. At first this might seem somewhat generalizing, for even darkness can connect. However Hesse's thoughts about the meaning of the "light" in life and the aloneness lead deeper. I remember a verse in the gospel of Luke. It says:

Your eye is the lamp of your body. If your eye is healthy, your whole body is full of light; but if it is not healthy, your body is full of darkness. Therefore consider whether the light in you is not darkness. If then your whole body is full of light, with no part of it in darkness, it will be full of light as when a lamp gives you light with its rays.[7]

Thereby we are in the middle of the problem. Apparently two thousand years ago it was important to appreciate that beside the outer light, there exists an inner, equally important light and that both lights are in related to one another. As decribed in the passage from Luke, the inner light within must not be obscured. Obviously it is in need of direct attention, otherwise there is a danger of the outer life becoming dark as well. As long as the inside is fully enlightened, there is a chance to keep a light, even in the darkness of outer life.

Hermann Hesse seems to fear the darkness, which, as said in the poem, can also bring about wisdom. We would say that darkness can bring light

---

7 Luke 11:34-36. Biblical references are from The New Oxford Annotated Bible: New Revised Standard Version with The Apocrypha, edited by Michael D. Coogan (Oxford: Oxford University Press, Oxford, 2010).

at the time when it is consciously searched for – by way of introversion. But with Hesse darkness separates and little is left but resignation, anxiety, or even fear. Could it be that the connection to the inner light is missing which could illuminate his darkness?

For sure: When fog gathers, all that just seemed to be under control becomes a riddle, security turns into insecurity and any community seems abolished. The senses are "foggy," one develops "foggy imaginations." One hears bells ringing without knowing where they might be hanging. The invisible becomes an intensively experienced fact. For the attentive mind everything natural turns into an immediate problem. There is no point in explaining rationally the differing origins of a state of fogginess. The mere existence of a state of fog throws people back onto themselves. The light of fog is "cold and moist by nature." It belongs to the feminine principle, like the moon and the earth out of which it rises.

In German superstition, fog is spun by witches, and "Brides of the wind" or – as in Silesia – "Puchweibla" brewed it, and by doing so seduced the wanderer.[8] What makes the shadow seem huge to us is a misconception of distances. In this context we remember the eeriness of the "Brocken specter" which mirrors its own shadow in colourful circles; or the "Erlking" with crown and tail who lets the son die in his fathers arms. The accounts of "Swan maidens" belong here too. They were understood to be allegories of fateful forces of nature. When floating fog is rising from the water it "condenses into clouds and moves across the sky like swans flying."[9]

According to Honorius of Autun the falling Satan ripped down a part of the stars with his tail and covered them with the fog of sin. Also, Senior, the alchemist, talked about the "tenebrae animae," the "darkness of the mind" and interpreted it as "evil earthiness."[10] For instance with Joel and Zephania in the Old Testament God appears in fog and darkness, threatening in his

8 *Handwörterbuch des deutschen Aberglaubens* [Dictionary of German Superstition], edited by E. Hoffmann-Krayer and Hanns Bächtold-Stäubli, vol. 6 (Berlin/Leipzig: Verlag Walter de Gruyter, 1934), column 986.

9 Emma Jung, "The Anima as an Elemental Being" in: Emma Jung, *Animus and Anima* (New York: Spring Publications, Inc., 1985, New Printing 2004), p. 49.

10 Marie-Louise von Franz, *Aurora Consurgens, A document attributed to Thomas Aquinas on the problem of opposites in alchemy,* translated from Latin into German with a commentary by Marie-Louise von Franz, translated by R.F.C. Hull and A.S.B. Glover (Toronto: Inner City Books, 2000), p. 204. The expression "tenebrae animae" appears only in the original German version.

fury.[11] On the other hand in Homer's Iliad the Gods use the fog to support their favourites and to misguide their enemies.

With Albertus Magnus, the teacher of Thomas of Aquin, the fog contains totally opposed aspects, which in this case are positive. In the *Biblia Mariana,* a collection of attributes in honour of Mary, he writes that Mary the mother of God is the "cloud of the overshadowing, cooling mist, ark of the covenant, rock from which water of grace or oil flows, star of enlightenment, shining lamp, 'best earth', sister of our poverty, sun, mount of benediction, bridal chamber of God's delight, window of escape or illumination… the tabernacle for God's union with human nature."[12]

In the creation myth of the Old Testament we find a similar positive aspect of fog:

These are the generations of the heavens and the earth when they were created. In the day that the Lord God made the earth and the heavens, when no plant of the field was yet in the earth and no herb of the field had yet sprung up – for the Lord God had not caused it to rain upon the earth, and there was no one to till the ground; and a stream would rise from the earth[13], and water the whole face of the ground – then the Lord God formed the man from the dust of the ground, and breathed into his nostrils the breath of life; and the man became a living creature.[14]

Here we come to a point where our wandering in the fog becomes really strange. In the context of the origin of life the fog even appears as the well of life. In the text of Albertus Magnus it is connected to the "bridal chamber of God's delight" and "the tabernacle for God's union with human nature." Therefore fog is connected to the feminine, to Mary, but also to earth, from which it emanates. And when it breaks out of the earth, God gives the human being the "breath of life." Could it be that the fog is a requirement for every creative act?

11 Joel 2:1-2: "… for the day of the Lord is coming, it is near – a day of darkness and gloom, a day of clouds and thick darkness!" Luther translates: "… a day of clouds, a foggy day!" Zephaniah 1:15: "That day will be a day of wrath, … a day of darkness and gloom, a day of clouds and thick darkness." Again here Luther says: "… a day of clouds and of mist."
12 M.-L. von Franz, *Aurora Consurgens,* p. 387.
13 Martin Luther translated: "And a mist would rise from the earth, and water the whole face of the ground."
14 Moses 2:4-7.

When the different amplifications of the symbolic image of "fog" are psychologically understood; summarily, they correlate with the indeterminable flowing contents of the unconscious, so changeable in their flow. After all, like nature spirits they hover over and enwrap. This is why Hermann Hesse's travelling in the mists appears so "strange" to us and for this reason is so worthwhile.

Etymological observations

Considering this not at all seldom oddity, it seems meaningful to me to look at the significance of the words "alone" and "lonely" in the light of etymology. The German word "allein," in English "alone," derives from the medieval German "al ein," meaning "being all by oneself." The syllable "al" enforces the old German "eino," in old English "all ana." And "all" includes the Indo-European word for "to grow" or the Gothic word "alan" meaning "to grow up" in the sense of "fully grown" or "complete." We find it again in the German word "alt" (old)[15] and this corresponds with the Latin "omnis," meaning "all, whole, over-all, pure." Therefore the meaning of aloneness in German as well as in English is "being all by oneself" or "nothing but being oneself." It means to have the chance to grow towards completeness. Actually, it is strange that in the face of these connotations, aloneness is so feared today.

In the old German dictionary written by Karl I. Trübner (1846-1907) we find a reference that combines the meaning of the German word "allein" with the German word "einsam," in English "lonesome."[16] The significance of this word has changed in the course of time. According to Trübner one can find this already in the 15th century. At that time it meant: "at one," "united," "harmonious." In this sense, Luther speaks of "lonely Christian truth." And in a document of 1635 we read of the "neighbourly and harmonious loneliness" between the county Hessen and the town Frankfurt. However "lonely" in the sense of "alone" we already find with Luther. But the word carries a negative connotation concerning humans or animals in the sense of "living alone." So it reads: "… I am lonely and miserable" or "I am abandoned and lonely." At the same time the word denotes certain

15 *Trübners Deutsches Wörterbuch* [Trübners German Dictionary], edited by Alfred Goetze and Walter Mitzka, vol. 1 and 2 (Berlin: Walter de Gruyter, 1955), keywords "allein" and "einsam."
16 For the following see *Trübners Deutsches Wörterbuch*, vol 2, keyword "einsam."

places or situations in order to describe their desolation, barrenness, still-ness and remoteness.

In the sentimental period of the 18th century, words like "lonely" and "loneliness" became fashionable and favourite words to describe a soulful atmosphere, which implied a state of feeling and contemplation, overriding the hustle and bustle of every day life. The primary negative association to the word is now being extended to a positive one, pointing to a substantial new value. As an example, *Trübners Wörterbuch* mentions the "rare meaning of the word lonely," namely "sole, unique, detached, single" and quotes Jean Paul writing in the 19th century: "Each peculiar style is good as long as it stays a lonely one and does not convert into any common one." This holds still to this day, so we say in German: "Jemand ist einsame Spitze," meaning "someone is on top."

A typical saying in compliance with this meaning we read in the work of the French moralist Nicolas Chamfort (1741-1794). He writes: "In solitude man is happier than being in the world. Could it be that in solitude one thinks about things where as in society we have to think about people?"[17] At this point the question arises, can we afford this solitude and is it morally responsible not to think about other people? And is this not the typical arrogance of an introvert when Chamfort goes on writing: "Weakness of character as well as emptiness of spirit, in one word, everything that hinders us from being alone with ourselves prevents many people from misanthro-py."[18] Or: "For most of the people being slaves, the reason is the same as the Spartans declared to be true for the slavery over the Persians: they could not say no. Knowing to speak out this word and being able to live alone – these are the only means to preserve freedom and character."[19] Holding such a brutal attitude, nobody wonders when Chamfort complains: "Sometimes we say about someone who lives by himself that he is uncongenial. This is as if someone is rumoured to be no friend of walks because he dislikes walking at night in the forest of Bondy."[20]

---

17 *Die französischen Moralisten* [The French Moralists], edited by Fritz Schalk, vol. 1 (München: Deutscher Taschenbuch Verlag, 1973), p. 301.
18 Ibid.
19 Ibid., p. 303.
20 Ibid., p. 301. The forest of Bondy was well known in French legends, see footnote 19, p. 381.

Against the Spirit of the Times

If we consider how strongly the Zeitgeist and collective perception are determined by our current evaluation of the experience of aloneness, we understand whether or not aloneness is regarded as something that is to be feared or to be achieved. We read in Jung:

> The spirit of the age cannot be fitted into the categories of human reason. It is more a bias, an emotional tendency that works upon weaker minds, through the unconscious, with an overwhelming force of suggestion that carries them along with it. To think otherwise than as our contemporaries think is somehow illegitimate and disturbing; it is even indecent, morbid or blasphemous, and therefore socially dangerous for the individual. He is stupidly swimming against the social current... To allow the soul or psyche a substantiality of its own is repugnant to the spirit of the age, for that would be heresy.[21]

The abyss between the individual and the representative collective being as described by C.G. Jung deepens and expands wherever individual development is confronted with a somewhat hidden obsession for submission under collective norms. The barbarism of a collective norm which no longer gives any room for individuality is illustrated by the following sentences of the Marxist philosopher George Lukacs:

> The lonely person embodies an asocial human-being, adverse to any progress, who at his core is a deadly enemy of the new society. He is a person who consciously takes up a position outside of the economical structure of socialism; one who removes himself from a community born of difficult struggle, who is therefore legitimately excluded by the new socialist community.[22]

Anyone who has not encountered the feeling of "loneliness" yet, will now be faced with it when confronting the concrete barbarism of such a collective norm [such as seen in Lukacs quote above]. Becoming aware of a situation where his identity is judged as "adverse" by collective norms is threatening,

21 C.G. Jung, "Basic Postulates of Analytical Psychology," *The Structure and Dynamics of the Psyche*, vol. 8 of *The Collected Works of C.G. Jung*, edited and translated Gerhard Adler and R.F.C. Hull (New York: Pantheon Books, 1960), § 653.
22 *Einsamkeiten. Ein Lesebuch* [Solitudes. A reading book], edited by Ilma Rakusa (Zurich: Verlag der Arche, 1975), p. 122.

especially when hundreds of people around him applaud and declare such norms as sacrosanct. To be not-part of such a "community of people"[23] will isolate and frighten even more, because the individual is no longer allowed to express himself and to reveal his otherness. Not only will he feel lonely, but he will experience what it can mean to be alone for real. In the extreme case of serious personal endangerment he will need all his strength not to panic. Obsessions like this of a dominant collective consciousness, bring into motion gigantic energies in the collective unconscious. These energies overflow the capacities of the individual to control himself and the ego becomes victim of the collective darkness. The experience of a forceful and anonymous dominance of the collective tears apart the conscious relationship between the ego and the unconscious.

The diary of Victor Klemperer (1881-1960) conveys an impression of such things. Klemperer, as a Jew, survived the Nazi terror regime in Germany with his "Aryan" wife. After an arbitrary arrest for no substantial reason, which was named "giving over," he writes in his diary on November 27th, 1938:

> At four o'clock I was on the street again with the curious feeling, free- but for how long? Since then we have both been unceasingly tormented by the question, go or stay? To go too early, to stay too late? To go where we have nothing, to remain in this corruption? We are constantly trying to shed all subjective feelings of disgust, of injured pride, of frame of mind and only weigh up the concrete facts of the situation. In the end we shall literally be able to throw dice for pro and contra.[24]

On December 2nd 1938 Klemperer writes:

> She told us how the SA had mounted the attack in Leipzig, poured gasoline into the synagogue and into a Jewish department store, how the fire brigade was allowed to protect only the surrounding buildings but not fight the fire itself, how the owner of the department store was then arrested for arson and insurance fraud. In Leipzig we also learned about the billion-mark fine the German nation had imposed on the Jews... Trude pointed out an open bay window on the other side of the

23 In German "Volksgemeinschaft."
24 Victor Klemperer, *I will bear witness. A Diary of the Nazi years 1933-1941*, translated by Martin Chalmers (London: Weidenfeld & Nicolson, 1998), p. 276.

street. It has been open for days; the people have been taken away. She wept as we drove off. On the way Eva's[25] nerves gave way... at home she had a screaming fit.[26]

Any human being delivered to such infamy needs all his strength not to lose his dignity before himself and the world, not to feel inferior and therefore lose his own inner freedom. This is, in such a situation, almost impossible. The human ego will feel overwhelmed, conforming to what C.G. Jung refers to as possibility or as a "vision" in a dream seminar:

> I see myself as this inferior, unfree, and foolish being, and I am also the one that can look at it and say: I am two, I am the one conscious function and I am another function also, that can look at this prostrate figure as if I were a god. We have acquired the divine quality of being able to look at ourselves... But we have acquired a mirror in ourselves which says: that is yourself, and in saying that we have a superior point of view. I look down upon myself as if I were a god, as if I were superior, and I *am* superior, that is my superiority.[27]

Wherever a totalitarian claim of the state determines what is allowed to be thought, wanted and felt – by means of destructive and murderous authority, there will be collective psychosis lurking at the other end of the spectrum. Psychologically understood, this provides the state with a power over the individual, which works like magic. It paralyzes: The person will freeze with an impression of choice, between nothingness and decay.

Dream of a seven year old boy, February 1933

Considering the age of the boy, his being still completely unconscious, the above described "vision" by C.G. Jung or a possible approach in this sense, could point to the fact that only by grace alone could a seven year old boy be saved from being broken. He was in a similar exigency as Victor Klemperer, being almost daily forced to watch his contemporaries getting whipped by SA people, who were authorized as so-called "teachers" to

25 Victor Klemperer's wife
26 V. Klemperer, *I will bear witness*, p. 277.
27 C.G. Jung, *Dream Analysis, Notes of the Seminar given in 1928-1930* by C.G. Jung, edited by William McGuire (Princeton: Princeton University Press, 1984), p. 586.

"re-educate" them for being children of opponents of the Regime. This was the method to exert "moral" pressure on parents – until it came to his turn. In 1933, one month after Hitler took over, the boy had the following dream:

> I am walking on a path up a mountain. At my left I look into a deep long drawn gorge, whooshing white-water. At the other side of this gorge there is a long chain of mountains as one can see in the Alps. I observe a thick, brown, mushy mass beginning to roll very slowly over all the mountain pikes down into the gorge. At my – quiet – side of the mountain there is a path leading upwards. On some sort of flat square with a railing towards the horizon, I see, black, a male figure standing there. It seems that the figure is wearing a long vestment reaching to the ground and on the head a large broad-rimmed hat, holding a big shepherd's staff in the left hand. He emanates silence. Motionless he looks out on the chain of mountains at the other side, which is getting rolled over by this awful, terrifying brown mass. I wake up by a buzzing noise and my tongue feels sulphurous. I felt queasy.

The somatic reaction at the end of the dream points to a strong emotional participation, highly difficult to support. The boy becomes witness to a dramatic event, a natural phenomenon, observing it from far away, but experiencing it as something irresistible, even agonising. If in a dream an invisible power is shifting the whole of an alpine chain of mountains with a mushy brown mass, the dreamer is encompassed by an emotional borderline experience. The dream shows a separation by a deep gorge between a here-and-now at the right side, and a sinister after world at the left. The setting is an alpine landscape, though in reality the boy had not seen any alpine landscapes. He knew them only from pictures in children books.

Symbolically mountains can stand for the child's growing up, a far off aim. However they can also be the expression of problems, elevating "like mountains" in front of us, problems we have to contend with. It is possible that problems of this kind can be constellated already in childhood as a task for the life to come. In this case they then represent the hindrance of the naturally given setting, which demands great effort to overcome and is not at all easy to achieve. Actually the mountain is something defined by nature as irremovable and massive "heavenly laws." It is all that limits and in fact gives orientation as well as challenges. In this tension of the opposites between the unconscious nature and the conscious human Ego, there is a chance, which contains the potential to learn something.

In the dreaming child's line of vision, on this side of the mountain, there is a path leading upward with the possibility to walk on it. This is an important fact! The other side of the mountain leads downward. There, a tremendous collective regression is taking place. Seemingly, the actual scheme of life of the boy contains the fact that he was forced to behold how this viscous, mushy, brown mass rolled slowly down over the edges of the mountains, devouring everything, transforming the mountain into something like a grave mound. Has a terrifying demon become lord over these mountains? We usually meet such demonic powers when the relationship to the soul gets lost, or when the soul is congealed in ideologies of the collective consciousness. If we understand mountains as symbolizing the place where the gods reveal themselves, expressing closeness to the spirit, the spirit will be completely suffocated by this brown mass.

Fortunately the side of the mountain where the boy stands is separated from the demonic side by a deep gorge with a flowing stream. For the time being, the boy is not threatened by the slowly approaching brown mass. Initially the stream as a symbol is remindful of the flux of life. It symbolizes the flowing energy of life as well as of the passing of time. Jung points to the fact that the living energy of the river "draws its dynamism from opposition. Without opposition, there is no energy. Where there is opposition, where the opposites clash, energy will result. The river is an eternal image."[28] In the dream of the boy, the river is imbedded in opposites: at one side there is the destructive, brown mass squashing everything, and at the other there is the impressive stillness of the elevation where the boy is standing. In these dramatic circumstances the figure of the shepherd is at his side as a moral support. He needs him most of all, because his flux of life is in so much danger.

The path in the dream is situated at the right side of the dreamer, at the conscious side. The observation of the boy is directed in a straight line up towards the dark figure with hat and staff. Such a figure often embodies an inner position. The position, which the dream offers here seems to be one of attentive observation about what is going on – without being the least influenced by any kind of anxiousness. Steadfastly, the dark figure gazes to the other side. The calmness of this shepherd shows an extraordinary

28 C.G. Jung, *Dream Analysis. Notes of the Seminar given in 1928-1930*, p. 704.

effective power. He emanates mana. His clothing and most of all the big staff, reminds the dreamer of a shepherd.

In olden times shepherds and sheepherder were known as "clever, wise people."[29] "They used incantations to charm away illness," they were blessed with the gift of foresight. In particular, people attributed to them the knowledge of a wholesome and powerful benediction against heavenly and earthly fire. "In antiquity shepherds were highly esteemed. It is not exceptional that sons of princes graze the herds personally," so it is said of the Trojan prince Paris. Some chief magistrates from antiquity called themselves "shepherds of the peoples." Also the Egyptian pharaoh is the "shepherd of the land and the sustainer of the peoples."

Being the son of a Prussian-protestant mother the dreamer was familiar with the picture of the good shepherd, who "protects" the human being like God. C.G. Jung brings to mind various figures of shepherds in the first centuries of Christianity. Christ is "The Shepherd of men."[30] He leads and holds together the herd and is in a larger sense the mediator between God and humans. It is to Him one gives the burden. He knows all the solutions. However when we look at the clothing of the dark figure with the wide-brimmed hat, the staff and long coat, it also reminds us of the Germanic god Wotan, who is connected here with the figure of Christ. The hat with the wide brim, as well as the staff and long coat, show dignity, authority and power. There is a sense of being protected. The hat, based on a rounded form, is reminiscent of a mandala. It covers "a sort of leading idea, covers the whole personality and imparts its own significance to it."[31] As a mandala it signifies the wholeness of the soul. To this Jung writes:

> In the last analysis every life is the realization of a whole, that is, of a self, for which reason this realization can also be called "individuation." All life is bound to individual carriers who realize it and it is simply inconceivable without them. But every carrier is charged with an

29 For the following see: Werner Danckert, *Unehrliche Leute. Die verfemten Berufe* [Dishonest people. The proscribed professions] (Bern/München: Franke Verlag, 1979), p. 176ff.
30 C.G. Jung, *Dream Analysis. Notes of the Seminar given in 1928-1930*, p. 184.
31 C.G. Jung, *Psychology and Alchemy*, vol. 12 of *The Collected Works of C.G. Jung*, edited and translated Gerhard Adler and R.F.C. Hull (New York: Pantheon Books, 1953), § 53.

individual destiny and destination, and the realization of these alone makes sense of life.[32]

The long robe of the figure in the dream also brings to mind the vestments of monks. The word "monk" derives from the Greek *monacos* meaning: "the unique, the solitary, the particular." Therefore, the clothing correlates with an attitude characterizing the bearer of this clothing, the dark figure, as one-of-a-kind.

What is threatening in the dream is the cohesive, brown mass heaving over the mountain chain. It calls to mind the *massa confusa* of the alchemists, an aspect of chaos and it shows the upcoming collective confusion at the time, brought about by the Nazis. It also shows the up rootedness of the dreamer and the total loss of security in social values he suffered. The problem the boy saw himself confronted with, which was brought on by the unconscious, obviously corresponds with a collective situation which, in another connection, C.G. Jung has described as follows:

> This end-result is... a false spirit of arrogance, hysteria, woolly-mindedness, criminal amorality, and doctrinaire fanaticism, a purveyor of shoddy spiritual goods, spurious art, philosophical stutterings, and Utopian humbug, fit only to be fed wholesale to the mass man of today. That is what the post-Christian spirit looks like.[33]

The boy wakes up with a sulphurous taste on his tongue, which makes him sick. At the same time he hears a "buzzing sound." A buzzing sound arises when energies rub against each other. There must be a constellation of extraordinarily strong dynamics. It creates sensation, taste, and releases a somatic reaction, nausea and vomiting.

From a Christian view, sulphur belongs to hell and to the devil. The first Book of Moses (Genesis) tells how God punishes the corruption of Sodom: "Then the Lord rained on Sodom and Gomorrah sulfur and fire from the Lord out of heaven; and he overthrew those cities, and all the Plain, and all the inhabitants of the cities, and what grew on the ground."[34] And in

---

32 C.G. Jung, *Psychology and Alchemy*, CW 12, § 330.

33 C.G. Jung, *Aion. Researches into the Phenomenology of the Self,* vol. 9/2 of *The Collected Works of C.G. Jung,* edited and translated by Gerhard Adler and R.F.C. Hull (New York: Pantheon Books, 1959), § 67.

34 1 Moses 19:24-25.

Revelation 14:9-12 one of three angels announces the judgement "against the Antichrist" in the following way:

> "Those who worship the beast and its image, and receives a mark on their foreheads or on their hands, they will also drink the wine of God's wrath, poured unmixed into the cup of his anger, and he will be tormented with fire and sulfur in the presence of the holy angels and in the presence of the Lamb... Here is a call for the endurance of the saints, those who keep the commandments of God and hold fast to their faith of Jesus.[35]

The word "sulfur" in German language is "Schwefel," in middle High German it is "swefel," "swebel," originally meaning "suffocating," "killing" or "shining substance." Strongly heated sulfur goes through different states of fluid aggregation, and can turn pasty and even a brown colour. There is a saying in the "Fichtelgebirge" such substances found in fields belong to a dragon who dropped them, and thus they called them "Dragonwax."[36] In the *Handwörterbuch des Deutschen Aberglaubens* [Dictionary of German superstition] it says:

> Superstition has it that the odour of sulphur is typical of evil spirits. The Devil, ghosts and the "Night-hunter" all carry the unpleasant odour of sulphur. In Tyrol there is a saying: "In sulfur sits the Devil, it is his favourite perfume, his smoking powder, because it burns well and smells bad. Poor Souls, having to suffer from pain, and endure the worst through sulphur... The hellish dragon smells like sulphur too; as soon as he releases his load one is contaminated life-long by the odour if one cannot escape it quickly."[37]

As is appropriate for his age, the dreaming boy had no idea about all of this. The dream narrates his personal situation at the time, what he had to endure without any understanding of it. In the sense of foreboding of what was to come, this archetypal dream, in its numinous sense, also shows the collective situation of the dreamer in all its abysmal content. The unconscious

---

35 Revelation 14:9-12.
36 *Handwörterbuch des deutschen Aberglaubens* [Dictionary of German Superstition], vol. 7, column 1458.
37 Ibid., column 1457f.

shows the boy what is approaching him and all of Europe: mass murder, war and devastation. But in the dark figure of the shepherd the dream also gives him hope. Calm and upright he stands in front of the boy on his side of the mountain. In him, the steadfastness of those who remain true to the will and the commandments of God, those "uncontrollable natural forces" as Jung once called them, is incorporated.[38] It is the regulating force of the self, and whoever builds upon what is presented by this force may unflinchingly go the way of individuation.

In this sense, the tortures of the SA people, which the boy had to watch and endure in a state of helplessness, were to constellate in his future life as an adult in a creative way. The tortures could even correlate to the initiation rites of young people in archaic cultures, about which our cultivated consciousness feels so terrible; they lead those concerned to the physical as well as the psychological abyss. The painfulness of this process forces the total capitulation of the ego, but also to the freedom of grown up life and the evolvement of social and religious relatedness. Under the dictum of pain, unconscious contents begin to press forth in such a way that the earlier ego-position will be changed inevitably. Whether the torture will destroy the individual, or be the crystallizing point of his completeness in the sense of the individuation process, is an act of Grace. It is the will of God, which manifests itself unadorned in such moments of destiny.

Those torturing the boy followed only the interests and manifestation of their own power and authority. They demonstratively wanted to humiliate and repudiate children who were not of parents conforming to the regime. However despite this, they actualised – with the will of God, *Deo concedente* – just the opposite. As the dream shows, the boy had a shepherd by his side, an inner authority, symbolizing the peace of divine providence.

On the dynamics of dreams

Searching for and finding the attitude that is "the right one" is in the end much easier thought or imagined than really found. Such critical life situations, weighing heavily in their dreadfulness, bring up a feeling of desperate abandonment and solitude. However the subjective feeling of hopelessness and the necessity of being forced to confront it is the indispensable requirement for the unfolding of a forward moving dynamic. "We

---

38 C.G. Jung, *Aion*, CW 9/2, § 48.

must not underestimate the devastating effect of getting lost in the chaos," Jung writes, "even if we know that it is the *sine qua non* of any regeneration of the spirit and the personality."[39] We are used to naming such situations "strokes of fate." Something operating outside of our rational consciousness is coming as a blow. Who, in this moment, thinks that distress can also be a positive value? Who thinks to search for the inner path firstly, especially when hardship hits us from the outside, a path that could bring about the basis for transformation and maturity as well as for salvation. In Hexagram 29 of the *I Ching* with the title: *The Abysmal (Water)*, it says in the comment to the second line:

> When we are in danger we ought not to attempt to get out of it immediately, regardless of circumstances; at first we must content ourselves with not being overcome by it. We must calmly weigh the conditions of the time and be satisfied with small gains, because for the time being a great success cannot be attained. A spring flows only sparingly at first, and tarries for some time before it makes its way into the open.[40]

Usually in such situations dreams have a signalling effect. In seemingly hopeless situations it is especially important to carefully consider the sources of our dreams, because in them we experience the force of our innermost nature speaking to us. Here an example:

Professional reasons once forced the separation of a passionately loving couple. They knew oceans would soon divide them. Later on, the man, 54 years old, described how he tried to prepare himself as best as possible for the moment of parting. It was understood that they would see each other again in due time.

He steadfastly promised himself to be brave. However, as soon as he saw the plane with his beloved slowly disappearing, he was overwhelmed by feelings of destruction and emptiness. A barely endurable endless grief set in, separating him from his surroundings. It seemed impossible to him to replace what he had lost by any other value. In one of the following nights he then dreamed:

39 C.G. Jung, *Psychology and Alchemy*, CW 12, § 96.
40 Richard Wilhelm, *I Ching or Book of Changes*, translated into English by Cary F. Baynes (Princeton: Princeton University Press, 1967), p. 116.

I see a fountain. In the middle of it, rising out of the depth, there is a pylon opening up into an elegantly shaped vessel. There is steam coming out. I have to wait before approaching the fountain.

Deeply moved, the man wakes up from this dream. What was its message? A fountain collects the water of a well. This is the water of life and carries a most important symbolic meaning. In Hexagram 48 of the *I Ching* it says: "The well is there for all. No one is forbidden to take water from it. No matter how many come, all find what they need, for the well is dependable. It has a spring and never runs dry."[41] The water in the fountain holds the meaning of wisdom and also carries a deeper meaning. It is the well of a refreshing spirit.

Out of this fountain rises a phallic male pylon. Normally a pylon is a supporting element, like a tower. The pillars of a suspension bridge, to which the supporting tensioning ropes are tied, are sometimes named pylons. In old Egypt such towers were flanking the entrance of temples. Therefore the symbolic meaning of the pylon is a creatively strong and supporting male life force.

The upper side of the pylon ends in a vessel formed like a bowl. This is a symbol of the feminine. In a text of Zosimos as well as in the 4th treatise of the *Corpus Hermeticum* it says, that God "created the humans as only half-conscious beings, and that he made a vessel *(Kratér)* to help them, filled it with Nous, that is, with spirit, and sent it to earth. Those humans who aspired to achieve broader consciousness... could dive into this *Kratér* to regenerate themselves and become *énnooi* there."[42] "*Ennoia*" means knowledge, or insight, the possibility of consciousness latently existing in the unconscious. The Holy Grail is also such a magical bowl. It [the Grail] has the power to give new life to humans by filling them with new spirit. In the dream steam rises out of the bowl as an expression of a creative dynamism. This takes place when the creative, the male pylon, conjuncts with the receptive, the bowl. The steam, though, also implies a process of distillation or cleansing.

---

41 R. Wilhelm, *I Ching or Book of Changes*, p. 188.
42 C.G. Jung, *Children's Dreams. Notes from the Seminar given in 1936-1940*, edited by Lorenz Jung and Maria Meyer-Grass, translated by Ernst Falzeder with the collaboration of Tony Woolfson (Princeton/Oxford: Princeton University Press, 2008), p. 224f.

However, what needs to be cleansed in the situation of the dreamer? At the time the dreamer started analysis, obviously the beloved woman had become the imago, the picture of his female soul, the anima. Her disappearance into the distance led to a destructively experienced loss of soul for the dreamer. The lover's farewell led to an obstruction in the energies of the soul and threatened the ego with overflowing feelings of abandonment and loss. When the union with the beloved woman was abruptly interrupted, the man was at the precipice of beginning to find his own soul again. And so, his aloneness became an important opportunity and a difficult task, asking of his strength to at least partially renounce the beloved image. For such a step one is in need of a human counterpart; this can often be an Analyst, one who patiently encourages him over and over again to hold on to the process.

Soon enough the dreamer had another dream offering him consolation and encouragement from his own resources, in spite of the separation and the pain that he could hardly bear.

> A team of doctors had developed an exceedingly simple therapy against cancer. The patient was to be provided with a large amount of salt. A reunion of Professors from all over the world was taking place who are examining this therapy. There was a great excitement because nobody had expected something like that. There would be salt at any time even if there was to be a war. It was almost a miracle.

The dreamer experienced this dream as an "enormous relief," he said. He had a gasp of relief as he woke up, and thought about the "salt of the earth" mentioned in the gospels.[43] The meaning of salt can be wisdom or bitterness. Both are frequently the impetus for a differentiation of feeling. Jung writes in *Mysterium Coniunctionis*:

> The failure of a pet plan, the disappointing behaviour of someone one loves, can supply the impulse either for a more or less brutal outburst of affect or for a modification and adjustment of feeling, and hence for its higher development. This culminates in wisdom if feeling is

---

43 Matthew 5:13: "You are the salt of the earth" and Mark 9:50: "Have salt in yourselves, and be at peace with one another."

supplemented by reflection and ration insight. Wisdom is never violent: where wisdom reigns there is no conflict between thinking and feeling.[44]

Therefore in the Analysis it was necessary to foster reflectiveness without hurting the feeling of the dreamer, so he could turn to his own soul and the *meaning* of the experience he had first perceived as bitterness.

Encounter with God in the air raid shelter, February 1945

Whenever the numinous starts to act in our life due to a helpless situation, slightly irrational phenomena occur. Later on, they can seem strange and cannot be explained rationally.

The evening of February 13, 1945, was a shrove Tuesday. Mrs. T. was together with her husband, in their shop at Prager Street in Dresden. Both of them planned to check and complete their bookkeeping that night. They had no idea how much "helplessness," planned with military precision, was already flying through the air. At 10:09 pm; just four minutes before the first waves of 2000 four-motored bombers would throw off their load; the local aerial defence – totally surprised – released an air raid warning. The couple believing that this alarm was only another precaution, at first considered whether they should enter the air raid shelter. But soon, hearing the terrible buzzing of the airplanes in the night sky, they hurried on downstairs. While they were still on the staircase to the shelter, the first of nearly 3000 tons of bomb – each of them weighed between four and eight tons – started falling on their area of the city, which would be a hundred percent destroyed within two hours.

Underground, the air pressure threw both humans around. The lights went out in an ear-piercing crack. Nobody but them made it to the shelter. The bomb-dropping, in the course of this first wave of attack, lasted for eight minutes during which neither Mrs. T. or her husband came to their senses. There was not even time for fear, even though everything was trembling, and cracking, and sparks flew all around them.

Then, there was silence. As they tried to open the escape hatch to see what was going on outside, they found it filled with rubble behind the iron door which rolled in towards them. When they opened the door leading

---

44 C.G. Jung, *Mysterium Coniunctionis*, vol. 14 of *The Collected Works of C.G. Jung*, edited and translated by Gerhard Adler and R.F.C. Hull (New York: Random House, 1963), § 334.

to the basement, the corridor was half collapsed. With the light of a torch they managed to crawl over the rubble, but access to the staircase was totally buried. The only way clear was to an iron door on the right leading out to a backyard. The key could be turned in the keyhole, but the iron door could not be opened an inch. Even though they tried running at the door with a broken ceiling beam, it would not move. It banged but it didn't open. Their cries for help went unanswered. They eventually decided to wait; thinking that: "Sometime someone will come, when everything is over!"

The two could not imagine what it looked like on the outside. They lit candles they found in the shelter to spare the battery of their torch. Suddenly bomb impacts started thundering again. All around them there was trembling: an infernal roar, twenty minutes long. They prayed the ceiling would hold up! They crouched in a corner next to the iron door, just in case parts of it should collapse. Luckily only a few chunks loosen. The dust evoked heavy fits of coughing. Then there was deadly silence again, after which they heard an eerie howling and roaring. They wondered if there was an opening somewhere? Where was it coming from? And if it was storming outside? Again they called for help, but nobody heard. As time went by, they got tired. Suddenly Mr. T. realised that the candle flames were slowly weakening. Was it the wick? But it could not possibly dwindle on all the candles simultaneously? More and more anxiety gave way to the fear that something must be wrong.

The couple had no idea that a wild fire storm was drawing with force across their area of the city, setting fire to even the asphalt. Flying back, the teams of British bomber pilots can see the light of the flames at a distance of 320 kilometres. 450 000 people lost everything they had, and at least 35 000 died of suffocation. If they were lucky to have not been torn apart by the bombs, the infernal blaze took away the oxygen from them.

In despair, Mrs. T. dropped to the floor, out of hope. But then she jumped up again, shaking her husband and screaming: "We have to get out of here! Do you hear me! We have to get out!" Desperately she rushed towards the iron door once more, hammering against it with some tool or other so that it banged. She screamed for help, then heard her husband saying the "Lord's prayer" and began to pray too. Afterwards they lay on the floor, exhausted and dumbly embracing each other. But then, Mrs. T. jumped up again suddenly and rushed towards the door in anger crying: "Lord! You cannot do this to us just like this! What did we do, that you are doing this to us? Open! Won't you open! Please open!"

Later Mrs. T. described it as follows:

> I had been drumming against the door and, bellowing the same over
> and over again as much as I could... and then all of a sudden... the door
> opens! I call: "Well, finally you are coming!" But there was no one, no-
> body and no one that could have done this! It was a miracle! I first had
> to cry and sit down. We then crawled outside and outside we did not see
> anyone either. And then we started running over rubble and ruins in the
> direction where there was no fire to be seen. This could only have been
> God's invisible hand that made suddenly the door swing open so easily!
> We could not find any other explanation, but it has happened anyway. I
> do not write about a vision to you for we have experienced this for real.

It is only with due respect that we can accept the assumption of Mrs. T., that
God lent his hand to her rescue. An argument stating that physical agents
took a part in this is trivial. Who would have provoked it? "To see through
a concrete situation to the bottom is God's affair alone," Jung writes. "We
may perhaps form an opinion about it but we do not know whether it is
finally valid."[45] Maybe one is nearest to God when, with accepting and
endurance, thinking ceases and the primitive instinct can stabilize; when
one does not *know* anymore but just *is*. Maybe only there and then one is
nearest to God – this holds also true for my own experience – and that is
when possibilities open up which cannot possibly be expected by way of
intellectual reasoning.

Jung once emphasized the fact that difficult, even seemingly hopeless
suffering also holds within itself the opposite pole. The pendulum of suffering can also be oriented towards a state of healing, conveying meaning.
Any winter, however strong, will finally grow into a new spring so one does
well to remember, that the "uttermost evil" is not necessarily leading to
the worst. The *I Ching*, in Hexagram 47, *Oppression (Exhaustion)*, says in the
comment to the first line:

> When adversity befalls a man, it is important above all things for him
> to be strong and to overcome the trouble inwardly. If he is weak, the
> trouble overwhelms him. Instead of proceeding on his way, he remains

45 C.G. Jung, "Good and Evil in Analytical Psychology." In: *Civilization in Transition*,
vol. 10 of *The Collected Works of C.G. Jung*, edited and translated by Gerhard Adler and
R.F.C. Hull (New York: Pantheon Books, 1964), § 862.

sitting under a bare tree and falls ever more deeply into gloom and melancholy. This makes the situation only more and more hopeless.[46]

And in Hexagram 29, *The Abysmal (Water)*, it says:

> Thus likewise, if one is sincere when confronted with difficulties, the heart can penetrate the meaning of the situation. And once we have gained inner mastery of a problem, it will come about naturally that the action we take will succeed. In danger all that counts is really carrying out all that has to be done – thoroughness – and going forward, in order not to perish through tarrying in the danger.[47]

The behaviour of Mrs. T. gives an example of how we should behave when completely alone and confronted with a hopeless situation. By referring to God or to something beyond the concretely tangible, it becomes possible to react out of the totality of ones humanness. Certainly, in her situation there was a "Daimon" at work, "a determining power which comes upon man from outside, like providence or fate,"[48] manifesting in the negative as well as in the finally positive way. The couple was manoeuvered into this awful situation, but were also rescued by it. This power was providence as well as destiny. "Divine powers" are "Powers of nature" and manifest in such situations.

Within the soul of Mrs. T. something happened that can be called "miraculous." Something totally unexpected. The pendulum changed from total exhaustion to furious provocation. Mrs. T. felt an urge to confront God directly: "You cannot do this to us just like this! What did we do, that you are doing this to us? Open!" It seems, as if it was about making God vigorously aware of what he is like – mortifying, violent, maybe even worse than the British who dropped the bombs? Most certainly this encounter did not match her previous perception of God.

"For you see, the Kingdom of God is within you."

In reality are we only free and one with ourselves at the moment when we are required to relate to God in a totally new way? And at this point, is a

46 R. Wilhelm, *I Ching or Book of Changes*, p. 182.
47 Ibid., p. 115.
48 C.G. Jung, *Aion*, CW 9/2, § 51.

turning to God a turning to the God within? "For in fact, the kingdom of God is within you" as it says in Luke.[49] And Meister Eckhart writes in his commentary:

> But a man in whom truly God is not but who must grasp God in this thing or in that from outside, and who seeks God in unlike ways, be it in works or people or places, such a man does not possess God. And it may easily be that something hinders such a man for he does not possess God, and he does not seek him alone, nor does he love or intend him alone; and therefore it is not only bad company that hinders him. Good company can also hinder him – not just the street, but the church too, not only evil words and deeds, but good words and deeds as well, for the hindrance is in him, because in him God has not become all things. Were that so, everything would be right and good for him, in every place and among all people, because he has God, and no one can take God away from him or hinder him in his work.
> On what does this true possession of God depend, so that we may truly have him?
> This true possession of God depends on the disposition, and on an inward directing of the reason and intention toward God, not on a constant contemplation in an unchanging manner, for it would be impossible to nature to preserve such an intention, and very laborious, and not the best thing either. A man ought not to have a God who is just a product of his thought, nor should he be satisfied with that, because if the thought vanished, God too would vanish. But one ought to have a God who is present, a God who is far above the notions of men... The man who has God essentially present to him grasps God divinely, and to him God shines in all things; for everything tastes to him of God, and God forms himself for the man out of all things. God always shines out in him, in him there is a detachment and a turning away, and a forming of his God whom he loves and who is present to him.[50]

---

49 Luke 17:21.
50 Meister Eckhart, *The Essential Sermons, Commentaries, Treatise, and Defense*, translated with an introduction by Edmund Colledge and Bernhard McGinn (New York: Paulist Press, revised edition, 1981), p. 252f.

What is Meister Eckhart's definition of "God"? He says, "… for he is one in that One where all multiplicity is one and is one unmultiplicity."[51] For God is wholeness before any separation. Logically, but for modern consciousness alarming in its consequence, Eckhart says, "… and it is God alone who performs all the man's works; for whoever causes the work, to him it belongs more properly and truly than it does to the one who performs it."[52] According to this, God becomes doer of all deeds. Isn't this tempting? Is this the result of surrendering to God with all of one's "soul"? But still it is correct when we remind ourselves of what we call "constellation." Something or someone "arranges" or "constellates"[53] the situations and moments of fate in our lives.

Late in his life, Ernst Ginsberg (1904-1964) fell ill of Amyotrophic Lateral Sclerosis (ALS); he was one of the best.actors and speakers ever known on the German stages. ALS consists of a rapidly proceeding degenerative illness of the central nervous system. The source of the illness is unknown. The related paralysis affects all the muscles of the face, lips, tongue, palate and larynx as well as the breathing. The capacity to speak and to swallow disappears totally. However, the patients' perception, their consciousness and intellectual capacities remain completely intact. Therefore the patients are in the unfortunate position to be fully aware of the degenerating process taking place. Reportedly Ernst Ginsberg, at the end of his tormented suffering, could only communicate through the movement of his eyes and eyelids. While he could still formulate words, he described his condition in a poem with the title *Tabula rasa*:

Tabula Rasa

Scattering of my hands
distorted joints
paralyzed haunches and you
you leaden lips –

In dreams alone still the beatitude of pacing
in dreams alone the delight of the tender embrace
in dreams alone the language .

51 Ibid.
52 Ibid. p. 251f.
53 Literally "constellation" means a specific pattern of the stars. Meant here is a fateful
   disposition or situation (the editors).

But when you wake
The jaws gape
For a single outcry.

But nothing rings
Out.[54]

In her introduction to Ginsbergs' memories, Elisabeth Brock-Sulzer wrote: "He had the need to bear witness once again, for whatever gave him the possibility to die the way he had died."[55] And so he reports:

I believe the first step towards any religion is the experience of that profound secret all of our being is embedded in: Birth, Love and Death. In no phase of my life, since my boyhood, could I understand the sober rationalists for whom a blade of grass is a blade of grass, a table is a table, and the heart is a heart; who are not touched by the absolutely incomprehensible mystery breathing in everything. Where I most deeply and inexplicably encountered the fact that the world and life remain a secret was in music. It is well understood that there are no rational explanations for its effect.[56]

And later he concludes:

However I won't end my little attempt to bear witness once again to my belief without confessing my helplessness towards this tremendous topic. Likewise I confess with gratitude that the belief, the joy, and the happiness have been a consolation and blessing in my life, and in the lives of my loved ones. At the time I am writing this I have had the grace to experience the ultimate confirmation and validity of this belief. Nothing but holding my glance to the cross enables me to endure this severe paralysis as I am facing death; which for a nonbeliever could only be ended with a deed like Hemingway's.[57]

It seems that when experiencing states of aloneness that come about as inevitable fate, our self-worth is not in doubt and not even of any consideration.

54 Ernst Ginsberg, *Abschied. Erinnerungen, Theateraufsätze, Gedichte* [Farewell. Memories, Essays on Theatre, Poems] (Zurich: Verlag der Arche, 1965), p. 254.
55 Ibid, p. 14.
56 Ibid, p. 16.
57 Ibid, p. 20.

The challenges involved evoke either rebellion or surrender, generating a quietness that cannot be rationalized or justified. In essentially endangering crises the measure changes and everyday worries become futile. However the "Kingdom of God is within you," and in this sense the wholeness and totality of one's nature enables the inner light to shine stronger and conveys meaning to the "All-one-ness" in the aloneness by an experience of reality and substance.[58]

58 Translated from German by Brigitte Jacobs-Fröhlich, Hedingen, Switzerland.

Claudine Koch-Morgenegg

The Great Mystery – Individuation in Old Age

> But the right way to wholeness is made
> up, unfortunately, of fateful detours and
> wrong turnings.
>
> *C.G. Jung*[1]

Like no other, C.G. Jung underlined the value, the dignity and the meaning of the second half of life for, in his view, the true task of the second half of life is to focus more deeply upon the unconscious. We find entry into this world, for example, through our dreams. For C.G. Jung, dreams are natural phenomena that are not influenced by consciousness. He writes, "The dream is a little hidden door in the innermost and most secret recesses of the soul, opening into that cosmic night which was psyche long before there was any ego-consciousness, and which will remain psyche no matter how far our ego-consciousness extends."[2]

And indeed, dreams can give the very elderly many new insights. The very act of focussing upon their dreams can have a fascinating effect. Many connections in one's own personal biography become clear, and for those who are willing to be guided by their dreams, to listen to their inner voice and to reflect upon their dreams in a genuine way, there are many treasures to be discovered within oneself that one did not know existed.

In my work with the aged, my focus is primarily upon their dreams. I

---

1 C.G. Jung, "Introduction to the Religious and Psychological Problems in Alchemy." In: *Psychology and Alchemy*, vol. 12 of *The Collected Works of C.G. Jung*, edited and translated by Gerhard Adler and R.F.C. Hull (London: Routledge & Kegan Paul, 1981), § 6.

2 C.G. Jung, "The Meaning of Psychology for Modern Man." In: *Civilization in Transition*, vol. 10 of *The Collected Works of C.G. Jung*, translated by R.F.C. Hull (London: Routledge and Kegan Paul, 1991), § 304.

often had the impression that my patients were waiting for someone to ask them about their dreams. They wanted to tell their dreams to someone who would take them seriously. To speak of them in a light-handed fashion is to dismiss their significance. For dreams describe an inner process. They are a part of one's ongoing development and they steer one towards reflection about who one is. They help the aged to master the final stage of their long life, for example, by uncovering buried experiences and by supporting the development of their inner potential, even in their final years.

By presenting the life story of a woman in her nineties, I would like to give some insight into the development and transformation that is possible in old age. My focus is mostly upon the voice of the unconscious that has its own unique viewpoint and pursues its own goals. Like every human life, Frau Suter's[3] life story is a mystery that cannot be put into words. I have nevertheless attempted to describe her journey. It mostly concerns a pivotal chapter of her life that allowed her to become what she had always been, and transformed her into being the person she had always had the potential to be. Her journey is a long one, through much darkness. For me, our relationship was an adventurous one that began in a puzzling way. And how it went on to develop moves and touches me deeply to this day. Who was this woman?

Frau Suter was born in Switzerland in 1908 as the only daughter of German parents. Her father was from Bremen, and her mother from Saxony. When the First World War broke out in 1914, her father had to return to Germany. Mother and daughter remained in Switzerland. Her mother had graduated from commercial college in Germany and was able to support herself and her daughter through this period by doing clerical work. After four years of war, her father was not permitted to return to Switzerland for, in Frau Suter's own words, there were sufficient architects at that time. He bided his time in southern Germany. They visited him regularly there. While her parents went out of an evening and celebrated being together again, Frau Suter remained at the hotel on her own. She pined for her absent mother. She suffered. Perhaps her mother was envious of her pretty, adolescent daughter. In any event, she prevented her from having a relationship to her father. This was very hard on Frau Suter. She felt rejected and unloved by both of her parents. In this situation, she had a dream that helped her to overcome her loneliness and sense of abandonment.

---

3 "Suter" is not her real name, it is a pseudonym.

The Childhood Dream

She is lying on a magic carpet and flying through the world on a great adventure. She has a bird's eye view of the world. Sometimes she flies down low, and then she flies back up high.

This is how her unconscious comforted her. Frau Suter read a lot of fairy-tales and identified with the heroes and heroines of these stories. She told me that this helped her. In 1919, her father was at last permitted to reunite again with his family. He found work as a bookkeeper in an engineering office in Zurich. In 1920, the family bought their own house. Shortly afterwards, her father invited some of his comrades-in-arms to his home. Together, they celebrated wild parties in the kitchen. Everybody had a good time. The adults sang, drank and ate together. It was the most wonderful time of her life, she told me. Frau Suter was eighteen years old at the time. Her parents sent her to Neuenburg where she studied at a commercial college. When she was twenty, she went to England to improve her English. Later, she spent time at various health resorts in Switzerland where she worked as a private secretary. Finally, she became a head secretary in Zurich and moved into her own apartment. In May 1938, her father fell ill with the flue. He was hospitalised and died there of an infection. Frau Suter met a man at the place where she worked and fell in love with him. He was still married. After his divorce, they married. A year later their son was born. Shortly after his birth, Frau Suter asked for a divorce. She moved back into her parent's home where she lived with her son and her mother for the next few decades. Her mother died when Frau Suter was seventy. A period then began in which she had a very close relationship to her son.

Prologue

Prior to our first meeting, Frau Suter had an unusual dream.[4] It preoccupied her and bothered her. She was puzzled by this dream. It seemed to suggest a hidden secret. According to her understanding of the dream, her mother forbade her to tell anyone "her secret." What was it that she was not allowed to tell? She wanted to get to the bottom of the secret and she sought after what had been covered up, hidden from view. Her thoughts circled around her inner wounds, around the painful experiences in her life. And strange

---

4   See dream below, p. 304: *The Secret in my Parent's Kitchen.*

fantasies began to arise that overpowered her. Frau Suter believed she had played a part in something quite shocking. She had the fantasy that she had destroyed what had once been a happy and joyful family. How dreadful to be guilty of such a thing! She felt she had to get on top of this dreadful feeling, this fantasy. And as she could not unravel the puzzle, she became unsettled. At some point the fantasies that were connected to the dream became threatening. They filled her with fear. A story had run its course. Something had gone wrong. Anger overwhelmed her, enveloped her. She was unable to control what was happening to her. She became bitter.

Essentially, she needed to put a stop to her thoughts and fantasies. But continuing in the same pattern had become compulsive. It prevented her from getting out of the situation under her own steam. There is something ecstatic about anger. Or she sometimes thought she might still get to the bottom of the secret – perhaps right now, if she just kept her focus upon it and gave it one last try. Much later it became clear that unlocking this secret meant recognizing how deeply wounded she herself was. But her mind protected her from the memory of the secret by burying it beneath the fog of forgetfulness. She was not yet ready. Frau Suter could not yet bear the truth. For her wounds were much greater and much deeper than a passing grievance – as she would later find out.

She did not know where her anger might lead and this unsettled her. Normally, anger has a goal. It wants to manifest something – for example, a separation and to get things going. Increasingly, Frau Suter became a victim of a dynamic that she was unable to escape from. As a result, fate led her towards its own inescapable goal, i.e. to having a deep relationship to someone – to me – something she had always wanted to avoid at any cost.

First Encounter

I met Frau Suter some time after her mysterious dream. I was working in a home for the aged at the time, and I was asked to see her. I ring her doorbell. The door opens only a crack. Frau Suter looks at me and says that she is fine, that there is nothing wrong with her and she does not need to see anyone. She rebuffs me. But then she says, *"Well, I suppose if you are already here you may as well come in."*[5] Barely in the room, she tells me where to sit. This is

---

5 Italics indicate that I am quoting from the protocols I wrote during our analytical hours.

where she always sits. Now I am to sit in that chair. She will sit in the other chair.

Frau Suter is a pretty, attractive, slim woman, who seems quite youthful. We sit down facing each other. Frau Suter is 93 years old and I am the same age as her son. We are silent for a little while. She looks me over warily. And then she tells me that she speaks to her son on the phone every day – so, she is not alone – and that about eight years ago, she came to the home just to try it out. She had kept her flat that is very close by. The latter had now become a burden. It was becoming increasingly difficult for her to make her way there as her sight was deteriorating. Her hearing was also poor and she now wore a hearing aid. And by the way, there is, she said, an "old age dream" she had had that bothers her and has puzzled her for a long time. She was sure this dream had something to do with her disabilities. It augured nothing good. She could tell it to me if I liked.

The Old Age Dream
I am walking through an empty town. There are only municipal build-ings in this town. I am walking through its districts. Nothing reminds me of any towns that I know. I come to a crossroad, and I should know whether to go left or right. I should go into the corners. How do I get out of here? I wake up.

The dream clearly has to do with her sense of hopelessness. But it does not frighten her. She is, she says, a divorced woman and she has a very close relationship to her unmarried son. Upon waking she thought, *"So now the dream has once again come and gone. I am not curious about where it (the path) leads. I am neither happy nor unhappy; it does not move me; I am simply curious."* For the moment, everything seems to be clear to Frau Suter. And yet the dream surprises her. It might be hinting at something she should know. She would, in fact, like to know what the dream might be telling her. But she is obviously afraid.

"How lonely she is," I think to myself. This empty town! There is no one to be seen or heard. There are only municipal buildings. A cool, rational spirit is in charge here. A town is a symbol of the archetype of the mothering feminine. There is an absence of speech, and an absence of relationship. This would appear to be a problem, one that goes very deep. I am moved by the dream.

After a little while, Frau Suter says, "Nothing reminds me of any towns that I know." She has the same dream repeatedly. And it is always a town with which she is not familiar. She searches for something she might recognize, but in vain. There is so much loneliness and hopelessness. Despite her daily contact with her son, she is unfulfilled. Emptiness surrounds her.

I bring to her attention that there is, indeed, a solution to her problem. It is said that she needs to go into the corners. She has a strong reaction to this. *"Why must I go there? I don't want to! How do I get out of there?"* Cool and aloof until that moment, she was now in the grip of naked despair. The dream is an imposition. Indignant and full of resistance, she says, *"How do I get out of there?"* One can hear her desperation. There is a way out of this terrible situation. But it requires Frau Suter to go "into the corners." Jung writes that in the corner – in one's own chaotic, personal unconscious – one finds "all that one would like to forget, and all that one does not wish to admit to oneself or to anybody else, and which one prefers to believe is not true anyhow. One therefore expects to come off best if one looks as little as possible into this dark corner."[6] Thus, she might encounter her shadow in these corners – perhaps even her great secret that frightens and terrifies her. No, anything but that! Understandably, she would like to quickly forget what she has discovered for, in the meantime, she is terribly frightened of the images in her dream! Her shadow might be even more sinister and threatening than what she already knows.

Frau Suter has had enough. Our talk is over. She stands up and goes to the door, with me following. On the way to the door, she discloses that whenever she feels bitter, she "dreams" of being on the carpet in her childhood dream. It is her way, encoded or indirectly, to draw attention to her despair. Through her childhood dream, she tries to avoid becoming bitter and to control the anger that she has evoked through her "arbitrary" and bizarre manner of dealing with her unusual dream of the secret. What Frau Suter chooses to do with her childhood dream – she dreams herself onto the carpet – as an adult is magic, as Marie-Louise von Franz explains in her book *Die Suche nach dem Selbst*: "Magic always links up to the willpower of the ego in order to protect itself against an approaching conflict."[7] Frau

---

6 Carl Gustav Jung, "The Psychology of Eastern Meditation." In: *Psychology and Religion: East and West*, vol. 11 of *The Collected Works of C.G. Jung*, edited by R.F.C. Hull (London: Routledge & Kegan Paul, 1986), § 939.

7 Marie-Louise von Franz, *Die Suche nach dem Selbst. Individuation im Märchen* (München: Kösel Verlag, 1985), pp. 98f. This quotation occurs only in the German version. See the corresponding English publication: Marie-Louise von Franz, *Individuation in Fairy Tales* (Boston/London: Shambhala, 1990), pp. 71f.

Suter uses magic when she is overwhelmed by threatening memories or fantasies from the unconscious. Thus, the conflict is not really experienced and there is no conscious integration of its contents. On the contrary! Frau Suter is left feeling disoriented, empty and bitter, as her "old age dream" shows. Her anger has a goal. It wants separation. This would mean she must firstly distance herself from her dream and its "secret." In other words, the "secret" cannot be approached directly. Several hurdles need to be overcome before the unspeakable thing can come to light.

Whilst taking my leave of her at the door, Frau Suter confides in me that she speaks to plants. The cyclamen that is standing near her window has blossomed three times. Something in her is longing for a life that will blossom once more. In front of me now is not a defensive, idiosyncratic woman, but rather a woman who is longing for human warmth and human relationship.

She wants me to visit her again. Not too often, but soon. Perhaps I could come next Tuesday? Scepticism, fear and distrust still have the upper hand. But her desperation seems to be even greater than she will admit. I stand there feeling somewhat helpless. But I am deeply moved by the encounter and agree to another visit.

This was the beginning of a lengthy relationship and a gripping, even dramatic, story. At first it was difficult for Frau Suter to trust her dreams. Her fear and the fiasco she had suffered by trying to understand her puzzling dream of the secret went deep. Nevertheless, she hoped to find her way out of her dreadful situation. We shared a world with each other in which she began to trust – a completely new experience for her as, up until then, she had never really opened herself up to anyone. She allowed herself "to get caught up in" our relationship. At first she lived completely in and with her inner images. I let her talk, listened to her, rarely asked her any questions, trusting that her dreams, her unconscious, would slowly lead her out of her desperation. In these early days of our relationship, her dreams were the only way to get a sense of what was going on inside of her for she was so sensitive, so vulnerable and so distrusting.

I can only present a small segment of the stony and painful path Frau Suter had to pursue here. The manner in which she had dealt with her dream about the "secret" had caused her to completely lose her way in life. So initially, I would like to show how her unconscious brought Frau Suter back onto the path of her life, in order to portray some of the important steps in her development, for example, what was the unspeakable thing that was referred to in that dream, and how was she redeemed?

Re-finding the Path of her Life

In the second dream Frau Suter told me she had to find her way down from the Fronalpstock in the canton of Schwyz. The Fronalpstock is a mountain she knows well. She is "up there" on the mountain with many people in the dream and they are admiring the view. She is deeply happy. Standing up there is exalting. But there is snow on the ground. She tells me that in summer there is no snow up there. The mountain with snow is an image of the bleakness of her life.

Frau Suter tells me that she had been on the Fronalpstock when she was around twenty-five years old. A man had an accident up there. *"Other skiers came and they knew what to do. I just stood there, stupid and forlorn."* But in her dream she is not as helpless as she presently feels. There are many other people there who could come to her aid. But this would mean including these people in her life. This horrifies her. She is accustomed to fighting alone, of finding her own way, even if it means being very lonely. The very thought of having to take all these strangers into consideration? No, anything but that!

The snow begins to melt, and her feelings come to life again. After a short while she said, *"It's not going to be a very pleasant descent."* It is quite an imposition to ask her to make the descent with all these people. That these people might be different sides of herself to which she has no relationship and who play no role in her life, she will not accept. It is almost too much that I even mention this. Her chagrin is very evident.

In symbolic terms, the Fronalpstock points towards the "Fron." Her path is a path of drudgery.[8] There is no need for me to explain this to her. It means that one gives and gets nothing back. So we could say it would be to recognize how and what one has lived only to discover that perhaps one's life was a failure. And this at ninety-three! This was a difficult decision. Frau Suter becomes pensive. She does not want to make any promises. But I should come back again.

Shortly before I leave, she mentions that her mother appeared in the dream and not only once. She said to her and to her son who was also present, *"So I shall not be coming back again."* Astonished, she says, *"But my*

---

8 "Fron" in German means drudgery or serfdom.

mother died twenty years ago," So no problem there. It is done. And that is true up to a point. But as Jung writes in his memoirs, the dead are the "voices of the Unanswered, Unresolved, and Unredeemed."[9] It is her mothering side that is being addressed here. If the mother leaves, it reflects her diffident, passive, impregnable manner.[10] In her dream, she and her son remain.

As I was leaving, she added, *"I ask myself what is the meaning of me going slowly blind."* It is, perhaps, about developing her inner self, of having a relationship to the person she is on the inside, in order to find her way back into life, and, perhaps, about letting go of her son, letting him enter life. And before completely closing the door, she makes it clear to me that she will only say as much as she chooses to say. She wants to stay in control. This is important to her. Nevertheless, she enjoys telling me her dreams. Nearly all our future meetings thus begin with a dream.

The Barn

I was together with a lot of people. We were in a very large barn. Above us were cross bracings made out of wood. They made me think of Noah's Ark. People were seated at tables. Others were standing, talking to each other. The barn was broad and high. We journeyed over the sea in this barn until we reached land.

The dream is neither uplifting nor oppressive, Frau Suter says. There were young and old people, all unknown. She is excited. She likes this barn, also the Ark. The barn represents a simple, humble attitude that could add breadth and height to her life. Again, there is reference to humility.

Symbolically, the barn and the Ark represent the protective lap of the mother. In this space, the dreamer is given the opportunity to speak of her experiences and her feelings and thereby bring stability to her feelings of self-worth. In connection with Noah's Ark, the Ark is also a symbol of there being an end, one that people have brought down upon themselves, as well as being a symbol of being rescued from ruin. One can view the journey across the sea as a time of transition in which one tries to engage with what one is feeling, and tries to take one's feelings seriously. And at some point, the Ark will dock on land. This would be an image of the dawn of a new era, or perhaps of death.

9   Aniela Jaffé (ed.), *Memories, Dreams, Reflections by C.G. Jung* (London: Flamingo, 1977), p. 217.
10 This is how she described her mother.

Here, the unconscious is showing Frau Suter how it wants to lead her. The dream has an effect. It is not about anything really disturbing, but just about "being," she says. She sums up the dream by saying, "*I want to be open for what wants to happen, but I don't want to have to deal with anything.*" She is ready to inwardly enter her "dream barn." But I should not expect too much. It is nice, however, that she is ready to set out upon her path.

She is barely in this barn when she confesses that she has had another dream of her mother. And once again she had it many times. This time she saw her mother elevated. It did not seem like a dream, more like reality. She had "to look up to" her.

Thus, it is about her relationship to her mother. Very enthusiastically she tells me about the wonderful relationship they had had with each other. She admired her mother's imperturbable calm. Indeed, she was her role model. Then her mood changes. Oppressed and sad, she says that after her father died, she consciously tried to strengthen her relationship to her mother, and sought out her company "*in order to give her the attention that father had given her.*" She tried hard to do the right thing. And at the end of her life, her mother had accused her of betraying her. She does not feel guilty. Her mother does not forgive her in the dream. She has been working on this in the past and she is still working on it.

She must overcome her mother for this is the inner force that is preventing her from being in life. Apparently her mother had always been jealous of her pretty daughter. Yet in the dream Frau Suter has to look up to her. She is probably not being completely honest with herself. Her unconscious has picked up on this. In fact, she is enormously angry with her mother. But she cannot allow herself to feel her anger. That would be the final blow to their relationship. And that would be impossible. She is still hoping that her mother will forgive her in a dream. But she probably never will. Feeling desperate and resigned, she says, "*If she wants to go, she should just go!*" She cannot stop her. Her bitterness seeps through these whispered sentences. Frau Suter is grieved and hurt. And possibly she is also afraid that at some point in her life she has failed. The unconscious now wants to redeem her from this terrible dependence.

When saying goodbye to me this time, Frau Suter says, "*When I die, I hope that my soul doesn't remain trapped in this room, that somebody opens a window.*" I promise her that when the time comes, I shall open a window. This calms her. This is how she draws my attention to things. She realizes that she has lost her soul and that she will only find it by going down into her own depths.

Before we part to celebrate the festive season, Frau Suter eagerly tells me a few stories from her childhood. She regresses into her childhood. C.G. Jung defines regression as adapting to the conditions of the inner world, as a process of spiritual regeneration, as "gathering inner strength." The unconscious seems to be preparing Frau Suter to finally be able to tell me her mysterious dream. Without being led to it, she would probably not be able to take the step. She is still in danger of avoiding any separation from her mother, i.e. in danger of remaining silent.

They are all stories in which she was hurt as a child. She describes how she always brought home animals as a child. *"Once it was a salamander. I asked my mother to give me a jar to put it in. The next day I had to take it to school to give it to my teacher. I don't know what happened to the salamander. I was heartbroken."* And then, suddenly, she is hard and assertive. She says, *"I am not so kind to animals now. For example, if there's a spider in my room, I squash it and throw it out of the window. I have become ruthless."* And quite soberly she continues, *"There is an even older dream that I still think about,"* and proceeds to tell me the puzzling dream I spoke of at the beginning.

The Secret in my Parent's Kitchen

I am in the kitchen in my parent's flat. Mama enters from the dining room/parlour that is opposite the kitchen. She comes into the kitchen, puts a finger to her lips, closes the kitchen door behind her and says, "Don't say anything. Not everyone may know this." I am puzzled. What has happened? I wake up.

Speaking to her so directly is not really her mother's normal way of speaking to her. She had had a great deal of self-control. *"One had to wring everything out of her. She was diffident."* The silence she asks for in the dream is like an unspoken code of conduct between the two of them, a code that she had adhered to until the present day.

That she was standing in the kitchen and that her mother came into the kitchen from the dining room was natural, she said. But she did not know why her mother had to close the door. She had not been able to solve this riddle. It probably has to do with how they got together. *"She (her mother) lost her husband through death. I lost mine (her husband) through divorce."* She tells me she is finished with our meetings for this year. She needs a holiday. She stands up and accompanies me to the door.

So there is a secret that needs to be kept. By putting her finger to her lips, her mother creates a taboo. If guilt and shame constellate in a family, most often a great silence ensues, the secret becomes taboo. The questionable thing may not be named, and it may not be spoken of. But this silence and keeping it in the dark has consequences. It prevents one from living one's own life.

The secret may not be spoken of. But it is in the kitchen, i.e. it is within the vessel of transformation. At first, Frau Suter interprets the secret that her mother makes her aware of in the dream as some form of guilt that she may not tell anyone about. But the unconscious is aiming at something quite different: it wants to bring the secret up from the depths into consciousness. It needs to be brought into the light as it has been poisoning Frau Suter from within for many years, and keeping her isolated. In the dream she and her mother share this secret. It is no longer a purely personal secret. It becomes a shared secret. According to Jung, this makes it less destructive. Jung elucidates, "If we are conscious of what we are concealing, the harm done is decidedly less than if we do not know what we are repressing – or even that we have repressions at all."[11] Frau Suter was not able to deal with what happened in the kitchen at that time. In symbolic terms, the kitchen is the place of transformation. It is where spiritual nourishment is made available and is digested. Some preparations must still be made before she will be able to bear the emotional tensions that are connected to it.

We meet again at the beginning of the new year. Frau Suter tells me the following dream that she had initially forgotten, but was able to later recall. She tells me that the dream is to be understood symbolically. It involves a confrontation. Actually, the dream describes her situation, the critical state she finds herself in.

The Tree of Life

I am walking along a path and come to an enormous area in which there are allotment gardens. I want to find our allotment. I see it. I continue to walk. I go up and, once on the other side, I descend a short way. When I was on top, I saw a little forest below me. I thought how beautiful

11 C.G. Jung, "General Problems of Psychotherapy." In: *The Practice of Psychotherapy*, vol. 16 of *The Collected Works of C.G. Jung*, edited by R.F.C. Hull (London: Routledge & Kegan Paul, 1981), § 125.

the trees were. I go down in order to look at the trees. And then I am standing in front of a tree up there. It has a powerful wonderful crown, and a wall runs vertically through the tree. The entire trunk is divided into two. Earth moving machines have removed the earth from this height. There is a wall running down the hill. Half of the roots are visible, and they are greatly entangled. The tree is healthy. Greatly excited, I woke up.

The allotment gardens refer to the time that mother and daughter were alone together. Her father had left for the war. It was a pleasant time. She is being drawn back to that time. She does not approach her goal directly. Instead, she "goes up around the top" and then comes down the other side. She does a loop, so to speak, in order to view her problems from behind, from a different perspective. This is how she sees the forest. The forest is the unknown, what is in the dark, a dangerous place where mysterious events take place, like in fairytales.

It is in the forest that the dreamer encounters the tree with the powerful crown. This tree is a symbolic representation of herself, of her personality. Every element of the tree represents an aspect of her personality. She says this tree was just as she likes a tree to be: it had no leaves. This makes it possible to see the form of its branches and she likes this very much. The crown and the roots of this tree are very similar. The tree's energy is concentrated at its centre. "A person whose roots are above as well as below is thus like a tree growing simultaneously downwards and upwards. The goal is neither height nor depth, but the centre," Jung writes.[12] For our dreamer, too, it would be important for her to find her centre.

The centre is the trunk. The trunk symbolizes her ego-identity, her value system of what is important. It represents her values and her beliefs. This trunk is divided, right down to its roots. It would appear to be an image of a very early inner split. Some aspect of her personality must have been removed beyond access very early in the dreamer's life. Something got split off, and was therefore no longer accessible to consciousness. This happens in order to make a traumatic, irresolvable or unbearable conflict bearable. As one's body is part of one's ego, any inner split destroys one's body image. Some part of one's body is no longer felt to be a part of the whole. It is split

12 C.G. Jung, "The Philosophical Tree." In: *Alchemical Studies*, vol. 13 of *The Collected Works of C.G. Jung*, edited by R.F.C. Hull (London: Routledge & Kegan Paul, 1981), § 333.

off. When this happens, one no longer feels connected to oneself, to one's fate or to other people. There is a disturbance in one's perception of being in a continuum and in one's connection to one's inner centre. In this sense, one could take the pathway to the allotment gardens to be a symbol of Frau Suter's search for what there still might be within her. Her life has proven to be empty. Perhaps she is also asking herself if her life up until now was not the life she was really meant to live.

She woke up "happy," she says. It was not as if the trunk had been damaged. But *"it stood right up the front, against the steep wall. One could see its roots."* Her confidence fades. What is going on? Her body image has been damaged. But she does not have any sense of this. She is poor at recognizing feelings, and even worse at expressing them.

The most important part of a tree is its roots. In order to grow, a tree needs to be able to grow downwards. Its roots bear and support a tree's trunk and crown. They keep it stable and firm. Its roots draw its life force up from the earth, sucking up water and nourishment and sending it upwards into even the tiniest branches of its crown. But the roots of this tree are visible. And there are earth-moving machines that are carrying the earth away. Earth-moving machines dig, excavate and create a dreadful inner emptiness that Frau Suter tried to fill with her fantasies, without having any creative effect. It is therefore not possible for any transformation to take place. Only fantasies remain. Much is unfinished or has not even been begun. Much has been left purely to fantasy.

Sad and resigned, she adds, *"I stand below while up above stands the tree with its roots in what is left of the earth."* Her unconscious wants her to finally take a look at her life, at her fate. She has reached a critical point. She has found something out in connection to the "secret in her parent's kitchen." And she cannot undo what has been done. Frau Suter is shaken up. The dream visibly affects her, wakes her up. She now sees it as a warning. For the moment, that is enough. She goes on to tell her next dream. In this dream she, her mother and her son leave her parent's house. This dream is based on reality, she says. When she is about to lock the front door, between the fourth room that has its own entry onto the hallway stairs and the front door, she sees dust, dirt and earth on the floor. She goes back inside, gets a broom and shovel from the kitchen and returns to the front door.

One could interpret the dust, dirt and earth to be a lack of fantasy, insight and inspiration that emanates from the spirit of her parents. To behave in the same way as her parents leads her into emptiness.

Once Frau Suter finishes telling this dream, she looks at me and tells me that the fourth room has its own story. Doors symbolize what is behind them, what has been fenced off and should remain hidden. She may not get to the bottom of this. It is not yet time. She understands this and says that there is nothing to be said about this right now. Of course she sweeps it all up. Thus, in her view, she has done what needed to be done. She takes a concrete view of things. Seen from a symbolical viewpoint, the fourth room seems to be connected to a taboo that she may not yet disclose. This appears to energize her.

And there is a vision that she absolutely wants to tell me of. The following visual impression she found to be particularly interesting.

Vision

An upended rectangle and whether it was standing on its upper or lower edge, it is not possible to say what is within it. On its upper edge was a face. It didn't say anything. I looked at it and then it went away. The colours – a combination of light blue and pink.

What is going on here? A face comes to life that is on top of a rectangle, and it evokes a deep longing in her. It is both very strange and very personal. "Light blue and pink" is a combination that she likes. "*It is poetic. The figure was ethereal, not supernatural. The face had a friendly expression.*" She is looking at something that was once silenced. Now, suddenly, it appears clearly in front of her. One could take it to mean a realm of the psyche that is capable of consciousness, one that gradually wants to show itself.

The feeling this face awakens in her is expressed here in the colours of light blue and pink. Light blue evokes a dreamy state. It softens any excitement and agitation. Light blue is often associated with the vastness of the sky. It is a colour that stimulates the search for one's inner truth, and helps one to reach inner peace. By contrast, pink is the colour of tenderness, romance and calmness. It connects the purity of white with the power of red. It mollifies and dismantles aggression and increases one's sensibility. It helps to give expression to one's feelings. Pink is feminine, playful, youthful – a typical colour for girls. She has had a very complex experience!

Visions often occur when a change is about to be made, when hope has disappeared, when traditions are no longer any help and structures no longer bear the load. Frau Suter has had a visual experience – a vision – that has moved her both emotionally and physically. Up until now she has tried to dismiss her own darkness that, earlier, had not been so threatening. But this darkness appears to be even deeper and greater. It would seem that not everything is (yet) lost. It is time, however, to face her life story. But this requires overcoming great fear and resistances. She states, *"One should let plants grow, even if they are crooked."* She appears to be exhausted and resigned. But she knows that she has to complete her journey within – that she has to face herself. She has been set a task in this life.

Before we part she adds, *"Nothing will be finished in my life. At some point I shall no longer be here and everything will remain unfinished, over. I feel caught in a dichotomy: on the one hand I am needed, but on the other hand I wish I could give in to the fatigue I feel towards life."* She is distraught, indecisive, and she does not know whether or how to go on.

After these dreams, Frau Suter fell ill. She had severe pneumonia. These dreams and her vision pushed her to her limits. We meet four weeks later. She describes to me how on one particular day she felt she was close to dying. She "turned over" in bed. She did, however, wake up again, and slowly she began to improve. Now she feels quite well.

Frau Suter is once again wrestling with herself – indeed, she is fighting. Her encounter with the unconscious challenges her, pushes her to her limits. And yet she chooses to continue. We arrange our next meeting. Before I leave, she remarks I must have noticed that she had not been open with me. She said she needed more time. I have the impression she wants to move forward, but she is still very afraid.

Half a year has passed. It is a Tuesday and Frau Suter is expecting me. I had not yet taken a seat when she says very excitedly – even anxiously – her father had appeared to her. She was surprised for she had not thought about him for ages. It was a short, impressive dream and it was the first time that an answer had come out of the unconscious. She really needs to tell me everything.

The Father

I am in a room in my parent's house and I am looking at the door. And then my Papa comes in, my dear Papa, and he has a moustache. I don't see him very clearly – it is all a bit blurry – and he is not wearing a suit, but a robe that covers him from head to toe. And we didn't speak.

She is surprised, shocked, that her father has a moustache in the dream. She does not like moustaches. Her father had a moustache upon his return from the First World War. This was the reserved, indifferent man who found it difficult to re-establish contact with his daughter. The war had ground him down. He had lost his soul. This had been a dreadful experience for Frau Suter at the time, which she did not like to recall. She went on talking, but the tone of her voice had changed:

> I woke up shocked about my own shock and I tried to become aware of what I felt about my unconscious working on an image of my father. I then had an urgent urge to go to the toilet.

And then the dream transformed into a vision[13]:

> I went to the toilet. Then I saw him. His robe was light blue, ethereal, and his face was – how shall I describe it? Absent, sympathetic, his eyes were upon me, watching me with interest. The rest of his face – perhaps he was amazed: is this the young thirty year old woman I left behind on earth, the child I knew? And he observed me. The transparent door stood between us, the door to "that Örtchen"[14] up there. It was not at all frightening. I felt happy. The transparent door stood between us, the door to "that place" up there.

And suddenly she began to panic and told many stories about her life, somewhat confused and without any connection, and ended with the following words, "*In 1942 my son was born. Shortly thereafter, I got divorced. My son was a big problem for me. I don't know if I shall ever talk about that – perhaps. It is so nice to have someone who is willing to share all this with me, to feel it all with me. I don't want to say anything about my marriage – perhaps later.*" We part. She remains behind, pensive.

Her encounter with her father was a big shock. What emotional security was taken away from her by it? It was her identification with her father,

13 Lutz Müller und Anette Müller (Hrsg.), *Wörterbuch der Analytischen Psychologie* (Düsseldorf/Zürich: Walter Verlag, 2003), pp. 455f. The vision is "like a dream, but one is awake. The vision is caused by the existence of a great tension between the unconscious and consciousness and an energetic gradient that flows from the unconscious into consciousness; then the vision erupts into consciousness as an autonomous sensory manifestation, leading to a breakdown of one's conscious attitude up to that moment, and it generates a new life direction, as it did, for example, for Saul in the New Testament who, after his vision, became Paul." (Translator)
14 "Örtchen" in German is a more colloquial word for "toilet," but it can also mean "little place." (Note by translator)

or with the fathering principle, that she later always referred to as "the construct." She had long realised this, but she had not been able to admit it. She explains that after her divorce, she had been like a father to her son, and his grandmother had been like a mother to him. That had been how she had lived from then on. It was a crazy decision with fatal consequences. Frau Suter had begun to identify with the masculine-fathering principle, thereby betraying her feminine development and her evolution as a woman. Her identity had been "derived" from her father and from the father complex, which meant she was neither real nor authentic. According to C.G. Jung, such a false identification represents a very real hindrance to individuality and it is an artificial deformity. Frau Suter is about to be confronted by this.

Initially, however, the image of her father in the dream is idealised. Frau Suter goes into raptures about it. But then the dream transforms into a vision, with a transparent door separating both of them, a door that brings brightness and light. While the previous situation was a glorification, it is now possible to actually see her father. It is not possible to have contact through glass, but one can see through it. The unconscious is revealing a division! And the toilet turns into "that Örtchen." While the word toilet is a more formal term that stands for hygiene and cleanliness, the associations to "Örtchen" are darker, not so hygienic, closer to what is instinctual and to one's drives. The "Örtchen" is also a place of dubious fantasies. Erotic and sexual fantasies occur there. What was previously dark and murky now suddenly becomes transparent. The taboo has been broken. The secret that Frau Suter had so desperately tried to uncover is briefly illuminated. The breaking of a taboo is a vital step towards becoming whole. But the secret may not be completely aired here. It is still too soon. Wounds to one's psyche are often surrounded by feelings of shame and guilt. If such experiences are dragged up into the light too quickly, old wounds are ripped open. What must be kept hidden, or what may be brought into the open, is decided by the unconscious. And in Frau Suter's case, her unconscious is being very careful!

Her father's moustache and his blue robe are attributes of the Nordic god, Odin! But where would one look to find her father's Odinic aspect? He had one! Upon returning from the war, he invited all of his past comrades-in-arms. In his kitchen, they sang and ate and celebrated. And her father sent his daughter on hikes with these men. Alone! She was thirteen, fourteen and fifteen at that time. Some of them were nice people, she said. But some were not.

These men returned from the First World War defeated. They were still infected by the war. The sinister and frightening events of the war were a part of their post-war "Odinic revelry." These were reflexes to the distress, defeats and traumas that needed to be contained within such compensatory reactions. It was the rage of the disappointed.

What it could mean for a young girl to be infected by such a frenzied atmosphere needs no elucidation here. Children are susceptible to rapture and are easily pulled into such an intoxicating atmosphere. This explains Frau Suter's shame, and her sense of disgrace that no one shared as no one understood what had actually taken place. The men had been unwittingly gripped by "the god of storm and frenzy," the "unleasher of passions and the lust of battle," this "superlative magician and artist in illusion who is versed in all secrets of an occult nature," as Jung wrote.[15] A traumatic experience has a numinous character. It is appalling, incomprehensible. Something befell the child or young woman that led to the trunk of her life tree being split in two.

In the dream vision, her father refers to "the child." This arouses the child in her soul. It is her inner child. If a child is neglected or physically abused by those in whom it has placed its trust, and upon whom it depends for love, it suffers a deep wounding. People who have been wounded in this way often reject their "inner child" for they find it dirty or revolting. But their "inner child" then awakens and asserts its right to be a part of life. This "rejected child" often leaves the person in question with a feeling of not being quite whole, of not being able to love deeply, and of not belonging in the world.

When Frau Suter tried to discover more about her secret, she probably became infected with that Odinic power, by he "who creates unrest and stirs up strife" that had come to life at the same time. Initially moved, she was then seized by this foreboding depth. "The dark, earthy, feminine side, with its... orgiastic characteristics" possessed her.[16] With her childhood dream and her fantasy of a flying carpet, she tried to escape these forces. Instead, she flew right into the hands of Odin, for Odin is the lord of longings. He is the typical spirit of magical thinking. He is the force that keeps the carpet in the air. The more Frau Suter progressed in her questionable development, the angrier she became.

---

15 C.G. Jung, "Wotan." In: *Civilization in Transition,* vol. 10 of *The Collected Works of C.G. Jung,* edited and translated by Gerhard Adler and R.F.C. Hull (New York: Panteon Books, 1964), § 373 and 375.

16 Ibid., § 375, footnote 3.

While telling me the dream, she mentioned that this was the happiest period of her life. She is protecting herself from the trauma that is threatening to destroy her. It is not yet time to identify her wounds by looking at what happened to her. No! Rather, our focus is upon her finally becoming centred within herself. Her unconscious has, in the meantime, torn down the blockades. The goal of this phase of her analysis was to get Frau Suter's life flowing again.

But she also mentions that she is missing the "construct," i.e. her identification with her father. She can no longer ride roughshod over everything, as she did in the past. She is beginning to feel things. She is starting to be moved by things, to be vulnerable. She tells me that she cannot let go of her father completely. He shaped the first six years of her life. As a child, she was her "*father's little butterfly.*" She admired her father greatly. He was a playful man with whom one could get up to all kinds of tricks. The butterfly has to do with one of her most wonderful experiences with him. She was five years old at the time. "*For example, he caught a butterfly for me with his hat. He placed his hat over it. I found it amusing. The butterfly tickled him. Then we both decided to let it go.*" This is an image of the very early erotic-sexual relationship between father and daughter, which she has not yet realized.

Frau Suter cannot yet truly comprehend and let in what is happening here. Her ego is still too weak. But the collapse of the "construct" is irreversible. Thus, she is no longer able to "*magnanimously and nonchalantly*" sweep aside any difficulty like her father used to do, and gone too is the attitude that when something goes wrong, one does not complain but says instead, "*Basically, life is wonderful.*" This way of living has now been destroyed. That period of her life casts a large shadow. But she was not simply a bad person. After the death of her father Frau Suter had to look after her mother who was in her nineties, and she had to take care of her son. She managed to do both things well.

The Transitional Space

The dreams we have discussed so far show how the unconscious led the dreamer step by step to destroy her "construct." It was a process that took place deep within her unconscious, without her having to feel threatened. It had to take place gently for Frau Suter was 93 years old at the time and extremely fragile.

She had already acknowledged the truth (see her dream, *The Father*). To look truth in the eye can wound one to the very depths of one's soul. What now followed was a period of transition. The barn in the dream became a "transitional space"[17] in order to gradually come to terms with and to accept "reality" in a playful way, before she could be confronted with the painful truth.

By 1935, C.G. Jung had already linked the analytical relationship and the realm of fantasy closely together. He writes, "I even make an effort to second the patient in his fantasies... All the works of man have their origin in creative imagination... My aim is to bring about a psychic state in which my patient begins to experiment with his own nature – a state of fluidity, change, and growth where nothing is eternally fixed and hopelessly petrified."[18] Thus, according to C.G. Jung, a person should not only develop himself, but he should also experiment with all of which he becomes conscious and try things out. And this, of course, holds true to the end of one's life.

It includes, for example, deducing "how it really was," or "how I truly am." The transitional space is a playroom in which one is free to discover a new identity. Within this space one's inner reality and one's outer life flow, and creative connections can be made between them.

The following dream leads Frau Suter into the cellar of her parent's house. To go into the cellar means to go down into one's own depths. At first, Frau Suter finds this "completely absurd." "What does that mean? What should I do down there?" In her view, the dream is completely beside the point, and has nothing to do with reality. It is as if what is taking place was not really happening. Thus, the transitional space manifests. It fuels questions being asked and fantasies being had. And Frau Suter asks herself where this giant of a man in the dream suddenly came from?

The Giant in the Cellar

I am in the cellar, in our cellar cubicle. And I see a man, a giant man, and somewhere at the back there is another man who is much smaller, and right at the back on the right is a small creature, a boy. The first

---

17 This is concept that was developed by the psychoanalyst Donald W. Winnicott. He used it to describe a space that existed between the inner and the outer world, i.e. between one's ego (me) and what is not me.

18 C.G. Jung, "The Aims of Psychotherapy." In: *The Practice of Psychotherapy*, CW 16, § 98f.

one, the hulk, the giant, has a knife in his hand, and he comes towards me, very leisurely and I am not afraid. I ask myself what I should do now? You have to kick him in his sensitive area. But I can't do it: I can't stand on one leg and do such a thing. What is going on here? I wake up, unafraid.

She is in the cellar cubicle that belongs to her parent's apartment and she encounters a giant. Giants personify affects. Why is she not afraid and frightened of such a powerful creature? Indeed, the giant does not impress her at all. It is quite unnatural to not be afraid of such a monster that, in addition, approaches one with a knife in his hand. It is not that Frau Suter does not have any feelings. On the contrary – she feels a great deal. But feelings frighten her because they make her vulnerable and defenceless. She has split off the feminine principle and thereby her personal feelings that could come to her aid in assessing this situation. Which explains her rational reaction that is cool-headed and disconnected. She does not take the giant seriously and turns him into something banal, thereby distancing herself from him.

In fairytales, giants live in forests, on a mountain or in a cave. They can easily rip trees out of the earth, and throw huge rocks into the air. "The giant is a mythological figure that represents chthonic nature, a purely natural being, against which one cannot protect oneself except by cunning" or by becoming conscious of what it means and why it is constellated.[19] Psychologically speaking, a giant is unformed emotions, for example, "enormous fear" or "enormous anger." Thus the giant in the cellar is an image of Frau Suter's anger, as well as her fear. If she realizes this, she will be able to defend herself against him.

The dream challenges her to take a closer look. It gives her a glimpse of a second, smaller man and a boy. This reveals that the giant is blocking her access to her own masculine energy. They would be masculine energies – for example, being active or setting oneself a goal. But she is not interested in the man or the boy right now. A giant is standing in front of her with a knife in his hand. This is curious, even exciting. In the dream, she wants to hurt the giant where he is sensitive. Frau Suter focuses upon this image, allows

---

19 C.G. Jung, *Children's Dreams. Notes from the Seminar given in 1936-1940 by C.G. Jung*, edited by Lorenz Jung and Maria Meyer-Grass. Translated by Ernst Falzeder with the collaboration of Tony Woolfson (Princeton/Oxford: Philemon Series, Princeton University Press, 2008), pp. 390f.

this dream scene to unfold in her fantasy and then says, *"One really cannot stand on one leg. It won't work."* Where is the problem? She does not dare to do him any injury where he is vulnerable. She is afraid to attack and offers the excuse: one cannot stand on one leg. To stand on one leg would indeed be possible, but her instincts are buried and her thoughts therefore block her spontaneity. And so she does not do it!

A knife means differentiation, becoming conscious, cutting away the veil of illusion. And this means becoming conscious of the fact that she does not have the courage to overcome the giant, i.e. to overcome her problem. A different strategy is needed. And that would be to react spontaneously. The giant is the anger she refuses to give in to, out of fear of hurting other people.

After having this dream, Frau Suter begins to be interested in the fate of her son who is dealing with the consequences of an earlier accident. She had felt hardly any emotion at the time of his accident. But now it is important to her that she finds out what she can do for him. She finds out more about his accident and reads a brochure with the title "Brain Damage from the Standpoint of the Brain-damaged." In any event, she must be more loving towards him. This new way of speaking about her son is very moving. She now allows herself to recognize someone in pain who gets pleasure from small gestures. She realizes that he is inwardly more independent than she is. She has become more considerate. She decides to alter her will. It is no longer appropriate. She will rip it up and write a new one.

The two other male beings in her cellar dream now become important. She repeatedly asks herself what they could represent. She has not yet understood. She will have to give it more thought. They would be a form of masculine strength that could help her to be courageous and to overcome the giant in some clever way.

A year has now passed. I meet Frau Suter on her way to the cafeteria. She is very excited. She needs a coffee. Then she tells me her dream. In the dream she is in a room where one wall no longer exists. The telephone rings. A female friend of hers answers the phone. *"And suddenly I hear the word 'buried'."* The dream has to do with a time *"of much rain and many floods."* She gave a lot of thought to the dream and then decided to tell it to me. She is struck by the word "buried." It has got to do with an everyday situation that must have been very bad. Something must have been broken, destroyed, died.

Frau Suter cannot be calmed down. She chatters on randomly about animals, research and technology. And finally she says we really must meet in her room next time. It is better to meet there. She can speak more freely there. She hopes she will live for many more years to savour all of this! We meet two weeks later. She is different. She has low blood pressure and feels weak. But she should be happy she is as well as she is. She had a momentary dream that she would like to tell me about. In this dream she is inside a circular structure and above her, through a window, she sees a large courtyard in which a very young man is standing, somewhat elevated. She is astonished and cries out in the dream, *"Who is that? Who is this man? How can I get up there?"* She sees a man the likes of which she has never seen before.

Frau Suter says she would like to know if she has, perhaps, met this man before somewhere without realizing it. Her ex-husband comes to mind. But there is no problem in this regard. They have made their peace with each other. She ponders on "the butterfly" that she once was for her father, on other childhood memories. This leads her to realize that men have played a greater role in her life than women. The latter have somehow always been a problem for her. She was often reproached for being too masculine. Nowadays, it hurts her to think about this for she thinks of herself as being feminine. Back then, she lived within her "construct" and was certainly often unfeeling and cold. The second man and the young boy in her dream are now coming to her aid. They represent different, softer masculine qualities.

In reflecting on her life, she realises that somehow she still misses not having the security of her "construct." And then she asks me, *"Do you know the fairytale "Kalif, the Stork" in which Kalif, together with his grand vizier, want to know what his people think of him and so, with the help of a magic word, both he and his grand vizier are transformed into storks and together they wander through his realm and experience a great deal. Then, one day they have to say a certain magic word to be able to become humans again. And I had to think about what this magic word might be for at least an hour as I could no longer recall it …. Sometimes one forgets a magic word, and it is wonderful when it comes back to one."* She asks if I would like to know the magic word? She tells me *"It is Mutabor."*[20] And she smiles at me, with a chuckle, pleased with herself.

She is able to identify with the images and symbols in this fairytale. This is a chance to find entry to something that cannot be spoken. She begins to understand that at some decisive point in her life she did something

20 Wilhelm Hauff, *Sämtliche Märchen*, ed. by Hans-Heino Ewers (Stuttgart: Reclam-Jun., 1986).

that channelled her life in a direction over which she had no control. She
was convinced she did it consciously. But now she is finding out that this
was not true: what she did was simply crazy. And the consequences weigh
heavily upon her. This is a creative, indeed, a masterly achievement. Frau
Suter confesses that after the death of her father she had had the chance to
change her life. But at the time she had not wanted to.

These reflections illustrate how Frau Suter playfully approaches difficult
experiences in her "dream barn." First came the magic word. She had had
to think long and hard about it. Finally, it came to her. She stuck with it.
She gave it her best effort. She was truly creative. The masculine principle is
evolving within her. It demonstrates in this instance that it is able to translate her inner images and ideas into words, to help them manifest in reality.
Her ponderings give her a brief glimpse into the mysterious unknown, her
personal animus. She longs for him, longs to encounter him once again. He
is standing behind a window. A pane of glass separates her from him on a
feeling level. But her heart is moved.

Frau Suter now reads a lot, reflects, and tries to understand. She tells me
that her eyes are slowly being opened. She has often read, "Peter Schlemihls wundersame Geschichte."[21] But it is only now that she realizes it is
important to have a shadow. Of Hesse's works, her favourite is "Hours in
the Garden."[22] In this book he describes his impressions and thoughts. He
wrote many beautiful poems. But this is her favourite work of his.

Lately, she has not avoided having contact with people. She has found
herself having "little chats" with people. She is actually quite shy about
having contact and sometimes she is afraid of people. Man is also a beast.
If she sees a large group of people, she flees if she can. It is not because she
despises people. Rather, it is because she is afraid of people. Wrestling with
her life and realising that she was often *"on the wrong track"* gnaws at her
health. Frau Suter is repeatedly ill with a high temperature, or intestinal
flue, or a cold. She vomits bile. This shows that her body is caught up in the
changes and transformation she is undergoing.

She is astonished to realize that even when she is not thinking about
it, life goes on within her nevertheless. That is an amazing and wonderful
thing. Indeed, one is always somehow in life's debt. Now it is time to let go

21 Adalbert von Chamisso, "Peter Schlemihls Wundersame Geschichte," in: Herbert
   Eulenberg (ed.), *Chamisso, Ausgewählte Werke* (Leipzig: Reclam, no date.), vol. 2, pp.
   299-359.
22 Hermann Hesse, *Hours in the Garden* (New York: Farrar, Straus & Giroux, 1979).

and to connect to something greater than she. Lately she has a sense of there being a religious element in her dreams. And now she feels God through her body. She feels safe.

Her new attitude is also reflected in a dream. A short while later Frau Suter dreams of a staircase made out of silvery wood. Her new attitude reflects a feminine force that has the potential to develop new abilities or aspects out of the potential that is there. In contrast to the "construct" that had something arrogant and cocky about it, the wood of the staircase is a material capable of undergoing great transformation, one that can age and rot. It is an image of the temporal, an experience that alters how she feels about her life. She says, "Frau Koch, in the last few months I have aged years, in what I feel, and in my body, in everything that troubles me." The old woman that she is at ninety-four now emerges.

And the silver? It represents the moon that is in constant flux. As an image of the feminine principle it points towards feminine values. And these are the very qualities she now feels within herself. She says, "Perhaps I have found my femininity, or I feel happy about my femininity. Who knows? Its texture was so fine, one wanted to continually run one's hand over it." This is her feminine instinct, her refined feelings, her sensuality and her emotional spontaneity that follows intuitions and the subtlest of inspirations. Furthermore, silver is a soft metal that melds easily. Perhaps she will succeed in connecting with other people and allow herself to be inspired by them. Her dreams have led Frau Suter to her sensuality. She is happy.

She tells me she is coming to have a feeling about life that is not so loaded with problems. But she still has so many unanswered questions. She needs to think about how to go on, what wants to happen? Frau Suter is happy to be able to talk about her problems. Our talks are important to her. Through them, she is learning how to talk about her thoughts and feelings. It is important to her that I understand her. She is now talking to her son. Her son was so frightened of her as a child. When he told her this, she was shattered. Now, she is gradually able to let him go, to set him free, but not without feeling pain at realizing how she let him down as a mother. She is developing compassion for him. She is able to make peace inwardly with her ex-husband. She explains, "*I now feel that I did truly love him. I used to be so angry. But what was has now faded. It has been a long journey. That these feelings have been able to mature, to take on another form, is simply wonderful. I have been chewing over these things for years. But now it feels as if it was worth it. Now I can once again recall all the good times."*

These are a few of the insights that shape her life, that allow it to really become what it is. Frau Suter is opening up, talking about things and she is enjoying it. And there is another new thing: lately, she has allowed herself to be "grumpy." It is a strange experience for her to quickly lose her temper, to lose patience and no longer have the strength to be more disciplined with herself. She can no longer brush things aside with a smile. This shows how the "construct" is "melting," little by little. It is a slow process that she describes as being *"an ambivalence between feeling responsible and trying to sneak out of taking responsibility."* This is sometimes difficult.

When Frau Suter opens the door to me after three and a half years, she appears to be deep in thought, and not at all how she usually opens the door – either cheerfully, or sometimes deeply angry and dissatisfied. What does this introspection and stillness mean? What is going on within her? I sit down on "my chair" and she tells me that in her dream she saw Rapunzel up in her tower.[23] And she could see her long plait and how the prince had to climb up it. She could really feel how it must have pulled on her scalp. It pulled so hard she had to lean forward.

And then she said, *"I am a Rapunzel!"* By this, she meant "I, too, have a destiny. I am a woman with the same destiny!" The mysterious stranger that she saw for the first time in the round construction and for whom she had such a deep longing has appeared. He must climb up to her. And he does so. She physically feels how he does it. It is her inner man, her animus. He is her inner guide, an inner attitude that is there to help her build a bridge between consciousness and the creative source of the unconscious.

The fairytale of Rapunzel could be an image of Frau Suter's relationship to her mother. In the fairytale, the mothering aspect is revealed to be a jealous sorceress who has her daughter completely under her control, and who tries to destroy her relationships. In the relationship between Frau Suter and her mother there was also distance and rejection that her mother rendered void by filling her daughter with guilt. Perhaps it was this shadow aspect of the mothering aspect or of the feminine aspect that whispered to her at the time, "Divorce is the only right thing to do. You will never be able to trust this man." Frau Suter does not see this yet. But her loyalty to her mother is being put into question!

---

23 See *The Complete Grimm's Fairy Tales* (New York/Toronto: The Pantheon Fairy Tale & Folklore Library, 1972), nr. 12, pp. 73-76.

She explains how desperate she had felt. And as she had many times before, she mentions a fairytale. *"Do you know the fairytale of the poor girl who has to sell matchsticks? It is cold. It is evening and the child should return home. But she has sold nothing. So she takes a whole bundle of matches and lights them and warms her hands with them. At that moment she needed them."*[24] She was describing to me how alone she had felt and how cold her life had been. But now she feels compassion towards herself and towards her suffering.

And she sums up her insights by saying, *"When things got too much for me, it was a kind of escape, an escape in order to survive and to find my way back to something positive again. I was so removed and alone with all that was not resolved within me. I simply wanted to put some distance between me and the world. It was the sort of isolation that was meant to protect me. But perhaps it is the isolation that everyone feels."* In a certain sense she was an orphan who lacked parental care and love. And as a consequence, she sometimes seemed "arrogant" and unapproachable to her fellow human beings.

The prince is pulling on her hair. Her animus is pushing into her life. She had so often lacked courage and decisiveness. There had always been this paralysing fear. And C.G. Jung once defined the animus of a woman as, "knowing what one wants and doing what is necessary to achieve it."[25] But the prince brings a whole new dynamic and vitality into her life. And her carpet has disappeared! She can no longer flee in her dreams to her magic carpet. At first, she is greatly disappointed – even angry – about this. Her carpet had always been her salvation. She had suffered so greatly at the hands of evil. Now, however, she can no longer flee to the realm of fantasy. She will have to face her conflicts. And they will come. When she is bitter, she will just have to bear feeling that way.

Her time in the "space of transition" is coming to an end. Here the two divided worlds could come together. A connection between her inner world and the real world outside has been established. Hope and trust are present. Much is now possible. It is as if life can now once again be lived.

More than four years have passed. In front of me now sits a mature woman. Her adolescence has yielded. She wears her hair tied back in a little ponytail. It gives her a serious, calm appearance. Her gaze is calm, concentrated. She feels she is indebted to many people. She hopes people

24 "The Little Match Girl," in: Hans Christian Andersen, *The Complete Fairy Tales and Stories*, © 1974 by Erik Christian Haugaard (First Anchor Books, 1983), pp. 306-308.
25 C.G. Jung, "Woman in Europe." In: *Civilisation in Transition*, CW 10, § 260.

will forgive her. Up until now, she has never felt grateful to the other people in the home. That has now changed. She is now grateful to the people who look after her – very grateful, indeed.

The Path into the World

She is "Lebens-müde" – tired of life. She eats very little, seems preoccupied and a little lost. In the first dream she has in this new phase of her life, Frau Suter sees a bed with a very strange mattress. An oval shape has been worked into the middle of it into which everything that happens can fit. One could think of it as being *"one of those things that has to do with burials."* But what should be buried there?

A mattress is a symbol of sexuality, birth and death. The oval space hints at something mysterious that she could now get to the bottom of. That she has an uncanny feeling is understandable. Many people appear in her dream. She is able to see how they enjoy each other's company. She is reminded of scenes in her parent's kitchen. A very deep change is being hinted at here. The "secret" should finally be dealt with, the trauma that she has repressed up until now. Only then will the way be clear for new possibilities in her life; only then will she be really able to live.

Barely has she finished telling me the dream when Frau Suter looks at me searchingly and says, *"I have thought of you so often. It's lovely you are here."* She is suddenly very lively and says very decidedly, *"And there is another dream. I have been having the same image for a long time."* She has had this dream at least a dozen times. *"And I was always wondering about it, and asking myself why. I didn't want to tell it to you, but that seems silly now. I have to tell it to you."* The moment has come for her to recall what happened. She wants to know – and she tells me the dream which I am repeating exactly as she told it to me.

The Abuse

I see myself lying there with a broken skull and various parts of me are kaput, my hands are scraped, I see myself lying there, somewhere, and everyone is here, those who I am referring to, the scent of fir tree branches is put over my face, hitting me, and of course sticking the pine needles into my face and into my feet, and it happens again and again. I am surprised and ask myself, "Why?"

In this dream, memories of the abuse she suffered return. Initially, it is an image that leads to the pain she had suffered. Then she feels the physical pain so acutely it is as if she were still that girl who suffered being abused. And she is meant to smell it again, experience it again with her senses, with these fir tree branches. She *"liked the scent very much, the resinous, herby smell."* She relives this traumatic experience at least a dozen times. She repeatedly wonders, "Why? Why?" She wakes up as her body is in so much pain. And then she thinks, *"What has happened to the child? Mothers normally always look after them."* But this was not the case with her. She remained loyal to her mother her entire life long, until her mother died. But her mother had not always been loyal to her. She knew this, but now she feels it. And it is difficult to bear.

The dreadful hitting that happens in the dream must apparently take place for her to realize what happened – so that she can be free of it! It is a kind of purgatory. Frau Suter now takes in what had happened to her. It becomes a part of who she is. Her suffering had forced her to become so withdrawn she could no longer feel who she was. The petrified realms of experience within her are now becoming accessible. It was a matter of her being able to once again be at home within her own body and in the world. The joy of life she had once felt, the energy she had once had, the vitality that had once been hers before she had this traumatic experience should all come back to life. For her story had basically stopped at the point where the trauma took place.

Only now can she share with me why she decided to get divorced. She tells me that after the birth of her son, her husband demanded to have a paternity test done as he suspected she had been unfaithful. Her mother, whom she thought would offer her support in this difficult situation, sided with her husband. She reproached her with being reckless, and accused her of having had many affairs. Frau Suter's world collapsed. She felt humiliated and betrayed by both of them. So she immediately demanded a divorce. And from that point onwards, she had been a father to her son. Her jealous mother had used her husband's distrust against her, and bound Frau Suter to her forever.

And the process continues. In one of her next dreams, Frau Suter encounters a white dog that draws itself up and barks at her furiously. She asks herself why the dog is barking at her. They know each other, after all. It is probably a dog she knows from her childhood. At that time, the dog was her loyal companion and friend. This dog represents being faithful, being

connected to human beings, loyalty, attachment as well as a connection to
the realm of animals. This encounter once again puts Frau Suter in touch
with her childhood when her instincts and feelings were still alive within
her, before she became petrified. Her new self-awareness enables her to confront her secret. Up until now she has tried to undo the abuse she suffered.
Distancing herself in this manner helped her to bear the unbearable. But
now the unconscious reveals the secret. She dreams the following – once
again not just once but many times:

The Secret
I am lying across something and a mob of people is having a party in
the room I am in and they hit me with branches of a fir tree. It is a sort
of ritual. They were giving me a beating. I was not naked, but undressed,
with only a nightdress on. And it was a huge party with all these male
people, and some women, but not all of them were recognizable, and
above all, not nameable. And it was strange; immediately afterwards I
was confused.

After telling me the dream, she cried out loudly, *"He abused me. I had to tell
it again. It is like a confession."* She allows herself to have her feelings and
gives herself over to her memories and to the emotions that are welling up
within her. And then she confides in me who had abused her; *"It was one of
my father's comrade-in-arms."* Her father had *"lent"* her to one of his friends.

Frau Suter had protected herself her whole life long by letting her
memories of the abuse she had suffered disappear by drawing a veil of
forgetfulness over them. She felt the only way to recover would be to undo
the past. This is impossible. In order to be healed, Frau Suter had to relive
what had happened.

It was an event that had severe consequences. *"This happened four or five
times in the dream. This is too important to forget. It was dreadful. It was 22nd
December. When I say it to you, it is as if I am also saying it to myself. It could also
be because of the fear of stepping over this threshold again. It was like a death. What
will the last chapter be like?"* She has faith that life could go on. Initially, it is a
true liberation – to face it, to accept it as a part of one's life, of one's identity.
This is how the unconscious helps her to overcome the abuse she suffered.
It does so in a dreamed ceremony with ritualistic acts, with a rite of passage.

Once again, fir tree branches are used. This is because it happened
shortly before Christmas. Every child looks forward to Christmas, to the

Christmas tree with its candles and coloured balls. And where light should have entered her life came darkness instead. This darkness overshadowed her almost to the end of her life. She felt completely lost. Her father was no longer her protector. The child could not go to her mother. Both parents played a role in the abuse, even if it was only the father who took an active part.

Being abused by the masculine is a thread that runs through Frau Suter's entire life. But now it has ended. She is *"wilting."* That is a good word to describe her state. And she sings the song of the Lorelei. "Lorelei" is the name of the legendary mermaids who, through their beautiful singing while combing their long golden hair, bring about shipwrecks for the seamen can no longer focus on their route through the dangerous currents and their vessels are shattered on rocky reefs. This song reveals a side of her that the masculine principle also abused. She had been a woman who enjoyed life. Indeed, she had been alluring to men. She can accept this now. She feels truly liberated.

She is very happy that I am going to see her again, that she may be in my company once again. She truly thought that now I knew everything, I would abandon her. For me as her therapist, this was a very moving, even unforgettable moment in our relationship. Relieved and happy, she confided in me that she no longer flew off the handle with people. She was able to remain very calm. She now has her anger under control and she is proud of it. She now lives in tune with her animal-vegetative nature. She is enjoying this and even finds it exciting sometimes. Will she surrender to her life and her fate? Or is something brewing beneath the surface? The serenity that she is trying to portray to me does not seem completely genuine. Something is off. Christmas is almost here. Hesitatingly, she confesses to me that she is dreadfully afraid of being beaten again in her dreams. But she knows she must keep moving forwards.

We meet again only in the New Year. Frau Suter has regained her composure; she seems lively and confident. She celebrated Christmas deeply within herself. It was lovely. She was not beaten again. It is over, finally, really and truly over.

The Search for One's Soul

The final chapter now begins. She wonders if she is still alive because she needs more time to digest everything, not swallow it whole. It is as if she is putting together the pieces of a puzzle. She does nothing other than turn over these last details again and again within herself. But things have been clarified. This mulling over things is more defined. It is no longer about forgetting or trying to undo things. It helps her to understand her life. It is a transition into an experience. In her dreams, she is working through the individual chapters of her life. It is always the same dream and yet it is always different. And at the end of the dream she sees a strange clock that wakes her up.

Indeed, a lot now appears to be different. Frau Suter realises that she did not marry to have a partnership. She wanted a child. This was the driving force. She made herself feel guilty. But it was not all her fault. She is turning into someone else. During this transformation, she dreams of municipal buildings that she had dreamt of much earlier in her life (see *The Dream of Old Age* above). But now these buildings have life in them. Many people are in them. And there is a lift in each building. The lift signifies a new level of experience being reached in her life. Who does she meet while she is in the lift? Does she go up or down in the lift? Perhaps it will occasionally get stuck. It represents the highs and lows of life that we do not always have under our control.

In retrospect, one could interpret the order in her first dream "to go into the corners" as a description of her path to find herself that would lead her through the labyrinth of her trauma. This path led Frau Suter back to her own experience of her body and to her feelings that had been split off. Whoever has suffered trauma knows the paralysing fear that also includes the feeling of being utterly lost in the world and of being robbed of one's own soul. This is now coming to an end in Frau Suter's life. But there is still one more very important dream that brings about a further release.

The Mountain of Fire

Fire is being spewed out of a mountain. Everything is flying out and everything is burning all around it. And in a certain area, if you go a certain way, smoke and flames are coming out of a crack. And then the earth shakes again.

Frau Suter says of this that it is an eruption of repressed anger. This anger that has been turned inwards underscores her paralysing fear, her passivity and her tendency to become resigned to things. Because she was afraid that she might hurt others (or herself), she flew around on her magic carpet to keep these feelings at a distance and to repress them, even before she herself could even feel them. But now this anger has dissolved itself into smoke. It went down very deep. It is a final upheaval, a decisive inner transformation. Odin does indeed come to mind. Very likely, Frau Suter was truly infected at the time when, with all the power of her secret, the trauma she had suffered, she had tried to tell what had happened to her. Now her anger is dying down. After this dream, her anger disappeared and never returned.

A short while later, a Japanese girl appeared to her in a dream. She was around twelve years old. Is this girl the girl she used to be? It returns. It was a lovely but puzzling experience. Now all is as it was before the abuse took place. Frau Suter feels healed and whole.

She is convinced that behind everything that happened in her life was an imp. This is how she describes it. When she now "hurtles" through all that happened to her in her life, she realizes that this imp was involved in all of it. He shows her how she did things that she should never have done. He shows her where she did not relent but where she should have relented. Well, one is always wiser in retrospect. That is just how it is. But now she is in control of this imp. He can no longer influence her from behind!

This imp brings back her vitality. This inner imp throws the dice and puts her life back together in a new way. He goes ahead, looks back and thereby links the wisdom of the future with the innocence of her child-hood. He dissolves all one-sidedness and softens what has become hard. He brings excitement back into her life. This imp facilitates "flexibility, creativity, thinking intuitively, tolerance and the ability to take criticism," writes William Willeford.[26] He represents an unconventional way of behaving that she needs to accept, that she needs to come to terms with. C.G. Jung thought of the imp as being an opposing tendency of the unconscious that "constantly breaks the consolidation of collective consciousness and thus keeps the door open for the influx of new creative contents.[27] He introduces fresh ideas and new energies.

It is impossible to pin down an imp. Perhaps we could say that now, in her great old age, he is an image of the redeeming factor in Frau Suter herself that has been pushing her towards individuation. He is that part of her – innocent and yet somehow knowing – that leads her towards self-knowledge. She tells me that the imp wants her to accept herself just as

26 Quoted by Gert Sauer, www.opus-magnum.de
27 Marie-Louise von Franz, *Creation Myths. Patterns of Creativity mirrored in Creation Myths* (Dallas: Spring Publications, 1972), p. 64.

she is. She is working on it. She offers me her imp. She no longer needs him. She hopes he will give me good thoughts – but also that he will sometimes fool me. And she laughs wholeheartedly. The imp should be a reminder to me of all the funny and unexpected things we have experienced together.

Indeed, in our relationship, she has been able to talk about some things in her life that she could never have done elsewhere. It has been so nice to be led. The sentence "Except ye become as little children, ye shall not enter the kingdom of heaven" now becomes important to her. One searches for God too much on the outside and He gets covered with pomp and words. God is within. She has understood that now. You cannot experience Him with your head, only with your feelings.

Now she is reclaiming her lost childhood – as it really was, with both shadow and sunshine! Now and again she has dreams that are preparing her for death. She succeeds in bringing early strengths back to life, and in connecting again to the person she was before the trauma. She regularly tells me of episodes from her childhood and youth that she now remembers and that were important to her. I should note them down. This heals the scar. This is how she wins back her life, her soul, in which the trauma becomes a faded memory of the past.

It was very difficult for her to accept that her mother had betrayed her, a betrayal that had profound consequences. Nevertheless, she found a place for her in her soul. There was reconciliation. This could not happen with her father. Too much had been destroyed. One can live with envy and jealousy. But there can be no reconciliation with abuse.

It is time for me to end. I was only able to present a small segment from a moving, difficult life story. Frau Suter lived another year. And then *"the circle of this life on earth closed."* She had the fantasy of becoming a star in the sky after death. I should look up occasionally. She would send me messages from above.

Epilogue

Together, Frau Suter and I experienced great steps forward, but also many steps backwards, and a great deal of desperation. As humans, we cannot avoid making the same mistakes again and again. If we know this, we can later recognize the dangers and weaknesses that lurk within us, and we can grow and mature because of them. At bottom, no one can avoid his or her fate. Very often old people think nothing matters any longer, their lives are no longer important. This is wrong. Every individual is important and has to walk his own individual path.

It is as if old age both supports and helps us to become authentic. Somehow, this has to do with dying. The more authentic I am, the more I am myself, which in turn helps me to accept my own mortality, but not, of course, without a little melancholy. Departing is natural: it is in accord with nature. The simple fact is, man is mortal.[28]

28 Translated from the German by Alison Kappes-Bates, Wädenswil, Switzerland.

Rudolf Högger

The Treasure Vase

On the many-sided Symbolism of an Archaic God-Image from the Stone Age to the Dreams of Modern Man

Prologue: How the Topic of this Presentation came to me

A few years ago, I was given the opportunity to participate in the initiation ceremony of Somi, a seven year old Hindu boy in Nepal. The festive occasion turned out to be a great personal experience for me. It opened my eyes to countless rituals and symbols, the meanings of which – at that moment – were unknown to me. Looking back, however, I gradually realize what treasures of the human soul presented themselves in the gestures and images of that ceremony and how meaningful these cultural riches can prove to be even for Western people. This is what I want to speak about today.

Somi's initiation ceremony lasted for about five hours, and it was one of its culminating moments when the father bestowed the "Sacred Thread" upon his son (picture 1). In the Hindu tradition, this thread is considered "the outward and visible symbol of the *Sūtrātman*, the Thread-spirit, on which all the individual existences in the universe are strung like gems, and by which all are inseparably linked to their source."[1] In other words, it is by

---

1 Explanatory footnote by Ananda K. Coomaraswamy in: Heinrich Zimmer, *Myths and Symbols in Indian Art and Civilization* (Princeton: Princeton University Press, 1974), p. 183. For more details see Rudolf Högger, *The Sacred Thread. The Development of Personality according to Hindu Traditions and Jungian Psychology* (Kathmandu: Vajra Books, 2014), pp. 30/31.

the Sacred Thread that Somi, from now on, would be connected with all other living beings and with the transcendent origin of his own Self.

Picture 1: Somi receives the Sacred Thread

Another prominent symbol marking Somi's initiation ceremony was the "treasure vase" (see plate 10, p. 234). It appeared in various shapes, mostly as a clay or copper vessel decorated with lucky symbols (e.g. with a *svastika*) and let a bouquet of leaves and flowers grow out of its narrow neck. Altogether, it seemed to express joy, growth, wealth and abundance. In Nepal and India, it is often referred to as *pūrṇa kalaśa* (sanskr.): "The vase of inexhaustible treasures."

At first sight, the symbols of the Sacred Thread and the Treasure Vase seem to have little in common. It is only now, at the end of an exciting journey of research and discovery, that I realize how closely the two are related. In the last part of this work, I shall come back to this important relationship and shall try to interpret it. But this will be possible only after we have drawn closer to the many-sided symbolism of the treasure vase. Therefore, I invite the reader to accompany me on the above mentioned journey and to jointly discover, perhaps for personal benefit as well, some of the jewels contained in it.

1. A Symbol linking different Cultures

Thanks to many earlier visits and observations in Nepal and India, I had already been familiar – to a certain extent at least – with the exterior appearance of the *pūrṇa kalaśa* even before I was given the chance to attend Somi's initiation ceremony. Thus, I had often noticed treasure vases painted at the doors of traditional Newari[2] houses in Kathmandu or Patan. According to informations of the inhabitants, they had been created at the occasion of a wedding taking place at the respective house and were supposed to bring good luck. Also, a wooden window frame, recently carved by a Newari craftsman according to ancient Newari tradition, was set by Somi's parents into the facade of their modern home. I had always admired this piece of craftsmanship whenever I had been a guest there (picture 2).

Picture 2: A treasure vase carved into a window frame

The salient features of the classic treasure vase as depicted by the Newars are modelled on the traditional Indian clay water pot with a flat base, round body, narrow neck and fluted upper rim[3]. There are leaves and flowers rising from its neck, but also broad leaves flowing from the rim downward. All these elements suggest an overflowing fullness of life and wealth which

2 The Newars constitute a segment of the Nepali population characterized mainly by their Tibeto-Urmese language. More than any other group, the Newars have shaped the culture of the Kathmandu Valley over the past centuries.

3 For more details see Robert Beer, *The Encyclopedia of Tibetan Symbols and Motifs* (Boston: Shambhala Publications, 1999), pp. 181ff.

seems to be originating in the vessel's body. Moreover, if the vase is placed on a lotus pedestal, as depicted in picture 2, the sacred character of the *pūrṇa kalaśa* is emphasised. It obviously represents much more than a simple folkloristic "lucky symbol."

When I began to trace the treasure vase not only in Nepal, but also on the adjoining northern and southern territories of Tibet and India, I realized that I was confronted with a symbol that clearly has no cultural delimitations. The *pūrṇa kalaśa*, both under its folkloristic and its sacred aspect, seems to be omnipresent in almost every cultural area of Asia and Europe. I discovered treasure vases that were painted in the most colourful manner on the walls of Buddhist cave temples in Western Tibet around one thousand years ago.[4] Equally lively and colourful appears the treasure vase on a Tibetan New Year's greeting card which I came across in a Patan Book shop (picture 3). And during my travels in India, I discovered many "flower pots" painted or modelled in clay on the walls of Indian village or town houses (picture 4).[5]

Picture 3: Tibetan New Year's greeting card

4   Namgyal Phuntsok, *Donggar Cave Murals in Ngari Prefecture* (Beijing: 1998).
5   These "flower pots" remind me of similar motifs found among the "sgraffiti" in the Canton of Grisons (Switzerland) or on marriage chests in many rural areas of Europe.

Picture 4: A treasure vase with birds

What, then – so I asked myself again and again –, is the secret power of a motif that is capable to touch the religious feelings of nomadic tribes in the Transhimalaya as well as those of sedentary farmers in the plains of India? What could be the meaning of a symbol which appeals both to Buddhists and Hindus and which has also found its place in the Christian culture of the European Alps? And above all: What was the significance of the treasure vases which were prepared for Somi's initiation and which adorned the sacred space within which the various rituals took place?

2. The Origin and Development of an archaic God-Image

Searching for answers, I was led back into the early period of Buddhist art and architecture, i.e. into the centuries just before and after the beginning of the Christian era. Around that time, the wonderful stone relief depicted in picture 5 was created. It shows a lush bouquet of lotus bulbs, lotus flowers, lotus leaves and lotus seedcases emerging from a round vessel, conveying an impression of growth, bloom and wholeness, contained and protected in a circle. In my eyes, the image, in all its simplicity, unfolds such an intensity that I cannot simply register it as a piece of art merely caused by the circumstances of time and culture. I am compelled to assume that it is of an archetypal nature. In other words: What the image mirrors is not only the beauty of plants; it reflects the beauty of the human soul as well, and thus becomes a symbol of psychic liveliness and creativity.

Picture 5: *Pūrṇa kalaśa* from the Stupa Nr. II in Sanchi (India)

The relief was found in Sanchi, one of the oldest Buddhist sanctuaries in Central India, world famous for the so-called Big Stupa (see plate 11a, p. 235). Jung was deeply moved by it and talks about its significance in his Memories.[6] The stupa presents itself to the visitor as an impressive hill covered by stone slabs and containing – according to Buddhist tradition – some relics of the Buddha. At the summit, a stone railing marks the sacred enclosure from which arises a triple parasol, ancient Indian emblem of royal power and authority. A paved footpath for meditating pilgrims encircles the stupa. It is protected by a massive stone railing, while broad stairs lead up to a second ambulatory pathway allowing for additional circumambulations. The access to this footpath is provided by four massive gateways (*toraṇas*) which mark the cardinal points. Their pillars and lintels are decorated with

6 Aniela Jaffé (ed.), *Memories, Dreams, Reflections by C.G. Jung* (London: Fontana, 1995), pp. 308f.

an unbelievable wealth of sculptured scenes and motifs from the Buddha's life.

During the early Buddhist centuries, Gautama, the Awakened-One, was never pictured in human form, but symbolically only.[7] On the sculptured *toraṇas* of Sanchi, he appears – among others – in the form of a parasol, a wheel, a throne, a tree or a stupa venerated by devotees. Also, and not surprisingly, he is represented as *pūrṇa kalaśa*. Plate 11b (p. 235) provides an example for this. The uppermost achitrave of the Northern Gate leading to the stupa is supported by two massive stone blocks adorned by treasure vases. Here, in addition to the lotus buds and flowers, the seedcases in the centre of the blossoms are given special prominence.

There can be no doubt: the motif of the treasure vase is much older than Buddhism. Most probably, the Buddhist sculptors borrowed it from ancient traditions and used it as a symbol for the Master because – as we shall see in a moment – the treasure vase had always expressed the mystery of divine creativity with which people were familiar. Thus, it may be assumed that the traditional forms of devotion towards that creative force governing the cosmos was transferred – together with the image of the treasure vase – onto the Enlightened-One, especially onto the mystery of his spiritual birth. Such a transfer testifies of the liveliness and spiritual fulfilment which the Buddha, as the harbinger of new possibilities of psychic development, was able to generate in the people of his time through his conduct and teaching.[8]

Our assumption, according to which the symbolism of divine creativity traditionally associated with the treasure vase was transferred upon the Buddha, must be further substantiated. For this, we turn to another type of symbol appearing on several gates of the Great Stupa. It is a female figure, larger than any other sculpture adorning the *toraṇas,* and she is placed most prominently, always in pairs, just below the left and the right end of the first lintel; she is not – as are almost all remaining figures – put in high relief, but is modelled in full round plasticity (see plate 12, p. 236).

The figure represents a *Śālabhañjikā,* "one who is shaking a tree," and she has played a key role in the history of Indian art throughout the past

---

7 The same holds true in the case of Christ during the early centuries of the Christian era.

8 For more details see Hans Wolfgang Schumann, *Die grossen Götter Indiens. Grundzüge von Hinduismus und Buddhismus* (München: Diederichs, 1996), pp. 203/204, also Heinrich Zimmer, *Philosophies of India* (New Delhi: Motilal Banarsidass, 1990), p. 20.

two thousand years.[9] Interpreting her posture and her gestures will be facilitated if we seek inspiration from folk customs practiced even today in remote areas of the country. There, in spring, young women would follow the ritual habit of embracing a tree with one of their arms – in exactly the same way as depicted on the *toraṇa*. With the other arm they would grasp one of the twigs bearing flowers and fruit, while with their heel they would vigorously kick the stem. The ritual aims at stimulating the tree's life sap and at promoting its bloom. At the same time, the young woman intends to partake in the rising strength and fertility of the plant. According to the world view governing such a ritual, all living beings – plants, animals, humans – are born and sustained by a single divine energy allowing them to interact and to support each other.

It is this concept of divine origin and creativity that links the figure of the *Śālabhañjikā* with the treasure vase. Their relatedness can be observed in many reliefs and statues originating from the early centuries of Buddhist art. As an example, we choose a sculpture from Mathurā, not too far from Sanchi, depicting a beautiful young woman who is clothed only in the adornment of rich ornaments (see plate 13 and picture 6). Whether the statue was ordered by a Buddhist or a Hindu patron is not known; both are possible. For centuries, this beautiful lady had been present in all parts of India and had been described and revered as goddess "Abundance" (*Śrī Lakṣmi*).[10] The analogies between her and the lady "Shaking the Tree" are striking. In our example, the goddess of abundance brings into focus – both with her eyes and her hands, her breasts and her sex – her divine capacity to create and to sustain life, as if this should be stressed. She stands on two lotus seedcases which – together with lotus buds and flowers – grow out of a round vessel. On the back of the statue (see right hand part of picture 6), this dense, lush web of plants unfolds from bottom to top and is enriched with a pair of peacocks courting each other.

9   The liveliness and sensuality of such female figures can easily be traced back to more ancient representations of so called *yakṣīs*, i.e. water or tree divinities which were venerated throughout India long before the advent of the Aryans. Today, similar figures adorn almost every Hindu or Jain temple. For more details see Ananda K. Coomaraswamy, *Yakṣas*, parts I and II (New Delhi: Munshiram Manoharlal, 1980).

10 Heinrich Zimmer, *The Art of Indian Asia. Its Mythology and Transformations*, vol. 2 (Princeton: Princeton University Press, 1960), plates 74 and 75, as well as Ananda K. Coomaraswamy, *Yakṣas*, parts I and II, (New Delhi: Munshiram Manoharlal, 1980), plate 49.

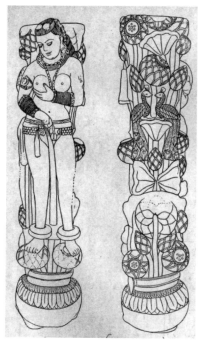

Picture 6: Statue of the goddess "Abundance" from Mathurā, front and back

In current literature, figures like the *Śālabhañjikā* of Sanchi or *Śrī Lakṣmi* of Mathurā are often interpreted as reminiscences of ancient fertility cults. This is not altogether wrong, as in both cases female sexuality is indeed praised without inhibition. However, by exclusively looking at the figures in such a perspective, we will not be able to understand their full meaning nor will it be possible to explain, why, e.g. "She who shakes the tree" would occupy the most prominent place among all works of art adorning the Buddhist sanctuary of Sanchi.

The numinous radiation of a goddess or a god cannot be comprehended by reducing her/his image to a metaphor of a physical or a biological phenomenon like fertility. Divinity always points beyond such realities, directing human attention towards the mysterious non-physical or non-biological background of phenomena. If this were not the case, the divine images would not be attributed a numinous character. What marks their difference from purely earthly phenomena is an inexplicable, ungraspable, unspeakable element sensed in so many life processes. "Divine" always points to an experience which cannot be understood in an everyday context alone nor be fully explained by observable circumstances.

In the case of the goddess "Abundance," this means: It is not so much biological fertility – not the observable processes of procreation, birth, growth, blooming, maturing, aging and dying – which are conceived as divine. Rather, what appears to be of a divine nature is that utterly unknown power who has created all these life processes, who has sustained them up to the present day and who has endowed them with meaning. Divinity is attributed to the mystery *behind* fertility, to life as an unending energy stream of unknown origin, as the unlimited power of renewal in all its human, animal and vegetable forms – in all its physical and psychic appearances.

Thus, in the sculpture of Mathurā (plate 13 and picture 6), we find three artistic elements united to express one common meaning: they are (1) the goddess Abundance (*Śrī Lakṣmī*), (2) the abundance of buds and flowers and (3) the vessel of abundance" (*pūrṇa kalaśa*). Each one of them mirrors the mystery of life and its creation. Female body, lush plants, and treasure vase are conjoined to form a triune god image pointing to the transcendent origin of all living existence. This, I believe, must be the key to any deeper understanding of the *pūrṇa kalaśa*. At the same time, it provides an explanation for why such earthy images like the *Śālabhañjikā* or the treasure vase have found their places at the gateways of the Great Stupa of Sanchi.

In the earliest history of both India and Europe, we find countless examples showing the close relationship between the female body, the fullness of vegetable life and the treasure vase.

We know of ritual vessels from Vedic times (second millennium B.C.), shaped in a form analogous to the female body and containing the life-giving *Soma* potation.[11] Similarly, a neolithic vessel from Romania shows vegetable decorations suggesting the breasts, the hips and the pubic triangle of a female body (picture 7), while at the lakeside of Zurich, a 6000 year old vessel was found shaped in the likeness of a youthful female upper body (picture 8).

11 Ajit Mookerjee, *Ritual Art of India* (London: Thames and Hudson, 1985), plates 34 and 35.

Picture 7: Neolithic anthropomorphic vessel from Romania

Picture 8: Neolithic vessel found on the shore of the lake of Zurich

3. The Symbolism of the Treasure Vase in Hindu Mythology

Indian lore of all tribes – both Aryan and pre-Aryan – is replete with stories and images of the "vessel of plenty."[12] One of the motifs belonging to all the traditions is the *akṣaya pātra* – the "Pot that will never be empty," which – as we know – also appears frequently in European fairy tales. Already in the *Mahābhārata*, the Indian "National Epic," the roots of which can be traced back to at least the fourth century B.C.E., this pot plays a prominent role. It is *Draupadī*, the wife of the five *Pandava* heroes, who received it as a divine gift at the moment, when the *Pandavas* were driven into exile in the forest. Henceforth, every day, out of the pot's unfathomable depth, *Draupadī* is able to bring forth sufficient food not only for her husbands, but also for the innumerable guests visiting the exiled princes in the wilderness.[13]

Throughout the ages, the *pūrṇa kalaśa*, as appearing in Hindu Myth, has frequently been depicted in wood or stone. Looking at some of these examples will provide us a more vivid idea about the vessel's symbolism in the Hindu world.

3.1 The Churning of the Ocean

This story – an ancient creation myth – is also told in the *Mahābhārata*[14]: In their never ending struggle for world supremacy, both the gods (*devas*) and the demons (*asuras*) tried to obtain the "nectar of immortality." However, the task proved to be too daunting for either party, as it meant nothing less than to churn the primeval ocean and to extract from it the coveted elixir like butter from milk.

As we can see in picture 9, gods and demons were left with no other choice but to make common cause with each other – for the moment at least – and to hope that the exclusive control over the nectar could be won later by trick or by force. They took Mount *Mandara* for the churning stick, firmly placed on the back of Lord *Viṣṇu* in his *avatar* (incarnation) as turtoise. The snake *Vāsukī* volunteered to take the role of the rope. The competing parties stood in line – *asuras* at the left, *devas* at the right. With all their joint forces they pulled the rope first in one, then in the opposite direction and thus maintained the alternating rotary motion of

---

12 See for example Lakshmi Lal, *"The Magic Bowl,"* in: Lakshmi Lal, *The Warlis. Tribal Painting and Legends*, (Bombay: Chemould Publications and Arts, no date), p. 22.
13 *The Mahābhārata*, edited by C. Rajagopalachari, (Bombay: Bharatiya Vida Bhavan, 1996), p. 137, chapt. XL.
14 Ibid., p. 67. chapt. XVII.

the churning stick. After tiresome efforts, wondrous objects appeared at the surface, including deadly poison, and – finally – the vessel with the nectar of life. Then, advised and assisted by *Viṣṇu*, the gods outsmarted the demons and took the elixir into their exclusive possession.

Picture 9: The churning of the ocean (Thailand, 11th century)

Through the course of history, in India as well as in neighbouring countries, the myth was often recounted and depicted in many variations.[15] Picture 9 hails from the *Khmer* culture of Thailand and was created in the eleventh century of our era. Its special feature is the round pot representing the primeval ocean within which the churning stick rotates. Undoubtedly, this

15 See for example P.K. Mishra (ed.), *The Bhāgavata Purāṇa. An Illustrated Oriya Palmleaf Manuscript*, parts VIII – IX, (New Delhi: Abhinav Publications, 1987), plates 11ff; Eberhard Fischer et. al., *Vishnu. Ein indischer Gott in vielerlei Gestalt*, (Zurich: Museum Rietberg, 2006), chapter 3.

pot is a treasure vase, a vase of abundance, and the fact that it is likened to the primeval waters brings out an additional aspect of its meaning. As *pūrṇa kalaśa* or as cosmic ocean it contains the unlimited possibilities of all existence. From its depth, all *nama/rupa,* i.e. "all that has a name and/or a form" is brought to the surface; and all will become submerged again in this womb of creation at the end of the time. In psychological terms, both the primeval ocean and the treasure vase are images of the collective unconscious, out of which our conscious world is born and into which it will return.

This myth – among others – conveys the message that fullness – *pūrṇa* – not only contains liveliness and bliss, but poison and destruction as well. At the same time, the most precious possession, i.e. the "elixir of immortality," can be brought up from the depth only by accepting contradictory movements (= churning) and at the cost of great pains. Moreover, it must be stressed, that "immortality" (*amṛta*), in the Indian context, does not have the same meaning as in the Western world. It does not suggest "eternal life," but rather "new" life, a life which is "ever renewable from within." We probably may come closest to the meaning of *amṛta* (literally: "non-death") if we conceive it as a "life inspired by meaning," or – in other words – a life that is not oriented towards earthly realities alone, but also towards a transcendent reality encompassing more than the realm of death. This realm beyond death is *a-mṛta,* non-death.

In the last part of this presentation, we shall come back to this word and to the mystery it implies.[16]

3.2 The Sage Agastya

The Sage Agastya, too, is already mentioned in the *Mahābhārata.*[17] Later, his story and his merits, were praised in many variations throughout the subcontinent. The one element, however, about which all legendary reports agree, is the concept according to which Agastya was born from a *pūrṇa kalaśa.* Thus, he is called *Agastya Kumbha Yoni,* which means: Agastya, who was born from a *kumbha.* The latter word means "pot" and is often used as a synonym with the word *kalaśa.* Not surprisingly, therefore, picture 10 shows the Sage sitting on a treasure vase.

16 For more detailed explanations on the concept of *amṛta* see Heinrich Zimmer, *Ewiges Indien. Leitmotive Indischen Daseins,* (Potsdam and Zürich: Orell Füssli, 1930), p. 30; Ananda K. Coomaraswamy, *Yakṣas,* parts I and II (New Delhi: Munshiram Manoharlal, 1980), p. 19; F.D.K. Bosch, *The Golden Germ. An Introduction to Indian Symbolism* (New Delhi: Munshiram Manoharlal, 1994), pp. 62ff.

17 *The Mahābhārata,* p. 108, chapt. XXX.

Picture 10: *Agastya Kumbha Yoni* … who was born from a *kumbha/kalaśa*

Agastya is revered as a culture hero. He is considered – among others – to be
the father of Indian medicine, the creator of several Indian languages and
even the author of the Rigveda. To herald these creative achievements, our
illustration shows him holding a vessel containing some healing ointment
in his lower, and a book in the upper left hand. More important than
these, however, are the *pūrṇa kalaśa*, on which Agastya is seated, and the
meditation band, which holds his knees. Both insignia point to the origin
of the Sage's creative power: it is born from the depth of the collective unconscious into which the Sage is diving in meditation. From there, from the
primeval ocean of the soul, he draws his wisdom. To illustrate this mystery,
there is no better means in Indian iconography than the treasure vase.

3.3 Mother Ganges

In many Hindu works of art, the treasure vase has also become one of the
insignia of the goddess *Gaṅgā*, the personification of the North Indian river

Ganges (picture 11). She is usually represented as a youthful woman riding on a *makara*, a mythic water animal combining the features of the dolphin and the crocodile. Like all *vāhanas* (vehicles) of Indian deities, the *makara* illustrates one or several characteristic traits of its rider. In him we encounter the mystery of creation and transience which, according to Indian tradition, is hidden in the depth of the waters, where all life originates and ends.

It is out of the *pūrṇa kalaśa* that *Gaṅga Mā* – Mother Ganges – pours not only the fullness of vegetable life but also the waters of that mighty river at the shores of which Indian cultures have blossomed. This motherly river has served, for thousands of years, as the life line of human creativity. It also receives the ashes of the dead and carries them to the sea. There, they are purified and prepared for a new beginning.

Picture 11: *Gaṅga Mā* riding on a *makara*

Gaṅga's name is derived from the Sanskrit root *gam*, which means "to go" or "to flow." She is the one "who goes" or "who flows," a symbol of the stream of life. *Gaṅga* is the mysterious power within human beings that encourages them to become seekers, to grow, to blossom and to mature. She also links us, deep within, with the primeval waters of the soul, where new beginnings are possible. The treasure vase in her hands points to the mystery of our own "being alive."

4. The Symbolism of the Treasure Vase in *Mahāyāna* Buddhism

In the world of Nepali and Tibetan Buddhism, too, the treasure vase appears as a symbol of deep religious significance. As in the previous chapter, I should like to illustrate this point by three examples.

4.1 The Birth of the future Buddha

In the imagination of his followers, the birth of prince *Siddhārtha*, the future Buddha, must have been an extraordinary, unheard-of and therefore utterly indescribable event. Not only at the level of millions of individuals, but also in historic dimensions, this birth brought about fundamental religious changes. How could the memory of that new beginning be adequately depicted? In order to make the impossible possible, i.e. in order to express the mystery in the form of an image, the artists of earlier centuries used – among other means – the triune symbolism, which was described in chapter two above: According to ancient tradition, female body, treasure vase and vegetable fullness were conjoined in a single image. By this, it was possible to convey something of the profound emotion and elevation that people throughout time may have experienced (and still may experience today) when meditating about the Buddha's birth. Plate 14 (p. 238) provides an example for this.

Filling the right half of the stone image, we find *Siddhārtha*'s mother *Māyā* in the guise of a *Śalabhañjikā*.[18] Her sensuous liveliness – if understood as outer appearance only – does not easily fit into our concept of Buddhist sobriety. If, however, we understand the figure in the same way as the *Śalabhañjikā* of Sanchi, i.e. as incorporating the divine mystery of creation, then her presence in the sacred scene makes a lot of sense.

The newborn child appears at *Māyā*'s right, He is already typified as the future Buddha by his lotus pedestal and a large halo. Like an adult, he stands upright and – by his gesture – seems to seek contact with the onlooker. Thus, he expresses a timeless quality, not depending on any growth or development according to human standards. He represents the archetypal (eternal) truth of the Buddha's message to the world.

Two celestial beings are hovering above the child/adult, dowsing him with water and flowers. Using their treasure vases, the angels solemnize a ritual which used to be – in ancient India – part of the initiation ceremony of a king, and which even today is performed during the initiation of

18 See section 2 above.

every Buddhist monk. Somi, the Hindu boy, was also bathed in this way when initiated to the Sacred Thread. The ritual symbolizes the "second birth," i.e. the awakening of the spiritual being within the physical man. In this perspective, we may interpret the *pūrṇa kalaśas* in the hands of the celestial beings as a symbol of the divine origin of the Buddha's spiritual achievement and religious message. In other words: It is from the *pūrṇa kalaśa* that flows the potential – inherent in every human being – to reach enlightenment and to become conscious. In analytical psychology, we would perhaps speak of the human potential for individuation.

In our image (plate 14), *Māyā*'s body and womb, the heavenly shower of blossoms and water, and the *kalaśas* held in angelic hands are arranged so as to form an integrated whole. They constitute the triune god-image, which antedates Buddhism by many centuries and which has played such a prominent role in Eastern spirituality ever since the beginnings of Buddhist art. I understand it as a timeless symbol of the miraculous impetus of all life – physical and spiritual alike.

4.2 Enlightenment and Compassion

A very similar symbolism becomes apparent in a Nepali scroll painting (*thaṅka*) from the 18th century (picture 12). In the centre of the *thaṅka*'s upper half, seated on a lotus throne, enhanced by three golden haloes, we recognize *Avalokiteśvara*. His name literally means "he who looks down (upon us) with grace." He is a *Bodhisattva*, who – according to the Mahāyāna Buddhist concept – represents an inner (psychic) helper on the way to enlightenment. The term can be translated as "he whose essence (*sattva*) is enlightenment (*bodhi*)." Thus, the *Bodhisattva Avalokiteśvara* is a symbol for an important aspect of enlightenment, more specifically for the inner human potential to develop compassion for other living beings and to support fellow humans on their personal quest for illumination.

In the lower half of the *thaṅka*'s central part, we notice a magnificently adorned treasure vase out of which three lotus stems emerge. The one in the middle yields that beautiful multicoloured lotus blossom which serves the *Bodhisattva* as a seat.

Picture 12: The *Bodhisattva Avalokiteśvara*; detail from a Nepali *thaṅka* (18th cent.)

The painting invites our eyes to an upward movement starting from the
treasure vase, following the central lotus stem, moving to the lotus flower,
reaching the *Bodhisattva* and finally his aureole. Does all this suggest a
spiritual development originating in the depth of the vase and culminating
in the *Bodhisattva's* haloes? If so, we might be permitted to interpret the
painting accordingly, namely as an image of the miraculous unfolding of
human consciousness from the unknown depth of the primeval waters
contained in the *pūrṇa kalaśa* to the enlightened mind of the *Bodhisattva*

reflected in his aureole. Similar to the stone image of the future Buddha's nativity (plate 14), our *thaṅka* also refers to the treasure vase as symbolizing the origin and potential of all psychic development and spiritual maturation.

In the two hands joined in front of his heart, the *Bodhisattva* holds an object which unfortunately cannot be clearly recognized in the present reproduction of the painting. It is a tiny treasure vase. In many similar paintings, *Avalokiteśvara*, instead of such a treasure vase, holds a diamond between his fingers. Since such a gem is usually understood to be a symbol of the highest truth or of enlightenment, we may safely conclude that – in the tradition of 18th century *thaṅka* painting – the same holds true for the treasure vase. It would then be a sign of the *Bodhisattva*'s spiritual perfection. Thus, in the course of Buddhist history, the treasure vase has not only become a symbol of the origin and potential of spiritual development, but also for the highest spiritual achievement, i.e. for enlightenment.[19]

4.3 The Mother of all Buddhas

In Tibetan Buddhism, achieved enlightenment is not only symbolised by the treasure vase, but is also represented in the form of a special goddess: *Uṣṇīṣavijayā*. The name means "supreme victory" and points to the ultimate overcoming of all attachments to the world and of all egocentricity. In the Museum Rietberg Zurich, we find a gilded bronze figure of this goddess. It was cast in Tibet in the 15th century A.D. (picture 13).

Uṣṇīṣavijayā is called "Mother of all Buddhas." She incorporates the mystery of that transcendent creative power which brings about the birth of the Buddhas and enables the human soul and spirit to unfold. She is the birth-giver *behind* all human births, the victor *behind* every human victory, the teacher *behind* every human teaching. To experience her power means to recognize, that the greatest mystery in the history of mankind is not our individual consciousness, but the archetypal potentiality inherent in all human beings to become conscious. *Uṣṇīṣavijayā* is the creator of this archetype, of this potentiality. From a psychological perspective, she is a symbol of the collective unconscious or the Self. In religious terms,

---

19 In Western Alchemy, too, according to Jung, the beginning and the end, the origin and the goal of the transformation process are called by the same term, i.e. "the Stone." C.G. Jung, *Psychology and Alchemy*, vol. 12 of the *Collected Works of C.G. Jung*, edited and translated by Gerhard Adler and R.F.C. Hull (Princeton: Princeton University Press, 1968), § 427, note 4.

however, she represents a transcendent power which is simply beyond human understanding and therefore unspeakable.

Picture 13: *Uṣṇīṣavijayā* (Tibet, 15th century)

Does it come as a surprise, then, that this goddess holds a treasure vase in her lap (picture 14)? Or does it rather remind us of the triune god-image, comprising female body, vase and vegetable fullness? How deeply rooted must this symbol be in the souls of women and men in Eurasia – perhaps in the whole world!

Picture 14: The treasure vase in the lap of the goddess; detail from picture 13

5. The Overarching Symbolism

In the first four chapters of this presentation, we have dealt with many examples of the treasure vase. Some of them already appearing in earliest history, others living on in actual folk culture, in Hindu myth and in Mahāyāna Buddhism. What we have found are innumerable variations in the details, but also a good number of common features characterizing all these "vases of plenty." Now, the question arises, whether an overarching symbolism might be discovered, linking past and present, even connecting different world religions like Hinduism and Buddhism. Where could such a reconciling symbol be found? What would it look like?

In order to find answers to these questions, we now enter the field of sacred architecture as it has developed over the last 2000 years in India, Nepal and Tibet. The focus will be on the Hindu temple and the Buddhist Stupa.

5.1 The Hindu Temple

During the Indian Middle Ages, starting from about the seventh century, it became a custom to crown the cupola or the śikara (tower) of Hindu temples by a kalaśa (also called kumbha). This development took place in the South as well as in the North of the subcontinent. Picture 15, which shows the upper part of a side-chapel of the Mālappaluvar temple complex, provides an example of it. The temple complex is situated in Tamil Nadu, South India. It was constructed in the eleventh century and is dedicated to the Sage Agastya.[20]

20 See chapter 3 above.

Picture 15: The treasure vase crowning the top of the temple

The circular keystone of the cupola is dented so as to appear like the sun in the zenith of the universe. Placed in the middle of this keystone, we notice a *pūrṇa kalaśa* showing a lemon-like object in its opening. In colloquial speech, this object is called *bijapūraka* (= lemon), but priests and architects interpret is as a bud, a seed, a jewel or a flame. All these terms point to something precious, to something growing, to the energy and sap of life.[21] The importance of the *pūrṇa kalaśa* and the *bijapūraka* within the overall concept of the temple can be realized by the fact that – by the vertical axis of the building – the bud or jewel or flame is related to the god-image placed below the pinnacle in the innermost part of the *śikara* (picture 16).

Picture 16: The temple towers (*śikarā*) of Osian, Rajasthan (7th and 11th century)

21 For more details see Ramachandra Rao, *Art and Architecture of Indian Temples* (Banga-lore: Kalpatharu Research Academy, 1993), pp. 87ff.

In order to deepen our understanding of the *kalaśa*'s significance at the top of the temple, we take a look at the *Kandariya Mahadeva* of Khajuraho (Madhya Pradesh) and its pinnacles (see plate 15, p. 239). We first consider the sacred building as a whole. It is conceived as an image of the universe und comprehends all the three worlds – Earth, Space, and overarching Sky. From a massive stone terrace representing the earth, the visitor is led over high stairs (lower right side of the image) to the entrance porch, from there to the central hall, the dance hall and, finally, to the ambulatory path which leads around the *garbha gṛha*, i.e. the "womb-house" or sanctum within the temple. For practical reasons, this long spiritual itinerary is laid out on the horizontal plane; symbolically, however, it constitutes an ascent in the vertical dimension. The pilgrim, on his quest for the absolute, is led from earthly existence through different spaces or halls (the roof pinnacles of which reach up higher and higher), until he arrives at the innermost centre of the highest temple tower. This chamber lies exactly below the peak of the main *śikara,* which represents the world mountain *Meru.* On its top, symbolically, the seeker reaches the sun shining from the zenith. It has taken the shape of that circular, dented stone plate which serves as the *śikara*'s key stone and which marks the uppermost limit of the universe.

Above the sun, however, *beyond* the universe and *beyond* everything that the human mind is able to comprehend, the treasure vase is hovering. Here, it is not a part of the human world, but is an image of the absolute, the indescribable "other," representing the origin and the goal of all human endeavour. The god-image deep below in the *garbha gṛha*, circumambulated by the pilgrim, is but an inadequate simile of that "other" sensed to exist in the realm beyond the sundoor.[22]

For obvious reasons, the terms *pūrṇa kalaśa* or "treasure vase," which we have hitherto used, are no longer adequate to describe that utterly different reality meant by the *kalaśa* at the top of the temple tower. Thus, the vessel holding the "bud" or the "seed" or the "jewel" or the "flame" is called *amṛta kalaśa* – "the vessel of non-death." This term is indeed an exact description of what the pilgrim envisages as her/his highest goal when visiting the temple. *Mṛta* means death; more precisely, it points to everything – literally everything! – which is part of this universe and is imaginable for human

22 For more detailed explanations of this symbolism see the following two essays of Ananda.K. Coomaraswamy, (1) *An Indian Temple. The Kandarya Mahadeo*, in Selected Papers, volume 1: *Traditional Art and Symbolism*, (Princeton: Princeton University Press, 1977), pp. 3-10; (2) *The Symbolism of the Dome*, ibid., pp. 415-458.

beings, be it our bodily existence or the objects of astrophysics, the concepts of natural science or the concepts of all humanities and religions. What all these "realities" have in common is the fact that they are dependent on measurable and describable causes and therefore bound to "die" sooner or later.

A-mṛta, however, which means "non-death," points to a totally different experience, to another quality of life, which is not dependent on outer causes, but – instead – remains receptive to be touched by a transcendent numen.[23] Such amṛta (non-death) has nothing to do with "eternal life," as it has occasionally been imagined in the Christian and the Muslim traditions. Amṛta, in the Indian tradition, is a symbol of a qualitative fulfilment of human life realized in the relatedness to transcendence.

The mystery of this transcendence was already praised in the earliest religious texts of the Hindus, for example in Book X of the Rigveda. The poet, however, refrains from providing any fixed description of yonder reality nor of the origin of all existence. Rather, he expresses his own wondering in the following question:

> "What was the germ primeval ... that was earlier than this earth and heaven, before the Asuras[24] and the Gods had being?"[25]

While the vedic poet was unwilling or unable to answer his question, sacred architecture in India "solved" the problem by using a very ancient image which had always been a symbol of the unspeakable: it is the treasure vase, now called amṛta kalaśa, which crowns the Hindu temple and – symbolically – the universe.

5.2 The Buddhist Stupa

While – during the middle ages – the amṛta kalaśa was given a prominent place in the metaphysical concept of the Hindu temple, it also entered the architectural language of forms of Mahāyāna Buddhism. Thus, it became an overarching symbol uniting the two religions at a very subtle level. An

---

23 Mircea Eliade, *A History of Religious Ideas*, vol. 1 (Chicago: The University of Chicago Press, 1985), p. 197.
24 On the *Asuras* and the Gods see para. 3.1 above.
25 *Rigveda* X, 5 in the translation of Ralph T.H. Griffith (New Delhi: Motilal Banarsidass, 1973).

example of this is the *Kumbum* of Gyantse in Southern Tibet, which was erected in the fifteenth century (see plate 16, p. 240).

Kumbum (tib.) means "(the stupa with the) 100 000 images." Like the Hindu temple, it is made in the likeness of the universe. A pilgrim would enter the huge building by a narrow door at the ground level and then, clockwise, follow the ambulatory path which is protected by a massive high wall. He would climb up to the first, later to the second, the third and fourth story, each time repeating his circumambulation. In the temple halls and chapels bordering the way, he would encounter the images of countless Buddhas and *Bodhisattvas* – according to tradition they number 100 000 – in order to meditate and to immerse himself into the spiritual presence of these innumerable enlightened beings. A Tibetan Buddhist author describes this inner journey with the following words:

> As he ascended from plane to plane, and circumambulated terrace after terrace, concentrating on every step he took, the devotee brought before his mind's eye the various stages of realization. With each story he ascended, he reached a higher plane of intuitive wisdom. At the very top (i.e. in the chamber hidden within the gilded copper rings below the honorary parasol, plate 16), all diversity disappeared, and the devotee was confronted with the ultimate integration of wisdom and compassion, mind and heart, feeling and knowledge, in the symbol of Dorje Chang (Vajradhara), the pure original consciousness who here functionally corresponded to the Ādi-Buddha, the primordial Buddha who resides in the very center of every being.[26]

Dorje Chang (tib.) or *Vajradhara* (sanskr.) is considered as the most sublime divinity in Tibetan Buddhism. In the top chamber of the *Kumbum*, he has been assigned the most prominent seat at the central wooden post supporting the parasol above. This golden umbrella is a symbol of the heavenly vault and – like in the Hindu world view – of the uppermost limit of the universe. Beyond that border, however, hovers the *amṛta kalaśa*, indicating that there is still another reality.

While the image of *Dorje Chang* (*Vajradhara*) – like the god-image in the sanctum of the Hindu temple – is but an inadequate simile of that other reality, in contrast the golden "vessel of non-death" expresses – more

---

26 Li Gotami Govinda, *Tibet in Pictures. A Journey into the Past*, vol. 1, (Berkley: Dharma Publishing, 2002), p. 77. Explanations in brackets by the author.

appropriately, although in a more abstract way – the ultimate truth. The statue of *Dorje Chang* inside the *Kumbum* is accessible for the devotee; the *amṛta kalaśa* with its crowning bud, or seed, or jewel, or flame, however, is not. It is beyond human accessibility and may therefore be comprehended as a timeless symbol of transcendence (picture 17).

Picture 17: The *amṛta kalaśa* on top of the *Kumbum*

With this, I come to an end of my search for the multi-layered symbolism of the treasure vase and turn back to the question asked in the introduction of this presentation: Which was the ritual meaning of the treasure vases that had been prepared for Somi's initiation and that contributed so much to the festive flavour characterizing the event?

In my view, the religious meaning of Somi's initiation conveys a message of transcendence, more precisely: a message concerning inner human orientation towards transcendence. The Sacred Thread is a symbol of such an orientation, and the treasure vases adorning the sacred enclosure, where the rituals for Somi took place, were apt to remind all those who were involved, but all onlookers as well, of *amṛta*, that quality of life which means "fullness" and which includes a spiritual relation to the beyond. According to my experience, this message is not only culture-specific, but of an archetypal nature. It appears in countless cultures of all times and in all parts of the world. This, perhaps, is one of the reasons why the rituals of

Somi's initiation have impressed me so deeply and have encouraged me to undertake some research with regard to their symbolism.

Epilogue: The Treasure Vase in the Dreams of Modern Man

To conclude, I should like to briefly mention three dreams which I have come across in my analytical work. I have the impression to understand them somewhat better since I have started to deal with the multi-layered symbolism of the treasure vase, especially with the triune god-image comprehending the female body, vegetable fullness and the *kalaśa*. Due to my studies of the treasure vase, each of these dreams spontaneously evokes in me some of the images with which I have become familiar during my research and which I want to share here. However, at this moment, I do not intend to delve into any form of dream interpretation; I would rather leave this task to the reader.

    I. A young mother, single, suffers from frequent self-doubts; in her dreams, she is often haunted by a threatening dark animus (picture 5).

One night, at the end of such a frightening dream, she sees – unexpectedly – a beautiful bouquet of flowers held in a round vase.

    II. In the middle of his life, a man meets, by chance, a women of his age. She had been his sweetheart at the time of primary school. For dozens of years, the former classmates had not seen each other. Now they agree to meet for lunch a few days later. During the meal, a conversation of unexpected intensity develops; both, the man and the woman, are moved and impressed. In the subsequent weeks, they exchange very personal letters.

During the night before meeting the woman for lunch, the man had the following dream (picture 7): *Right in front of me and quite close, I see the beautiful lower body of a naked woman. It is suntanned, but it does not arouse me; rather it calls for consenting warm feelings.*

III. A woman in the second half of her life has to take a painful decision. Is she to follow her reason or her feelings? Now, she dreams (picture 12):

A beautiful Buddha sits in the midst of colourful flowers growing out of a round vessel.

Picture Credits

Plates

Cover page: *Speculum humanae salvationis* (15th cent.), © Bibiothèque Nationale de France, Paris, Ms. Latin 512, fol. 34.

Plate 1: © Foundation Peter and Sibylle Birkhäuser-Oeri, Binningen/CH.

Plate 2: Photo Felix Leyer, Adligenswil/CH.

Plate 3: Photo Felix Leyer, Adligenswil/CH.

Plate 4: *Psalter of Robert de Lisle*, (1310/1330), Arundel 83 II, fol. 125v, London British Library, Faksimile, edited with a commentary by Lucy Freemann Sandler (Graz: Akadem. Druck- und Verlagsanstalt, 2008).

Plate 5: Photo Andreas Schweizer, Zollikon/CH.

Plate 6: *Aurora Consurgens* (15th cent.), © Zentralbibliothek Zürich, Ms. Rh. 172, fol. 24v.

Plate 7: Rudolf Gamper and Thomas Hofmeier, *Das Alchemiehandbuch des Appenzeller Wundarztes Ulrich Ruosch* (Basel: Schwabe Verlag, 2002), p. 37.

Plate 8: Rudolf Gamper and Thomas Hofmeier, *Alchemische Vereinigung. Das Rosarium Philosophorum und sein Besitzer Bartlome Schobinger* (Zurich: Chronos, 2014), p. 65.

Plate 9: Roman Vishniac, Hasidic man wearing a *shtreimel* (fur hat) on the Sabbath, Kazimierz, Krakow, ca. 1935-1938, © Mara Vishniac Kohn, courtesy International Center of Photography.

Plate 10: Photo Rudolf Högger, Langenbruck/CH.

Plate 11a and 11b: Photos Rudolf Högger, Langenbruck/CH.

Plate 12: Photo Rudolf Högger, Langenbruck/CH.

Plate 13: © National Museum of India, New Delhi.

Plate 14: © National Museum of Nepal, Kathmandu.

Plate 15: © Martin Hürlimann, by courtesy of Anna Schindler.

Plate 16: Yu Shao and Peng Shen (eds.), *Selected Tibetan Jtaka Murals* (Beijing 1982), p. 23, figure 11.

Pictures

Foreword

Speculum humanae salvationis, (15th cent.), © Bibiothèque Nationale de France, Paris, Ms. Latin 512, fol. 34.

Regine Schweizer-Vüllers, "He struck the rock and the waters did flow"

Picture 1: Jo. Jacobi Mangeti, *Bibliotheca chemica curiosa,* 2 vols., Genf 1702, reprint Arnaldo Forni Editore (without particulars), vol. 1, p. 442r.

Picture 2: Johannes Rhenanus, *Solis e puteo emergentis sive dissertationis chymotechnicae libri tres,* Frankfurt 1613, in: C.G. Jung, *Alchemical Studies,* vol. 13 of *The Collected Works of C.G. Jung,* translated by R.F.C. Hull (Princeton: Princeton University Press 1967), picture B7 (following p. 152).

Picture 3: Samuel Langmeier, Zurich/CH

Picture 4: Jo. Jacobi Mangeti, *Bibliotheca chemica curiosa,* vol 1, p. 442r (detail).

Picture 5: Stoltzius of Stoltzenberg, *Chymisches Lustgärtlein,* with an introduction by Ferdinand Weinhandl, reprint of the edition Lucas Iennis, Franckfurt 1624 (Darmstadt: Wissenschaftliche Buchgesellschaft, 1975), figure LXXVI.

Tony Woolfson, "I came across this impressive doctrine"

Picture 1: Manuel Bachmann and Thomas Hofmeier, *Geheimnisse der Alchemie* (Basel: Schwabe Verlag, 1999), p. 166.

Picture 2: Gershom Scholem at Eranos, August 1951. Photo Margarethe Fellerer, © Fondatione Eranos, Ascona/CH.

Picture 3: Kabbalistic Scroll (1605), Bodleian Library, Oxford, in: Avram Davis and Manuela Mascetti, *Judaic Mysticism* (New York: Hyperion, 1997), p. 184.

Picture 4: Robert Fludd, *Utriusque cosmi maioris,* vol. 2, Frankfurt 1621, in: Alexander Roob, *The Hermetic Museum. Alchemy and Mysticism* (Cologne: Taschen Verlag, 1997), p. 318.

Picture 5: *Miscellanea d' Alchimia* (15th cent.), in: Alexander Roob, *The Hermetic Museum. Alchemy and Mysticism,* p. 307.

Marianne Jehle-Wildberg, Stations of a Difficult Friendship

Picture 1: Congress in Weimar (1911), in: Marianne Jehle-Wildberger, *C.G. Jung und Adolf Keller. Über Theologie und Psychologie. Briefe und Gespräche* (Zurich: TVZ, 2014), p. 28.

Picture 2: M. Jehle-Wildberger, *C.G. Jung und Adolf Keller,* p. 28 (detail).

Picture 3: Adolf Keller, at the age of about 70 years, in: Marianne Jehle-Wildberger, *Adolf Keller (1872-1963). Pionier der ökumenischen Bewegung* (Zurich: TVZ, 2008), p. 521.

Picture 4: Handwriting of Adolf Keller, in: M. Jehle-Wildberger, *C.G. Jung und Adolf Keller,* p. 172.

Picture 5: Handwirting of C.G. Jung, ibid., p. 173.

Picture 6: Cover of Time Magazine, February 14th, 1955, ibid., p. 2013.

Rudolf Högger, The Treasure Vase

Picture 1: Photo Rudolf Högger, Langenbruck/CH

Picture 2: Photo Rudolf Högger, Langenbruck/CH

Picture 3: Tibetan New Year's greeting card from a bookshop in Patan, Nepal (without date, indication of the artist nor the publisher).

Picture 4: Photo Rudolf Högger, Langenbruck/CH

Picture 5: *Pūrṇa kalaśa* from the Stupa nr. 2 in Sanchi, India, © Archaeological Survey of India, New Delhi.

Picture 6: The goddess "Abundance" from Mathurā, in: Ananda K. Coomaraswamy, *Yaksas,* parts 1 and 2 (New Delhi: Munishiram Manoharlal Publishers, 1980), plate 49.

Picture 7: Neolithic vessel from Romania, in: Florin Drasovean, Manuela Wullschlegel, Laurent Chrzanovski, Jacques Charmay, *Neolithische Kunst in Rumänien,* Catalogue of the exhibition *Steinzeitkunst. Frühe Kulturen in Rumänien* (Olten: Historical Museum, 2008), plate 102, © arte'm sri.

Picture 8: Neolithic vessel found on the shore of the lake of Zurich. The vessel was unearthed in "Zürich – Kleiner Hafner." With kind permission of the "Amt für Städtebau – Unterwasserarchäologie Zürich."

Picture 9: The churning of the ocean (Thailand, 11th cent.), © Musée Guimet, Paris, Réunion des Musées Nationaux.

Picture 10: Mary Shepherd Slusser, *Art and Culture of Nepal. Selected Papers* (Kathmandu: Mandala Publications, 2005), figure 23 (following p. 635).

Picture 11: *Gaṅgā Mā* riding on a *makara,* © National Museum of India, New Delhi.

Picture 12: The *Bodhisattva Avalokiteśvara,* detail from a Nepali *thanka* (18th cent.), in: Hugo E. Kreijer, *Kathmandu Valley Painting – The Jucker Collection* (London: Serindia Publications, 1999), p. 45.

Picture 13: *Uṣṇīṣavijayā* (Tibet, 15th cent.), © Museum Rietberg, Zurich.

Picture 14: Detail from picture 13.

Picture 15: Ananda K. Coomaraswamy, *Essays in Early Indian Architecture,* edited by Michael W. Meister (New Delhi: Indira Gandhi National Centre for the Arts, 1992), figure 71.

Picture 16: The temple towers (*śikarā*) of Osian, Rajasthan (7th and 11th cent. respectively), © Asia Society, New York.

Picture 17: The *amṛta kalaśa* on top of the *Kumbum,* © Robert Schmid, Erlinsbach/CH, 3wimage.

Authors

Rudolf Högger, Ph.D., studied History, German Literature, Theology and Jungian Psychology. He spent his professional career in international development cooperation, focusing mostly on Asian countries. His key interest was always directed towards the cultural, religious and psychological background of so-called development. From 1988 until 2005 he lectured about these topics at the Swiss Federal Institute of Technology in Zurich. In 1993, he published the critical study *Naga and Garuda – the Other Side of Development*. His second book *The Sacred Thread – About the Development of Personality according to Hindu Traditions and Jungian Psychology* appeared in 2014. Högger is the chairman of the Board of Trustees of the Tibet-Institute Rikon. He lives in Langenbruck, Switzerland.

Marianne Jehle-Wildberger, lic. phil. I, completed her studies in History, German literature and History of Christianity at the university of Zurich. She is married to the theologian Frank Jehle with whom she has two grown sons. From 1970 to 2001 she taught History and German at the Pre-College and the Teacher's College in Sargans, Switzerland. She is engaged in projects for the current refugees. Marianne Jehle-Wildberger has published several books on historical subjects, among others *Adolf Keller. Ecumenist, World citizen, Philantropist* (2013), *C.G. Jung und Adolf Keller. Briefe und Gespräche* [C.G. Jung and Adolf Keller. Letters and Discussions] (2014).

Claudine Koch-Morgenegg, lic. phil. I, is a graduated business economist FH who originally worked in business administration. She studied psychology, psychopathology and history of art at the University of Zürich. Later she graduated as analytical psychologist at the C.G. Jung Institute of Zurich in Küsnacht, and she also possesses a diploma as gerontologist INAG. At present she is a practicing Jungian analyst and works as lecturer, training analyst, and supervisor at the C.G. Jung Institute of Zurich. Her emphasis is on dreams – especially on dreams of old people – and on art in general.

Andreas Schweizer, Dr. theol. (Ph.D.), is a practicing Jungian analyst in Zürich. He studied theology and comparative religion in Zürich as well as Egyptology with Prof. Erik Hornung in Basel. He has been training analyst since 1986, first at the C.G. Jung Institute of Zurich in Küsnacht and currently with The International School for Analytical Psychology Zurich (ISAP). He is president of the Psychology Club, founded in 1916 by C.G. Jung, and was for fourteen years president of the Eranos Conferences in Ascona. He has published numerous essays and books, including *The Sungod's Journey through the Netherworld* (2010).

Regine Schweizer-Vuellers, Ph.D. studied German literature with special emphasis on the Middle Ages and European folk literature. She is a Jungian analyst in private practice in Zurich, Switzerland. She works as a training analyst, supervisor and lecturer. She served at the Inaugural Board of *The Research and Training Centre in Depth Psychology According to C.G. Jung and Marie-Louise von Franz*. Her interests include medieval mysticism, alchemy, fairytales, legends and folksongs. She has published various psychological interpretations. Her book *Die Heilige am Kreuz* [The Feminine on the Cross] explores the feminine aspects of the Christian God image in folklore and mysticism from the Middle Ages until 19th/20th century.

Murray Stein, Ph.D., is a graduate of the C.G. Jung Institute of Zurich (1973) and of Yale University (1965), Yale Divinity School (1969) and the University of Chicago (1985). He is a founding member of The Inter-Regional Society of Jungian Analysts and the Chicago Society of Jungian Analysts. He was president of the International Association for Analytical Psychology (IAAP) from 2001 to 2004 and President of The International School of Analytical Psychology Zurich from 2008-2012. He has lectured internationally and is the author of *In MidLife, Jung's Map of the Soul, Minding the Self,* and *Soul – Retrieval and Treatment* as well of numerous articles on analytical psychology and Jungian psychoanalysis. He is the Jungian editor for the *Edinburgh Encyclopedia of Psychoanalysis* as well as the editor of *Jungian Psychoanalysis*. He lives in Switzerland and is a Training and Supervising Analyst with ISAP Zurich. He has a private practice in Zurich.

Hermann Strobel, Dr. med. Dent., was born 1927 in Dresden, Germany. He studied dentistry in Heidelberg. Later he came to Switzerland where at first he worked as a dentist. At the same time he trained in analytical psychology at the C.G. Jung-Institute Zurich and worked over years as an analyst, training analyst and lecturer, at home and abroad. He was the author of several publications, among others the book *Das Zahnweh, subjektiv genommen... über Zähne, Zahnschmerzen, Zahnärzte und ihre Bedeutung für den Seelenfrieden* [The toothache, taken subjectively... about teeth, toothache, dentists and their importance for peace of mind]. He was well known for his psychological interpretations of films, in particular his interpretation of the film *Hiroshima mon Amour* by Alain Resnais und Marguerite Duras. Hermann Strobel died in March 2006.

Tony Woolfson, Ph.D., grew up in Glasgow, Scotland, before moving to Canada in 1969. He earned post-graduate degrees in Political Science, and wrote his doctoral thesis on Jean-Jacques Rousseau, the Citoyen de Genève. He was a university teacher of Social Sciences and Humanities for many years before turning to Jung in mid-life, especially in the study of religion. He now lives in Zurich where Jung is at the centre of his lecturing, teaching, and writing. He is a Scholar and Translator with the Philemon Foundation, collaborating on English language translations of Jung's unpublished works. He is also collaborating on the first English translation of Marie-Louise von Franz's monumental work *Symbolik des Märchens* [Symbolism of Fairy Tales].

* * *

English Titles from Daimon

Ruth Ammann - *The Enchantment of Gardens*
Susan R. Bach - *Life Paints its Own Span*
Diana Baynes Jansen - *Jung's Apprentice: A Biography of Helton Godwin Baynes*
John Beebe (Ed.) - *Terror, Violence and the Impulse to Destroy*
E.A. Bennet - *Meetings with Jung*
W.H. Bleek / L.C. Lloyd (Ed.) - *Specimens of Bushman Folklore*
Tess Castleman - *Threads, Knots, Tapestries*
- *Sacred Dream Circles*
George Czuczka - *Imprints of the Future*
Renate Daniel - *Taking the Fear out of the Night*
Eranos Yearbook 69 - *Eranos Reborn*
Eranos Yearbook 70 - *Love on a Fragile Thread*
Eranos Yearbook 71 - *Beyond Masters*
Eranos Yearbook 72 - *Soul between Enchantment and Disenchantment*
Michael Escamilla - *Bleuler, Jung, and the Schizophrenias*
Heinrich Karl Fierz - *Jungian Psychiatry*
John Fraim - *Battle of Symbols*
von Franz / Frey-Rohn / Jaffé - *What is Death?*
Liliane Frey-Rohn - *Friedrich Nietzsche, A Psychological Approach*
Marion Gallbach - *Learning from Dreams*
Ralph Goldstein (Ed.) - *Images, Meanings & Connections: Essays in Memory of Susan Bach*
Yael Haft - *Hands: Archetypal Chirology*
Fred Gustafson - *The Black Madonna of Einsiedeln*
Daniel Hell - *Soul-Hunger: The Feeling Human Being and the Life-Sciences*
Siegmund Hurwitz - *Lilith, the first Eve*
Aniela Jaffé - *The Myth of Meaning*
- *Was C.G. Jung a Mystic?*
- *From the Life and Work of C.G. Jung*
- *Death Dreams and Ghosts*
C.G. Jung - *The Solar Myths and Opicinus de Canistris*
Verena Kast - *A Time to Mourn*
- *Sisyphus*
Hayao Kawai - *Dreams, Myths and Fairy Tales in Japan*
James Kirsch - *The Reluctant Prophet*
Eva Langley-Dános - *Prison on Wheels: Ravensbrück to Burgau*
Rivkah Schärf Kluger - *The Gilgamesh Epic*
Yehezkel Kluger & - *RUTH in the Light of Mythology, Legend*
Naomi Kluger-Nash *and Kabbalah*
Paul Kugler (Ed.) - *Jungian Perspectives on Clinical Supervision*
Paul Kugler - *The Alchemy of Discourse*
Rafael López-Pedraza - *Cultural Anxiety*
- *Hermes and his Children*
Alan McGlashan - *The Savage and Beautiful Country*
Gregory McNamee (Ed.) - *The Girl Who Made Stars: Bushman Folklore*
- *The North Wind and the Sun & Other Fables of Aesop*
Gitta Mallasz - *Talking with Angels*
C.A. Meier - *Healing Dream and Ritual*
- *A Testament to the Wilderness*
- *Personality: The Individuation Process*
Haruki Murakami - *Haruki Murakami Goes to Meet Hayao Kawai*

English Titles from Daimon

Eva Pattis Zoja (Ed.) - *Sandplay Therapy*
Laurens van der Post - *The Rock Rabbit and the Rainbow*
Jane Reid - *Jung, My Mother and I: The Analytic Diaries*
of Catharine Rush Cabot
R.M. Rilke - *Duino Elegies*
Miguel Serrano - *C.G. Jung and Hermann Hesse*
Helene Shulman - *Living at the Edge of Chaos*
D. Slattery / G. Slater (Eds.) - *Varieties of Mythic Experience*
David Tacey - *Edge of the Sacred: Jung, Psyche, Earth*
Susan Tiberghien - *Looking for Gold*
Ann Ulanov - *Spiritual Aspects of Clinical Work*
- *Picturing God*
- *The Female Ancestors of Christ*
- *The Wisdom of the Psyche*
- *The Wizards' Gate, Picturing Consciousness*
Ann & Barry Ulanov - *Cinderella and her Sisters*
A. Schweizer / R. Scheizer-Villers - *Stone by Stone: Reflections on Jung*
Eva Wertenschlag-Birkhäuser - *Windows on Eternity:*
The Paintings of Peter Birkhäuser
Harry Wilmer - *How Dreams Help*
- *Quest for Silence*
Luigi Zoja - *Drugs, Addiction and Initiation*
Luigi Zoja & Donald Williams - *Jungian Reflections on September 11*
Jungian Congress Papers - *Jerusalem 1983: Symbolic & Clinical Approaches*
- *Berlin 1986: Archetype of Shadow in a Split World*
- *Paris 1989: Dynamics in Relationship*
- *Chicago 1992: The Transcendent Function*
- *Zürich 1995: Open Questions*
- *Florence 1998: Destruction and Creation*
- *Cambridge 2001*
- *Barcelona 2004: Edges of Experience*
- *Cape Town 2007: Journeys, Encounters*
- *Montreal 2010: Facing Multiplicity*
- *Copenhagen 2013: 100 Years on*

Our books are available from your bookstore or from our distributors:

AtlasBooks
30 Amberwood Parkway
Ashland OH 44805, USA
Phone: 419-281-5100
Fax: 419-281-0200
E-mail: order@atlasbooks.com
www.atlasbooks.com

Gazelle Book Services Ltd.
White Cross Mills, High Town
Lancaster LA1 4XS, UK
Tel: +44 1524 528500
Fax: +44 1524 528510
Email: sales@gazellebookservices.co.uk
www.gazellebookservices.co.uk

Daimon Verlag - Hauptstrasse 85 - CH-8840 Einsiedeln - Switzerland
Phone: (41)(55) 412 2266   Fax: (41)(55) 412 2231
Email: info@daimon.ch
Visit our website: www.daimon.ch or write for our complete catalog